DAT

THE MISSOURI SESQUICENTENNIAL EDITION

WILLIAM E. PARRISH

GENERAL EDITOR

A HISTORY

UNIVERSITY OF

OF MISSOURI

VOLUME III 1860 TO 1875

WILLIAM E. PARRISH

MISSOURI PRESS

Copyright © 1973 by The Curators of the University of Missouri
University of Missouri Press, Columbia, Missouri 65201
Printed and bound in the United States of America
Library of Congress Catalog Number 76-155844
ISBN 0-8262-0148-2   All rights reserved

PREFACE

Missouri, with its thriving river port St. Louis, dominated the trade and commerce of the upper Mississippi River Valley in 1860. Because the increasing competition of the railroads had already begun to draw much of her traffic from the East, however, she was forced to divert some of her attention away from the Southern trade centers along the river and focus on connections to Eastern markets. The state had undergone considerable change in the 1850's with an influx of Northern- and foreign-born population. Industry had grown to supplement her agricultural and commercial interests. This situation presented a challenge to the authority of dominant Southern-oriented political rulers.

The momentous issues of the Civil War had a strong emotional hold on most Missourians. Aggressive leaders on both sides at the state level quickly shattered the hopes of the majority for some kind of neutral stance within the Union. Thereafter, the state and its people were torn apart by divided sympathies and the horrors of a ferocious guerrilla warfare. Out of this turmoil there arose a Radical whirlwind which ended slavery and sought to give Missouri a new constitution to equip it for "modern times." As a result, the postwar period became almost as turbulent as the war years. The forces of change proved politically vindictive against many members of the prewar establishment, fearful lest they disrupt the new order that had been set in motion. This attitude touched off a reaction that restored Missouri to the Conservative fold by the mid-1870's, although the progress of Reconstruction was by no means eradicated.

In this third volume of the Missouri Sesquicentennial History, I have tried to portray the tumult of these times and to give an impression of their impact upon the history of the state and the lives of its people. Designed to detail the state's development and the role it has played both regionally and nationally, this series was undertaken by the University of Missouri Press to mark 150 years of statehood. The University of Missouri generously agreed to underwrite leaves and research assistance for the five authors to enable them to complete their work. Each author is a specialist in his field, and the volumes are based on extensive research in both primary and secondary sources. Because the volumes are general surveys of each era, footnotes have been limited to explanatory matters. The reader will find a more detailed bibliographic essay accompanying each volume to direct him to materials used and to offer suggestions for further study. Subsequent volumes will trace Missouri's story during the age of the Populists and the Progressives, and from World War I to the present.

I have drawn heavily on research done for two previous studies I have written concerning this period of Missouri history. I have benefited greatly from reactions of colleagues in the history profession and of students to these earlier efforts. The subsidization of the current project by the University of Missouri has made possible additional research in recently discovered materials and allowed me to develop studies and investigate those areas beyond the scope of the other works. In these new endeavors many persons have aided me in the pursuit of a comprehensive picture of Missouri at the mid-nineteenth century. I am especially indebted to my long-time friend Richard S. Brownlee, Secretary and Director of the State Historical Society of Missouri, Columbia, for his encouragement and helpful conversations over the years. His excellent staff provided generous assistance. Particular thanks there must go to James W. Goodrich, Mrs. Elizabeth Comfort, Mrs. Goldena Howard, Mrs. Henrietta Krause, Mrs. Alma Vaughan, and Mrs. Nancy Prewitt. Appreciation is also due the staff of the Missouri Historical Society, St. Louis, and the Reeves Library at Westminster College, Fulton, Missouri, for their help in securing materials. Lawrence O. Christensen of the University of Missouri, Rolla, devoted part of his busy schedule to providing me with valuable insights into the postwar black community of St. Louis. Michael Burlingame of Connecticut College kindly permitted me to read his senior thesis on Carl Schurz's early senatorial career, written at Princeton University, and a seminar paper on Liberal Republicanism in Missouri, delivered at Johns Hopkins University. I was fortunate to have L. Steven Demaree as a research assistant. His diligent work on various aspects of research and in initially organizing the bibliographical essay proved most helpful.

My final word of special thanks to HelenSue, Beth, and Billy, who entered my life midway through this project. Their sympathetic help and understanding through a long summer of writing made the final completion of the task a much more pleasant one.

The author alone is responsible for any errors of fact or interpretation.

W. E. P.
Fulton, Missouri
December, 1972

CONTENTS

CHAPTER I

WAR COMES TO MISSOURI

The dusty streets of Jefferson City were crowded on the evening of January 3, 1861, as citizens and visitors hastened to the State Capitol on the brow of the hill overlooking the Missouri River. A tense mood charged the air as the Hall of Representatives rapidly filled. Promptly at eight o'clock the Speaker of the House, John McAfee of Shelby County, convened the joint session of the Twenty-first Assembly to witness the inauguration of Missouri's fourteenth governor.

Claiborne Fox Jackson, upon whom all eyes focused that evening, had traveled a long road to arrive at this moment. A native of Kentucky with Virginia antecedents, the new governor had come to Missouri at the age of twenty. He had settled originally at Franklin, then moved to Arrow Rock where he engaged in mercantile practice. The people of Saline County first sent him to the legislature in 1836, and from that time politics became his principal profession. During the following decade he became a leader in the "Central Clique," which, in alliance with Sen. Thomas Hart Benton, ruled Democratic politics and hence the state. At the close of the 1840's, he helped engineer the Senator's downfall through his Jackson Resolutions, which called for the extension of slavery into new territories. While this move caused a split in Democratic ranks, the party managed to smooth over its differences at election times and thereby maintain control of state government throughout the 1850's. Jackson served as an agent of reconciliation during the last years of the decade and was rewarded by being named Missouri's first state bank commissioner in 1857 even as he held the position of state Democratic chairman.

The new Governor had come through a rough canvass in the election of 1860. After securing the Democratic nomination in a close convention fight in April, he had had to confront the na-

I

tional schism of his party. Forced to declare his choice between Stephen A. Douglas and John C. Breckinridge, he elected the former as the standard bearer of the regular Democracy even though in principle he sympathized with the latter. Immediately, Jackson precipitated a split within his own ranks as Breckinridge's supporters nominated an opposition slate for governor and lieutenant governor.

Jackson's principal opposition came not from this group, however, for the bulk of the Democracy rallied behind him—at least through the state canvass. Rather it loomed in the form of Sample Orr, an obscure farmer-lawyer from Greene County, who suddenly appeared at a Jackson rally in Springfield on June 15 to announce his independent candidacy and challenge the Democratic nominee to a debate. Jackson attempted to ignore this upstart, but Orr clung doggedly to his heels as he made his canvass from town to town. Whenever his better-known opponent finished speaking, Orr would climb to the platform and hold the audience a bit longer with his ready wit and moderate counsel on the burning issues of the day. When Robert Wilson of Andrew County declined the Constitutional Union party's nomination for governor, its leaders rallied behind Orr and declared him their nominee at a giant ratification meeting in St. Louis early in July.

Both Orr and Jackson canvassed the state strenuously during the final month before the state election, to be held in early August.[1] The Breckinridge nominee, Hancock Lee Jackson, failed to unite the anti-Douglas leadership in his cause. The Republican candidate, James B. Gardenhire, held such slim hopes that three days before Missourians went to the polls he urged his supporters to vote for Orr in the hope of thwarting the Democrats.

In a close contest, Claiborne Jackson emerged victorious with 74,446 votes to Orr's 66,583. Hancock Jackson and Gardenhire trailed far to the rear with 11,416 and 6,137, respectively. Most of Gardenhire's support came from the St. Louis area with its strongly antislavery German population.

Three months later, Missourians went to the polls again to vote

1. Most states held their elections separately from the national contest at this time.

in the national election. An attempt had been made in the interim to persuade the Governor-elect to switch his support to Breckinridge, but Jackson refused to get involved in the presidential canvass. He remained nominally a Douglas man while doing nothing to secure the Illinoisan's election. When the November ballots had been counted, they revealed a Douglas victory in Missouri over John Bell, the Constitutional Unionist, by the narrow margin of 429 votes (58,801 to 58,372). Many of Jackson's earlier supporters had gone over to Breckinridge who polled 31,317. Lincoln received nearly three times Gardenhire's vote but still ran a poor fourth with 17,028.

In both elections, the vast majority of Missourians revealed a desire for compromise on the great issues facing the nation. They had overwhelmingly rejected the candidates of the sectional parties, yet the presidential nominee of one of these groups had been elected, precipitating a political crisis of major proportions.

As Jackson stood to take the oath of office on January 3, he faced a constituency that, with their counterparts North and South, looked to the immediate future with concern and dismay. South Carolina already had withdrawn from the Union, and the states of the lower South were about to follow her. Economic paralysis gripped the nation in the wake of the political uncertainties. A little more than a month earlier, all of Missouri's banks except one had suspended specie payment. Jackson had had two days' warning of the move when he received the request that he not invoke the penalties requisite under the law for such a suspension. Indeed, he was asked to recommend that the legislature "sanction the continuance of such suspension for such a period as the public interests will permit," which he did. A few days later, on December 9, an anxious mother in St. Louis wrote her son in Saline County, "The times were never so hard in St. Louis as they are now, money is scarce and labour is scarcer, hundreds of industrious men are out of employment and the amount of distress in this City never was so great." Given these circumstances it is small wonder that the new governor's audience waited anxiously to see what course he would chart for the state in the days ahead.

One of Jackson's contemporaries described him as "tall, erect,

3

and dignified; a vigorous thinker, and a fluent and forcible speaker, always interesting, and often eloquent." He waxed strongly on this particular evening, placing the blame for the current crisis squarely at the feet of Northern abolitionists who threatened millions of dollars of Southern slave property. Like many another of Southern leanings, he equated the election of a "Black Republican" president with an abolitionist triumph. Hence, while regretting South Carolina's hasty action, he could not really blame her. He only hoped that it might not lead to an even more fatal error—"an attempt at coercion" by the Union.

"So far as Missouri is concerned," he informed his listeners, "her citizens have ever been devoted to the Union, and she will remain in it so long as there is any hope that it will maintain the spirit and guarantees of the Constitution. But if the Northern States have determined to put the slave-holding States on a footing of inequality . . . then *they* have themselves practically abandoned the Union, and will not expect our submission to a government on terms of inequality and subordination." Jackson recommended the calling of a state convention in the immediate future to determine what the true state of affairs was and what Missouri's course should be. And "In view of the marauding forays which continue to harass our borders, as well as of the general unsettled condition of our political relations, a due regard to our honor and safety requires a thorough organization of our militia."

In the days that followed, the Governor worked arduously to activate the militia in anticipation of Missouri's withdrawal from the Union in the immediate future. His principal aide in this effort was Lt. Gov. Thomas Caute Reynolds, who, if anything, believed more ardently in secession than his chief. A native of South Carolina, Reynolds had graduated from the University of Virginia and then gone on to receive his degree of doctor of laws (*summa cum laude*) from the university at Heidelberg. After performing diplomatic service at Madrid, he had settled into a comfortable law practice in St. Louis in the early 1850's and had become United States district attorney and an active participant in Democratic politics. A brilliant man who "bored into the heart of every question with the pitiless auger of com-

4

mon sense," Reynolds could also be impetuous and proud.

The Lieutenant Governor had just returned from secret conferences with certain Southern congressional leaders in Washington where they had discussed how best to carry out plans for secession. Early on the morning following Jackson's inaugural, he convened a meeting in the Capitol's basement to report to those of like mind, both in and out of the legislature, and to formulate plans. All agreed that in any confrontation St. Louis would be vital to determining who would control the state. Here stood a United States arsenal containing some sixty thousand stand of arms, two hundred or more barrels of powder, and other implements of war. The city had a Free-Soil administration under Mayor Oliver D. Filley and was the home of Free-Soil Congressman Frank Blair, a member of one of the nation's most influential families and a close friend of President-elect Lincoln. Blair had been quite active in the Republican cause, organizing the antislavery Germans into Wide Awake clubs for purposes of political demonstration during the recent election. Even as the secessionists met, he was working quietly to disband these groups and broaden his base through reorganizing them, along with members from all pro-Union factions in the city, into Home Guard units.

Reynolds and his cohorts agreed to advocate Jackson's announced program and to add to it a measure that might give them a modicum of control in St. Louis—the establishment of an independent police board appointed by the Governor. The board was instituted by late March with Jackson making his initial appointments on the eve of the firing at Fort Sumter. In the meantime, Reynolds went to St. Louis for a mass meeting to rally fellow secessionists there to the cause. Out of this came the organization of Minute Men, another paramilitary group, to offset Blair's Home Guards. Soon both outfits were drilling secretly in various halls around the city. At the same time, Jackson authorized Brig. Gen. Daniel M. Frost, who commanded the state militia in the St. Louis area, to seize the arsenal if necessary to keep it out of hostile hands. Frost immediately went into consultation with Maj. William H. Bell, the arsenal's commander, who was a native of North Carolina and sympathetic with the secessionists. He came away with assurance that Bell would co-operate with the state forces when the proper time came.

As the General Assembly got down to work on the Governor's program, it reflected existing political divisions, although not in proportion to the votes in the recent election. Malapportionment and holdover senators gave the Breckinridge Democrats a combined plurality of 62 in both houses as compared with 46 Douglas Democrats, 44 Constitutional Unionists, and 13 Republicans.[2] Thus, by combination, the moderates could block such stringent Jackson proposals as virtually unlimited gubernatorial power to completely reorganize the militia and the sending of representatives to the convention of seceded states called for at Montgomery, Alabama.

The Assembly did approve his recommendation for a state convention; but, in so doing, they seemed merely to respond to public opinion as expressed through the editorial columns of the state's newspapers and the accounts therein of numerous mass meetings supporting such a move. To make certain, however, that the convention not take precipitate action, the legislators approved a moderate proposal requiring a statewide referendum on any act of secession. In place of sending representatives to Montgomery, it designated five men to go to Washington to sit in the convention called by Virginia in the hope of working out a peaceful solution to the pending crisis.

Although Governor Jackson and his friends hoped that the election for a state convention would vindicate their cause, most Missourians continued to follow their inclinations of the previous fall by voting against extreme solutions. With candidates running, not under partisan labels, but as Conditional or Constitutional Unionists, Unconditional Unionists, and States' Rights or Anti-Submission men, the voters chose the representatives of the first two groups by a resouding margin of approximately 80,000. Not a single avowed secessionist secured election, and only four known Republicans, all from St. Louis, won.

For all their concern with the protection of slave property and the preservation of the rights of Southerners, the Jackson men

2. The proportions were approximately the same in both houses.

had failed to adequately take into account the changing conditions in Missouri. The state's over-all population had climbed nearly 75 per cent during the previous decade to 1,182,012, of whom 114,931 (1 in 9) were slaves. This was a vastly different ratio from the 1 to 4½ of thirty years earlier. Most of these Negroes lived in counties with borders that lay within fifty miles of Missouri's two great rivers. With only 59 of the state's 24,320 slaveholders owning more than 40 chattels, it can readily be seen that Missouri was not a land of large plantations. Twenty-five per cent of these owned only one slave while more than 70 per cent had less than five, which would indicate that most Missouri slaves were either household servants or worked as farm laborers in small groups.

By contrast with this decline of slavery in both percentage of population and economic importance, the state's white population had nearly doubled in the 1850's—much of this due to immigration, which in increasing numbers came from the Northern states and abroad. Indeed, while the percentage of native Missourians had remained relatively stable at 44 per cent and that of Southern-born had increased 44 per cent, the population of those of Northern birth had jumped 180 per cent while that of foreign birth rose 110 per cent. By 1860 Northern- and foreign-born outnumbered the Southern-born within the state's population for the first time. Those emigrants from the North tended to settle in the southwest prairies and the more fertile of the Ozark regions, the upper tier of counties beyond the recently completed Hannibal and St. Joseph Railroad, and in and around St. Louis. The foreign-born concentrated almost entirely near St. Louis, although they spread out along the Missouri River as far west as Cole County. Marion County in the northeast, Buchanan and Platte counties at the opposite end of the state, and Cooper and Lafayette counties in west-central Missouri had also absorbed a considerable influx of foreign-born settlers. The majority of these were German and Irish, with the former outnumbering the latter two to one. Both of these ethnic groups were antislavery and to a considerable extent anti-Negro. These newcomers had not yet emerged to a dominant position politically as illustrated by the makeup of the new convention, in which all but 17 of 99 members had Southern origins. Still, they had to be reckoned with. Another five years and a new convention would present a different story.

In addition to changing population trends, the state's economic patterns were slowly shifting. With the inching of the railroad south and west across the Illinois prairie, more and more freight traffic moved east rather than south along the rivers. The bridging of the Mississippi by the Rock Island Railroad near Davenport, Iowa, in 1856 and the completion of the Hannibal and St. Joseph Railroad across northern Missouri two years later helped to divert considerable trade away from the Missouri River line into St. Louis, to the advantage of that growing lakeside community, Chicago. Even though the river traffic south to New Orleans still represented the major portion of Missouri's trade, a large part of it was ultimately destined for eastern markets. This made secession even less desirable, because the new connections to the East could carry much of the cargo that had been shipped on the river.

Further, as the state's largest newspaper, the *Missouri Republican* at St. Louis, pointed out, secession would leave the state practically isolated in a sea of Union territory even if Arkansas should withdraw. There was virtually no possibility that a Southern confederacy could dominate the Mississippi as far north as St. Louis. The South had little to offer Missouri economically, for its free-trade policy would destroy her hemp industry and it had no capital with which to help develop the state's considerable mineral potential. Capital could come only from the East. To cap it, the *Republican* argued, secession would harm rather than protect Missouri's slave property, for with so much free hostile territory around her, the temptation for flight might be nearly irresistible. These sentiments had been reiterated in numerous mass meetings in the month prior to the election.

For all their Southern antecedents, the delegates to Missouri's state convention readily agreed that secession would not be wise economically. They gathered initially at Jefferson City on Thursday, February 28, but finding the crowded facilities in the Cole County courthouse not to their liking, they accepted the prearranged invitation of the Mercantile Library Association of St.

Louis to adjourn over the weekend and reconvene to its spacious quarters. There they spent eighteen days in deliberation, hearing, among others, the recently returned delegates from the Washington Peace Convention who reported that it had ended in failure because the Republicans had refused to cooperate.[3]

In the course of the deliberations Hamilton R. Gamble emerged as the convention's dominant figure. A prominent St. Louis attorney with extensive property interests and a former judge of the Missouri Supreme Court, Gamble was a conservative ex-Whig who had come out of semiretirement in Pennsylvania to seek a convention seat at the urging of his brother-in-law Edward Bates and others. He caught the popular imagination with a stirring pro-Union speech at a courthouse rally in early January. Nominated by both Conditional and Unconditional Unionists, he led the St. Louis ticket. Now his colleagues showed their esteem by making him chairman of the Committee on Federal Relations. As such, he wrote the report the convention adopted with minimal opposition.

Through the report, the delegates rejected secession and called upon Missouri to "labor for such an adjustment of existing troubles as will gain the peace, as well as the rights and equality of all the states." To ensure states' rights, the report approved the Crittenden Compromise which Congress had just rejected and urged the calling of a national convention by the state legislatures to provide a constitutional guarantee of slavery. Supposedly, this body would implement the recently passed congressional amendment for that purpose. Pending further attempts at compromise, the convention urged that neither North nor South take military action against each other. In this connection, Gamble agreed to amend the report to advocate that federal troops be withdrawn from "the forts within the borders of the seceding States where there is danger of collision between the State and Federal troops."

3. One of the Missourians attending, Alexander W. Doniphan, had written home earlier that most of the Republicans who were at the convention had gone there to seek office from the incoming Lincoln administration, and they were using their presence at the meeting as a means of having their expenses for the trip paid by their respective states.

Of the other amendments proposed, only one received serious consideration. It sought to assure that Missouri would join her Southern sisters if the North rejected compromise for coercion and the rest of the border states left the Union; it failed 70 to 23. Many of those who favored it later went South when the final crisis came. Included among them was Sterling Price, the convention's president.

Having completed its work, the convention adjourned until the third Monday in December, 1861, with the proviso that a select committee of seven might reconvene it earlier if necessity arose. It thereby kept the door ajar for possible further action, but probably few realized the direction of such a course. Here, in March, 1861, three weeks before the firing on Fort Sumter, Missouri's representatives had spoken in favor of Union and compromise. Like their delegates to the Washington Peace Convention, however, they would discover that the latter was impossible unless the North would accept the new status quo, which it did not.

The bombardment of Fort Sumter and the coming of the war brought Missourians face to face with the reality most of them had tried thus far to avoid. The President promptly called for 75,000 three-month volunteers to quell the rebellion and assigned each state a quota through the War Department. In response to the request that Missouri furnish 4,000 men, Governor Jackson gave a sharp negative. In the heat of the moment many Missourians sided with him to resist the coercive policy upon which the United States was about to embark.

Congressman Frank Blair returned to St. Louis from Washington even as the Governor made known his reply. He promptly wired the Secretary of War, offering to muster his Home Guards into service to fill the state's quota. A quick affirmative came back and with it orders recalling Gen. William S. Harney, the departmental commander, to Washington. A conservative Regular Army veteran, Harney had sought conciliation between state and federal authority. He had been moving too slowly in securing the arsenal and its property to please Blair and his friends. They wanted action.

The departure of Harney catapulted to prominence a hitherto

relatively obscure officer, Capt. Nathaniel Lyon, who had arrived at Jefferson Barracks from Fort Riley just two months earlier. A New Englander by birth, Lyon had witnessed at first hand the attempts by Missourians to impose slavery on Kansas in the 1850's. This experience had served to strengthen in him already existing antislavery feelings. No stauncher Unionist could have been found to aid Frank Blair's cause. The two of them had been working in harness since shortly after Lyon's arrival in February to make certain that the valuable arsenal remained safely in Union hands. Now, with Harney out of the way, they moved quickly to muster the Home Guards into federal service and distribute arms to them. They sent the arsenal's surplus across the river for the use of Illinois troops; then, Lyon dispatched four companies to occupy buildings and ground surrounding the approaches to the arsenal in the event secessionists carried out recent threats. Even as he did so, new orders arrived from Washington authorizing the muster of an additional ten thousand men under his personal command "for the protection of the peaceable inhabitants of Missouri." Should occasion warrant, he might also proclaim martial law in St. Louis.

The mustering of the German Home Guards increased tensions in the city. The guards sought to carry out their directives with a zeal that only further angered Southerners, who were already resentful of these upstarts whose ways and ideas had begun to change St. Louis during the past decade. The Southerners looked to Governor Jackson for action. It was not long in coming. On the same day he declined to furnish troops for the Union cause, Jackson met covertly with his St. Louis militia commander, General Frost, and the other secessionists in the area. Out of this conference came a decision to call a special session of the legislature "to place the State in a proper attitude of defense" while ordering the militia into training musters at various points around the state.

Mustering the militia was designed to serve as a coverup for an attempt by Frost to seize the arsenal by placing his encampment on a high rise to the south of that facility. To provide the necessary artillery to accomplish that mission, Frost suggested and Jackson agreed to dispatch secret envoys to seek aid from both the Confederate government at Montgomery and the recently seceded state of Virginia. The two governments responded readily. Virginia authorized the sending of twenty-two guns. Jefferson Davis ordered two 12-pound howitzers and two 32-pound guns forwarded to Frost. He assured Jackson that "our power to supply you with ordnance is far short of the will to serve you" and expressed the hope that it would not be long before Missouri's star joined the others in his nation's flag. Through his Secretary of War, the Confederate President sent a request that the state provide a regiment for service in Virginia. Governor Jackson replied that he could not make such a strong commitment so soon. When the time came, however, he felt confident that Missouri would furnish 100,000 men to the Southern cause.

The quick actions of Lyon and Blair thwarted the immediate plans of state officials, although their projected program still went forward. The latter scurried around St. Louis and elsewhere to purchase the necessary arms and supplies to equip the proposed militia musters. Secessionists in the western part of the state seized without authorization the small federal arsenal at Liberty with its four brass guns and fifteen hundred stand of arms.

The legislature assembled on May 2, while the militiamen went into a week's encampment around the state four days later. When Lyon declined to yield to the prosecession police board's request that he withdraw all his troops from their positions outside the arsenal, Frost established Camp Jackson, named for the Governor, in a wooded valley known as Lindell Grove, near Grand and Olive streets. This position, as state officials knew only too well, made the militia powerless to accomplish their ends. In addition, the encampment amounted to only seven hundred men, against Lyon's ten thousand. Further, with all of its surplus arms having been sent to Illinois, the arsenal had lost much of its importance.

Two days after the establishment of Camp Jackson, the arms and ammunition sent by Jefferson Davis arrived from down river. They had been taken from the federal arsenal at Baton Rouge and concealed in boxes marked "marble Tamaroa." Militia officers met the shipment and took it to Camp Jackson where the cases remained unopened.

General Lyon now became convinced that the encampment presented a hostile threat and that it must be seized to prevent an attack. To confirm his suspicions, he disguised himself as Frank Blair's blind mother-in-law and took a ride through the area in an open carriage on Thursday afternoon. There he saw small Confederate flags flying from some of the tentpoles and noted handmade signs at the intersection of two streets designating them as "Davis" and "Beauregard" avenues.

Lyon summoned the Union Safety Committee that evening to announce his plans and to seek their approval. He found them divided. While agreeing that the stolen federal property from Baton Rouge could not be ignored, some argued that it be resecured by serving Frost with a writ of replevin through a federal marshal. Lyon overrode their objections and prepared to move out the following day. Ignoring Frost's protests that the militia had done nothing illegal, his troops surrounded Camp Jackson and demanded its surrender within a half hour. The relative difference in size of forces made resistance futile, so Frost complied. The Union troops thereupon placed the militia under arrest and marched them to the arsenal.

All of this activity attracted a crowd as many St. Louisans, some with relatives or friends at the encampment, rushed westward to see what was happening. Among them was William Tecumseh Sherman, who had moved only recently to the city to assume the presidency of the street railway company after a slow-moving Lincoln Administration had been unable to make up its mind on an appointment for him. By his own telling, Sherman had been offered Harney's post by Blair at the time of the general's recall and had turned it down. He had gone with his children to the arsenal the previous day for one of the visits that had become a regular habit with him. There he found Lyon "running about with his hair in the wind, his pockets full of papers, wild and irregular, but I knew him to be a man of vehement purpose and of determined action." Now he discovered to what purpose.

As Sherman reached the end of Olive Street opposite Lindell

Grove, he saw Frank Blair's regiment lined up on either side of the thoroughfare with ranks open and the militia prisoners between them. The procession moved out toward the arsenal with a band at its head playing a martial tune. The crowd was composed of citizens of mixed sympathies who begun to grow restive. Some cheered for Jeff Davis and Southern resistance while cursing the Germans; others encouraged the Union forces. Sherman headed into the park where he soon witnessed an altercation between a drunk who had tried to cross the military lines and one of the Home Guards. Having been treated rather unceremoniously, the drunk whipped out a pistol and fired toward the troops, who stopped in place and loosed a volley over the heads of the crowd. In the confusion, Sherman lost track of events. He seized his son and fell to the ground for protection; then he hurried back toward the city. Later reports revealed that twenty-eight persons had been killed and many others wounded in the ensuing melee.

An investigation by Lyon exonerated the troops, but regardless of the riot's instigator, war had come to Missouri. In St. Louis many Southern sympathizers panicked as rioting continued through the night. In a rare instance of cooperation between federal and local authorities, the disturbance was brought under control, but the following weekend a considerable number of citizens packed what belongings they could gather and headed down river or into the county "to escape the Dutch."

As numerous observers indicated later, life was never the same after the incident at Camp Jackson. It forced Missourians to get off the fence and make immediate personal choices. Tensions in the state had been mounting since the bombardment of Fort Sumter, and Lyon's movement against Camp Jackson released them in full fury. William F. Switzler, the conservative pro-Union editor of the Columbia *Missouri Statesman*, later recalled: "Nothing equal to it in the intensity of popular delirium occurred during the war." Many Missourians, in an emotional reaction, rushed to the defense of the state—some to regret the ultimate direction in which this action would take them later. Those who came forth strongly for the Union found their course difficult over the next few months, especially in areas outside St. Louis where they had little official protection.

While one can argue, as some do, that for Lyon to have restrained himself would simply have postponed the inevitable,[4] it is difficult to justify his action. For all his assertions to the contrary, the encampment did not pose a direct threat to his military position. It had been scheduled to break up the next day. Its numbers were less than 10 per cent of his, with little to back them up, while he could call in additional troops from surrounding states, as he did a month later. By his own admission in his official report, many of the muskets later found at the camp were in pieces, "all separate, and apparently without ever having been put together." While the theft of federal arms from Baton Rouge was genuine cause for some action, the use of the writ of replevin, as suggested by one member of the Union Safety Committee, might have accomplished the purpose of asserting Union authority while keeping tensions at a controllable level.

Missouri had already spoken in favor of the Union through its state convention; and, although the compromise it had hoped for at the national level had failed, fewer than one fourth of its members would defect from their original Unionism in the tumultuous days that followed. For all Lyon's lumping of the Governor and legislature together in one pro-Southern bag, Jackson had been having continuing difficulty with the General Assembly. The moderates were in control at Jefferson City, and, after sitting for a week in special session, the General Assembly seemed no more ready to pass the Governor's new militia bill than it had at its earlier meeting.

But when Claiborne Jackson entered the Hall of Representatives early in the evening of May 10 with the news of the events at Camp Jackson, resistance crumbled rapidly. The Governor's bill, which provided for the enrollment of every able-

4. This view was popularized by John Fiske, *The Mississippi Valley in the Civil War* (Boston, 1900) and John McElroy, *The Struggle for Missouri* (Washington, D.C., 1909), among others, and eventually was stated in many textbooks. It is not very widely accepted today, although Albert Castel implies that he supports it. See *General Sterling Price and the Civil War in the West* (Baton Rouge, 1968), p. 22.

bodied man under the state flag for its defense, passed through both houses in fifteen minutes, and Jackson promptly signed it into law. Subsequently, that same evening the General Assembly enacted another measure granting the militia all funds reserved for the state's schools and charitable institutions. It also authorized a loan of $1 million from Missouri's banks as well as the issuance of an additional $1 million in state defense bonds.

Toward midnight, the legislators were summoned once again by the ringing of church bells to hear that "two of Mr. Blair's regiments were on the way to the capital." Although this news turned out to be wild rumor, in its wake the startled Assembly rushed through legislation that gave Governor Jackson carte blanche in organizing the state's defenses. The thwarted executive had been released from his cage, and he promptly made the most of his opportunity. He had already sent some detachments to guard the approaches to Jefferson City at the bridges of the Pacific Railroad over the Gasconade and Osage rivers. Although no attack came, in the excitement some of the troops fired the Osage bridge, partially destroying it. The Governor, on learning of the accident, promptly ordered that the bridge be repaired the next morning.

While panic reigned in St. Louis and Jefferson City as well as elsewhere in the state, General Harney returned from Washington to resume his command. He had been captured by Confederates at Harpers Ferry, Virginia, on his way east, taken to Richmond where he refused to align with the Southern cause, and then released. Once arrived at Washington he had persuaded General-in-Chief Winfield Scott, a close personal friend, and the War Department that his firm but conciliatory policy would hold Missouri for the Union. Now, he promptly released a proclamation approving the capture of Camp Jackson and scoring the General Assembly for its new legislation. He promised to maintain order in the city and did so while avoiding a declaration of martial law. Warrants were secured from the Federal District Court authorizing the United States Marshal, accompanied by troops, to search out and seize all illegal arms caches in the city. All trains and other transportation entering and leaving the city were searched to prevent the movement of contraband.

Upon learning that secessionists were harassing loyal men at Potosi on the Iron Mountain Railroad, Harney sent a request to Scott for reinforcements and arms and dispatched troops there to relieve the situation and secure its vital lead works. They arrested fifty troublemakers and then paroled all but nine of the leaders, whom they brought back to St. Louis prisoner. A few refugee families began to arrive from towns along the Pacific Railroad, but apparently Harney sent no forces in that direction. Enlistments continued apace with nine hundred Irish being formed into a separate regiment and a group of native Missourians organizing an outfit of Zuaves.

Governor Jackson, meanwhile, moved forward with his reorganization of the militia (now termed the Missouri State Guard). Somewhat reluctantly because of past differences, but at the insistence of Lieutenant Governor Reynolds, he named Sterling Price to head the new organization. A former governor and a hero of the Mexican War, Price had chaired the recent convention. He was only one of several prominent Missourians who, previously neutral, had offered the state their services. He and Jackson now worked vigorously to prepare Missouri for what they considered inevitable conflict. Eight district brigadiers were appointed, with orders to enroll every eligible man in their areas. More than one thousand volunteers had already poured into Jefferson City itching for a fight. They were quickly mustered and stationed at the nearby fairgrounds pending further action.

While Missouri rapidly became an armed camp, alarmed conservative Unionists dispatched James E. Yeatman and Hamilton R. Gamble to Washington to plead with the Administration for a tactful firmness. Countering them was Franklin A. Dick, Frank Blair's brother-in-law, who hastened to the nation's capital to urge a free hand for Lyon in carrying out the work he had begun. Fearful that Harney would stand in the way, Dick sought that general's complete and final removal. Yeatman and Gamble, however, looked upon Harney as the only one on the scene who could restore saneness and order.

In the ensuing debate in the Administration, Atty. Gen. Edward Bates gave strong backing to the conservatives while Postmaster General Montgomery Blair sided with his brother. The two men would usually remain on opposite sides of debates over Missouri policy during the next four years. This time Lincoln, in typical fashion, tried to steer a middle course. He agreed, with some reservations, to an order for Harney's removal, which was to be forwarded to Frank Blair through his brother. But this order was to be held in abeyance by the Missouri congressman for the time being, to give Harney a chance to accomplish his mission. The President feared that an immediate change would lead to accusations of vacillation in the Administration and would "dissatisfy a good many who otherwise would be quiet." But, in the end, he allowed Frank Blair a free hand to serve the order whenever he deemed it necessary. At the same time, the War Department issued orders confirming Lyon's appointment as brigadier general of the volunteers he had recently mustered in for three years' service.

Frank Blair received the news of these events on May 20. That same day Sterling Price arrived in St. Louis for consultations with General Harney. The following morning they issued a communiqué to announce their agreement for keeping the peace in Missouri. Essentially, they were to embark on a cooperative venture, with Price responsible for maintaining order outstate and Harney looking after the St. Louis area. So long as Price kept his part of the bargain, the Union commander would not move troops beyond the confines of the city and its environs. Harney accompanied the announcement with a proclamation calling upon the people of Missouri "to observe good order, and respect the rights of their fellow-citizens, and give them the assurance of protection and security in the most ample manner." Price returned to Jefferson City where he promptly ordered the dispersal of all troops, except one St. Louis company, to their home districts where they would be organized under the law. Harney had urged him to suspend all militia operations but supposed the guard would be the means by which Price tried to keep order.

The Harney–Price agreement displeased the extremists on both sides; and, whether by design or otherwise, it failed in its purpose.[5] The guardsmen at Jefferson City were obviously disappointed, and at one point it appeared they might mutiny. Having been called to defend the state capital, it now appeared, on the surface at least, that no crisis existed; but many were spoiling for a fight. Their tempers were probably not cooled by the revelation that a misguided Unionist had attempted to poison their bread supply. He had approached an aged Negress who lived near their bakery and tried to persuade her to put arsenic in their flour, with the promise that once this had been done Frank Blair would come to Jefferson City to set all the slaves free. She wisely had reported him to the authorities.

By May 26 most of the troops were on their way home. Thomas W. Knox, the correspondent of the *New York Herald*, encountered them at the Jefferson City depot when he arrived from St. Louis that afternoon. Knox had reached Missouri ten days earlier with Albert D. Richardson of the *New York Tribune* to cover the stirring events there. In the wake of the Harney–Price agreement, he had decided to see for himself what was going on in the capital. After two days at Jefferson City, he was convinced that the state authorities were merely playing for time. He found the Confederate flag flying at Camp Frost, where

5. The motivations of Jackson and Price in concluding an agreement with Harney have been the subject of considerable controversy among historians. One group contends that Jackson and Price was merely stalling for time and had no intention of remaining neutral for long. Therefore, the agreement could serve as a cover for further preparations to carry Missouri into the Confederacy. See Arthur R. Kirkpatrick, "Missouri in the Early Months of the Civil War," *Missouri Historical Review*, 55 (April, 1961), 235–66, and Castel, *General Sterling Price*, 14–22. Other historians state that the views of the two men were different. While accepting Jackson as an avowed secessionist, they argue that Price served as a moderating influence and genuinely hoped that neutrality might be maintained through this agreement. See Allan Nevins, *The War for the Union*, I (New York, 1959), pp. 126–29, and Robert E. Shalhope, *Sterling Price: Portrait of a Southerner* (Columbia, Missouri, 1971), pp. 160–64. Yet another interpretation is that of William H. Lyon who contends that both Jackson and Price now accepted neutrality as the only hope for Missouri in view of superior Union military force. See "Claiborne Fox Jackson and the Secession Crisis in Missouri," *Missouri Historical Review*, 58 (July, 1964), 422–41.

two companies of guardsmen remained, from the staff in front of the governor's mansion, and elsewhere in town. Rumor was rife that Jackson was conferring with a secret agent from Richmond; negotiating with John Ross, the president of the Choctaw Nation, for aid; and sending wagon trains to Arkansas to pick up arms.[6] The Governor managed to spare Knox fifteen minutes for an interview in a local bar. The reporter noted in his dispatch the following day, "The Governor is a shrewd talker, and one cannot 'make much out of him.' His face is indicative of treachery, and no one ever so insane would select Claib. Jackson as a model of all the masculine virtues. He affects a deep regret at the recent occurrences, and hopes all difficulties will soon be settled."

It appears almost certain that these hopes pointed in the direction of some kind of arrangement with the Confederacy. Jackson's private correspondence, such as is extant, indicates his concern to move as quickly as possible toward secession. He had already dispatched agents to Little Rock and Richmond to seek military aid from Arkansas and Confederate authorities. Yet, in all of this, there seems to have been an unfortunate working at cross purposes by state officials, which apparently grew out of mutual distrust. When Lieutenant Governor Reynolds informed Jackson around May 18 or 19 that he planned to visit the Confederacy and offered to take any messages the Governor might wish to send, the latter simply informed him that he already had an emissary there. He gave no further details. In reality, Reynolds had decided to make the trip because of his apprehensions that Jackson had been immobilized through fear of federal authorities. He planned to make a direct appeal to Jefferson Davis for troops to hold the state, but he said nothing of this to the Governor. He did take Price into his confidence, however, and the latter sent along a written request to the same effect. According to Reynolds, the guard commander's parting words were: "Get Jefferson Davis to send in Confederate troops as soon as possible."

The two men had gone to the Jefferson City depot together on May 20—Price to entrain for St. Louis and his meeting with Harney, Reynolds to go to Fort Smith, Arkansas. It was not

6. None of these rumors have been substantiated by historical evidence.

20

until the Lieutenant Governor reached his destination that he learned, through the press, of the real purpose of Price's mission.[7] Jackson and his guard commander had decided to keep this plan from Reynolds for fear that his objections might ruin their negotiations.

Meanwhile, the more ardent Unionists of St. Louis felt that Harney had betrayed them. James O. Broadhead of the Union Safety Committee complained to Montgomery Blair: "We fear that no good will come of the arrangement but that it will only result in putting off the evil day until such time as the enemy will be better prepared to make resistance." Reports that seemed to confirm Broadhead's suspicions began flowing into St. Louis from all parts of outstate Missouri almost immediately. They told of the organization of the Missouri State Guard and the subsequent harrassment of Union citizens in various locales, some of whom were reported fleeing from their homes in central and western Missouri. At St. Joseph, a mob had surrounded the post office and the Germans' Turner Hall and forced the lowering of the Stars and Stripes.

Harney was concerned and, acting partially under pressure from an anxious Administration, wired Price concerning these outrages and a rumored invasion by Confederate forces from Arkansas. The guard commander replied that he knew nothing of the latter but would resist it with everything he had, a rather ironic twist in view of the Reynolds and other missions. As for the distresses of the Unionists, Price considered these reports grossly exaggerated. Where they had occurred they were the work of "irresponsible individuals," and he would do his best to quell them.

Harney seemed relieved by these assurances, but Blair refused to accept them. On May 30 he delivered Lincoln's order to remove Harney from his command.[8] Nathaniel Lyon automatical-

7. Reynolds was particularly puzzled by the part of the agreement in which Price promised Harney that he would resist any Confederate invasion of Missouri. This stipulation was contrary to every plan he had made with Price. It marked the beginning of Reynolds's suspicions of Price's motives, a situation that would plague their relationship throughout the war.

8. General Harney spent the remainder of the war in retirement.

ly succeeded him. The new commander immediately pushed the enrollment of additional volunteers in St. Louis and began recruiting in the villages along the Pacific Railroad to the west. Writing The Adjutant General of the reported Confederate threat through Arkansas, he asked for standby authorization to call in Iowa and Illinois troops. Price immediately moved to ready his forces. While publicly urging calm and asserting his hope that Lyon would not move beyond St. Louis, he sent secret orders to his district commanders to hasten their respective enrollments and get their men ready for action.

Many conservatives still hoped to avert open hostilities. They supported Harney's plea for reinstatement, but to no avail. When all else seemed hopeless, they arranged a conference in St. Louis between the leaders of both sides. Undoubtedly Jackson and Price attended because they felt the need for more time to get their forces ready. Lyon, in an uncompromising mood, probably looked upon it as a sop to those Unionists who had criticized him for being too rash. Whatever the case, he and Blair, accompanied by an aide, went to the Governor's suite in the Planter's House late in the morning of June 11. For the next four hours, they debated with the state officials over the right of the Union to raise Home Guards in the interior and to station forces there against an anticipated invasion. When it became obvious that agreement was impossible, Lyon intoned slowly and with great emphasis: "Rather than concede to the State of Missouri for one single instant the right to dictate to my Government in any matter however unimportant, I would see you, and you, and you, and every man, woman, and child in the State, dead and buried." Then, having risen to his feet, he sternly announced: "*This means war.* In one hour one of my officers will call for you and conduct you out of my lines." Without waiting for a reply, he turned on his heel and stalked out of the room.

The startled state officials did not wait for an escort. They hastened to the railroad yards where they commandeered an engine and sped down a cleared track to Jefferson City. Stopping only long enough to fuel the engine and burn the bridges over the Gasconade and Osage rivers behind them, they arrived in the capital at two o'clock the next morning. While they were

22

en route, they discussed what action they should take. Governor Jackson outlined a proclamation through which he would sound the tocsin for resistance. In it, he reported the futile interview and then called for fifty thousand volunteers to fill the ranks of the State Guard. The executive's secretary, Thomas L. Snead, who had attended the Planter's House conference, hurried from the train to get the document ready for distribution. By dawn it was going to all corners of the state with directives to the district commanders to assemble their men at a convenient place and have them ready for instant service in the field.

Brig. Gen. John B. Clark of the North Missouri District received orders to proceed with his command to Boonville, which Price had earlier determined would make a better defensible position than Jefferson City if Lyon moved up river. Boonville stood at the edge of the northwestern corner of the state, which had a relatively pro-Southern population. Here the guard could rally and, with anticipated Confederate help from Arkansas, hold the western third of Missouri, pending additional recruitment. Jackson had ordered the armory and workshop removed to Boonville ten days earlier. Now state officials hastily packed records and other necessary items for shipment to the temporary capital. Missouri's authorities pulled out on the afternoon of June 13 after word arrived that Lyon was preparing to embark for Jefferson City. Theirs would be a government-in-exile from that time forth.

Forty-eight hours later Lyon arrived at the capital with three steamboats and two thousand men. Thomas W. Knox, the *New York Herald*'s correspondent who accompanied the expedition, reported that they had found sentiment along the river banks strongly in favor of the Union with Home Guard units having been hastily formed to protect the railroad from further damage. This was not too surprising in view of the large numbers of Germans in these counties.

Finding Jefferson City deserted, Lyon remained only twenty-four hours before continuing upriver toward Boonville. He left behind a small garrison under Col. Henry Boernstein's command. These troops occupied the Capitol where Albert D. Richardson, the correspondent of the *New York Tribune*, found them a day or two later cooking on the grass, "standing in the shade of its portico and rotunda, lying on beds of hay in its passages, and upon carpets in the legislative halls." Richardson, who had been on an excursion to Cairo, Illinois, had missed the Planter's House conference and Lyon's subsequent embarkation. Now Colonel Boernstein showed the correspondent around the occupied city. At the governor's mansion Richardson noted "Sofas were overturned, carpets torn up and littered with letters and public documents. Tables, chairs, damask curtains, cigar-boxes, champagne-bottles, ink-stands, books, private letters, and family knick-knacks were scattered everywhere in chaotic confusion. . . . Beds were unmade, dishes unwashed, silver forks and spoons, belonging to the State, scattered here and there." Then ironically, "The only things that appeared undisturbed were the Star Spangled Banner and the national escutcheon, both frescoed upon the plaster of the gubernatorial bedroom."

Lyon meanwhile had routed the state forces at Boonville with little difficulty. Upon his arrival, Price had learned that Federal troops from Kansas threatened Lexington, a city he deemed vital to his plans. He hastened to Lexington and left only about five hundred men behind at Boonville. Jackson assumed personal command of these troops, and, when Lyon appeared on the morning of June 17, the Governor ordered a charge. With raw, undisciplined troops the situation quickly became a fiasco. When news of the events at Boonville reached Price at Lexington the following day, he realized his original line of defense had become untenable. He ordered retreat to the southern border while he went ahead to try to secure help from the Confederates in Arkansas.

The incident at Boonville could hardly be called a skirmish, but the dispatches Knox, Richardson, and other correspondents sent east reported the vigor with which Lyon acted, and he became an overnight hero. Here, obviously, was the man of action the people were looking for in that initial summer of what they hoped would be a short war. Operating in generally hostile territory with a minimum of logistical support and supply, Lyon proved to be a remarkable organizer who understood quite readily what the situation demanded in Missouri. Simultaneous-

24

ly with his own advance on Jefferson City, he had dispatched approximately nine hundred Home Guards under Col. Franz Sigel down the line of the southwestern branch of the Pacific Railroad to Rolla. From there they were to march overland to Springfield so they would be in a position to insert themselves between Missouri forces coming from the north and any Confederates advancing from Arkansas. Sigel's advance occupied Springfield on June 23 and then moved on west as Lyon, hampered by bad weather, remained at Boonville, waiting for reinforcements and supplies. The fiery German finally intercepted the retreating Jackson and his forces near Carthage on July 7. Although outnumbered four to one, Sigel charged the state troops only to be brushed aside after a brief encounter. The way was now open for the State Guard to complete its retreat into the southwestern corner of Missouri, its morale somewhat improved by its victory over the Germans. Sigel made his way back to Springfield to await the coming of Lyon.

Meanwhile, at Lyon's instigation, troops were pouring into Missouri from all sides—Kansas, Iowa, Illinois. Maj. Samuel D. Sturgis entered the state from Fort Leavenworth with 2,300 men; quickly the Stars and Stripes flew once again at St. Joseph. Then, at Lyon's direction, Sturgis headed south toward Lexington and Price. Even as he did so, Lyon ordered all river traffic stopped along the Missouri. Union patrols were set up at all major crossings, and an improvised gunboat, the *John Warner*, roamed between Boonville and Kansas City destroying boats and rafts the enemy might find useful.

At the other end of the state, the First Iowa Volunteers reached Hannibal around midnight of June 14 while Lyon was on his way to Jefferson City. The next day they quickly deployed along the line of the Hannibal and St. Joseph Railroad, which had been completed across the state just two years earlier. Thus they brought another vital thoroughfare under control and further handicapped Price's operations and recruiting in north Missouri. The Iowans faced a difficult assignment, but they were capable of meeting it. At Macon, where they established temporary headquarters, they took over the prosecession *Missouri Register* and renamed it *The Whole Union*. They managed to get out one issue before being ordered up to join Lyon at Boonville. They found several Confederate flags flying in Macon and surrounding neighborhoods. These were lowered quickly, and the regimental fife and drum corps serenaded those who were willing to raise the Union colors. To persuade the populace of the importance of loyalty to the North, the Iowans developed regimental orators who gave "red-hot, spread-eagle Union speeches" to any person or group who would listen. At the same time, they had more serious work to accomplish as the Southern sympathizers in that region turned to the type of warfare that was to plague Missouri throughout the remainder of the conflict—guerrilla hit-and-run tactics. Trains rarely came in without bullet scars from bushwhacker attacks, and the bridge guards got little sleep at night.

Upon being ordered to Boonville, the Iowans turned their duty in north-central Missouri over to men from Illinois. While they were en route on the line of the North Missouri Railroad, they encountered a variety of adventures. They iron-plated the engine of their train to make it bulletproof and removed the doors from the cars "so that the boys could jump out and shoot." The road lay through heavy timber, and they came under sniper fire almost immediately. At one clearing they noticed a farmer plowing. As the troop train came into sight he stopped his team and "began gesticulating and shaking his fist at the train." One of the company, in response, drew a bead on him and splintered the handle of his plow. The farmer hit the dirt and remained there until the train passed.

At one or two stops the Iowans received warnings from blacks of various secession patrols in the neighborhood. At another crossing they were greeted by "an old negro woman, [who] yelled and danced and shrieked and acted like a howling dervish." The men encouraged her, and the obviously antislavery regimental historian later wrote, "It was a wild, hysterical outbreak of joy . . . a sight never to be forgotten; she seemed to know what the war was about."

Lyon remained at Boonville until July 3, hampered by problems of equipment, supply, and weather. But he used this time to get his men ready for the campaign ahead of them. An extraordinarily intense man, Lyon also proved a stern disciplinarian. Journalist Franc B. Wilkie, who arrived with the First Iowa and would soon become the correspondent for the *New York Times*, has left a vivid picture:

> When he first looked at one the stormy expression would settle into his eyes, and a fierce questioning would light them with a moody gleam; a moment later, the storm-clouds would roll away as one spoke to him, and would pile up again as he began to reply. He was intensely loyal and earnest in his views of the war and his hatred of the treason of the people of the South. He was a strict disciplinarian, and was severe and unsmiling when with the soldiers. I have seen him dismount from his horse to kick a soldier who was lugging off some article of property belonging to a citizen, and at the same time [he] would overwhelm the offender with opprobrious epithets. He was known among the regulars as "Daddy"; and when the cry was passed along, "Daddy is coming!" everything would be quiet as death. He was often seen, when in camp, wandering absently about, plucking his long beard with one hand, apparently noticing nothing, and yet permitting no detail to escape his observation. . . . I do not think he knew the meaning of fear, and had he lived, there would have been another name well to the front in the list of the great ones, at the close of the contest.

Two days before Lyon advanced toward Springfield to rendezvous with Sigel and Sturgis, President Lincoln appointed a new commander for the Department of the West. As an old friend of the Blair family and the son-in-law of the late Thomas Hart Benton, John Charles Frémont seemed an ideal choice. He was thoroughly acquainted in the area, which had served as a launching station for many of his expeditions to the West. Frémont had become the Blairs' candidate for the post after Missouri's conservatives demanded a commander more experienced than Lyon—and one less rash, to their way of thinking. Attorney General Bates, backed by General Scott and Secretary of War Cameron, had persuaded Lincoln to detach Missouri and place it in the Department of the Ohio under Gen. George B. McClellan at Cincinnati. But this arrangement proved unwieldy, because that officer was fully occupied with a projected campaign in western Virginia. He had given Lyon free rein but little help in the way of organization and supply at the St. Louis base.

Frémont was not to be much of an improvement over Mc-Clellan. He took three weeks getting to his post, using that time to gather supplies in the East and organize his staff. He finally arrived at St. Louis on July 25 with virtually a blank check from the President for carrying out his mission—in essence, the "clearance of all rebels from Missouri, and a movement down the Mississippi upon Memphis." He found the situation confronting him a chaotic one. With Lyon at the front, jealousies among supply officers in St. Louis had created enormous confusion in procurement and the forwarding of needed goods. Few of the original three-month volunteers showed any desire to reenlist as their initial terms expired.

While Lyon, who had reached Springfield twelve days earlier, called for more men in the face of a buildup of state and Confererate forces, Frémont also had demands for reinforcements along the Mississippi, where Cairo appeared to be threatened. Maj. Gen. Gideon J. Pillow had moved up from northeastern Arkansas to occupy New Madrid on July 28 with approximately five thousand troops. He was soon followed by Maj. Gen. William J. Hardee, who moved on Greenville farther west with another twelve hundred. They hoped to be augmented by a force of Missouri State Guard being formed by M. Jeff Thompson, who had just been named commander of the southeastern district of that organization. Thompson, an ardent secessionist and mayor of St. Joseph, had left his home to go to Virginia before any military activity occurred in Missouri. He had reached Memphis when he decided to return, because Lyon had repudiated the Harney–Price agreement and moved on Jefferson City. A born leader, he had quickly catapulted himself to the head of the State Guard forces then rallying in the Bootheel region.

With only limited troops at his disposal, Frémont decided that Cairo and the line of the Mississippi were more critical to his defense posture than southwestern Missouri. Hence he personally conducted four thousand reinforcements there. Simultaneously he wired Lyon to fall back on Rolla if he thought his forces insufficient to hold the area beyond that railhead. The fiery Lyon refused to retreat because he believed his army to be the only checkmate against the loss of western Missouri, which he had done so much to secure.

After the state forces had retreated from north of the Missouri River and brushed past Sigel near Carthage, they had concentrated around Cowskin Prairie in the extreme southwestern corner of the state. There General Price worked hard to whip them into fighting shape, and somewhat reluctantly, a Confederate general, Ben McCulloch, joined him from Arkansas. He was not impressed with Price's efforts. Despite urgings from Lieutenant Governor Reynolds and Edward C. Cabell, whom Governor Jackson had sent east, his government held back on giving him complete freedom of operation where Missouri was concerned. Jefferson Davis had developed a basic distrust of Claiborne Jackson since the Harney–Price agreement and, further, hesitated to commit himself in an offensive operation against a state still in the Union.

McCulloch, afraid that Lyon's advance might jeopardize his own defensive position if not stopped and learning of Pillow's incursion, agreed to a joint operation under his personal command. With a combined force of between thirteen thousand and fourteen thousand men, McCulloch and Price advanced toward Springfield in early August. Lyon, with only half that number, determined on an attack in the belief that his men were better equipped than the state troops and that the element of surprise might bring about a Union victory or at least so maim Price as to delay major action further.[9] He did catch the Confederates quite by surprise near Wilson's Creek, approximately ten miles southwest of Springfield, on the morning of August 10. A fierce battle ensued, in the course of which Lyon fell mortally wounded. By afternoon the superior numbers of the Confederates began to affect the outcome of the battle. Sturgis, who had succeeded to the command, ordered a retreat to Springfield. The Confederates, too exhausted to follow, left off the engagement, but two days later, they occupied Springfield with no additional fighting as the Union troops fell back on Rolla. The future of Missouri seemed to lie in the balance.

9. Lyon also underestimated the strength of McCulloch's supporting Confederate forces.

CHAPTER II

MISSOURI IN TWO NATIONS

In the wake of the Union military sweep across Missouri, the politicians on both sides of the conflict went to work to determine the state's political future. The flight of Gov. Claiborne F. Jackson and his staff from Jefferson City created a power vacuum at the capital. Col. Henry Boernstein, whom General Lyon had placed in command there, simply closed the various offices, pending further orders. The only official of note to remain behind had been Atty. Gen. J. Proctor Knott, but when he refused to take an oath of allegiance to the United States, Boernstein kept him prisoner. State Treasurer Alfred W. Morrison was discovered in Hermann, where he was arrested by Home Guards. They returned him to Jefferson City where Boernstein released him after securing his records. It quickly became obvious that some kind of civilian responsibility was needed to coordinate the efforts of the Federal Government with those of Missouri's Unionist citizenry, who still formed the bulk of her population.

To this end, some suggested the appointment of Frank Blair as a provisional military governor, but the St. Louis congressman-turned-military commander wisely discouraged this action. Most of the responsible citizens favored recalling the state convention that had earlier declared Missouri's loyalty. Before adjourning on March 22, 1861, a special committee had been created with power to reconvene the convention should an emergency arise. A majority of that group issued a proclamation on July 6, declaring that the extraordinary conditions facing the state required a meeting of the convention. They called it into assembly at Jefferson City on the 22nd.

Approximately 80 per cent of that body gathered during the last ten days of July to debate Missouri's future. It quickly became evident that not all those sympathetic to the Southern cause had joined Jackson. Twenty to twenty-five members led by Uriel Wright proposed that the convention simply urge the Lincoln Administration to immediately acknowledge Confederate independence and give the border states their option, through voluntary elections, of Union or secession. More than twice as many Unionists countered this proposal with resolutions declaring that the state's executive branch had "expatriated" itself and committed treason in opposing federal forces. They demanded that the executive offices be considered vacant and that a provisional government be established to cooperate with the Union.

The convention sent all proposals to a select committee, which was soon dominated by Hamilton R. Gamble. He had returned belatedly from the East at the urging of Edward Bates and other friends, but once on the scene he took charge. Despite opposition by the Wright recalcitrants, under his influence the resolutions proposed by the Unionists were adopted, and the convention was given the power to make appointments to fill these vacancies until an election could be held in November. The convention also abrogated the recent militia act passed by the legislature and reinstituted that of 1859. In an obvious indication that they considered their exercise of sovereignty only temporary, the members unanimously voted to submit their decisions to a referendum that fall.

The pro-Jackson men had argued, unsuccessfully, that the General Assembly alone had the power to impeach and that the convention had usurped the state constitution. When they lost, nine of them refused further participation; others had already left for home. The remaining sixty-five delegates unanimously elected Gamble, Willard P. Hall of St. Joseph, and Mordecai Oliver of Greene County to the respective posts of governor, lieutenant governor, and secretary of state.[1]

1. The action of the convention in overthrowing Jackson and the General Assembly was of questionable legality, as several delegates pointed out during the debate. When confronted with arguments that the convention was usurping constitutional authority, Gamble had only one answer: any convention chosen by the people "has all the power that the people could have if they had all assembled in one vast plain, unless there has been some limitation on the power." The 1861 convention was faced by a great crisis caused by extraordinary times. Since Missouri was in a

All three men had long records of public service. Gamble, a native Virginian, had come to Missouri in 1818, had mixed a legal career with occasional politics, and had risen to the state Supreme Court in the early 1850's. Hall was also born in Virginia although his antecedents had been Massachusetts Puritan. After receiving his degree from Yale, he had followed an older brother to Missouri in 1840. Three years later he established his law practice at St. Joseph, taking time out for service in the Mexican War and three terms in Congress immediately thereafter. A strong supporter of Stephen A. Douglas in the 1850's, his politics neatly balanced Gamble's Whig background. Hall had been a conciliatory force in the state convention and was Gamble's personal choice for the second spot. The head of the Provisional Government wanted a younger man as his chief lieutenant in view of his record of poor health. In the turbulent days that followed, Hall amply rewarded Gamble's faith in him. The remaining member of the new executive trio also belonged to the legal profession. A native Kentuckian, Oliver had moved to Missouri at an early age. Like Gamble an ex-Whig, he had served two terms in Congress during the 1850's. He was a staunch Unionist and the only one of the three newly elected state officials to come from outside the ranks of the convention.

In his inaugural address, Gamble indicated his genuine reluctance to undertake the burdens of office under existing circumstances. He pleaded for the cooperation of all, regardless of past political differences, inasmuch as "It is utterly impossible that any one man can pacify the troubled waters of the State." If they all worked together, much good could be accomplished; if not, the people would have to contend with additional turmoil. The new governor received extensive praise from all quarters. President Lincoln immediately extended him official recognition. But in the days ahead, Gamble was to discover only too well the burdens of public office and political decision.

Even as the new executive spoke, the man he had supposedly

---

deplorable condition, some action was necessary to ensure that responsible authority would manifest itself in handling the affairs of state in conjunction with the Union, whose military forces now occupied much of the state. In such circumstances, consitutionality lost to expediency.

deposed alighted from a train at Memphis, Tennessee, with new determination to regain his lost power. Claiborne Fox Jackson had spent the preceding week in Richmond, Virginia, where he had gone with former Sen. David R. Atchison to seek Confederate aid. Jefferson Davis had become increasingly wary of aiding Missouri, because he did not trust Jackson. In addition, he had determined upon a defensive course of action for his new nation. Until Missouri formally joined the Confederacy, the President's constitutionalism barred him from giving help. But Atchison's intervention during the personal visit of the Governor to Richmond had overcome Davis's reluctance. The former senator had been a warm friend of the Confederate President since their university days at Transylvania forty years earlier. As one of the leaders of the Southern ultras in the early 1850's, Atchison had worked closely with Davis and Robert M. T. Hunter, at this time the Confederate Secretary of State, to advance the cause of states' rights. He persuaded the Confederate leaders of Jackson's sincerity in wishing to declare Missouri a member of the Confederacy and of the state's importance to the Southern cause. As a result, Davis had promised the Missouri leaders that his government would undertake to pay their soldiers in the field as soon as Congress could appropriate the necessary funds.

Jackson and Atchison remained in Memphis overnight, then headed for New Madrid to join General Pillow's "Army of Liberation." There they found Lieutenant Governor Reynolds and M. Jeff Thompson. Lengthy conferences followed to determine the best political course to follow in light of the developments in Richmond. All agreed on the need to establish a legal basis for further negotiations with the Confederacy, hence, on August 5, the Governor issued a proclamation declaring Missouri an independent and sovereign state. He claimed authority under the legislative act of May 10, which had given him carte blanche power in defending the state against Federal invasion and pointed to numerous violations of the Constitution and of Missouri's sovereignty by Union authorities. Whether the act gave him legal justification for his moves has been seriously questioned.[2]

2. Significantly, the Confederacy did not recognize Missouri until after

Jackson and Atchison left New Madrid the following day to return to Memphis where they learned that the Confederate Congress had appropriated $1 million for Missouri troops cooperating with its armies. The Governor immediately wired his agent at Richmond to assure President Davis his full cooperation and enclosed a copy of his proclamation. He now hoped that a giant pincers movement could be mounted by Pillow, cooperating with Thompson and the State Guard in the southeast, and by Price and McCulloch in the southwest. But when Gen. Leonidas Polk, Pillow's immediate superior at Memphis, indicated that his forces were not strong enough for such a campaign, Jackson and Atchison hastened westward to rejoin Price.

Price had been having difficulties, but in spite of them he was on the move. He and McCulloch had disagreed after the battle at Wilson's Creek about the desirability of reoccupying northwestern Missouri. Lyon's retreating army left only nominal Union forces in the western part of the state, and Price considered this situation a golden opportunity militarily. He also believed the move was a political necessity, given the recent action of the state convention. Only in this way could Price secure additional recruits and persuade his supporters of the viability of the Confederate cause. McCulloch claimed that he feared the extension of his meager forces so far north and that he lacked sufficient ammunition for such a venture. In reality, he considered the Missouri troops raw, poorly disciplined, and militarily incompetent. He saw Price as little more than a self-seeking politician and distrusted him accordingly. Consequently, the Confederate general and his command soon withdrew into Arkansas.

Price went ahead without him. On August 20 he issued a proclamation in which he stated his intentions and denounced the Provisional Government. Five days later he left Springfield to go to Lexington. That pro-Southern town on the Missouri River was held by a small garrison of thirty-five hundred under Union Col. James A. Mulligan. In spite of numerous warnings, including a plea from Governor Gamble on September 13, Frémont,

the General Assembly had ratified Governor Jackson's action in November, 1861.

34

commander of the Department of the West, underestimated the danger and urgency of the situation there. He did not order reinforcements until the 14th, by which time Price had already invaded the town. Then, for various reasons, these troops failed to reach their destination. Mulligan held out until the 20th when, after a spirited defense, he capitulated.

Price's victory at Lexington underscored Governor Gamble's growing concern over General Frémont's management of military affairs in Missouri. Gamble wrote one of his supporters in Washington: "He [Frémont] is incomprehensible to me. We have lost Lexington. We will soon lose the whole state." The two men had been disagreeing with one another almost from the outset of their virtually simultaneous assumption of power in late July. Frémont had demanded certain appointments be made in the volunteer regiments of the Governor, and Gamble did not feel entitled to make them. The general had also requested the removal of the Jackson-appointed members of the St. Louis Police Board and their replacement by his own choices. Gamble agreed on this point, although he did not move as quickly as Frémont would have liked.

Relations between them reached a boiling point, however, when the Governor, without prior consultation, sought to reorganize the state militia under the recent action of the convention. On August 23 he called for forty-two thousand six-month volunteers. Two days later he wrote President Lincoln to complain about abuses committed by Federal troops from outside Missouri and Home Guards while maintaining order in rural areas. He felt that their lack of understanding of the people's basic conservatism tended to heighten tensions and produce needless violence. It was his hope that in setting up the militia, it would be possible to allow Missourians to patrol their own domain and lessen the dependency on outsiders. To sustain these troops, however, he would need Federal support, particularly in the form of money and material, since Missouri's treasury stood depleted.

This action infuriated Frémont, who saw in these moves an attempt by Gamble to usurp his authority. When the Governor followed his letter with a visit to Washington at the end of

August, Frémont wired the President a terse message: "Will you allow me to suggest that for the present no authority be given to Governor Gamble to raise regiments in Missouri?" Lincoln, however, was impressed by Gamble's sincerity. The Governor's way had been well prepared by Attorney General Bates, his brother-in-law, and by Charles Gibson, his nephew, who had been recently appointed solicitor of the United States Court of Claims. Gamble received the promise of arms for the use of his militia and a loan of $200,000 from the Federal Government to sustain them. Undoubtedly Lincoln hoped that by this means existing Federal troops could be released from duty in Missouri to perform more pressing service elsewhere.

While Gamble was in Washington, Frémont became embroiled in two other controversies, on both of which the Governor opposed him. The first centered around Frank Blair, who had become disillusioned with the commander of the Department of the West after the defeat of Lyon. Blair blamed Frémont for his friend's disaster and argued general incompetency against the man whose appointment he had helped secure. Gamble had carried a note bearing these complaints to Frank's brother Montgomery, to be used with Lincoln. Shortly thereafter, Frémont arrested the outspoken Blair on charges of insubordination, which only heightened Frank's determination to be rid of him.

The second, and by far the more serious, controversy occurred when Frémont proclaimed martial law on August 30. The proclamation began: "Circumstances, in my judgment, of sufficient urgency render it necessary that the commanding general of this department should assume the administrative powers of the State." Thereupon Frémont extended throughout the entire state the process of martial law already invoked some time earlier in St. Louis. Anyone found with arms within Union lines would be shot, upon being found guilty by a court-martial. Those who had taken up arms against the Union would forfeit all property, including slaves, who would be freed.

Such a policy ran directly counter to what Governor Gamble was trying to accomplish in the restoration of full civil government and the establishment of a state militia to keep order. It seemed to threaten his promise of August 3 that amnesty would be extended to those who had taken up arms but now desired to return peacefully to their homes and occupations (a pledge Lincoln had promptly seconded). It also undermined Gamble's assurance of that same date that his administration would brook no interference with slavery.

Frémont's proclamation came without warning as the commander seemed to be trying to shore up his shaky position. It alarmed not only Gamble but Lincoln and Union leaders in the other border states as well. The President lost no time in making his feelings known. In a special dispatch on September 2, he revoked the order to shoot those discovered to have arms, because he feared such action would lead to Confederate retaliation. He urged Frémont to reconsider his emancipation policy and bring it into line with the congressional action of August 6 which granted freedom only to those slaves who were forced actively to participate in the war against the Union. When Frémont refused to do this, Lincoln rescinded that part of the commander's proclamation as well.

Through all of this, Frémont raised up enemies both in Missouri and in Washington. They did not hesitate to seek his removal. Price's victory at Lexington, which made his forces appear to be a threat to northwestern and central Missouri, only added to their determination. Frémont secured a temporary reprieve, however, by announcing that he was taking the field personally in the hope of destroying the enemy and clearing the state, an action the Lincoln Administration had been pressing for some time.

This action, coupled with McCulloch's continued intransigence, forced Price to abandon his advanced position on September 29 and retreat slowly into southwestern Missouri. While he had not accomplished his dream of freeing Missouri from Union control, he had achieved a measure of personal satisfaction, and his exploits had begun to launch him toward a fame which some feel he later took too seriously. He raised the hopes of secessionist sympathizers considerably, even though many of them in the eastern part of the state were not in much of a position to aid him directly unless he could move in their direction.

Price had captured large quantities of materials as a result of his endeavor. These supplies included 7 cannon, more than 3,000 badly needed rifles, 750 horses, and a wide variety of accoutrements. Even with the additional supplies he had to leave several thousand would-be recruits behind for lack of arms. Although he augmented his retreating force by approximately 50 per cent, most of those who joined him were raw, undisciplined farm boys who needed extensive training in the art of fighting a war, preparation Price and his subordinates were not really equipped to give them. With Frémont on the move with 38,000 men, Price, with approximately 18,000, had little choice but to fall back toward a more defensible position.

Governor Jackson had rejoined Price just before the battle at Lexington. He used the dramatic moment of victory to issue a call for a special session of the General Assembly to convene a month later at Neosho. Although he did not specifically mention his intent at the time, it was at this session that he proposed ratification of his secession proclamation. The Confederate Congress, following up its appropriations bill to aid Missouri troops, had passed legislation on August 20 authorizing President Davis to enter into alliance with Missouri, pending her final admission into the Confederacy. The Confederate troops could be used to support state forces, and Missouri volunteers could be recruited into Confederate service. The acceptance of the state to full partnership would follow upon receipt of notice from Governor Jackson that she had ratified the Confederate provisional constitution.

After he received this invitation, Jackson dispatched two agents to negotiate with Confederate authorities simultaneously with his call for the special session. They were Edward C. Cabell, who had served previously, and Thomas L. Snead, his personal aide. To facilitate their endeavors he gave them unlimited power within the general outline of their instructions by ratifying whatever action they took in advance. Cabell and Snead hastened to the Confederate capital by way of Arkansas, where they sought, in vain, to persuade McCulloch to reinforce Price and provide him badly needed military supplies. For all Price's success, the Confederate general still held him and his army in disdain. Once in Richmond, the Missouri emissaries began negotiations with Secretary of State Hunter that resulted in an offensive-defensive alliance on October 31. Three days earlier at Neosho, what remained of the Twenty-first Missouri General Assembly[3] had passed an ordinance of secession, which Governor Jackson signed at Cassville on November 3. By the end of the month notice of this legislation had reached Richmond, and Missouri (in reality, the government headed by Jackson) was formally received into the Confederacy.

Meanwhile, General Frémont's campaign had achieved nothing. As the commander advanced into the field, he found himself the victim of increased political sniping to the rear, some of which he had brought on himself. Burdened by the numerous problems of requisition and supply attendant to the preparation of an army for the field, he had made himself increasingly inaccessible at his St. Louis headquarters, and had surrounded himself by a personal guard of approximately three hundred soldiers, most of whom he had recruited in Europe. They held fancy titles, wore gaudy uniforms, and had difficulty communicating with those who wished to see the general. Frequently, Frémont could be seen riding in their midst down the dusty streets of St. Louis while those who wished to talk with him might wait for hours in his anteroom and never see him.

To his credit, it must be said that Frémont began to bring order out of the chaos he had found when he arrived in St. Louis. Occupation of the Brant mansion enabled him to concentrate under one roof all of the administrative offices of his department. He worked energetically to secure, both internally and externally, the city and surrounding area to the Union. But he also, as so many others before and since, found himself victimized in his choice of subordinates. One of those close to him wrote after his removal:

> There was a great amount of labor performed day and night but there appeared to be no proper system or method. Some of his most

3. The records of this meeting of the Twenty-first General Assembly do not indicate who attended, by rollcall or otherwise. It has been generally assumed that a constitutional quorum did not appear, but those present acted anyway. The only available journal is that of the Senate, which was published after the war.

intimate friends were undoubtedly cheating and circumventing him, I thought. He is no judge of men at all, it seems to me, and he can readily be imposed upon by plausible knavery. I think he is honest and honorable himself, but too impulsive and too impressionable.[4]

In the process of equipping his forces, considerable graft became evident. Disgruntled contractors began to join the chorus of the politicians who were opposed to Frémont. Many of the contractors were friends of Frank Blair who did not feel that they were getting what was due them in relation to the congressman's efforts on their behalf. The story of Frémont's subsequent loss of command in Missouri becomes exceedingly complicated.[5]

President Lincoln tried to discern the true state of affairs from the rumors of total demoralization that made their way eastward. He finally issued orders for his commander's removal. Rather than implement them immediately, however, he sent Secretary of War Simon Cameron and Adj. Gen. Lorenzo Thomas to Missouri to make a personal investigation. With the information they would gather, Cameron should make the final decision on the general's status. Although their subsequent investigation at St. Louis and in the field confirmed much of the dissatisfaction with Frémont and its causes, Cameron agreed, at the general's request, to give him additional time to defeat the enemy. The reprieve proved to be temporary. A caustic report by Thomas and continuing rumbles out of St. Louis from sources the President considered reliable led Lincoln to overrule Cameron on October 24.

By the time the orders for Frémont's removal reached him, he had advanced to Springfield and believed that he stood on the brink of a major battle and a great victory. Although Price and McCulloch, joined now by necessity, were prepared to fight, they were not within striking range. On November 4 Frémont yielded his command to Maj. Gen. David Hunter and returned to St.

4. Allan Nevins, *Frémont: Pathmarker of the West* (New York, 1955), p. 496.
5. For a thorough analysis of Frémont's one hundred days in Missouri, see Nevins, *Frémont: Pathmarker of the West*, pp. 480–549, and William E. Parrish, *Turbulent Partnership: Missouri and the Union, 1861–1865* (Columbia, Missouri, 1963), pp. 48–76.

Louis. His career in Missouri had lasted exactly one hundred days. During that time he had stirred up considerable controversy and touched off, in part, the bitter factionalism that would rent Missouri politics throughout the remainder of the war. With his strong stance against the secessionist element in St. Louis and his antislavery proclamation, he had gained a considerable following among the German radicals. They gave him a large reception upon his return to St. Louis, and he became increasingly a figure of martyrdom to them as they sought to propel Missouri along a more liberal course.

Frémont's replacement, General Hunter, retained his post only a week before being transferred to the command of the newly created Department of Kansas. In that time, however, he reached the decision to abandon the campaign against Price and pull back to winter quarters at Rolla and Sedalia. President Lincoln had already advised this action, although he left the final decision to Hunter. By his retreat Hunter allowed Price to occupy Springfield once again.

It seems probable that, had Hunter pushed the offensive as Frémont had been planning to do, he might have cleared southwestern Missouri of pro-Confederate forces. His troops outnumbered those of the Confederacy at least 2 to 1, and his men were generally better trained and equipped. With Price and McCulloch cooperating only when they could not avoid it, Hunter seemingly had numerous advantages. But as frequently occurred during the war, the amount of information his intelligence forces provided him was almost totally inadequate. Both he and his successor Maj. Gen. Henry W. Halleck were convinced that the Confederates confronted them in force with the real possibility of inflicting disastrous losses if Union troops remained too far from a base of supplies.

Price wished to pursue the fleeing Federals in an effort to open the way for new recruits and to encourage his supporters in the interior of the state. McCulloch refused to support him because of what he considered foolhardiness in the face of the military reality of too few men, who were inadequately supplied and trained. Price went anyway, making winter camp at Osceola on the Osage River. By his movements he threw panic into Union men and brought hope to Confederate hearts. Thomas W. Knox recalled later that the Federal retreat set off much covert activity by St. Louis secessionists. They expected Price to invest the city by Christmas. "It was known that a goodly number of Rebel flags had been made ready to hang out when the conquerors should come," wrote the *Herald* correspondent. "Sympathizers with the Rebellion became bold, and often displayed badges, rosettes, and small flags, indicative of their feelings. Recruiting for the Rebel army went on, very quietly, of course, within a hundred yards of the City Hall." Shortly after assuming command, General Halleck seized the secessionist headquarters and brought this activity to an end. Some consternation occurred among leading pro-Union citizens when officials discovered a book that appeared to contain an execution list headed by the name of Frank Blair.

Although in Union reports, the size of Price's army was estimated at 30,000 to 50,000 men, he had a mere 12,000, and many of them were leaving him as their six-month terms expired. As their militia ancestors in previous wars, these men wished to go home for the winter, since it appeared there would be no more campaigning until spring. Most of them were in dire need of clothing and equipment. Due to the lateness of Jackson's agreements with the Confederacy, they had not been paid since their enlistment. Price had little choice but to grant them furloughs. Many of them never returned. To overcome these difficulties, on November 26 he issued a call for 50,000 men, with some results. A recruiting party sent to Lexington brought in 2,500 volunteers. Many men stayed home either because they could not penetrate Federal lines along the river or the Hannibal and St. Joseph Railroad or because they had determined that they could serve better as guerrillas. This activity increased enormously as the war progressed. Many of those who became guerrillas preferred action closer to home because of the depredations being visited on their localities by Federal troops from outside the state.

Both Governor Gamble and General Halleck sought to bring order out of the mounting chaos. Gamble had recalled the state convention in October to recommend another reorganization of the militia and to put Missouri's finances in order. It responded by declaring eligible for service by volunteer enlistment all physically able white males between the ages of eighteen and forty-five who had taken a test oath of loyalty to the Union. They would receive pay only when on active duty. Any company mustered into state service could enter that of the Federal Government if it so desired. The convention then directed Gamble to go to Washington to work out some plan of cooperation between this force and the Federal army. Since it was anticipated that many would enlist for home defense who would not join the Union military, the Provisional Government anticipated that the Lincoln Administration would provide financial help to keep them in the field and release Regular troops for service elsewhere. Without such aid there could be little hope of raising many state enlistments.

To provide some political leverage for the Provisional Government internally, the convention required that all civil officials take a test oath within sixty days. Therein they swore allegiance to both state and Federal constitutions, and agreed not to take up arms against the government of either or give aid or comfort to their enemies. Those failing to take the oath would forfeit their offices, with the Governor making appointments to fill the vacancies for the remainder of the term.[6] In addition, the convention followed up Gamble's earlier offer of amnesty to any of Price's disillusioned followers who wished to return home peacefully by extending them protection if they took the test oath. Because of the tumultuous conditions throughout the state, the convention also postponed the scheduled elections from November, 1861, to August, 1862.

Governor Gamble promptly went to Washington, where he secured the backing of the Administration for his new militia plan. Such forces as the state could raise would "be armed,

6. Most state officials refused to subscribe to the test oath, so Governor Gamble made wholesale appointments in mid-December, 1861. These positions included the state treasurer, attorney general, register of lands, and the three justices of the state Supreme Court. A month later, Congress expelled Missouri's two United States senators, Trusten Polk and Waldo P. Johnson, for supporting the Confederacy. To replace them, Gamble appointed John B. Henderson of Pike County and Robert Wilson of Andrew County.

equipped, clothed, subsisted, transported, and paid by the United States during such time as they shall be actually engaged as an embodied military force." While the Governor could appoint the various officers, he was required to give the over-all command to the Federal departmental commander or someone designated by him. Halleck promptly selected Brig. Gen. John M. Schofield to head the new force. It was a fortunate choice. Schofield had taught at Washington University before the war and served Lyon as adjutant at the battle at Wilson's Creek. He was a West Point graduate and well understood Missouri's internal problems. He and Gamble would work well together during the next two years. By April, 1862, approximately 13,800 men had enrolled in the Missouri State Militia (M.S.M.) under its new commander and had begun to relieve Federal troops of garrison and patrol duties around the state.[7]

At the same time, Halleck sought to move against the guerrillas with punitive orders that separated them from the treatment accorded Regular troops. He proclaimed that anyone caught in the act of burning bridges or destroying railroads or telegraph wires would be killed immediately and that anyone so accused would be tried by military commission with death the penalty to those found guilty. Captured Regular troops would be treated as prisoners of war, but guerrillas would be treated as "mere freebooters and banditti" and receive little mercy. When General Price protested, Halleck replied that he could give no quarter to any marauder not in uniform.

Simultaneously, Halleck ordered assessments against all Confederate sympathizers in St. Louis to underwrite the cost of caring for the refugees who had been flooding into the city during November and December. Persons suspected of disloyalty could escape payment by signing the convention's test oath. Few did, and much bitterness resulted among the "secesh," as they were called. Halleck decreed that his subordinate commanders in the countryside could impress the slaves of known secessionists, and indeed the secessionists themselves if necessary, to re-

---

7. In addition to the militia, Missouri furnished 109,111 volunteers and draftees to the Regular United States Army.

pair damaged railroads and telegraph lines. Damages would be assessed against the towns or counties in which they occurred unless it could be proved that the striking force had been too great to be resisted.

Halleck backed the Provisional Government fully by requiring the oath of all city officials, business and educational leaders, attorneys, jurors, and railroad officers. The last named also had to file bonds guaranteeing that they would not knowingly employ anyone who had not taken the oath. To cap it all, Halleck directed, at Governor Hall's request, that all future voters would be required to take the oath before exercising their franchise.

The increasing burdens of the strife-torn state rapidly brought Halleck to the conclusion that Price must be driven from Missouri once and for all. Halleck was under pressure from Lincoln to cooperate with commanders farther east to clear the line of the Mississippi southward, but he reported that he could not spare the troops to do so long as Price continued to be a threat in the southwest. The State Guard commander had withdrawn from Osceola in late December to more comfortable quarters at Springfield. His effective force had been reduced to less than seven thousand men. Throughout all of his maneuvers in western Missouri during this period, he fired off letters to Confederate officials complaining bitterly about McCulloch's lack of support. When the Richmond authorities called McCulloch into question the controversy boiled over into the public press. Jefferson Davis attempted to resolve the issue through the appointment of a new trans-Mississippi commander. After some difficulty, he chose Maj. Gen. Earl Van Dorn for the post. The whole affair tended to worsen Price's already growing martyr complex and to leave with the Southern citizenry a picture of him as a gallant soldier who was inadequately supported.

Halleck assigned to Maj. Gen. Samuel Ryan Curtis the mission of driving Price southward. Curtis had been serving in various capacities around the state since he led the first Iowa troops into Missouri in mid-June. He gathered twelve thousand recruits and began the push from Rolla on January 26, 1862. His quartermaster Capt. Philip H. Sheridan left a vivid description of their difficulties in his memoirs:

The roads were deep with mud, and so badly cut up that the supply trains in moving labored under the most serious difficulties, and were greatly embarrassed by swollen streams. Under these circumstances many delays occurred, and when we arrived at Lebanon nearly all the supplies with which we had started had been consumed, and the work of feeding the troops off the country had to begin at that point. To get flour, wheat had to be taken from the stacks, threshed, and sent to the mills to be ground. Wheat being scarce in this region, corn as a substitute had to be converted into meal by the same laborious process. In addition, beef cattle had to be secured for the meat ration. By hard work we soon accumulated a sufficient quantity of flour and corn meal to justify the resumption of our march to Springfield.

Price and his troops, encountering many of the same difficulties as Curtis's men, evacuated Springfield without a struggle on February 12. He left behind considerable supplies and equipment because he lacked transportation to take them with him. Curtis did not hesitate to follow him. Leaving Sheridan to coordinate the task of supply, Curtis forced the guard rapidly southward until they crossed the Arkansas border on the 17th. It was two and a half years before Price returned to Missouri. During the preceding eight months, his army had marched more than eight hundred miles, had fought in five battles, and engaged in approximately thirty skirmishes. He had yet to lose a fight, but given inadequate support from the Confederacy and faced with a serious loss of morale among his forces, he had no choice but finally to quit the state.

Three weeks later on March 7 and 8 Curtis and Price met at the battle of Pea Ridge. The weary Missouri troops had been augmented by reinforcements that were commanded by Van Dorn, McCulloch, and Albert Pike, who brought two thousand Indians into the fray, but poor tactics led to the defeat of the Confederates and their subsequent retreat deeper into Arkansas. The events at Pea Ridge ended any further threat to Missouri from the Confederacy in the immediate future except for the guerrillas.

Claiborne Fox Jackson had rejoined Price just prior to the battle at Pea Ridge. He had been scheduled to go to New Madrid on March 3, where a session of his General Assembly had been called, but the apparent futility of such a meeting, coupled with the impending battle, changed his plans. After the sessions of the legislature at Neosho and Cassville, the Governor had spent a month with General Thompson in southeastern Missouri, trying to increase the morale of the state troops there and to persuade as many of them as possible to enlist in Confederate service. Price had been undertaking a similar recruitment campaign among his men. Neither attempt met overwhelming success, apparently because of disillusionment by many of the men with the lack of Confederate support thus far and particularly with Jefferson Davis's refusal to name Price to the trans-Mississippi command.

In mid-December Jackson headed for New Orleans, stopping briefly at Memphis to confer with Gen. Albert Sidney Johnston. It had been hoped for a time that after Johnston was appointed to command the western Confederate defenses, he might help launch a two-pronged attack to regain Missouri, but he did not. Jackson spent another month in the Crescent City, seeking supplies and funding for the state troops; he was moderately successful in both missions. Unfortunately, many of the guns he procured burst when Thompson's troops fired them; but the state defense bonds, which the Governor managed to float, provided the first pay for these same men in several months.

Thompson had to evacuate his forces from southeastern Missouri in mid-March as the Union push to clear the line of the Mississippi got underway. He fell back toward Arkansas and eventually made juncture with the Confederate forces of Van Dorn and Price near Des Arc. Price had just received a commission as a Confederate major general. Simultaneously, the Missourians learned that Van Dorn's army had been ordered east of the Mississippi by General Johnston in the wake of the disasters at Forts Henry and Donelson.

The five thousand men whom Price and Jackson had persuaded to enter Confederate service feared they were betrayed in this action. They considered their purpose to fight in the trans-Mississippi and, more particularly, to liberate Missouri. Van Dorn persuaded them that their transfer into Tennessee was temporary, and he promised them that they would return west of the Mississippi after the emergency. Price, in resigning as commander of the State Guard on April 8, made an impassioned plea, "Soldiers, I go but to mark a pathway to our homes, follow me." Many guardsmen demurred, deciding that the time had come for them to return to their homes in Missouri either individually or in small groups. Some of them became active guerrillas; others joined Gamble's militia to curtail the activities of their former comrades. Those guardsmen who did not choose Confederate enlistment or return home remained as a state force serving as an allied unit to the Regular troops. They went with Price briefly, but, after the action around Corinth, returned to Arkansas in July where they were assigned to the army of Maj. Gen. Thomas C. Hindman.

Governor Jackson remained west of the river. Although his movements are somewhat difficult to trace, he apparently established his headquarters or temporary capital at Camden, Arkansas, about seventy-five miles south of Little Rock. His wife and family, accompanied by twenty handpicked slaves, had gone south some time during the winter; Jackson eventually settled them on a farm in Red River County, Texas. In July, he met with the governors of Louisiana, Arkansas, and Texas in Marshall, Texas, to discuss the problems of the trans-Mississippi Confederate states. The executives made several recommendations to Jefferson Davis, most of which he eventually adopted. That fall Jackson conferred with former United States Sen. Waldo P. Johnson, now in Confederate service, and Gen. Theophilus H. Holmes, commanding the trans-Mississippi area, about setting up reception camps for those Missourians going south to join Confederate service. By November, Johnson had established two such outposts—one in northern Arkansas and a second, just over Missouri's southern border in Oregon County, Missouri.

Jackson meanwhile had contracted a bad cold, which apparently developed into pneumonia. He had suffered from stomach cancer for several years and also had tuberculosis. Whatever the case, the pneumonia proved fatal. After a confinement of several weeks, he died near Little Rock on December 7, attended by three physicians, one of whom was Dr. Joseph McDowell, whose

Missouri Medical College in St. Louis had been confiscated and turned into a Union military prison. His family had arrived from Texas a few days earlier to be at his bedside. However one may judge the actions of Claiborne Fox Jackson in terms of practical wisdom in 1861, it must be said that he had chosen that course he sincerely believed to be best for his state and the South and that he was deeply attached to both.

Jackson's passing did not end Missouri's government-in-exile. Lt. Gov. Thomas C. Reynolds had been living in self-imposed retirement in his native South Carolina since December, 1861. Upon receiving word of the Governor's death from Confederate Sen. John B. Clark of Missouri, he hastened to Richmond to confer with Jefferson Davis and other Confederate officials. On February 14, 1863, he issued a proclamation to Missouri's Confederate sympathizers and soldiers, formally announcing Jackson's death and his own assumption of power.

Numerous problems faced the new executive: the records of the Jackson government had to be found and straightened out; financial accounts with the Confederate Government and other creditors settled; and liaison reestablished between state and Confederate officials. Reynolds's most immediate problem was the controversy over Sterling Price's demand that he and his command be returned west of the Mississippi. In dealing with this he proved to be an able diplomat. Price had come east in late January to press his claim. Reynolds used his long-standing friendships with President Davis and Secretary of War James Seddon to serve as go-between and ultimately to arrange a satisfactory transfer. Throughout this and other discussions the new governor continually stressed the need for understanding and cooperation between state and Confederate officials, which would stand him well over the next two years.

Reynolds headed west by way of South Carolina in mid-March. After pausing briefly in Mississippi to visit the remaining Missouri troops there, he continued to Shreveport, Louisiana, to confer with Gen. E. Kirby Smith, the commander of the Trans-Mississippi Department. With the fall of Vicksburg on July 4, this region would become almost an autonomous division of the Confederacy, and Reynolds and Smith would work together closely on many of its problems. From Shreveport the new governor went on to Camden, Arkansas, where he found most of the papers of the Jackson government. There he maintained his capital and began systematizing the affairs of his administration.

In late June Reynolds transferred his headquarters to Little Rock. When the city fell to Union forces early in the fall, he wandered first to Arkadelphia and then to Washington, Arkansas, before returning to Shreveport. He finally established a capital at Marshall, Texas, for the remainder of the war. He had been impressed by the small community in east Texas when he attended a governors' conference there in August. It was only thirty miles from Smith's headquarters at Shreveport. As chairman of the Committee of Public Safety, which emerged from the August meeting, he served as one of the general's principal advisers.

During the later years, Missouri's government-in-exile existed largely as a military organization. It had no state territory to administer and few civil functions to perform. Yet, Missouri's Confederate soldiers and exiled citizens needed an organized entity to represent them in their dealings with the authorities at Richmond and their agents. As an officially recognized member of the Confederacy, with senators and representatives in its congress, the Reynolds government had legitimate status. Its head never gave up hope that an invasion of Missouri might restore him to full power at Jefferson City, and when Sterling Price attempted such a move in the fall of 1864, Reynolds went with him. In the meantime, his regime served as the covert agent in the state for Confederate recruiting through letters of authorization to those who pursued guerrilla warfare.

As vacancies occurred in Missouri's ranks in the Confederate Senate, Reynolds named replacements. The original holders of the seats, together with Missouri's House delegation, had been named by the legislature at Cassville. Provisions had been made for the subsequent election of House members but never carried out. Finally, when nationwide elections were being held in May, 1864, for the Second Confederate Congress, Reynolds coordinated balloting for Missouri's House delegation among the various camps and stations where his constituency was located.

Inevitably, the question of Reynold's own legal status came up as the time for regular elections approached. Technically, under Missouri's constitution, a governor succeeding to the office because of the death or disability of his predecessor was required to call a new election within eighteen months. Yet, in Reynolds's case, this could not be done because that same document provided that such an election could be held only within the confines of each of Missouri's townships. The Governor sought to evade the dilemma, however, through the provision that an executive should hold office for four years or until a successor should be duly elected and qualified. In support of this stipulation, former Governors Price and Trusten Polk somewhat reluctantly gave him their written endorsement. Pending a return to Missouri, where legitimate elections could be held, this provision continued to be the reed on which Reynolds relied for his power.

While Claiborne Fox Jackson and Thomas Caute Reynolds struggled with the difficulties of a government-in-exile, Hamilton Rowan Gamble and Willard Hall were dealing with the ever-increasing problems of strife-torn Missouri. In the wake of General Curtis's victory at Pea Ridge and Sterling Price's subsequent transfer east of the Mississippi in the spring of 1862, many former state guardsmen began filtering back into Missouri. Some returned to their homes peacefully. Others determined that they would do what they could unofficially to harass efforts of the Union there. As the countryside thawed out from the long winter, guerrilla activity increased measurably.

In addition to those Confederate sympathizers who acted strictly on their own, Missouri soon found itself overrun with irregular detachments organized under the Confederate Partisan Ranger Act of April 21, 1862. Maj. Gen. Thomas C. Hindman, commanding the Confederate District of Arkansas, commissioned at least a dozen Missouri officers early that summer to return to their respective areas as recruiters for both Confederate Regulars and for guerrillas who could be left behind.

As the Union campaigns down the Mississippi and into Tennessee gained momentum that spring, Missouri was increasingly depleted of Union troops forcing General Schofield to rely more heavily on the new M.S.M. With the departure of General Halleck for the battlefront in early April, Schofield assumed almost total responsibility for defending the state. This arrangement received official recognition from Halleck on June 1, when he created the Military District of Missouri. Schofield promptly divided his new command into five subdistricts, each headed by its own M.S.M. officer. Throughout, he received the full cooperation of Gamble and the Provisional Government.

Three days earlier, on May 29, Schofield had laid down his program for ridding the state of its mounting guerrilla warfare. "The time is passed," the general declared, "when insurrection and rebellion in Missouri can cloak itself under the guise of honorable warfare." He ordered his men to shoot on the spot any marauders "caught in arms" from that time forward. He called on all of the state's citizens to cooperate with the militia in detecting and punishing outlaws. Failure to do so would brand one as disloyal. To avoid the excesses of the previous year, however, Schofield warned his own men "not only to abstain from molestation, but to protect from injury all loyal and peaceable citizens." In the heat of action, the militia sometimes found the line he had drawn a thin one. They unfortunately allowed themselves on occasion to fall victim to old grudges that had created many of the same problems that outsiders had caused in 1861.

Confronted with a worsening situation by late June, Schofield ordered that all "rebels and rebel sympathizers" be held responsible in their property and persons for damages done by the guerrillas. For every Union soldier or citizen killed, they would forfeit $5,000; for those wounded, $1,000 to $5,000. The cost of destroyed property would have its full value assessed against and collected from the disloyal citizens who lived in the neighborhood. All money collected in this way would go to the heirs of those killed, to the person wounded, or to the property owners. The general directed his district commanders to set up boards of assessment in each county for the purpose of enrolling all rebels and rebel sympathizers and distributing among them the responsibility of paying for any damages reported.

A month later, on July 22, Schofield called for an all-out enlistment of the state militia in order to exterminate the guerrillas infesting Missouri. Through this action, every able-bodied white male between the ages of eighteen and forty-five was forced to make a choice: he could take the oath and enroll for militia duty; he could refuse and be placed automatically on the assessment list as disloyal; he could hasten to join the nearest guerrilla band; or he could leave the state.

The success of Hindman's irregulars and the continuation of a high level of guerrilla activity indicated that many hitherto silent secessionists chose one of the latter two courses. Yet Union men generally responded to Schofield's call with enthusiasm. Adj. Gen. William D. Wood reported, following an inspection trip through central Missouri, that he received but one request everywhere: "*Give us arms and the authority*, and our country shall soon be rid of rebels and guerrillas."

By November, 1862, seventy regiments (approximately 52,000 men) had been organized into what became known as the Enrolled Missouri Militia (E.M.M.). They served on call in their respective areas as needed. The Federal Government agreed to forage, subsist, and transport them when they were in actual service on order of the Governor while the state assumed responsibility for their pay. To this end, Schofield and his district militia commanders had already been levying assessments against those who were disloyal. A new General Assembly, elected that November, enacted a program of taxation and Union Military Bonds to raise additional money. This program became particularly important when Gamble and Gen. Samuel R. Curtis, who became commander of the new Department of the Missouri in September, disagreed late in the year over assessments. As a result, President Lincoln ordered the permanent suspension of that policy.

The effectiveness of the M.S.M. and the E.M.M. is difficult to determine. The troops undoubtedly pacified many local areas for varying lengths of time. Most of them fought well when necessary. Many who served in this capacity would not have volunteered for Regular Union service, although it should be noted that enlistments from the state in the Federal army climbed steadily throughout the war until more than 100,000

Missourians had joined by the end of the conflict. Some abuses no doubt crept into the militia system. In many local situations, assessments led to confiscations as it became necessary to arrange subsistence for various unit on duty. Local militia officers did not always exercise due care in making certain that only the acknowledged disloyal suffered in these cases. Sometimes they settled old grudges with disagreeable neighbors. Wherever such instances came to their attention, Governor Gamble and the district commanders constantly sought to remedy them.

Many of the more ardent Unionists, especially in St. Louis, distrusted the decision to rely on the enrollment of local militia. Tending still to look upon outstate residents as pro-Southern at heart, they doubted the reliability of Missouri as opposed to Federal troops should there be a showdown in an all-out defense of the state. It was stated emphatically in the policy of the new enrollment that disloyalists should not be organized into companies "nor required nor permitted to do duty in the Missouri Militia." Yet some careless officials did, mistakenly or otherwise, allow registered or known rebel sympathizers, including some returned secessionists, to enroll. Probably the best-known example of this type of enlistment was the "Paw Paw Militia,"[8] made up largely of disloyal men in Clinton and Platte counties. They were organized, with the sanction of Governor Gamble, by Col. James H. Moss in the summer of 1863 to serve strictly as local home guards. It was the contention that a strict application of the oath in this area simply would not bring sufficient enrollments. Supposedly the Paw Paws would be largely limited to guard duty with minimal opportunity for contact with the Confederate enemy, but when called upon to face organized irregulars in the summer of 1864, many of them showed their true colors. In the long run, it must be said that their enlistment probably did more harm than good from both the military and political standpoint.

A great deal of prejudice existed against the state militia

8. The origins of the term "Paw Paw Militia" are not clear. Some have supposed that it derived from the tendency of the troops to camp among the paw paw bushes of the Missouri River bottoms. Others attribute it to their alleged sympathy with the bushwhackers.

among the Germans. They resented Governor Gamble's insistence on a separate Missouri force after he had instigated the breaking up and federalizing of their Home Guard units. Many of them had been promised that they would not have to see action beyond the state's confines, only to find themselves later serving farther south.

Inevitably the whole matter of the militia became involved in the emerging political division within the Unionist ranks. The appointment of many officers gave Governor Gamble a considerable patronage plum, which he used judiciously. Undoubtedly he tended to favor his own conservative element, but there were any number of later Radical politicians who had received their starts as militia officers. By alienating the Germans, Gamble also caused Frank Blair to be opposed to him. When a group of St. Louis Unionists, led by Henry T. Blow, went to Washington early in August, 1862, to seek the removal of Schofield on grounds of inefficiency and the diminution of Gamble's influence in military affairs, they claimed Frank Blair backed them. Blair denied this statement, but made it quite clear to both General Halleck and Frank's brother Montgomery that he believed the Governor had carried his military authority too far.

Gamble, aware of his critics, defended the militia in an open letter that same month. He praised their service and declared it unfair to criticize them or him when "the need for the militia is plain." In writing to General Halleck, who had just become general-in-chief of all Union forces, the Governor again praised "my pet State Militia" and reported that they "fight well." He even carried his program of home defense one step further by asking that some of the Missouri volunteer regiments be sent back to reinforce the militia against the anticipated continuation of guerrilla activity. If possible, he hoped President Lincoln might suspend the recent draft in Missouri in the hope of encouraging enlistments into the militia. Then, significantly, he closed his letter to Halleck: "General Schofield is doing well, according to my judgment."

In the case of the controversy over the militia, Lincoln faced the first of a growing number of problems from Missouri that were to plague him throughout the rest of the war. As guerrilla warfare wracked the western border, where William Quantrill was on the rampage, and the organization of the E.M.M. went forward in the early fall of 1862, the cries of both sides deafened Lincoln. The growing split in the Unionist ranks and the increasing concern for political advantage by both groups led the President by May, 1863, to write one group of St. Louis Radicals: "It is very painful to me that you in Missouri cannot or will not settle your factional quarrel among yourselves. I have been tormented with it beyond endurance for months by both sides. Neither side pays the least respect to my appeals to your reason."

Dr. Charles R. "Doc" Jennison and Sen. James H. "Jim" Lane had begun raiding western Missouri once again in reaction to Quantrill. Among their new activities they engaged in kidnapping or enticing Missouri slaves to help fill Jim Lane's "nigger regiment." The Kansas senator prided himself on his black "recruits." He taught them that Missourians were traitors and had no rights that they were bound to respect. He armed them without any Federal authority and sent them back into Missouri to seek more recruits from among their fellows. Between the Quantrill and the Lane–Jennison raiders, it appeared that the entire area might erupt in prolonged and bloody chaos.

Schofield had been recommending a tighter, more unified structure of command. He especially favored a common command for Missouri and Kansas to eliminate rival jurisdictions along the border. The Department of the Mississippi, established in March, 1862, when Halleck took the field, had proved quite unwieldy. It had subsequently been divided into various districts, which had gone their own ways following Halleck's transfer to Washington that summer. Now, to secure greater coordination, as well as to solve some of the boiling political controversies, the Department of the Missouri was created with its headquarters at St. Louis. It included Missouri, Kansas, Arkansas, and the Indian Territory. Lincoln selected Major General Samuel R. Curtis, the hero of the battle at Pea Ridge, to be its new commander. He had been active since that time in consolidating Union control over northern Arkansas.

A disappointed Schofield resigned his post as head of the state militia and of the Military District of Missouri to request an active field command. Halleck realized Schofield's chagrin at not receiving the larger appointment and wrote a letter to him stating that the selection of Curtis was "the only way of cutting the knot" of political demands upon the President. With western politicians, including the Blairs, "pulling all kinds of political wires to cut up the West into departments for the benefit of each." The charge of Curtis could be defended on the ground that he was the ranking officer in the area. It might have been added that he had served well in Missouri in several capacities during 1861 and was probably as familiar with her problems as any officer who might have been chosen.

If Lincoln hoped that the appointment would solve his problem, however, he would be disappointed. Curtis and Gamble were soon at odds over who should control the militia and whether or not it was wise for these troops to have such a large role. As already seen, they also became embroiled in an argument over assessments until Lincoln resolved the issue by curtailing the practice. In the meantime, Curtis, in part under pressure from the War Department, had stepped up confiscation procedures, including the freeing of the slaves of known rebels, and the banishment of Southern sympathizers. All of this displeased Gamble and the conservatives, particularly since Curtis and his agents were not always careful in differentiating between conservatives and rebels. Gamble had from the first regarded martial law as repugnant. He had been working against great odds to restore respectable civil government. He undoubtedly regretted the removal of Schofield, with whom he had been able to work closely and effectively.

Consequently, the Governor began a campaign for another change of commanders. Curtis was accused by his enemies of mismanagement of his responsibilities and of cotton speculation. Although the general provided seemingly satisfactory explanations to the President, Lincoln became increasingly concerned over his inability to get along with Gamble and the state's other recognized leaders. The Governor had found erstwhile allies in the Blairs, who had hoped that Frank might have the departmental command. In the end, Lincoln gave in by dispatching Maj. Gen. Edwin V. Sumner to replace Curtis on March 10,

1863. Unfortunately for all concerned, Sumner died suddenly while en route to his new post, and the President had to begin the entire process again. He hesitated another two months while the cries of the Gamble's men grew louder. Curtis, realizing the awkwardness of his position, indicated that he wanted a transfer. Finally, after much deliberation, Lincoln replaced Curtis a second time and returned the command to Schofield in the hope that this would promote harmonious relations between the civil and military authorities. This move was successful, but in the meantime a new controversy had arisen that would finally divide the Unionist party and add to Lincoln's grief.

CHAPTER III

LIFE IN WARTIME MISSOURI

As Thomas W. Knox, the *New York Herald* correspondent who reported the first year of fighting in Missouri, rode from Springfield to Rolla in November, 1861, ahead of Frémont's retreating troops, he "found many houses deserted, or tenanted only by women and children. Frequently the crops were standing, ungathered in the field. Fences were prostrated, and there was no effort to restore them." It was a disturbing picture, and as Knox later remarked, "The desolation of that region was just beginning."

This description could have applied just as aptly to the entire state of Missouri. The battling armies had already passed through the southwest twice, and another campaign would take place there that winter before Price's forces were driven permanently from the state. In northern Missouri, Maj. Gen. John Pope had been trying during the fall to curb depredations by guerrillas. He had arrived there in late July to find "the whole country in commotion, bridges and railroad tracks destroyed, or in great danger of being so, and the entire population in a state of excitement and apprehension." Much of this chaos could be attributed to secessionists anticipating Price's quick success in taking over the state, but the situation became increasingly aggravated by Pope's tactics, particularly the unlicensed and often indiscriminate raiding and pillaging by his occupying forces. The general charged each county with the responsibility for enforcing the law within its area through committees of public safety. He expected these groups to call out their citizenry as militia when guerrillas appeared. Failure to do so would result in the introduction of Federal troops, who would be sustained by local resources and paid by countywide levies. Pope assured Robert T. Van Horn: "I am satisfied that peace can be kept if the people will interest themselves in keeping it & I have therefore furnished them with a very strong inducement to do so."

Unfortunately, even where area leaders were willing to undertake such responsibility, they seldom had the means or sufficient support to carry it out. It became increasingly necessary for Pope to send in troops to repel guerrilla depredations, and he and his men assumed that the failure of the local residents to resist these attacks indicated rebel sympathy. When county authorities could not meet the levies imposed on them, the general simply ordered his troops to take what they needed, and they did so without concern for the owner's political sympathies. Within a month after Pope's arrival in northern Missouri, J. T. K. Hayward, president of the Hannibal and St. Joseph Railroad, began sending letters of complaint to all authorities. Having initially welcomed the Federal protection that Pope's troops afforded his railroad, Hayward now wrote Governor Gamble: "The Union cause in our section of the State is being greatly injured by the bad management of our military affairs. The outrages committed on the people by the soldiery . . . are all causing Union men to leave."

On the western border, a similar situation existed. Kansas Jayhawkers, led by Jim Lane and Doc Jennison, moved into the area in the summer and fall of 1861 for the ostensible purpose of protecting government supply trains and property from Price and his marauders. As veterans of the bitter border warfare of the 1850's, Lane and Jennison found it impossible to think of Missourians as anything other than slaveholders and natural enemies. Consequently, they looted and burned indiscriminately wherever they went. In the process, they turned many a Union supporter into an anti-Union guerrilla.

Because of the Kansans' activities, a major force of Southern irregulars was formed, which plagued western Missouri for the next three years. Led by William Clarke Quantrill, a twenty-four-year-old ex-schoolteacher who had already participated in several skirmishes during his four years on the border, this band had its first formal encounter with the Jayhawkers in mid-December when it intercepted Jennison's raiders as they were looting a farm home in Jackson County. From that time forward, the fame of Quantrill's guerrillas spread until they achieved the status of legendary folk-heroes among the border population.

In response to Governor Gamble's protests against the mounting depredations of Union forces, General Halleck acknowledged the depth and consequences of their offenses. He wrote in mid-December, "I am doing all in my power to prevent outrages of the kind you refer to, but the want of organization & discipline of the troops, and the inefficiency & bad character of many of the volunteer officers are such that I cannot yet entirely prevent them." In following months, Halleck and his successors did make a real effort to curb excesses. The increasing use of state militia by the spring of 1862 helped considerably, although some of the militiamen took advantage of their newly found power and harassed neighbors with whom they disagreed politically or otherwise.

In reality, maintaining order in what continued to be a bitterly divided state did not prove to be easy for either Federal or state forces. Much of the difficulty lay in the desire of many Missourians with strong Southern sentiments to be neutral in a struggle that would not tolerate such a stance. Once pent-up resentments had been released in the turmoil of 1861, it became difficult to quench them. Many of those who followed Price later took advantage of the amnesty the Provisional Government offered in the winter of 1861, so they could return to their homes and try to resume peaceful pursuits. Frequently, however, their neighbors, who had not wavered in their all-out Unionism, refused to forgive them the temporary "error of their ways." Honest differences of opinion, which in peacetime might have caused nothing more than a good argument, now resulted in bloodshed.

Not only did divisions exist among neighbors but also many families were at bitter odds among themselves. In July, 1862, Mrs. Bethiah Pyatt McKown of St. Louis wrote her son John in central Missouri of such a tragedy. The McKowns had Southern sympathies, which they had evidenced rather strongly in the opening year of the war. One of their daughters, however, had acquired a "wiseacre of a husband one of the Blackest of Black Republicans." The husband and his wife's brother William operated stores opposite one another in downtown St. Louis. As the resentment over political differences continued to build up, an open encounter became inevitable. During an argument over the constitutionality of Lincoln's conduct of affairs, the Republican brother-in-law accused McKown of disloyalty and demanded the surrender of a gun and a sword he possessed. McKown refused, then reconsidered, only to learn that his accuser had reported him to the provost marshal. William decided not to take his chances with military justice. To quote his mother, "They miss'd him and he got off, and now where he is we know not, for he has left for parts unknown."

Another St. Louisan noted the effect of divided loyalties on the city's youngsters when she recalled many years later:

> Some of those who had discarded the flag instructed their children to walk around and not under it, should they meet it on their way to school, while the Unionists taught their children to keep as near to it as possible. With these counter influences, the children of '61–'65 were veritable little warriors, with their tongues, if not with more deadly weapons. . . . From the day of the capture of Camp Jackson there was an estrangement between friends and neighbors —a condition that extended, more or less, to all departments of social and business life.

Churches were among those institutions that were affected. Galusha Anderson, one of the prominent Baptist pastors of the city, recalled later that many ministers refrained from discussing the burning political issues to avoid alienating either faction within their congregations. Anderson's Southern parishioners criticized him because he continued to pray publicly for the President of the United States after Lincoln had been elected to the office. When his anger at the sight of a secessionist flag flying near the church led him to preach a strongly pro-Union sermon one Sunday evening and close the service with the singing of "America," the Southerners sought his ouster. A mob that was intent on disrupting the service appeared on the Sunday morning following the provocative sermon. The pastor happened to be out of town on his honeymoon, and a visiting clergyman took his place. As the substitute prayed, a brickbat came through the window. He continued as several of the mob entered the back of the auditorium. Then, seeing that the regular pastor was not present, they dispersed. What would have happened otherwise, no one could tell. The secessionists failed to relieve Anderson of his post but thereafter allowed their section of pews to stand noticeably vacant.

Few congregations or denominations escaped such division. Where pastors tried to remain aloof, they received criticism from the Unionists. The most noted case of this type of treatment involved the Reverend Samuel B. McPheeters of the Pine Street Presbyterian Church in St. Louis. He argued that his congregation "owed its allegiance only to Jesus Christ." When President Lincoln asked for a day of fasting and prayer that fall on behalf of the Union cause, McPheeters, among other ministers, declined to participate because of his fear that it would split his congregation, which contained many Southern sympathizers. The Unionist members became increasingly impatient with his attitude.

Matters came to a head when, at the close of a morning service in June, 1862, McPheeters baptized Sterling Price Robbins, an infant whose parents belonged to his church. A committee now approached him to ask that he make his political position known to the congregation. He declined to be specific but reminded them that he had taken the oath of allegiance prescribed by the state convention. The affair turned into a feud that lasted the entire fall and was publicized by the press. It reached its climax in December when the leader of the opposition persuaded the provost marshal general to banish McPheeters and his family from Missouri. The loyalists charged McPheeters with allowing his family, some of whom openly sympathized with the South, "to seduce him from an open and manly support of the Government into active sympathy with the rebellion" and with refusing to follow the President's requests to the various churches for their concerned prayers.

While ordering McPheeters to settle his affairs within ten days and relocate somewhere "North of Indianapolis and West of Pennsylvania" for the duration of the war, the provost marshal general also directed that the control of the church be turned over to a committee composed of three men from the Unionist faction. McPheeters was extremely angry, and, instead of following the order for exile, he went to Washington where he approached the President through a close friend, Atty. Gen. Edward Bates. Lincoln listened sympathetically. Then, apparently convinced of McPheeters's sincerity, he ordered the banishment rescinded and the church restored to the control of its ruling session. Discord continued to mar both this group and the congregation, however, until McPheeters, after his case was carried to the church's national governing body, left for Kentucky to seek a more hospitable pulpit.

The sentence of banishment was not unique to McPheeter's case. Nor was the problem of military interference with internal church policy. In Hannibal, the district commander ordered the closing of the Roman Catholic church because it refused to raise the American flag in accordance with his directive that it be flown over all public buildings. Most clergy had to take the Provisional Government's test oath as a prerequisite to performing marriages. By the spring of 1864, Gen. William S. Rosecrans, who then commanded the Department of Missouri, had extended this requirement to anyone attending a church convention.

All of these procedures constituted part of the system of martial law, which flourished throughout the war and touched the life of every citizen at many points. General Frémont had first invoked martial law in St. Louis County on August 14, 1861, as a means of providing greater security within the district where his headquarters were located. It immediately became necessary to have a military pass if one wished to enter or leave the area. Three newspapers, which had taken a hostile attitude toward the war in Missouri and the Union military effort, were ordered to cease publication. With the help of Governor Gamble, Frémont reorganized the heretofore Southern-oriented St. Louis Police Board and transferred most of its power to the office of the provost marshal. Directives went out from that office forbidding the sale of firearms without a permit or the carrying of concealed weapons by unauthorized personnel. To help curb off-hour activities by Frémont's troops, all places of amusement had to close on Sunday and by 10:30 each week night. No liquor could be sold after noon on Sunday, in the hope of ensuring a sober work force the following morning.

Just as St. Louisans were beginning to become accustomed to these new regulations, Frémont extended martial law to the entire state on August 30. Every subsequent commander maintained the system with varying degrees of intensity until Gen. John Pope and Gov. Thomas C. Fletcher officially revoked it by joint proclamation in March, 1865. During its lifetime, martial law embraced a variety of edicts and programs, depending upon place and circumstance. It by no means eliminated civilian courts or controls but relegated these functions to military supervision when demanded by the exigencies of war.

The provost marshal system was fundamental to the operation of martial law. It comprised the basic police power within the state. Under the direction of the provost marshal general, attached to military headquarters in St. Louis, district provosts and their deputies were "especially intrusted with the peace and quiet of their respective districts, counties, and sections; and to this end may cause the arrest and confinement of disloyal persons, subject to the instructions and orders of the department." Treatment of supposed secessionists was handled on a purely arbitrary basis by the local officers. Mere suspicion of pro Southern sympathies or activities frequently proved sufficient for at least temporary detention in a nearby stockade. Depending upon the seriousness of the alleged offense, the prisoner's case could be handled locally by a military commission, or it could be forwarded to St. Louis. There the suspect was confined at one of two places—the Myrtle Street prison or the Gratiot Street prison. Myrtle Street prison had been a "slave pen" before the war, and the abolitionists and many Negroes thought it appropriate that it now be used to house secessionists. Gratiot Street prison occupied the former Missouri Medical College, "a large octagonal building of gray stone, with arched and square windows ... surmounted by the oddly shaped dome, and flanked by two wings." Its proprietor, Dr. Joseph McDowell, had gone to the South, accompanied by one of his sons, in the aftermath of the incident at Camp Jackson. Another son had been captured when he returned to St. Louis on a recruiting mission for Price's army.

The people who were detained in these facilities included political prisoners, army deserters, those arrested for criminal activity, and Confederate prisoners of war. For most of them, these institutions were temporary way stations. Political prisoners usually had a fairly prompt hearing before a military board, which resulted in their being released on bond or banished, depending upon the severity of their case. If they had been involved in serious guerrilla activity, they could be sentenced to death or permanent imprisonment. In the latter case, they were usually transferred to the new federal prison at Alton, Illinois, which opened in February, 1862. Most Confederate prisoners of war were sent to this facility after they had been processed at Gratiot Street.

St. Louis prisons were typical of their kind. Their major problem was crowding. Equipped to handle 500 prisoners comfortably, Gratiot Street prison accommodated 800 by November, 1862. Authorities reopened Myrtle Street prison, which had been closed for sanitary reasons. There they placed 150 in a facility designed for no more than 100, but this action did little to relieve the crowded conditions. Within a few days, a new influx of prisoners sent Gratiot Street prison's population soaring to 1,100. An epidemic of large proportion was caused by the inadequate quarters, with 235 reported sick in one week and many dying for lack of medical attention. Although Alton prison was already filled to capacity, the provost marshal general reduced the number of prisoners at Gratiot Street through transfers, until, by the end of the year, the population was down to 570. Thereafter it fluctuated between 600 and 750.

Under these circumstances, the improvement of prison conditions was difficult no matter how good the intentions of the authorities. Some prisoners, of course, remedied the situation by vacating the premises at any opportunity. Quite a few disguised themselves as Negro laborers until it became necessary to restrict the use of these workers. Thereafter, the easiest means of exit lay through the cellars or over the rooftops of the adjacent

Christian Brothers Academy. The latter route, of course, exposed the fleeing prisoner to the gunfire of any guard who happened to spot him. These guards displayed little hesitancy in shooting any moving object. Indeed, they were instructed to fire at anyone coming out of a window, who did not retreat immediately upon being ordered to do so. Most outstate facilities were similar to those in St. Louis—makeshift buildings frequently confiscated from secessionists or local jails designed for far fewer prisoners.

Proving loyalty in war-torn Missouri was not easy, and undoubtedly many innocent persons suffered at the hands of provosts and militia, who were responsible for maintaining order. Those who criticized military policy publicly did so at some risk. If they spoke out too vociferously, especially in the rural areas, they could be the victims of arbitrary arrest, regardless of their past loyalty rating. Even government officials were not exempt, as Sample Orr, the state's register of lands, discovered in November, 1862. The 1860 gubernatorial candidate of the Constitutional Union party had taken a somewhat conservative tone in a public speech at Jefferson City, which led the district military commander to arrest him for what he considered "disloyal sentiments." The personal intervention of Governor Gamble was required before Orr regained his freedom.

The basic means used by officials to determine one's political allegiance were test oaths and performance bonds. They were initially required by the Provisional Government of those who had served in Price's State Guard and who accepted its offer of amnesty in the fall of 1861. As guerrilla warfare increased that winter, however, these processes were extended by the provost marshal general to anyone suspected of disloyalty. It is difficult to ascertain how many people this procedure affected, but the number mounted into the thousands. In the Liberty district alone, according to press reports, bonds had been required of 612 men by the end of 1862. Their amounts ranged from $1,000 to $10,000 and totaled $840,000. The provost at Palmyra claimed to have taken in more than $1 million from "several thousand traitors" during the same period.

Many Missourians probably had to stretch their consciences considerably to take the oath, yet the alternatives were such that they had little choice if they wanted to remain in their neighborhoods. Refusal usually led to arrest with subsequent imprisonment or banishment. The system was pervaded with abuses as the provosts or militia commanders exercised a highly arbitrary power over suspects. Force of circumstances, such as pressure from a guerrilla relative or a change of heart, led many citizens to violate their oaths of loyalty. In these instances, immediate death or forfeiture of bond and seizure of property usually resulted. Confiscation of property was not uncommon in any case if a military force needed supplies or forage while on duty.

Additionally, persons suspected of Southern loyalties might be subjected to assessments of varying amounts as military authorities needed monies to underwrite a variety of special expenses. General Halleck had instituted this policy in St. Louis in December, 1861, to provide funds for the growing stream of refugees inundating the city. Noting that until then the cost of providing for these persons had been taken care of by voluntary contributions from Unionists, he decided the task ought to be underwritten "by the charity of men known to be hostile to the Union." They, after all, had contributed to the problem, either directly or indirectly, through their encouragement of Price or the guerrillas.

Halleck consequently appointed a board of five assessors to draw up a list of those who had fled South and left families behind, or who had remained and had given aid or comfort to the enemy in any form, including their utterances. Should these not volunteer a contribution, the board would assign them an amount. The general estimated the need at $10,000. Within a few days the board had compiled a roster of 300 names. The first 64 people received their "Christmas greetings" on December 20. "You are hereby notified that, pursuant to General Orders No. 24 . . . directing a levy upon the friends of the enemy for charitable purposes, you have been assessed the sum of. . . ." Noting several "fashionable and wealthy ladies" among the group, the *Missouri Republican* commented that these would now "have an additional reason to indulge in their very common and delicately insinuating taunts and sneers against the 'prevailing dynasty'."

Protests could be filed, but they had to be accompanied by unqualified proof of loyalty. Failure to pay within a specified time could lead to additional penalties and, ultimately, to the confiscation of goods. One prominent physician, who refused to acknowledge a $300 levy, later confided in his diary: "I had certainly violated no law, civil or military, but was quietly practicing my profession, when . . . my house was entered in broad daylight by United States Police Officers and robbed." Halleck's men took the doctor's buggy, a set of harness, two damask-covered rosewood sofas, six damask-covered rosewood chairs, one rosewood center table with an Egyptian marble top, and one rosewood piano. The victim of this "raid" estimated the value of these items at $2,000. Shortly thereafter, he left the city to join Price. A merchant, who underwent a similar experience, decided to seek redress through the city's courts. He obtained a writ of replevin for eighty boxes of Star and Adamantime candles that had been taken from his warehouse. When he went with the sheriff and an impromptu posse to serve this on federal officials at the storage depot, he met armed resistance. A local paper reported the next morning: "The Sheriff concluded that his duty did not require him to be absolutely riddled with Minie balls and to sacrifice the lives of his undisciplined corps, and therefore gracefully ordered a retreat." Military power usually proved absolute.

The application of assessments spread throughout the state by summer with the monies being used to cover a wide variety of military expenses including indemnities to Unionists who had been wounded and to the families of those who were killed. Because local boards were appointed by the various district commanders in charge of the assessments, fraud and corruption inevitably crept into the system. By December, 1862, complaints had become so strong that the matter came to the attention of President Lincoln, who ordered the program suspended.

General Frémont had suppressed three newspapers in St. Louis immediately after his proclamation of martial law. Such action became a common occurrence during the first year of the war and continued occasionally thereafter. The *Shelby County Weekly* might proclaim on its masthead: "Free as the wind, pure and firm as the voice of nature, the press should be"; but when

Union troops disagreed with its policies, they ransacked its offices. What furniture and other items they did not want for themselves, they threw into the street. The paper, which had begun publication only three months earlier, ceased to exist. Some pro-Southern editors quit publishing voluntarily and joined the Price–Jackson forces. The *Missouri Register* at Macon, which the men of the First Iowa took over and rechristened *The Whole Union* for one issue, was a case in point.[1] Another was the *Platte Argus* at Platte City. Its owner followed Price south from Lexington in September with press and equipment to begin publication of the *Missouri Army Argus*, the official newspaper of the State Guard.

With General Halleck's assumption of the departmental command in December, 1861, the system became tighter. The requirement of a license for the shipment of goods from St. Louis offered an effective means of controlling the flow of printers' ink and newsprint to editors of questionable loyalty. By early January, 1862, editors had received an order that they submit one copy of each issue to the provost marshal general's office for examination. An increasingly strict censorship of war news and expressions of antiadministration views followed. Editors were soon required to take the test oath if they intended to continue their operations. On occasion, papers from outside the state of "copperhead hue" were banned, and by war's end, books and other publications were also censored.

Hardly any area remained untouched by the dislocations of war. In the rural regions, one never knew when he might be visited by guerrillas or militiamen with varying demands. Property was no longer sacrosanct, and life became cheap. Pillage and assassination were commonplace. The weekly press reported enough atrocities on private citizens committed by both sides to fill a long book.

As a result of these and related forces, many Missourians, both white and black, became people on the move. The refugee problem, with which both military and civilian officials had to deal, assumed major proportions. Because of its size, location, and relative safety St. Louis became the focal point of many of these

1. See pp. 25–26.

migrations. It also bore the brunt of Unionist refugees from Arkansas, who were driven from their homes because of adherence to the Northern cause.

The city received its first major inundation in the winter of 1861–1862, as a result of the fighting in southwestern Missouri and northwestern Arkansas. In his reminiscences, Thomas W. Knox, the *New York Herald* correspondent, described a typical case. By the time he interviewed the family, all that remained were an old man and his grandson. The old man, a native of Pennsylvania, had emigrated to the Fayetteville area of Arkansas in the 1830's. When the war broke out, his two married sons were living near him on adjacent farms. The eldest had been impressed into the Confederate Army in the fall of 1861 and died shortly thereafter. The younger son had been killed in his own home when he failed to report for service as directed. The two widows and their children took refuge with the grandfather, but the entire group soon received orders to clear out because of the old man's northern birth and the younger son's "disloyalty."

Although promised two days to make preparations, the family found an enforcement squad at their door within ten hours. This posse allowed them only one wagon to carry what possessions they could. These vigilantes confiscated any item of value and followed them all the way to the Missouri border. As the family moved down the rutted road on their way north, they could look back over their shoulders and see their homes being put to the torch. After they reached the state line, they still had two hundred miles to go to reach a Union camp. It was a bitterly cold winter, and only four of the party survived the trek to Rolla. The two women died there from the effects of exposure, leaving only the grandfather and young child to continue to St. Louis by train. The story of these Arkansans could be duplicated many times over in Missouri as well.

To care for these helpless victims of the war, some of the concerned women of St. Louis organized the Ladies' Union Aid Society. They secured an old mansion on Elm Street to serve as a way station for receiving the refugees on their arrival and meeting their needs until more permanent locations could be found for them in the city or beyond in some other Northern state. This home could accommodate sixty people at one time.

Ten times that number passed through its portals during the first year of operation. By September, 1863, a second home had been opened on Walnut Street. These places housed both whites and blacks. The Elm Street home had originally provided the Negroes with quarters at the rear, but later, segregation apparently broke down. Reverend Galusha Anderson mentioned at least one instance of a recently arrived family of poor whites who complained bitterly about being moved in next door to a fugitive black. He recalled, "These refugees were clothed in rags and were barefooted. The unkempt hair of the wife and mother was a mass of matted tangles. In their cheerless apartment there was neither stove nor bed. They slept on straw and ate from the hand of charity." Yet their black neighbor had already obtained a broom and cleaned his quarters. He had secured an old stove, some coal, a bedstead, and a washbasin to make the place liveable. The abolitionist minister could not help noting the contrast.

Initially, the refugee homes were supported by voluntary contributions from Unionists and compulsory assessments on Southern sympathizers. After President Lincoln suspended the latter in early 1863, the Federal Government underwrote the cost of rations and fuel while the local quartermaster covered the rent out of his departmental budget. By then, homes similar to the ones in St. Louis had been established at Pilot Knob, Rolla, Springfield, and Cape Girardeau. All of them were supervised by agents of the Western Sanitary Commission.

This organization had had its origins in the need to provide some care for wounded soldiers after the fighting in Missouri during the summer and fall of 1861. Prompted in part by his wife and by the Reverend William G. Eliot, General Frémont established the five-man commission of private citizens on September 5. Like its larger counterpart, the United States Sanitary Commission, this group's original purpose was to cooperate with the medical director of the Department of the West in establishing and maintaining hospitals under acceptable sanitary conditions. To this end, it quickly secured a five-story marble-fronted building in downtown St. Louis, which it refitted as "City General Hospital." Within two months, it opened five additional hospitals of varying sizes to take care of the growing numbers of wounded, and by the war's end had expanded the total to fifteen with accommodations for six thousand patients.

The recently organized Ladies' Union Aid Society promptly volunteered its services to perform many of the necessary chores connected with this work. Its members rolled bandages and secured clothing. They visited the men on the wards, bringing them various small articles, reading to them, and writing letters home. Many performed nursing services. Some undertook charity work to help the families of servicemen who had come on hard times because of the absence or disability of a father or son. Nor was theirs a ministry to one side, for they also went to the prisons to see to "the needs of the enemy."

Not to be outdone by the Union women, those of Southern sympathies sought to aid their own. Their leader was Mrs. A. J. Coons, who "by her eloquent appeals, found favor with the Federal officers, who opened to her the doors of Confederate prisons and hospitals." She and her friends distributed food and personal items to the prisoners and in the process helped several to escape under the disguise of feminine garments. When Mrs. Coons tried to promote a bazaar at Mercantile Library Hall for needy Southern soldiers, Federal authorities decided she had overstepped her bounds. They arrested her and a number of her compatriots and banished her to Illinois. According to one friend writing years later, however, Mrs. Coons entered and left the city freely thereafter in a variety of disguises and continued her activities as much as circumstances allowed.

The Western Sanitary Commission did not limit its efforts to St. Louis. When General Frémont took the field in October, 1861, it pioneered, under his orders, the concept of hospital cars. Two cars on the Pacific Railroad were outfitted "with berths, nurses and all necessary arrangements for cooking." It also devised "the flying hospital," or "hospital on wheels" to accompany the army on the march. In the wake of the fighting at Forts Henry and Donelson in February, 1862, one of the commissioners went down the Mississippi to Cairo and Paducah with doctors, nurses, and volunteer workers to take supplies for the sick and wounded there. The medical director in Paducah gave them the use of a steamboat on which they transported many of the wounded back to St. Louis. From this beginning, the floating hospital joined its counterparts on land, and by 1865, the Commission had four such operations within the western theater. In addition, it sent workers and supplies to a variety of stations throughout the Mississippi Valley, frequently in cooperation with the United States Sanitary Commission.

James E. Yeatman, St. Louis banker, entrepreneur, and philanthropist, headed the Western Sanitary Commission. A man of vast energy and dedication, he served tirelessly and without compensation in this important work. Not content with a narrow role, Yeatman and his fellow commissioners[2] constantly anticipated other related needs that had to be met. In March, 1862, they established a hostel for discharged and furloughed soldiers who passed through St. Louis. A sort of early U.S.O., it could house as many as 100 at any one time. More than 71,000 military personnel enjoyed its services before it ceased operations in May, 1866.

The Commission helped organize the Freedman's Relief Society as the number of fugitive slaves increased markedly in 1863. This new group took over the responsibility for housing these unfortunate persons in the old Missouri Hotel and provided a hospital for them on Sixth Street. It tried to find permanent locations outside strife-torn Missouri for many black refugees. It also worked at Benton Barracks with black army recruits and their families. Here the Commission underwrote the cost of basic educational instruction for both adults and children. That winter, it aided in organizing a Negro board of education to undertake the work of Negro schools in St. Louis generally. By early 1864, it had established a Freedmen's Orphans' Home to care for abandoned youngsters found by its agents throughout the Mississippi Valley.

The following winter, the Commission brought into being the Soldiers' Orphans' Home, located in Webster Groves, to minister to those who had lost their fathers during the war. The orphanage was managed by the Ladies' National League. This group gave an opportunity to serve to those not interested in actively participating through the Ladies' Union Aid Society. Until now, its primary purpose had been fundraising.

The question of funds was a constant concern for the Western

2. The other members of the Western Sanitary Commission were Carlos S. Greeley, J. B. Johnson, George Partridge, and William G. Eliot.

Sanitary Commission. Although it received extensive aid from the War Department, voluntary contributions formed the backbone of its budget. These contributions were solicited nationwide. Here it ran into competition with the United States Sanitary Commission, whose officers remained irritated throughout the war because the St. Louis group would not subordinate itself to their control. Outside the Mississippi Valley area, the Western Sanitary Commission had its principal financial support in New England, from whence many of its more active members had come originally, and in California. All told, it distributed approximately 4 million articles to soldiers, refugees, and freedmen with an approximate value of $3.5 million. In addition, it received cash gifts of not quite $771,000.

By far, the greatest portion of the cash gifts were donated through the Mississippi Valley Sanitary Fair at St. Louis, which the Commission sponsored for three weeks beginning May 17, 1864. Modelled after similar endeavors undertaken previously in other cities, the fair was a tremendous success and netted $554,-591 for the cause. Housed in a specially constructed building five hundred feet long that stretched from St. Charles Street to Olive Street along Twelfth Street, it attracted huge crowds to view the many displays and purchase the variety of souvenirs contributed from all parts of Missouri and the nation. Here one could stroll through the floral park or take advantage of a skating rink. The gallery of fine arts included "a wreath wrought of hair collected from the heads of a large circle of United States generals, and nearly all the members of the President's Cabinet—some forty distinguished personages—thus entwined in capillary union." A book of autographs and photographs of the contributors, which was raffled off at the close of the exhibition, accompanied this item.

Patriotism was the motif from the display booths of war trophies and merchandise to the variety of restaurants and food counters where the women of the community "cooked and washed dishes for the Union and where the hungry ate for the same lofty purpose." The Germans operated a beer garden, much to the dismay of several Protestant ministers who sought to dissuade them. Martial strains of military bands constantly filled the air while drill teams performed at an improvised theater, which also presented patriotic dramas and other amusements.

Standing guard at the various entrances was a specially picked company of Negro soldiers. Blacks mingled with whites along the avenues within the building "without complaint or a murmur," according to Anderson. There was at least one untoward incident, however, when the Reverend Henry A. Nelson of the First Presbyterian Church entered one of the restaurants with some black ministers. At first refused service, the indignant Nelson held his ground until one of the waitresses finally agreed to take their orders. Times were changing in St. Louis, but slowly. Although outstate Unionists could not match the grandeur of the Mississippi Valley Sanitary Fair, they did promote bazaars and benefits of various kinds, where possible, to underwrite the Commission's work or similar activities in their locales.

For all those who sought to assume the kinds of responsibility represented by the work of the Western Sanitary Commission and its auxilliaries, many others sought to evade any role at all. By 1863, as conditions worsened, a considerable group of Missourians decided simply to pull up stakes and head West. The weekly press began carrying frequent accounts of wagon trains leaving for California and intermediate points. Quite a few were Southern sympathizers who were tired of trying to maintain their neutrality in the midst of hostile forces or fearing the possibility of a new specter—the military draft. Others, merely weary of the turmoil around them, sought what they hoped would be a calmer clime.

Efforts by various interests, such as railroads, speculators, government officials, and churches, to promote new immigration to replace the population that was being lost were usually futile as long as the war continued.[3] Few people had much inclination to emigrate into such a troubled area. The various travel and trade restrictions imposed under martial law did little to enhance Missouri's demonstrable assets. Missourians learned to live with these conditions, but not without a great deal of grumbling, some of it justified by the corruption that permeated the system.

The provost marshal had required passes for travel to and

3. These efforts did begin to bring results promptly after the war ended. See pp. 198–201.

from the city as early as August, 1861. One had to prove loyalty, of course, to secure one. Baggage of those travelling on public conveyances was subject to military check to make sure that goods were not being transported to the enemy. For the convenience of transients, inspectors would visit the hotels to inspect the luggage of departing guests. If it passed inspection, it would be sealed and a permit issued, so it would be allowed to be taken through the train or boat terminal without further delay.

By early 1862, General Halleck had regularized the whole procedure through a directive giving supervision of the movement of all goods and persons to Treasury customs officials. This brought into play a variety of licenses and permits for river boats, railroads, and stage lines. Merchants found it necessary to have every shipment leaving the city approved. A 5 per cent tax was collected on all goods shipped down the Mississippi. District and local commanders supplemented Halleck's basic program as needs dictated in their respective areas. In some cases, these additional restrictions included the licensing of business houses to ensure their operation only by "loyal" men.

Opportunities for bribery and graft were abundant. St. Louis merchants complained of being discriminated against in favor of their Chicago rivals who were not restricted. Newspaper reports of such instances were numerous. One wholesale grocery firm, for example, received an order from a Kansas customer for 250 barrels of salt. Upon applying to the Treasury agent for a shipping permit, the company was informed that he would approve shipment of no more than 10 barrels at a time. This inconvenience caused the customer to cancel the order and place it with a Chicago firm. In Lexington, which had a reputation for being pro-Southern, Gen. Ben Loan proscribed "uncooperative" merchants in wholesale fashion during May of 1863.

After the fall of Vicksburg that July, Secretary of the Treasury Salmon P. Chase lifted restrictions on through traffic from St. Louis to New Orleans while continuing to require permits for intermediate shipments. The Union Merchants Exchange, which had broken away from the Chamber of Commerce in 1862 over political differences and ultimately superseded that organization, sent a delegation to Washington in September to meet with Chase and President Lincoln. The St. Louisans produced evidence of discriminatory practices, especially in relation to their Chicago rivals, and as a result secured the lifting of the 5 per cent tax with retroactive reimbursement. Other restrictions continued until war's end, however.

While government contracts helped to bolster the economy of St. Louis, they did not completely offset losses caused by the inconveniences of the permit system and the over-all disruption caused by the war. By mid-1863, the St. Louis business community also faced a shortage of labor, which drove wages up and led to increased efforts at unionization by various groups of skilled workers seeking to preserve wartime gains. Mechanics who had received $1.50 a day in 1861 were receiving $3.50 to $4.00 by 1864. As many employers began to hire a large number of apprentices to fill out their work force, the journeymen began to suspect that attempts were being made to overstock their ranks in an effort to drive wages down. When certain establishments refused to limit the number of apprentices they hired, the mechanics struck those shops and began to harass workers who did not cooperate. Many of the factories had government contracts, and their proprietors appealed to General Rosecrans. He responded on April 29, 1864, with General Order No. 65 forbidding such activities and requesting of employers the names and addresses of anyone they knew thus engaged. In the weeks that followed, military force was applied not only to the mechanics but also to striking coal miners, tailors, and printers.

All of this trouble threw the working community in turmoil. Petitions were circulated throughout St. Louis calling upon Rosecrans to be more sympathetic with the mechanics' cause. In these documents, workers proclaimed:

> We could believe you never would have promulgated Order No. 65, but for reasons of military necessity, and as loyal men we regret if the operations of the Government have been impeded by the course those mechanics interested felt called upon to take . . . [but] inasmuch as the "bosses" are few in number and more easily controlled, are rich and better able to make sacrifices, if need be, and believing that the mechanics have at least as fair a claim of justice as they for their cause—we invoke you to issue an order requiring the "bosses" to limit the number of apprentices to one for

every five journeymen employed in their establishments, thus ending the controversy, and, as we believe, on the side of justice.

General Rosecrans did not reply, and ultimately the controversy subsided.

Unionization continued with varying results in different trades. A new threat to at least one group of workers surfaced in August when the proprietors of the Lindell Hotel, the largest establishment of this type in St. Louis, discharged their white waiters because of a wage dispute and hired blacks to replace them. The white chambermaids threatened to strike in protest but apparently reconsidered when faced with the realization that blacks could do their work equally well also. The Radical party's *Missouri Democrat* praised this "forward move" by the hotel with the pungent observation: "When properly drilled, the black boys make excellent waiters, and can afford to work for lower wages than white men, as they do not spend much for whisky and theater tickets." By the fall of 1864, the Workingmen's Union of Missouri appeared to serve as an umbrella for the specific crafts organizations which had emerged. It not only coordinated efforts on "bread-and-butter" issues but also sponsored such social activities as the First Annual Workingmen's Ball that October. In the postwar years, those who had a skill benefited from all of this union activity.

Business outside of St. Louis languished except in those places, like Rolla and Jefferson City, where military outposts were maintained. The situation was particularly bad through 1862 as guerrillas roamed over vast areas with minimal resistance in places. Property values in St. Joseph declined from $5,126,249 in 1860, to $3,267,025 in 1861, to $2,456,641 by 1862 before beginning a slow climb back. Kansas City was a beleaguered town in a sea of constant turmoil, which left it "shabby and dilapidated," according to one observer. "The streets were not repaired, the taxes were unpaid, the revenues uncollected, city warrants were worth from 50 to 60 cents on the dollar." During the invasion of Missouri by Sterling Price in the fall of 1864, Congressman James S. Rollins, who lived in Columbia, complained to Frank Blair, "We are now as completely in the Confederate States here, as if we were in Augusta, Georgia. We have no connection with the U. States, not having received a mail for three weeks! Half of our people are ruined, and the rest will be."

Farming became increasingly difficult. The massive flight of slaves by 1863 and 1864[4] and the increasing demands for men to fill the ranks of militia and army created a critical shortage of labor in agriculture as well as industry. The continual destruction of buildings and crops and the confiscation of goods by one side or the other left those who remained with little desire to do more than scratch out a bare subsistence. As the war died out in the spring of 1865, much of rural Missouri was again the victim of devastation as roaming bands of bushwhackers, who were turning increasingly to simple outlawry, plagued the countryside. Many of these men were returning Confederates without prospects for employment or a friendly reception in their former homes. Others merely took advantage of a disorganized society to gain whatever plunder they could. In spite of the circumstances, Missouri agriculture was to make a remarkable recovery in the remaining years of the decade, as will be noted later.

Money was scarce throughout the war. All of Missouri's banks except one had suspended specie payment in November, 1860. Most of them managed to remain open during the war by agreeing to honor each other's notes, but Missourians were inundated by a sea of paper money, the value of which, like that of its counterparts elsewhere, fluctuated considerably, depending upon circumstances. The lack of small coinage upon which everyday trade depended so heavily was particularly noticeable. Postage stamps became a popular substitute early in the war, although warm weather would frequently make them sticky in pockets and billfolds, causing all kinds of problems for the user. By August, 1861, the Bank of St. Louis began issuing fractional currency, even though state law forbade the practice. Other banks followed suit, and the Federal Government did likewise after its suspension of specie in early 1862. These small pieces of paper, in a wide variety of denominations from three to fifty cents, came to be known variously as "postage currency" or "shinplasters." Small and easily torn, they quickly became dirty and tattered, but because they were necessary they were kept in cir-

4. See p. 104.

culation, with few people paying much attention to their condition as they passed from hand to hand.

The war took its toll of Missouri's cultural life as well. Public education, which was just beginning to progress in 1860 after two decades of struggle, collapsed almost entirely outside of St. Louis and some of the other larger towns. Approximately 175,800 students, slightly less than half of the potential number, attended public schools in 1860. Missouri's 240 private academies and other institutions enrolled 20,000 more. The state had contributed $262,234.52 in aid to its schools that year. Then came the crisis of 1861. The General Assembly suspended the Public School Fund to provide monies for the State Guard in the wake of the incident at Camp Jackson that May. Although the state convention rescinded this action in October, neither it nor the state legislature made any effort to distribute the fund again until 1864. In an effort to effect budget economies, the same meeting of the convention abolished the post of state superintendent of common schools and transferred its duties to the secretary of state. It also eliminated the county school commissioners outside of St. Louis County.

Consequently, without leadership or state monies, only the larger communities managed to keep their operations viable and then generally on a reduced level. Only about a third of the districts held classes in 1862. St. Louis, which enjoyed excellent educational leadership during this period, experienced a drop in its enrollment by more than 50 per cent. Lack of funds forced the closing of its evening division, which had enrolled 1,149 students in 1860–1861. It had operated the only high school in Missouri until St. Joseph opened one in March, 1861. Operations were suspended at St. Joseph High School that fall for the duration of the war, but St. Louis High School maintained a fairly steady level of approximately 250 pupils. By 1863–1864 the entire city school system had regained its 1860–1861 level. Outstate, however, public education was restored a little more slowly. There the ravages of war had taken a heavier toll in burned-out buildings, shifting population, and lack of concern.

Higher education also suffered severely. Most colleges outside St. Louis suspended operations in the fall of 1861. Although some held periodic sessions thereafter, their historians almost universally report that records are too scanty to know really what kind of operation they maintained, if any. Quite a number of pro-Southern students had attended Saint Louis University, and their excitement over the Camp Jackson affair forced the premature closing of that institution in the spring of 1861. By fall, however, calm had generally been restored on campus, and classes resumed with only nine of the "Southerners" enrolled. Although some of its professors faced the possibility of the military draft later in the war, the War Department granted indefinite furloughs to those educators who applied for them, which enabled them to remain at their posts. Washington University carried on its work without interruption, graduating its first class in 1862. Its founder, the Reverend William G. Eliot, was an ardent Unionist and a member of the Western Sanitary Commission.

In central Missouri, two institutions maintained a regular schedule, although each suspended briefly. Established in 1839 as a capstone to the public education system, the state university at Columbia had received no state appropriations in the prewar era. It subsisted instead on student fees and a small income from federal land grants. It had been caught up administratively in the political turmoil of the 1850's, but it was beginning to make progress under a new president when the war broke out. Although enrollment dropped by half to sixty students in the fall of 1861, the University remained open. Continuing operation was a struggle, given the reduction in fees and the defection of one professor and several trustees to the Confederate cause. By early 1862, the number of students had dwindled to thirty-six. A permanent military garrison had taken over the main building. With salaries $7,000 in arrears, the curators decided in mid-March to discontinue operations. Seniors were allowed to complete their work under whatever arrangements they might make with cooperative professors. The rest of the students went home. Largely due to the persistence of President John H. Lathrop, the school reopened in November, but only twenty-three students appeared. The military continued to occupy the campus for the remainder of the war. By 1864–1865, enrollment had climbed to sixty-nine. Only the efforts of concerned faculty kept the institution alive.

Twenty miles away, a similar dedication kept Westminster College open. Several institutions had been opened in the community of Fulton in the 1850's with the establishment there of the state lunatic asylum, an institute for the deaf and dumb, and two girls' academies in addition to Westminster. All of them suspended operations when the war broke out. The superintendent of the school for the deaf discontinued instruction in July, 1861, taking a handful of students with him to his Audrain County farm where he remained for two years. The state hospital sent its patients home in October, shortly before Union troops moved into Fulton to occupy its grounds. It would not reopen until the fall of 1863.

Westminster alone carried on. Although the college did not begin its regular session until December, 1861, this delay was due to the difficulty of calling a trustees' meeting. Then a controversy with the president over a matter of student discipline the previous spring brought that official's resignation. Still, the college enrolled forty-three that winter. When the editor of the local paper wrote at the end of April, 1862, deploring Fulton's decline and particularly the demise of her institutions over the preceding eighteen months, he received a prompt and sharp rejoinder from Westminster's acting president for deprecating the efforts of those who were "doing all we can to advance the interests of the College and instruct the youth committed to our care." Although the faculty did not find their task an easy one in a community noted for its strong Southern sympathies, they continued, and by 1863–1864, enrollment had increased to better than a hundred.[5]

Some mention has already been made of the divisions that war caused in Missouri's churches. Many in the rural areas found it necessary to close their doors for reasons similar to those affecting the schools. Most of the statewide governing bodies of the various denominations discontinued meeting because of the

5. The only other outstate college to maintain continuous operations, as far as this writer has been able to ascertain, was St. Vincent's in Cape Girardeau.

difficulties of wartime travel. An attempt by the Baptist General Association to convene in 1862 was disrupted by Federal troops. The Presbyterians had difficulties at their state meeting in 1864 because of a requirement by General Rosecrans that all those attending such an assemblage take the test oath. A band of bushwhackers broke up a Methodist revival meeting at Pilot Knob in the summer of 1864, and then confiscated for themselves the sumptuous meal the members had provided for postservice fellowship.

In spite of such instances as these, however, churches continued their activities. Revivals particularly attracted large crowds, perhaps because the people welcomed any diversion from the depredations going on around them. The large number of converts, reported periodically in the press, indicated that the uncertainties of life in wartime made religion a major concern for many Missourians. In St. Louis and elsewhere, Unionist churches sponsored mass prayer meetings on behalf of the war effort. Galusha Anderson reported that those in the city attracted as many as fifteen hundred to two thousand on occasion. At the close of each session, the entire group would rise and with upraised right hands repeat in unison a pledge of allegiance.

Such fraternal organizations as the Masons and the Odd Fellows kept their groups intact, although many lodges became inactive. The Masonic order, for example, had 225 lodges in Missouri in 1861, but the following year its grand secretary indicated that only 88 had filed any kind of report. While noting the unreliability of the mails, he also observed that many local units were struggling under great odds to maintain themselves. Masons in the southwestern part of the state were particularly disturbed because "many of the lodge rooms had been burned and their jewels and furniture destroyed." Membership in the Odd Fellows dipped from 4,880 in 1861 to 3,111 the following year and did not take an upward swing again until after the war.

The conflict brought a virtual halt to many of the amusements and entertainments that Missourians had enjoyed earlier. Agricultural fairs, which had blossomed in the 1850's, ceased their operations for the duration of the war in view of the depredations of the land. Even St. Louis's Agricultural and Mechanical Exposition, which had begun to attract national attention, went into abeyance. Depending upon conditions at any given time, such occasional amusements as trotting matches, concerts, or amateur theatrical performances might be mentioned in the weekly out-state press; but these occasions were not numerous, although their number had increased somewhat by 1864.

Because traveling was difficult, theatrical groups limited their performances to St. Louis and occasionally St. Joseph, Rolla, or some other town easily reached by rail. Individual entertainers still did some touring. One such was the actor John Wilkes Booth. He appeared on numerous occasions at DeBar's Grand Opera House in St. Louis—sometimes with a local company in a Shakespearean production, again in a program of solo readings. Early in January, 1864, Booth was detained in St. Joseph, en route from Leavenworth, because the railroad was immobilized by snow. The local citizenry was delighted to have the well-known Thespian in their midst and persuaded him to give his readings at Corby's Hall. The local paper carried the story the next morning with Booth's name headlined just below its mast-head which called for "Abraham Lincoln for President." St. Joseph had two saloon–variety halls during the early 1860's with occasional traveling troups making appearances. By 1864 they were attracting a new, war-born phenomenon—panoramic battle scenes that brought the Eastern combat directly to the door-step of an area which had already seen too much of its own.

Conditions had improved sufficiently by that summer for four circuses to tour the state. In May, G. F. Bailey's Quadruple Combination Circus played Prairieville, Bowling Green, Louisiana, Palmyra, and Canton. Palmyra and Canton were also visited by John Robinson's Menagerie and Circus in July. James Melville's Australian Circus toured more extensively, playing at fifteen towns across northern Missouri during the last two weeks of June, then coming back for a swing through west-central Missouri the first week in August. Mabie's Grand Menagerie and Moral Exhibition closed out the circus season with appearances in nine northeast Missouri towns in late August and September just the war was becoming more active elsewhere because of Price's raid.

St. Louis, with its large population, relative safety, and accessibility to travel, enjoyed a continuing variety of entertainments during the entire war. The *Missouri Democrat* noted in late January, 1862: "It is gratifying to know that, despite the peculiar positions of the times, our citizens seem determined to enjoy themselves. Our public places of amusements are all well patronized—better so, perhaps, than in any other city of the Union." Part of the sizable clientele was due to the influx of military personnel who sought diversions from the preoccupations of war. Indeed one genteel devotee of the legitimate theater later scored the owner of a local music hall for playing to these demands of the soldiers with "stage exhibitions . . . of the most reckless and abandoned kind. Song, broadly indecent, appealing to the lowest instincts, dances, vulgar and wildly grotesque, recitations as vile as anything in Joe Miller's or George Buchanan's suppressed books."

For those with different tastes in the field of entertainment, St. Louis had its Philharmonic Society, a choral and orchestral group organized in 1860 and dominated by German musicians, which maintained a regular series of concerts throughout the war. Amateur theatricals also came into vogue, with such groups as the St. Louis Dramatic Association making periodic appearances. On the professional level, DeBar's Grand Opera House booked not only John Wilkes Booth on a regular basis but also other noted performers. One of these was Laura Keene, who included "Our American Cousin" in her repertoire during a three–week stint there in December, 1863. A year and a half later, she and Booth would keep a rendezvous with President Lincoln at another performance of that same play at Ford's Theater in Washington.

Missourians also had a rendezvous with the future, even as they sought diversion from the burdens of life around them in their war-torn state. As the conflict swept through Missouri it brought vast change. No one remained unaffected. It produced a turmoil and a division which those who lived through it never forgot. It also created a social and political revolution as the overriding issue of slavery rose to demand the attention of all classes of society.

CHAPTER IV

A NEW DIRECTION

As guerrilla warfare mounted in the summer of 1862, with all the attendant problems discussed previously, the Gamble administration faced yet another dilemma that would tax its resources and those of most Missourians to the utmost. On March 10, President Lincoln had called together the Congressional representatives of the border states to discuss his proposal of four days earlier that the legislature go on record as favoring gradual, compensated emancipation through a cooperative program with the states. Although the men from the border areas gave little encouragement that their states were interested, Congress approved his plan by early April.

In his first proclamation after taking office, Governor Gamble had placed his administration squarely behind the preservation of slavery. The purpose of assuming this position was to place at ease the minds of many of those who had supported him in the overthrow of the Jackson administration and the establishment of a bonafide Union government. For those slaveowners who wished to take their chattels south, he had instituted a pass system, which the military duly recognized until the arrival of General Halleck in November, 1861. Halleck stopped the practice on the ground that those going to the South could carry important information to the enemy. Subsequent efforts to secure approval for renewing the policy never materialized.

Gamble's was to be a basically conservative regime, and he made it clear from the first that Jacobinism was furthest from his mind. When General Frémont sought to free the slaves of Missouri rebels later that month, Gamble ardently opposed him at Washington. Lincoln was not ready for such a drastic program in the fall of 1861, and consequently, Frémont's policy was reversed.

Frémont had struck a responsive chord among many of the more radical St. Louis Unionists, however, and thereby touched off a latent antislavery sentiment that was especially prevalent within the German community. Albert D. Richardson, the correspondent for the *New York Tribune*, accompanied Frémont into the field in late September. He reported that slaves flocked into the general's camp at Springfield and that Frémont would not permit any to be returned to their masters. The same reporter had written earlier that Federal troops operating in southeastern Missouri were freeing slaves and engaging them as servants to the officers at "fair wages." Apparently, Frémont was trying to follow Maj. Gen. Benjamin F. Butler's "contraband" policy with regard to runaways and thus bring his actions into line with the recent Confiscation Act, as directed by President Lincoln.

When General Halleck assumed the command of the Department of the West in November, he quickly put a stop to this practice. In General Order No. 3, he directed that all runaways be excluded from within his lines because such slaves frequently proved to be a source of information for enemy intelligence. In reply to the inquiries he received to clarify the order, Halleck stated that he intended to leave the question of master-slave relationships to civil authorities. He did not wish any of his officers to act either "in the capacity of negro-catcher or negro-stealer." The new commander made no effort, however, to interfere with various blacks working at different military camps around the state whose antecedents might have been forgotten over a few months time. As for the sixteen blacks who had returned with Frémont's army and were remanded to the city jail for sale as slaves under state law, he ordered that they be freed by the provost marshal general, although they were to work for the quartermaster's department until they had paid for clothing and other necessities the army had given them. When the St. Louis police began the policy that winter of taking into custody any black they found on the street and holding him as a runaway subject to sale if his owner was not found, Halleck ordered the practice stopped except when they had a specific court order.

The turbulent times made the plight of the Negro a difficult one. Accounts of runaways in the Missouri press increased that winter. One paper, the St. Joseph *Journal*, perhaps with tongue in cheek, accused the slaveowners themselves with creating the problem. "The secessionists have charged that the purpose of this war was to free the negroes and have talked so much about it, that it is no wonder their negroes leave them. They may blame themselves for the present stampede among slaves." Whatever the case, the desire for freedom on the part of the blacks themselves became increasingly evident. The Reverend Galusha Anderson, a prominent abolitionist Baptist minister in St. Louis, noted the clandestine departure of two "faithful servants" from the household of one member of his congregation who was a local banker. This parishioner had invited his pastor for dinner shortly after Anderson's arrival in St. Louis. During the evening, the banker had gone out of his way to reiterate the blessings of the "peculiar institution" for all concerned and to point out the well-being and happiness of his slaves. His words came back to haunt him when they ran away early in the war.

The number of slaves that fled to the various military outposts around the state or found their way into St. Louis during this early period cannot be ascertained. But as the movement continued in the spring of 1862, a small number of Missouri Unionists began to raise serious questions about the continuation of a slave system they considered a prime cause of the war. These and other Unionists realized that there would be little room for such an anachronistic institution in the postwar world. Some, such as B. Gratz Brown, had urged some type of gradual compensated emancipation before the war. They had done so largely on grounds that this would redound to the advantage of the white laborer and help attract Eastern immigrants and capital. Almost universally, they coupled emancipation with colonization to rid Missouri of the possibility of free Negro competition for labor. Few, if any, had been ardent abolitionists of the Garrisonian type.

With a statewide election scheduled to be held in August to choose a successor to the Provisional Government, the budding emancipationist group began to think in terms of the possibilities of political power. Old party labels were increasingly losing their meaning in the light of the many new issues raised by the war and its projected aftermath. Not surprisingly, Brown, chairman of the Republican state central committee, deemphasized party allegiances when he called a convention to select candidates for the fall election. Rather he urged all those interested in a "humane, economical, and constitutional method" of emancipation to meet at Jefferson City on June 16. To further promote his cause, Brown helped organize the Missouri General Emancipation Society that spring.

Governor Gamble returned to Missouri in mid-March after a two-month stay in the East, occasioned by state business and ill health. He found public sentiment favorable toward him. General Halleck's firm policy in dealing with secessionist sentiment that winter, coupled with his obvious willingness to work closely with the Provisional Government, gave Unionists encouragement. In his responses to various letters and petitions, Gamble made it known on May 12 that, although he preferred private life and would not actively seek public office, he would not refuse to serve if called upon to do so. The public generally understood this statement to be an indication of his willingness to run for governor, and other would-be candidates quickly dropped by the wayside.

Inasmuch as certain procedural problems had to be resolved before the coming election, Gamble called the state convention back into session the first week in June. Foremost among these matters was the need to redistrict the state because of the addition of two congressional seats after the 1860 census. Some arrangement also had to be made for absentee voting by Missouri's servicemen. The convention had little difficulty in resolving these and other problems. Perhaps the most lively topic concerned which offices should be submitted to a vote in the fall election. A committee-proposed ordinance that would keep the Provisional Government in office until the 1864 elections, the normal end for the Jackson administration, went down to a narrow defeat. Probably few of those delegates voted against the proposal because they were dissatisfied with the existing administration. Rather, they anticipated that Gamble and Hall would be candidates for their respective offices that fall, with little or no opposition, and a popular vote would provide them with a legitimate, electoral base. They were extremely surprised when it was announced that the two men looked upon the outcome of the vote as a censure of their administration .

The following morning, out of consideration for the feelings of Gamble and Hall, the convention by large majorities voted to reconsider and then passed, 45 to 21, a resolution that the Provisional Government be continued for two years. Local, legislative, and congressional races would go forward that fall as previously scheduled. To reinforce their support, the convention members unanimously adopted a resolution declaring their "undiminished confidence in the ability, integrity and patriotism of Governor Gamble and the other officers" whom they had elected a year earlier.

In the light of subsequent events, it was unfortunate that Gamble and Hall took the attitude they did. All indications are that the Provisional Government enjoyed a great deal of public support in the summer of 1862. No serious rivals had appeared to challenge its two leaders. In any election, the test oath, which the convention strengthened at this session, would prevent most of the non-Unionist element from voting. The split that appeared in Unionist ranks that fall over emancipation and the use of the militia did not become serious enough to hurt the Provisional Government until after the newly elected legislature convened. Had Gamble and Hall had the legitimacy of a legal election behind them by the winter of 1862–1863, they would have had a much easier time facing the problems that confronted them during the next two years. These issues mounted steadily following the convention's adjournment. Attacks on the Provisional Government grew in intensity. Its failure to stand before the people for election undoubtedly increased its vulnerability to these criticisms.

Some citizens had hoped that Gamble might confront the convention with the growing concern over emancipation and particularly Congress's proposal to cooperate with the states in effecting this policy, but he made no mention of it in his opening message. In spite of the omission of any such statement, a group of St. Louis conservatives led by Samuel M. Breckinridge advocated an emancipation ordinance designed to end the importation of slaves and to free all those born after January 1, 1865, when they reached age twenty-five. They favored accepting the congressional offer of aid to provide some type of compensation to owners. They would leave the final decision, however, to a popular referendum at the 1864 election.

Breckinridge argued that the war had doomed slavery in Missouri and urged that recognition of this fact would greatly facilitate the state's postwar economic development. Action now on his moderate proposal would hopefully forestall a bitter struggle within the Unionist ranks, he warned, and perhaps prevent more radical solutions later. But he spoke in vain. At this early stage, few of his fellow conservatives could read the future as clearly as he. They tabled the ordinance, 52 to 19, on motion of Congressman William A. Hall, the Lieutenant Governor's brother.

Although he agreed with the convention's action, Governor Gamble became concerned about the group's abrupt negativism. At the close of the session, he sent the members a special message asking for a more positive response to the congressional offer. While he did not expect a reconsideration of the Breckinridge ordinance, he did think the convention should clarify the reasons for the decision to decline the open hand of a Congress that had been quite generous to Missouri in other matters. The members responded with a carefully worded resolution, which indicated that the majority did not feel authorized "to take action with respect to the grave and delicate questions of private right and public policy" set forth in the congressional offer, although they desired "to recognize the liberality displayed therein" and to express their appreciation for it.

Gamble promptly received a letter of commendation for his action from Sen. John B. Henderson, who had been one of the few border-state congressmen to approve Lincoln's proposals the previous March. Henderson believed that the border states should acknowledge the concern the President had displayed in their behalf. He warned prophetically: "We cannot secure interest in slave property by closing our mouths and ears in Missouri whilst events here are daily demonstrating to all who take the time or pains to think at all that if this war continues (and I think it will continue long enough to accomplish this end) slavery will be forever destroyed in the United States."

Two days after the delegates at the state convention had completed their work, approximately 195 emancipationists, respond-

ing to the call of B. Gratz Brown, descended upon Jefferson City.
In a series of fiery speeches, their leaders denounced the Provisional Government for its refusal to stand the test of a public
election and referred to a Gamble dictatorship. They deplored
the failure of the convention to take advantage of the congressional offer of aid in emancipation and urged the legislature,
which would be elected that fall, to remedy that situation. From
this meeting there began to emerge the nucleus of a Radical
party that would become a major force during the next year
and a half.

The changes that were occurring in Washington advanced
the emancipationists' cause. There, Congress, under pressure
from the Radicals, pushed through a plan for compensated
emancipation in the District of Columbia and strengthened the
Confiscation Act. Failing to secure any satisfactory response on
emancipation from the border states, Lincoln began to think in
more drastic terms, culminating that September in his Emancipation Proclamation.

By that time, the Missouri election campaign was in full
swing. The press in Missouri struck up a lively debate over the
merits of emancipation within the state and the attendant problems that should be expected if the policy were adopted. While
Lincoln's new program did not affect Missouri directly, it did
tend to push many politicians there one step further to the left
of the positions they had held earlier that summer. The Brown
Radicals, glorying in the epithet "Charcoals" which their opponents hurled at them, began to discuss more immediate action and the desirability of enlisting Negroes in the armed
forces. The Breckinridge Conservatives, whom the Charcoals
labeled "Claybanks" because of their supposedly colorless middle ground, concentrated on making certain that the transition
from slavery to freedom would be a gradual one with adequate
compensation to the owners. Governor Gamble joined their
ranks that fall as more moderates began to realize that emancipation was inevitable. The thought of Negro enlistments was
anathema to them, in part because they feared it might be the
first step toward full equality. Some, like Frank Blair, still hoped
that there could be a complete separation of the races through a

scheme for colonization. A small group of Conservatives clung adamantly to the belief that slavery could survive the war. In Columbia, the *Missouri Statesman* dubbed these individuals "Snowflakes" because they were "more concerned about the white man than about the nigger."

Seventy-six thousand fewer Missourians voted that fall than had done so two years earlier. The turmoil that disrupted many areas and the rather stringent test oath adopted by the convention undoubtedly contributed to the small response. The returns clearly indicated that the candidates who were elected favored some form of emancipation, but the new legislature could not be said to reflect either a strong Charcoal or Claybank majority. Indeed, except for the more ardent St. Louis Radicals, most emancipationist candidates had been deliberately vague as to how they would carry out such a policy. The nine newly elected congressmen included four future Radicals, three Claybanks, and two conservative Democrats.

When the Twenty-second General Assembly convened at Jefferson City on December 29, 1862, Governor Gamble urged a program of gradual emancipation, which he hoped Congress might underwrite financially. But the legislature could not muster a majority to support any particular scheme and wrangled away its time until adjournment with nothing accomplished. Nor did congressional efforts fare any better as Sen. John B. Henderson and Rep. John W. Noell introduced bills that were widely at variance in their terms concerning both compensation and the requirements whereby Missourians might secure such aid.

The failure of the General Assembly to enact an emancipation measure caused Governor Gamble to call the state convention for one last time to deal with that issue. It became necessary to hold a special election because the state convention had declared a number of its seats vacant at its last session. This gave an opportunity for further contest between Charcoals and Claybanks, and in the filling of one of the vacant St. Louis seats, it propelled a new Radical champion into the head of the coming struggle.

The Charcoals had swept the St. Louis municipal elections

that spring and were brimming with confidence. They anticipated nominating B. Gratz Brown for one of the convention
vacancies, but he tarried on an Eastern trip until it became obvious that he could not return in time to file the oath that was required for candidates. Brown had no desire to become embroiled
in convention politics. Knowing that Gamble would have his
own way at that meeting, he was concerned with building up a
Radical party to challenge the moderates and the Conservatives
over the long future and perhaps pave his way to a seat in the
United States Senate.

In view of Brown's reluctance, Chauncey I. Filley, the new
Charcoal mayor of St. Louis, and other Radical leaders enlisted
Charles D. Drake to run. A recent convert to emancipation,
Drake accurately depicted his situation in his highly self-centered
autobiography. "Up to this time I had been only a private in the
Missouri division of the great Union host, but now it was sought
to put me where I should inevitably have to lead a forlorn hope
against the compact and disciplined majority in the Convention." Drake was a former law student and close friend of Governor Gamble, and in the 1850's, he had been successively a
Whig, a Know-Nothing, and a Douglas Democrat. He had
spent one highly controversial year in the legislature just before
the war, where he antagonized the Germans and their political
allies through his advocacy of strict blue laws. Since then he had
shunned an active political career, but he was a skilled orator
and frequently in demand to address the public on ceremonial
and other occasions. As late as July, 1861, he had denounced agitation against slavery, but during the following winter, he underwent a metamorphosis and began to score slavery as the
principal cause of the war and all of the subsequent evils visited
upon Missouri. The next logical step was advocation of emancipation, and Drake was soon preaching this theme as opportunity
allowed.

Drake's candidacy provided the Charcoals with a well-known
platform personality, which was quite important in view of the
brief span of six days remaining until the election. His Claybank
opponent, James E. Yeatman, was one of the most respected
Unionists in St. Louis as head of the Western Sanitary Commis-

sion. Drake and Yeatman really differed little in their announced platforms, an indication that few politicians, whatever their label, had a definitive program at this time. Drake demanded emancipation "in the most speedy manner consistent with good order" while Yeatman desired slavery "abolished in the shortest possible time consistent with true humanity and common justice." But the new Radical, having broken with his old law mentor, attacked the Gamble administration for its supposed intransigence in dealing swiftly with rebel elements. This criticism would become one of the main Radical themes of the future. It helped bring the still suspicious Germans into line behind Drake under pressure from the Radical press. He defeated Yeatman by a narrow margin, and B. Gratz Brown would soon find that because of his reluctance to confront Gamble directly, his leadership of the new party he was molding was being threatened.

The results of the convention session were just as the Charcoals had anticipated. Governor Gamble announced in his opening message that, after a two-year absence from the group, he would resume active participation in its deliberations. His colleagues promptly named him chairman of the committee charged with introducing an emancipation ordinance. After a long and sometimes vitriolic debate in which Drake emerged as a fairly effective leader of the Charcoal opposition, the convention decided that slavery would be abolished in Missouri on July 4, 1870.[1] The ex-slaves would remain under the supervision of their former masters for varying periods of apprenticeship, depending upon their age on the date of emancipation. When Drake attempted to secure a referendum on the ordinance, Gamble objected, and the convention sustained him.

During the train ride back to St. Louis after the convention's adjournment, Senator Henderson approached the embittered Drake with the plea, "Come now, Charlie, declare in favor of the Ordinance, and let the whole matter be settled." The new leader of the Radicals refused with the rejoinder, "No, I'll go before the people, and smash your Ordinance and you too."

1. Drake on behalf of the Charcoals first proposed January 1, 1864, as the date for emancipation, but he later indicated that they would accept November 1, 1866. Both were too soon for the Claybank majority.

Henderson, however, proved a bit too adroit for the Drake on-slaught that followed.

Drake took up the cudgel in a St. Louis speech on July 9, eight days after this conversation. Reviewing the convention's recent work, he set the theme for the days ahead:

> Governor Gamble and those who act with him, saw that a public sentiment was rising, over our whole State, in favor of the removal of the curse of Slavery from our soil; that the people were rapidly wheeling into line in favor of *immediate* Emancipation; and that they also demanded the election of a Governor and other State officers, in lieu of those set over them by the Convention. It was necessary, in some way or other, to thwart this movement, or it would sweep the Governor and his party overboard, whenever the people should have access to the ballot-box. How was it to be done? To take issue with it, was certain destruction to him and his parti-sans. There was only one other way, and that was to take the wind out of the sails of the Emancipationists, by calling the old, almost defunct, pro-Slavery convention together, and let it ordain Emanci-pation, at such time as it could be cajoled or frightened into adopt-ing, no matter how distant or protracted, and then go before the people as they are now doing, and demand and urge acquiesence in its action as a final settlement of the whole matter! It was a cun-ning game, well played, and doubtless expected to be successful. It was a bold game, too, as it had need to be; for upon its success de-pended, perhaps, the maintenance and consolidation of enormous power in the hands of the Governor and his parasites. But it was no honest game, and it will not win, if the people come to under-stand it, as I doubt not they will.

During the remainder of the summer, Drake and other Radi-cal leaders made certain that the citizenry was aware of their message. They toured central and western Missouri extensively and spoke almost daily to a growing number of citizens who shared their sympathies. President Lincoln became their unwit-ting ally when they came into possession of a letter the President had written his new departmental commander, Gen. John M. Schofield. In it, he warned Schofield to avoid the factionalism that had plagued General Curtis, his predecessor, and caused his removal. While Lincoln had not been able to ascertain any actual wrongdoing on Curtis's part, the President thought that the former commander had allowed himself to be used by the emerging Charcoal group in "a pestilent factional quarrel" with the Gamble administration. Then said Lincoln, in a sentence which the Radicals seized upon: "After months of labor to reconcile the difficulty, it seemed to grow worse and worse, until I felt it my duty to break it up somehow, and as I could not remove Governor Gamble, I had to remove General Curtis."

The *Missouri Democrat* printed Lincoln's entire letter on June 27. Its publication incensed Schofield to the extent that he demanded that the editors tell him how they had obtained a copy. When they declined to answer, he arrested one of them and then released him on oral parole with ten days to reconsider. At this point, the President found himself right back in the middle as the Radicals accused Schofield, a known friend of Gamble's, of being partisan. Lincoln asked his commander to drop the matter; Schofield did, somewhat reluctantly. But the Radicals continued to emphasize the affair at their rallies. As far as they were concerned, they now felt confident that had the President been able to remove Gamble, he would have done so.

The Governor did not hesitate to express his views in the snowballing political melee. He had known nothing about the letter prior to its publication, but he interpreted it the same way the Radicals did. He sent Lincoln a stinging defense of his actions in which he denied that he had ever served the cause of factionalism. He assured the President that his efforts had been motivated solely by a sense of duty to his state and country. Gamble believed that it was by seeking to rise about faction and protect all Missourians from those with "the thirst for vengeance" that he had brought on much of the difficulties that now beset him. Whatever the case, he considered his position weakened in the eyes of the people of Missouri by the publication of the President's letter.

Gamble could have gone further by pointing out that he had resigned his post at the last session of the convention only to have both that body and General Schofield persuade him to reconsider. The general had reasoned that nothing positive would be gained by such a move and that the whole result might be "confusion worse confounded." Yet Schofield refused to be pinned down to certain prior guarantees when the Governor urged him to institute a specific program of cooperation. Although the *Missouri Democrat* had indicated that many considered the whole matter a deliberate move by the Governor to gain sympathy and support, there is no evidence that Gamble's resignation was not sincere. He was plagued by ill health and weary of the increasing criticism being heaped upon him. Yet he recognized, especially in view of the publication of Lincoln's letter, that to insist upon resigning might be understood as a victory for the Radicals, whom he had now come to fear where Missouri's future was concerned. The Conservative cause needed leadership, and Gamble felt dutybound to provide it. That group's press, led by the *Missouri Republican*, breathed a sigh of relief.

Lincoln, in replying to what his secretary had called a "very cross" letter, told the Governor that he had declined reading the correspondence personally "as I am trying to preserve my own temper, by avoiding irritants, so far as practicable." But he hastened to reassure Gamble: "I was totally unconscious of any malice, or disrespect towards you, or of using any expression which should offend you, if seen by you."

This assurance soothed the Governor temporarily. He had other problems to worry about that summer. With the coming of warm weather, guerrilla activity once again began to increase. After wintering in Arkansas as part of Gen. Jo Shelby's command, Quantrill's raiders returned to Missouri some time in late April or early May. This seemed a signal for other groups and individual guerrillas to emerge from their hiding places. That summer the militia was given the major responsibility for containing them, because Schofield forwarded most of the volunteer regiments in Missouri and Kansas to the Vicksburg campaign.

Unfortunately, the new commander continued his predecessor's policy of attaching western Missouri counties to Kansas when he determined the boundaries for military districts. On June 9, he divided the old Military District of Kansas into two new ones with Maj. Gens. James B. Blunt and Thomas Ewing, Jr. in command. Both men were ardent Radicals, and Ewing was a political sycophant of Sen. Jim Lane and a brother-in-law of Maj. Gen. William T. Sherman. Not trusting the Missouri militia to maintain order in their part of his district, Ewing relied on Kansas troops whose "loyalty was unquestioned." Actually, this policy simply aggravated an already difficult situation.

With the circumstances on the border steadily deteriorating, Ewing wrote Schofield on August 3 to propose the mass evacuation of those known to have aided or abetted the guerrilla cause. Although he had some misgivings, the departmental commander finally agreed to the move on the 14th with the proviso that it be limited to the smallest number of people possible because of the expense involved and "the suffering it may cause to children and other comparatively innocent persons." That same day, disaster struck one of several makeshift prisons in which Ewing had incarcerated the mothers, wives, and sisters of those men suspected of guerrilla activity. When it collapsed from overloading, five women were killed and several others seriously injured. The rumor quickly spread that Ewing had deliberately planned the tragedy. Although no evidence exists to support this accusation, the grieving guerrillas needed no proof. When Ewing's new order for evacuation followed quickly, they were spurred into action.

The result was a raid on Lawrence, Kansas, by the Quantrill gang in which some 150 men and boys were gunned down leaving 80 widows and 250 orphans. Property damage totaled more than $2 million. The guerrillas struck so swiftly and unexpectedly that they lost only one of their own; he had stayed behind in a drunken stupor and had been shot by an Indian. His body was torn to pieces by a vengeful mob. The guerrillas seemed to vanish. The border was aflame. For a few days afterward, it appeared that Kansans would make a retaliatory strike into Missouri as Jim Lane led the cries for vengeance. He blamed Schofield and, indirectly, Gamble for being lax and demanded more positive federal action. The Radical press did not hesitate to blame the Governor for the occurrence of the tragedy. The *Missouri Democrat* went to the extreme of accusing him of supporting Quantrill. Indeed, it charged him with personal responsibility for failure to contain the guerrilla leader.

Schofield hastened to the border to calm the troubled situation. Without waiting for his superior's arrival, Ewing had carried his evacuation policy to its ultimate in his General Order

No. 11, dated August 25. Through this order *all* persons in Jackson, Cass, Bates, and the northern half of Vernon County, who lived beyond a mile's distance from a Union military post, were required to leave their homes within fifteen days. Those who could prove their loyalty could remain at a post in the area; all others would have to move completely outside the military district. To enforce the order, Ewing utilized the Fifteenth Kansas Cavalry under Doc Jennison, whom most Missourians hated bitterly. The Kansans carried out their assignment with a vengeance. The Lexington *Union* reported in mid-September that no less than five thousand refugees had crossed the Missouri River there within a week. Many had to leave furniture and clothing for lack of adequate transport.

Much of the border area lay in ruin within two weeks and became known for years as the "Burnt District." In Cass County, which had a population of ten thousand before the war, only six hundred remained; Bates County suffered to an even greater degree. One officer wrote his wife on September 10: "It is heart sickening to see what I have seen since I have been back here. A desolated country and men & women and children, some of them allmost naked. Some on foot and some in old wagons. Oh God." Although called upon by Acting Governor Hall to rescind the order, Schofield felt he could not do so for fear of antagonizing hostile Kansans who were threatening to retaliate. Later that winter, however, he mitigated its effects somewhat through the appointment of a new district commander who allowed those not "disloyal or unworthy" to return to their homes.

In the midst of all this turmoil, the Radicals climaxed their summer political campaign with a mass emancipation convention at Jefferson City, which was attended by seven hundred delegates from three-fourths of the state's counties. No hall at the capital could house that large a crowd, so they gathered in front of the state house early on the morning of Tuesday, September 1, to march en masse to the nearby fairgrounds. There they launched the Radical Union party, which swept into power fourteen months later. Taking their cues from Charles D. Drake's keynote address, the delegates called for the resignation of the Provisional Government, the removal of General Schofield, the appointment of a committee of seventy to carry their grievances to President Lincoln, and the establishment of a committee of public safety to supervise the protection of the loyal citizenry. They advocated the immediate emancipation of Missouri's remaining slaves and the enlistment of free blacks into the armed forces. Finally, they endorsed B. Gratz Brown and Maj. Gen. Benjamin F. Loan of the M.S.M. for the two Senate vacancies that the legislature had to fill at its forthcoming session, and nominated candidates for a special state Supreme Court election, which Gamble had recently called.

At the end of the month, Drake led the seventy-member committee to Washington, where Lincoln allowed them to cool their heels for three days before receiving them. The President had been overwhelmed throughout September by Conservatives and Radicals alike who tried to influence him to their political advantage. Lincoln finally granted Drake and his followers a full hearing but with doors locked and reporters barred. His infinite patience manifested itself throughout as he heard their complaints and discussed them with the delegates in detail. Yet he gave no hint of an answer to their concerns except to admonish them for their attacks on General Schofield, whom he warmly defended.[2]

The Radicals returned to Missouri to launch their campaign for the judicial election scheduled for early November. It set the tone for all their subsequent efforts. On platform after platform throughout the state, Conservatives were branded as "Copperheads" who were not true supporters of the Union, as Radical speakers "waved the bloody shirt" and revealed an unrelenting attitude of vindictiveness toward anyone who questioned their program. The Radicals sought to promote themselves as progressives whose policies could ensure a favorable atmosphere in the state for the attraction of immigrants and outside commercial investment. They appealed to the working class to join in the battle of democracy versus aristocracy by contending that Conservative circles held them in disdain as "poor white trash."

2. The President drafted his formal reply to the Radicals on October 5, although he did not send it to Drake until October 14. He rejected their demands and indicated once again his strong approval of Schofield's conduct. Lincoln's answer was so damaging to the Radical's cause that Drake withheld its publication for another ten days.

They admonished the eligible soldier electorate to vote as they shot—to uphold the "loyal men" in their attempts to secure protection at home for all "true" Unionists.

As the political group in power with considerable civil and military patronage at their disposal, the Conservatives did not deem it necessary to undertake a formal party organization. They backed the incumbent judges, whom Governor Gamble had appointed in 1862, and answered the Radicals' charges mainly through their press. They pictured their Radical opponents as mere opportunists who were primarily concerned with political gain. They often placed their foes on the defensive by directing public attention to incendiary statements made by the Radicals wherein their foes sometimes appeared as desperate men ready to undertake revolution, if necessary, to secure their ends. The Conservatives, in a blatantly racist appeal, also accused their opponents of pushing more immediate emancipation for the purpose of foisting equality of the Negro upon the state.

The returns from the election were close, and the final outcome was not determined for several weeks. The validity of the soldier vote caused a major dispute, with the Conservatives charging fraud in some returns and the Radicals claiming that many legal ballots went uncounted. The official returns, when finally announced, revealed a Conservative victory by a count of 43,180 to 40,744. General Schofield reported to the President that it had been a quiet election, and most of the outstate press confirmed his opinion. In this initial test of strength, the Radicals received their strongest support in the southwest, which had been wracked so heavily by guerrilla warfare; in the extreme northern parts of the state, where many citizens had free-state ties; and in St. Louis with their large German vote. The Conservatives dominated the central and southeastern counties along the rivers, where the large landowners concerned with the security of their slaves and other tangible property resided.

While disappointed by their setback in the judicial contest, the Radicals moved forward by consolidating their strength in the General Assembly, when it reconvened in December. They managed the election of B. Gratz Brown to the Senate for a four-year term, replacing Conservative Robert Wilson, who had been serving by appointment of Governor Gamble. At the same time, they supported the reelection of moderate Sen. John B. Henderson for a full six-year term. Henderson had been a Douglas Democrat before the war. He came from Pike County and had been active in the state convention and the state militia before Gamble sent him to the Senate in 1862. There he became one of the few border-state congressmen to try to help Lincoln with his program of compensated emancipation. In the recent election, Henderson had campaigned actively for the Conservative candidates. As the political winds shifted, however, he moved gradually closer toward the Radical ranks, and although never a leader in the new party, he cooperated with that group once it achieved power.

Henderson was already advocating that the Lincoln Administration renew one policy that was especially important to the Radicals—the recruitment of blacks into the armed forces. General Schofield had initiated such a policy in line with congressional provisions at the time he resumed command in late May, 1863. Governor Gamble consented, with the proviso that recruitment be limited to the slaves of disloyal owners, but Col. William A. Pile, whom Schofield placed in charge of the program, found it difficult to comply with this qualification. Too many of his field agents were willing to take blacks wherever they could find them.

In the wake of Missouri's emancipation ordinance that July, many slaves simply decided to extend the limits of its application where possible. Reports of flights became numerous, and many allegedly tried to take additional property of their masters with them. Some were victimized by unscrupulous whites who promised to lead them to freedom upon payment of goods or money, and then stranded them after payment had been made. In the western part of the state, Gen. Tom Ewing encouraged them to leave their masters by ordering his subcommanders to protect any slave wishing to flee to Kansas. The number of blacks in the border counties was soon diminished. In eastern Missouri, the *Canton Press* reported slaves escaping with increasing frequency until finally, on June 16, 1864, it simply stated that the "colored element in this place has about cleaned out."

When the Radicals met at Jefferson City in September, they endorsed the recruitment policy as Drake admonished:

I have no squeamishness about arming the Negro. I am no half-breed unionist, sensitive about seeing white men alongside of the "American citizen of African descent." No traitor is too good to be killed by a Negro, nor has any traitor a right to insist on being killed by a white man. If for the sake of slavery he turns traitor, let former slaves be his executioners; it is a just and fit retribution.

As protests from loyal slaveowners mounted, however, on October 1 Lincoln ordered the curtailment of Negro enlistments. Schofield had already drawn up a plan, with Senator Henderson's endorsement, for compensating loyal owners $300 out of the substitute fund for each slave recruited. The President waited until after the judicial election to approve it. The program met with mixed results. Many of the provost marshals, to whom the recruiting was entrusted, refused to actively pursue the endeavor because of their Conservative outlook. Others moved vigorously.

Lincoln established a special board to determine the validity of owners' claims where their slaves decided to take this step toward freedom. Some masters encouraged their slaves to enlist so they could collect the bounty, because they assumed it would be the only way to receive compensation for the loss of their property. As time wore on, more Missourians became reconciled to the program, especially as they realized that every slave recruited could count toward the state's draft quota. Reports of Negro enlistments became a regular feature in the state's newspapers. Many of the blacks recruited were runaways, and the *Canton Press* reported that their masters preferred the government taking them to allowing them to roam without restraint or means of support. Some owners stubbornly resisted the inevitable, however, as witness the report of August 20, 1863, in the St. Joseph *Weekly Herald*, that 85 slaves had been shipped from there to Kentucky to protect them from molestation. By war's end, Missouri had officially furnished 8,344 blacks, including 665 who served as substitutes for white draftees, to the nation's armed forces. Undoubtedly, there were many others from Missouri who enlisted in neighboring states after flight from the state.

Schofield's policies meanwhile continued to be attacked by Missouri Radicals. Brown accused the commander of working to block his election to the Senate and threatened to oppose his permanent promotion to major general. After several weeks of wrangling, Lincoln sought to combine the Missouri problem with another one to the mutually satisfactory settlement of both. Maj. Gen. William S. Rosecrans had lost favor with Generals Grant and Sherman as a result of his behavior in the Chattanooga campaign. Schofield, on the other hand, rated well with them. Thus, the President proposed an exchange which Senators Henderson and Brown approved—the appointment of Rosecrans as commander of the Department of the Missouri and the nomination of Schofield for the permanent rank of major general with a command in the field.

The turnover in military commanders at St. Louis coincided with a change in civilian leadership on the state level of government as well. Governor Gamble had been plagued with ill health throughout the war. Several times he had undergone treatment in the East while there on official business. During all of the turmoil over Quantrill's raid on Lawrence the previous fall, he had been in Philadelphia recuperating from a freak accident that had resulted in a fractured elbow. Upon his return, however, he had plunged vigorously into the judicial campaign while also getting ready for the new legislative session. But a few weeks after it convened, Gamble slipped and fell on the ice while descending the Capitol steps. He severely reinjured his yet unmended elbow and went to St. Louis to recover. There, weak and with low resistance, he contracted pneumonia. By mid-January, 1864, his condition had become critical. Just before noon on the 31st, he died.

Lt. Gov. Willard P. Hall immediately assumed the governorship and made clear, in his first message to the General Assembly, that he would try to carry out Gamble's policies. The state stood much in debt to the departed leader. Although in the end he was too conservative for many Missourians, he had inherited an exceedingly difficult situation in 1861 and performed a highly creditable job in dealing with it. Indeed, his conservatism and moderation were important staying factors in the whole drama of Missouri during the Civil War, as his policies kept many loyal to the Union who might otherwise have gone over permanently to the Confederacy or at least refused cooperation with the Northern war effort. Through the militia Gamble made it possible for many to perform valuable service for the Union cause who would have had little inclination to do so had Missouri pursued a more radical course. Many of those who had fought for the South early in the war returned to their original allegiance as it became obvious that the Federal authorities would not dictate state policy. The Governor's legal–judicial outlook, coupled with a Southern background, prevented his moving more readily on the social issues of the day, especially emancipation. Hence he was pushed by events rather than leading them as time went on. But he had followed his conscience, and, in the long run, his steady hand made possible a smooth transition of political power.

The Radicals had continued to gain strength as the legislative session progressed that winter. Shortly after Hall became governor, they pushed through a bill calling for a referendum that fall on a new state convention to consider emancipation, suffrage, and constitutional revision. The previous December, Hall had cast a tie-breaking vote in the Senate to table the measure. But when the Radicals revived and passed it by a large majority, he signed it in the confidence, as he wrote James S. Rollins, that it would be defeated at the polls. The Radicals, equally confident that the public would pass a referendum, provided for convention members to be chosen at the same election.

This new issue gave additional importance to an already crucial election. That fall the people of Missouri would have their first opportunity to choose a full slate of state and local officials since 1860. Both Conservatives and Radicals were determined to make the most of this chance, for those chosen would generally have a four-year lease on their respective offices. Underlying the entire scene in a rather significant way was the matter of presidential politics. While many leaders in both groups were not enthused about the possibility of Lincoln's reelection, most of the responsible ones realized the importance of a tie to the National Union party, as the President had redubbed the Republicans.

The Conservatives made their move first when the *St. Louis Union*, which Frank Blair had established as his personal political newspaper two years earlier, hoisted Lincoln's name to its masthead the first week in January. This endorsement was made apparently only after some strong pressure from Blair's friends overcame a desire by "some of our truest and best men" to maintain neutrality a bit longer. R. J. Howard, in reporting the matter to Montgomery Blair, correctly noted that "unless this step is taken we in Missouri have no status, no ground to stand upon." After they declared their preference for the Presidency, the Conservatives began organizing Lincoln clubs across the state. The one in St. Louis sent out a call on April 11 for a meeting there on May 18 under the banner of the Unconditional Union (Conservative) party to choose delegates to the National Union (Republican) convention at Baltimore.

The *Missouri Democrat* bitterly denounced this meeting as "bogus Unionism" and accused the Conservatives of attempting to divide the Radical party, "the true Union force" in Missouri. Undeterred, the Conservatives selected twenty-two delegates, headed by Governor Hall, to go to Baltimore with instructions to vote for Lincoln's renomination. They strongly endorsed the President's war policies and called for full cooperation with him. While favoring a constitutional amendment to abolish slavery, they went on record as approving the geographical segregation of the Negro. Lacking a concrete organization, the Conservatives established a state central committee with power to call a convention after the national meeting to nominate a state and electoral ticket.

The Radicals converged on Jefferson City for their state convention a week later. Fresh from a strong victory in the St. Louis municipal elections, their ranks were divided over the presidential issue. Many of the more fervent spirits within the Missouri party, as well as the national Radical movement, considered Lincoln's policies too conservative. They feared the implications of his amnesty proclamation of December, 1863, which they thought too conciliatory toward former rebels. They condemned him for not having gone beyond the Emancipation Proclamation of January 1, 1863, and ardently demanded further action to free the slaves in the border states. For this purpose, they had called a Slave-State Freedom Convention at Louisville in late February. Charles D. Drake and others had thwarted their attempts to turn that meeting into a political rally for Secretary of the Treasury Salmon P. Chase or some other anti-Lincoln candidate. Undaunted, certain Missouri Radicals, led by Gratz Brown, had joined with others of like mind to call a national Radical convention at Cleveland in late May to nominate a "true" Union ticket.

The Radical majority at Jefferson City, however, determined to send delegates to the National Union (Republican) convention at Baltimore. This decision caused some of the Germans to walk out because they feared that the national party would automatically endorse Lincoln's renomination. When it became obvious that, for all of this, the state convention remained in an anti-Administration mood, they returned and helped push through a resolution endorsing the one-term principal for the Presidency. The Radicals then selected twenty-two uncommitted delegates to go to Baltimore. They voted to sustain the Federal Government in a vigorous prosecution of the war but called for a purge of those elements within the cabinet who were not in step with the Radical program for a more stringent reconstruction. They also protested the Lincoln Administration's continued support of the Provisional Government while rejoicing at the prospect of imminent deliverance of Missouri from Conservative control.

Unlike their Conservative rivals, the Radicals nominated a state ticket for the fall campaign. It was headed by Thomas C. Fletcher of Jefferson County. A compromise choice for governor, Fletcher had been an active Republican and emancipationist since the 1850's. He had been a delegate to the 1860 national convention where he supported Lincoln. A native Missourian, he was only thirty-seven years of age and was an attractive candidate. He had been engaged in railroad and town building before the war, but during the conflict, he enlisted in the Missouri Volunteers and had risen to the rank of colonel with command of a brigade in Sherman's Army of the Tennessee at the time of his nomination. The other nominations were largely to Radical legislators with a judicious geographical and factional distribution. All of the men except George Smith, the candidate for lieutenant governor, were less than forty-five years of age.

As a result of these two conventions, Missouri sent rival delegations to the National Union conclave at Baltimore. There, in a series of intricate political maneuvers, the credentials committee recommended and effected seating the Radical group. To the dismay of many, the Radicals then became the one discordant note in the proceedings; they were the only delegations to cast their first ballot vote against Lincoln's renomination. The Missourians supported Gen. Ulysses S. Grant, to no avail, whereupon their chairman graciously moved to make the President the party's unanimous choice. Most important to Missouri in the proceedings at Baltimore was the official acceptance given the Radicals by the national party. Although some of their number had gone to Cleveland to aid in the nomination of John C. Frémont on a Radical ticket instead of to Baltimore, that movement ultimately collapsed, and the party was unified by the time of the fall elections.

The rejection of the Missouri Conservatives at Baltimore left that group in an untenable position politically unless it wished to divide the Union vote. Some Conservatives quietly supported Lincoln's reelection while refraining from any activity at the state or local level. The rest drifted into the ranks of the Democratic party, which the remainder of Missouri's "old guard" resuscitated. Meeting at St. Louis in mid-June, the Democrats chose a slate of delegates to attend the national convention at Chicago. There they supported Maj. Gen. George B. McClellan, the eventual nominee of the party. Upon their return, the state central committee called another convention to select a state ticket. It was headed by Thomas L. Price, prominent Jefferson City businessman and real estate promoter, who had been a staunch Benton Democrat in the 1850's. Price had long been active in party politics and had served briefly both in the Missouri General Assembly and the national House of Representatives.

All of the political activity operated against a background of increasing unrest and military action in Missouri. After a comparatively quiet winter, widespread guerrilla warfare had erupted again in the late spring of 1864. Raids by the Kansans had touched off retaliatory bushwhacker activity. But much of the new violence, which increased in June and July to unknown proportions, obviously was designed to serve as a prelude to something bigger. Reports kept filtering through to General Rosecrans of an imminent invasion from Arkansas, and he readied his troops. With the help of Governor Hall, Rosecrans urged closer coordination between state and Federal troops and even accepted some of the militia as six-month volunteers in the Union service.

In Shreveport, Louisiana, Gen. Edmund Kirby Smith, commander of the Confederate Trans-Mississippi Department, was preparing a major advance into Missouri in mid-August. While he did not carry out his plans because of orders from Richmond to divert all his available infantry to the defense of Georgia and Alabama, Kirby Smith did determine upon a cavalry raid which would hopefully divert reinforcements from Sherman's Army, secure badly needed men and supplies, and frighten the North on the eve of the national elections.

Gen. Sterling Price and Gov. Thomas C. Reynolds had been urging the Confederate commander to such action all summer, and Kirby Smith now chose Price as the logical leader for such an expedition. At a briefing session in Shreveport on August 4, he ordered the Missourian to prepare for the operation immediately with St. Louis as his principal objective. Seizure of that metropolis would "do more toward rallying Missourians to your standard than the possession of any other point" while also furnishing Price with military stores and supplies of all sorts. With the guerrillas already active, the presence of a Confederate unit might serve as a magnet for recruiting badly needed volunteers into the Southern ranks. So that he could recruit as many men as possible, Price, if forced to retreat, should move west along the Missouri River into Kansas and then return to Arkansas by way of the Indian Territory, accumulating every type of supply en route. Kirby Smith urged Price to keep a firm reign on his men during the campaign and not allow wanton destruction or the taking of personal revenge. Learning of the planned invasion, Governor Reynolds signified his desire to accompany the raiders. He and Price had not seen eye to eye on a variety of issues during the past year, and deep smoldering resentments had begun to build up. Each had supporters, and Reynolds now feared that Price might use his occupancy of Missouri soil to hold some kind of election that would seek to establish a legitimacy for a new state government, military or otherwise.

In preparation for his raid, Price sent orders to guerrilla leaders in Missouri to increase their activities north of the Missouri River in order to draw troops away from St. Louis and the southern part of the state. They immediately went into operation. Especially effective was an offshoot gang from Quantrill's raiders, led by Bloody Billy Anderson. They dashed thither and yon through central Missouri north of the river in August and September, always one jump ahead of the pursuing militia. The climax of their activities came on September 27 when Anderson and thirty of his guerrillas rode into Centralia on the North Missouri Railroad. They spent the morning terrorizing its citizens and looting various stores and homes. In the midst of the chaos, the Columbia stage rolled into town with Congressman James S. Rollins among its passengers. As one of the guerrillas held a pistol under his nose, Rollins did a fine bit of impromptu acting to convince them of his Confederate sympathies. They released him to scurry into hiding in a nearby attic but kept his valise from which they extracted a number of souvenirs.

Toward noon Anderson's men heard the whistle of a train coming from the east. They promptly blocked the track with railroad ties and hid until the engine hove into view. Then they fired through the windows of the cars to force the passengers to get off the train and give up their valuables. Among those who had boarded the train at St. Charles were twenty-five unarmed Union soldiers who were going home on furloughs. Discovering their presence, Anderson lined them up on the station platform and ordered them to strip off their uniforms, so his own men could use them. Then the guerrilla chieftain turned to Little Archie Clement, his second in command, with instructions to "muster out" the enemy. Clement, a perpetual smile on his twisted face, did so with a vengeance, firing point blank at the stunned troops with a pistol in each hand. Only one escaped; Sgt. Thomas Goodman of the Missouri Engineers had the audacity to step out when Anderson asked if any present were officers or noncommissioned officers. Thereby he attained a reprieve as Bloody Billy ordered him out of the line of fire. The Centralia "massacre" completed, the guerrillas fired the train and sent it at full speed down the track with its whistle tied down. Then they rode out of town to continue raiding elsewhere.

While the guerrillas thus caused havoc within Union lines

in Missouri, Price arrived at Pocahantas, Arkansas, on September
13 to organize his Army of Missouri consisting of twelve thousand men. It was, in some respect, a ragtag group. About one-
third of the complement were conscripts and deserters, recruited
when Kirby Smith held back on the number of Regulars in order
to increase the force he was sending east of the Mississippi. Many
of these last-minute additions were unarmed. Unfortunately,
Price also found himself hampered by dissension among his subordinate commanders and the lack of confidence at least two
of them had in his military ability.

For all of this, he got underway and crossed the Missouri border on September 19. After two years and seven months he had
returned for what he hoped would be a triumphal march. It
turned instead into a disastrous retreat. As Price regrouped at
Fredericktown on the 24th he learned that two forces blocked
his path into St. Louis: a small garrison of fifteen hundred men
near Pilot Knob under Gen. Tom Ewing and the Sixteenth
Corps, diverted from Sherman at the last moment, under Gen.
A. J. Smith just south of the city. Although urged by Jo Shelby,
one of his division commanders, to bypass Ewing and strike
directly for St. Louis, Price decided to eliminate the force at
Pilot Knob first so there would not be the threat of a flank attack by Union forces. His tactics for accomplishing this defeat
proved abominable, however, and resulted in heavy losses. While
Ewing abandoned his position, the gain proved negligible for
Price. Fearful now to attack St. Louis, he turned west toward
Jefferson City. Finding Union troops entrenched there on October 2, he circled the capital and moved on to Boonville without fighting.

General Rosecrans called out the local militia on October 9 to
serve within their own counties. Four days later, he took the
field to pursue Price, who continued moving westward toward
the Kansas border. There the Confederates found themselves
caught in a vise between the advancing Union troops to the east
of them and another force, under General Curtis, moving in
from Kansas. After three days of fighting, climaxed on October
23 by the battle of Westport, Price and his men retreated down
along the Missouri–Kansas line with Federal forces pursuing
them the entire distance. On October 30, the Confederates re-

entered the northwest corner of Arkansas. By that time, less than a week remained until the election. Price's raid had brought campaigning to a standstill. But Col. Tom Fletcher, the Radicals' gubernatorial nominee, had returned home in time to participate actively with Missouri troops against the invaders. His Democratic opponent, Thomas L. Price, though no relation to Sterling, suffered by the similarity of their names and his own inactivity, even though he held a militia commission.

Nearly 52,000 fewer Missourians went to the polls in November, 1864, than had done so four years earlier. Many citizens were disfranchised because of the test oath. Still others had fled the state. The turbulence that was still prevalent in many sections undoubtedly kept voters home also. Whatever the case, the Radicals made a clean sweep of the contest. Fletcher triumphed by approximately a 40,000-vote majority with Lincoln securing the state's electoral vote by the same margin. The Radicals carried both houses of the new General Assembly by large majorities. As with their statewide ticket, the emphasis here was on younger men; 56 per cent of the Radicals who were elected were under the age of forty-five. By far the largest group professionally within the ranks of the new Radical legislators were farmers who outnumbered lawyers 36 per cent to 19 per cent. Approximately one-fourth of those elected had served in the previous session, but for the most part they were inexperienced when it came to the tasks that confronted them. Inasmuch as many of them had short political careers, full-scale biographies of the majority of Radical legislators in this and subsequent sessions are difficult to find. Hence the political antecedents of only a few are known. Legislative records indicate, however, that the overwhelming majority had come to Missouri prior to the Civil War with two-thirds of them having immigrated before 1850. Fourteen per cent were native Missourians while one third had come from Northern states, half of this number from Ohio. Of the 22 per cent of Southern origins, most had come from Tennessee and Virginia. The new group of Radical legislators was 8 per cent German, while the origins of the other 8 per cent were unknown. In the congressional races the Radicals swept every district except the First, where a split in their ranks enabled Democrat John Hogan to go to Washington. The proposal for a new state convention carried by 29,000 votes with approximately three-fourths of its delegates elected from Radical ranks.

Such a sweeping success cannot be attributed solely to the test oath requirements, as some have claimed. The Democratic (Conservative) ticket carried only fifteen counties in this election, half the number that would consistently appear in that party's column in later contests during Reconstruction. For the most part, their faithfulness to the party of the "right" can be attributed to either a relatively large Negro population or a high per capita value of real and personal property, or in some cases both. The Radicals were undoubtedly aided by their ability to link themselves with the Lincoln Administration and the National Union party. The military successes of Generals Grant and Sherman that summer and fall seemed to bring war's end in sight and helped the Administration ticket in Missouri as elsewhere. The Price raid, coming after a renewal of intensive guerrilla warfare, contributed to a general dissatisfaction over the Conservatives' seeming ineptness. The death of Governor Gamble early in 1864 had removed their strongest political figure, and no one really rose to take his place.

Beyond all this discontent with the old administration, most Missourians seemingly believed that new times demanded new leadership. As they faced a future fraught with many problems, social and economic, they handed the Radicals the reins of power in a decisive fashion. Governor Fletcher, in his inaugural address on January 2, 1865, presented the challenge to the Twenty-third General Assembly: "Being victorious everywhere, let magnanimity now distinguish our action; and, having nothing more to ask for party, let us, forgetful of past differences, seek only to promote the general good of the people of the whole commonwealth." The inability of the Radical Union party to respond to Fletcher's vision brought quick dissension and led to its ultimate and permanent downfall five years later.

CHAPTER V

RADICALISM IN THE SADDLE

The members of the General Assembly showed little enthusiasm as they plodded routinely through the business at hand on the afternoon of Wednesday, January 11, 1865. Many glanced often toward the doors at the back of their respective chambers as if they anticipated some kind of interruption. Shortly after three o'clock the messengers for whom they had been waiting arrived. Hastening to the rostrums these handed the clerks copies of a telegram from St. Louis that announced that Missouri's slaves were now and forever free men. The recently convened state convention had just passed an emancipation ordinance by an overwhelming vote, and it took effect immediately.

The legislators greeted the news "with vociferous and prolonged applause." Both houses immediately adjourned to reassemble with a large group of private citizens in the Hall of Representatives for a celebration. As various state officials began expressing their exuberant feelings to the crowd, Governor Fletcher hurried in, accompanied by a special committee. He spoke only briefly, yet his partisan audience cheered loudly when he proclaimed the convention's action as merely the first step toward "the truly radical policy" that would characterize the new Missouri.

With the strains of "John Brown's Body" still ringing in their ears, the gathering dispersed to get ready for another, more formal celebration to be held that evening. Returning to his office, Fletcher drew up an official proclamation to announce the important event. That night there resounded from the Capitol such shouts and singing that the Radical editor of the *Missouri State Times* commented: "We hope that our Callawegian neighbors across the Big Muddy were not seriously disturbed, or caused to apprehend an early visit from the Apocalyptic Gabriel, or any other unwelcome stranger. But if they take the papers they will soon learn that 'THE DAY OF JUBILEE HAS COME'." Callaway, the state's fourth-largest slaveholding county, had already received the news that its convention delegate had cast one of the four votes against the ordinance. The extremely conservative county would have to be satisfied with that.

While there was no great rejoicing in "The Kingdom,"[1] as Callaway would quickly become known, or in other Conservative counties, celebrations similar to that in Jefferson City occurred in every community where any sizable group of Radicals resided. St. Louis held its official observance on Saturday, January 14. Whites and blacks mingled together as they thronged the streets, which were gaily festooned with flags and banners. Midafternoon ceremonies culminated in the firing of a 60-gun salute and the reading of Governor Fletcher's proclamation by one of the local members of the convention. That night excited spectators enjoyed a fireworks display augmenting brilliant illuminations on many of the downtown storefronts.

The Radical Union party had begun its work of ushering Missouri into the postwar world. The state convention, which passed the emancipation ordinance, had opened its deliberations in Mercantile Library Hall in St. Louis only four days earlier. Of the sixty-six delegates, approximately three-fourths were Radical. Like their counterparts in the legislature, they tended to be young men without much previous political experience. Two-thirds of them were less than fifty years of age; half that number was forty or younger. Only three had served in the wartime convention. Whereas that body had been dominated by Southerners

1. References to Callaway County as "The Kingdom of Callaway" can be found in the Missouri press as early as 1865. By local tradition, the term derived from an agreement signed between a local defense group and state militia forces in October, 1861. The local group had been called out because the county had information that the militia planned to "invade" Callaway, which had been occupied briefly by German Home Guards earlier that summer. According to the agreement, Union forces would stay out of Callaway if the small group disbanded and the Callawegians caused no further trouble. The local group complied, but a few days later Union forces occupied Fulton, where they remained for the duration of the war. As party to a "solemn agreement," however, Callaway had become "The Kingdom." For the views of the commanders of the respective sides, John B. Henderson (M.S.M.) and Jefferson Jones (Callaway County), with regard to their agreement, see their correspondence in the Columbia *Missouri Statesman*, February 17 and 24, 1871.

and lawyers, the new group contained more farmers and doctors than any other profession. Not quite half the delegates had their origins in the free states and abroad. The previous convention had been dominated by the strong personality of Governor Gamble; the new assemblage would be strongly influenced by an even more aggressive figure, Charles D. Drake, who had been Gamble's chief antagonist in the final session of 1863.

The legislative act of 1864, which had provided for a new convention, stressed two functions other than its concern for action on emancipation: (1) the disfranchisement of those of questionable loyalty to the Union, and (2) the consideration of whatever additional constitutional amendments might be deemed necessary for the promotion of the public good. Instead Drake persuaded the delegates at the convention to resolve that they would undertake the drafting of an entirely new constitution. Although a large group of dissidents both inside and outside the convention, opposed this decision, they were unable to out-maneuver Drake, who rapidly became the most powerful figure at the proceedings in St. Louis.

In his highly egotistical autobiography, Drake noted that while most of the delegates were "sensible, upright, and worthy men . . . only a very small number of them had ever had experience in lawmaking." Hence, as a leading member of the St. Louis bar and a former legislator, he felt obligated to furnish guidance. To this end he made a careful study of the existing Missouri constitution and those of other states before the convention got underway. By mid-December, 1864, he had already begun a basic draft for a new document. When the convention met, Drake presided until permanent officers could be elected. He was unanimously chosen vice president and, in the months that followed, also served as chairman of two key committees and a member of two more. His most important work occurred on the floor of the convention and in the committee of the whole, however, as evidenced by the frequency with which his name appears throughout the pages of the convention journal and the proceedings. He proposed the basic working organization that the group adopted and saw to it that the various committees were aware of his ideas.

As the proceedings of the convention dragged on in the wake

of the emancipation ordinance, opposition slowly began to build against Drake and his methods. While many agreed that Radicalism should be promoted, they did not see the need for a completely new constitution, nor did they appreciate the arrogant way in which he projected his ideas. Drake was so convinced of his own infallibility that he insisted that his own special phraseology be used for particular clauses.

The situation reached a turning point during the first two weeks of February. Led by the German delegates, whose enmity for Drake went back to his Know-Nothing days as a legislator in the late 1850's, moderates and conservatives began to question some of his proposals and the length of time it was taking to get committee action on different measures. The Germans suspected Drake's motives in opposing suffrage for aliens and in insisting that, in counties entitled to multiple representation, the legislators be elected from single-member districts. Particularly in St. Louis, the proposal for single-member districts would diminish German voting power, which was highly concentrated in certain areas. They also disliked what they considered his narrow definition of religious freedom. He advocated taxing church and other charitable properties and restricting the property holdings of the church to those actually used for purposes of worship. All of these proposals, to them, reflected an anti-Catholic bias. Moderates and conservatives, at the same time, took alarm at Drake's attempts to secure civil and other rights for the new freedmen.

When the showdown came, however, Drake rallied a hard core of St. Louis supporters with a majority of the outstate Radicals whom he had been cultivating through regular speaking tours to their areas over the past two years. The latter accepted his firebrand type of Radicalism because, as one of them from northwestern Missouri put it, he had come to the convention "to protect the interests of the loyal men who had been ground to powder." They also shared his prejudices against the Roman Catholic Church and the German liberals. By a vote of 34 to 14, they defeated a motion by the dissidents to finish the work of disfranchisement and adjourn. Then, with five additional delegates balking at the idea of a complete rewrite, the convention decided 29 to 19 to accept a Drake resolution calling for an entirely new constitution. The direction the convention would take was determined, and, as one of the German leaders declared later, it became a day "upon which barn-yard fowls pair off. A *Drake* set up the *quack* that there was an attempt to break off the Convention. Several *geese*, mistaking this drake for the real *gander*, followed him." Many of Drake's opponents thereafter absented themselves from the proceedings for they found the "Drake's bitters," as another delegate put it, more than they cared to consume.

Given this strong division of feeling among the delegates, which was also reflected outside the convention in various meetings and resolutions, one must confront the question as to why the Drake men insisted on a completely rewritten organic law. Undoubtedly, most of them believed sincerely that the new era called for the elimination of the remnants of conservatism to ensure the complete triumph of Radicalism. Drake continually reiterated this idea with his references to the mandate the voters had handed the convention in the 1864 election. He and his followers held a basic distrust of the General Assembly as an instrument for accomplishing permanent change. If and when the legislature fell once again into conservative Democratic hands, the work of economic and social progress for both races could be quickly and effectively undone if it had no firm constitutional foundation. Drake made his feelings quite clear.

> We intend to erect a wall and barrier in the shape of a constitution that shall be as high as the eternal heavens, deep down as the very center of the earth, so that they [the Democrats in the legislature] shall neither climb over it nor dig under it, and as thick as the whole territory of Missouri so that they shall never batter it down or pierce through it.

For this purpose, the convention imposed numerous restraints on the general legislative process. Some of them were procedural in nature, as in the case of requiring passage of bills by an absolute majority of both houses and the recording of votes when division occurred. Other restrictions sought to limit special legislation if a general law already existed that was relevant to the concern. There had been much abuse of this prerogative by prewar Legislatures. The convention continued the authority of the General Assembly to propose constitutional amendments

but made it mandatory that they be submitted to popular referendum with publication four months before the election. Any
call for a new constitutional convention would also require
voters' approval as would the work of that body before it could
replace the document currently being drafted.

A principal concern of the delegates was the disfranchisement
of the "rebel" element, which the legislative act in 1864 had
specifically admonished them to secure. Disagreement centered
here, not on the object to be accomplished, but again on the
means to the end. The moderates wished to meet the problem
with a simple ordinance similar to that used for emancipation.
Drake saw the need to make it an integral part of the new constitution. He consequently pushed through committee at an
early date a proposal for an elaborate "iron-clad oath" requiring
an individual to affirm that he was innocent of any one of eighty-
six different acts of supposed disloyalty against Missouri and the
Union. These acts included taking up arms in rebellion; giving
help, comfort, countenance, or support to anyone who did so;
contributing money, goods, letters, or information to the enemy;
advising anyone to enter Confederate service; expressing sympathy for the rebel cause or for any specific foe; engaging in guerrilla warfare or aiding and abetting those who did. The oath
would be a prerequisite for voting and for holding public office,
as well as for jurors, lawyers, corporation officials and trustees,
teachers, and ministers. The General Assembly could revoke it
only by an absolute majority of both houses and not until January 1, 1871, as a requirement for voting and four years later in
the other cases.

Many moderates and Conservatives objected to the stringency
of the Drake program and sought to limit its application particularly to the period after December 17, 1861, so that those who
had taken advantage of the Provisional Government's offer of
amnesty would not be affected. Many believed that the simpler
test oath established during the war would be sufficient for the
present situation. The more ardent Radicals disagreed, citing
numerous atrocities by guerrillas in the rural areas and instances
where those who had taken the oath had later been discovered
in violation of it. They backed their concerns with resolutions
from meetings of Radicals across the state that demanded strin-

gent measures. In the end, they won with only one alteration of any consequence in Drake's original proposal. This provision required ministers to take the test oath before they would be allowed to teach or preach. Drake would merely have prevented them from performing marriages on the ground that this function was a civil action. During the heated debate that ensued, one of the opponents, Dr. Moses L. Linton of St. Louis, contended that the whole philosophy of the extreme oath reminded him of the "Code of Draco."[2] Thereby, the term "Draconian Code" was first used; in the months to come, Drake's opponents would apply it to the entire constitution.

To reinforce its efforts to ensure the purity of the electoral process, the convention also required the General Assembly to provide for a systematic biennial voter registration. Thereby, those who falsely swore their loyalty could be detected by registrars who would have the final authority in determining the validity of each oath. The Radicals contended that anyone guilty of treason would probably have few qualms about committing perjury in addition.

Meanwhile, pressure was building for more immediate action to purge the state's judiciary of potentially hostile conservative forces. A resolution to this effect had been introduced early in the session and then allowed to languish in committee because of Drake's concern for incorporating some such arrangement into the constitution rather than for taking special action. But with the ending of the war and of martial law later that spring, the demands for a quicker solution increased. Drake consequently gave his assent to the "Ouster Ordinance" in mid-March and actively led attempts to prevent its being watered down. In its final form, it declared vacant, as of May 1, the offices of all judges and clerks of the Missouri Supreme Court, the circuit courts, the county courts, and the special courts of record and of all county

2. Dr. Linton's remark had reference to the first codification of laws in ancient Greece in the seventh century, B.C., by a man named Dracon. Although he did not establish any new laws, his work of systematizing the existing practices of the courts brought the harshness of society into bold relief. Upon their realization of the extremity of the law, especially as it applied to homicide, the common people are said to have cried out: "The laws of Dracon are written in blood. These are not the laws of Dracon, but of dracon (dragon)."

recorders, circuit attorneys, and sheriffs. Passed by an over-whelming vote of 43 to 5, it created approximately eight hundred vacancies, which the governor had the power to fill. To celebrate the occasion, Dr. Linton, one of the convention's really sparkling wits, sent to Drake's desk one of a series of barbed epigrams with which he frequently goaded the Radical leader:

> Disloyal judge, all agree
>   Should be decapitated;
> So just is this that such a point
>   Should not have been debated.
> And those who are good Union men,
>   Unfaltering, firm, and hearty,
> Shall be turned out, that *Radicals*
>   *May harmonize their party!*

The members of the convention voted on the constitution the afternoon of April 8. After each delegate had had the opportunity to explain his stand, it carried, 38 to 13, although some of those voting in favor indicated that they would not endorse its ratifi-cation. At this point, they merely desired to bring the work of the convention to an end. Others, while not enthused, believed it the best document that could be obtained under the present circumstances and assumed that as flaws developed they could be remedied by amendment. Those who voted negatively were the Germans and the Conservatives, who generally believed that the convention had acted more drastically than was originally intended. Drake later contended in his autobiography that most of the thirteen members who did not attend when the final roll-call was recorded would have opposed the constitution had they been there. A scanning of the list of absentees would tend to verify this statement. Most had been boycotting convention ses-sions for some time.

In spite of the controversy it engendered because of its more negative portions, the constitution produced by Drake and his followers reflected generally the progressive ideas that typified the national Radical movement. While restrictive of the General Assembly in some areas, it provided, for the most part, a broad framework within which that body could establish progress for the encouragement of industrial and corporate growth and the orderly development of Missouri's natural resources. To ensure a broadly based public education system for both races that was essential to the state's progress, the delegates made adequate provision for an equitable method of financing schools. They shortened the terms of elected officials while broadening the power of referendum at both the state and local level, so the people could exercise greater control over government. Blacks received all civil rights except suffrage and officeholding.[3]

Although it came to be known as "Drake's Constitution," the St. Louis lawyer occasionally had to compromise to meet the temper of his rural followers. In one such case, he anticipated without success a controversy that exists in modern times. Arguing that under the old apportionment system a majority of the House of Representatives could be chosen by only one-fifth of the total vote cast in any given election, he proposed establishing 100 districts based on population, without regard to equal representation of counties. This proposal proved too extreme for outstate colleagues. They retained the previous method, although they agreed to change the divisor for the determination of additional seats from 140 to 200.

Drake had early seen the wisdom of using a popular referendum on the finished document as a means toward mollifying some of the opposition. To assure the best possible results, however, he inserted provisions calling for the use of the Iron-Clad Oath in determining the eligibility of voters and for the canvassing of Missouri's soldiers in the field. The convention set June 6 for the election, which would give ample time to explain the issues to the people. Drake assumed full responsibility for leading the struggle for ratification. He issued a series of seven letters in the *Missouri Democrat*, which other Radical papers also printed, and then went on an extensive speaking tour. Only through the new constitution could the Radicals have a means of "fixing Missouri firmly on a foundation of Loyalty," he argued. Failure now would doom any future effectiveness of the party.

Not all Radicals agreed. Prominent among the dissidents was Governor Fletcher, who believed that the convention had usurped too much legislative prerogative, thereby placing the

3. Many of these provisions will be discussed in more detail in subsequent chapters.

needs of the time into a structure that might be too inflexible to
be suitable in the future. Simple legislation might be "more easily altered or repealed as experience may show to be our best
interest." The Governor particularly questioned the proscriptive
limitations on voting and hinted that he would like to see the
blacks enfranchised. He declined to take an active role in opposing ratification, however, which forced the constitution's foes to
turn elsewhere for help. They obtained it from some capable
Conservatives in the *Westliche Post*, the state's leading German
newspaper, published at St. Louis. Prominent among these Conservatives were former Atty. Gen. Edward Bates, who had recently returned from Washington, Dr. Linton, and William F.
Switzler, the editor of the Columbia *Missouri Statesman*, who
had been a convention delegate. In an unsigned verse that smacks
of Linton's touch, some Conservative summarized the opposition's theme quite succinctly:

> All sorts of folks met on a time,
>   And came to the conclusion
> That they were just the sort of men
>   To make a Constitution.
> The time set for their vengeful work
>   Was in a Revolution,
> When they might vent their spite and put
>   It in a Constitution.
> They then mixed up a mighty oath
>   Of very strong solution,
> To be gulped down with other things
>   In this strange Constitution.

Bates assured the document's opponents that they should have
no qualms about taking the Iron-Clad Oath, even though they
considered it illegal prior to any ratification of the constitution,
because only in this way could they exercise their free choice. If
they were to sidetrack the constitution, they must play the Radicals' game, at least temporarily.

While the question of loyalty versus disloyalty dominated the
ratification campaign, it did not receive exclusive attention. The
Radical press also stressed as a secondary theme the idea that
the constitution represented the only possible way to social and
economic progress. Its acceptance would open the door for a

flood of immigrants and capital, who were merely waiting to see what course Missouri planned to take before committing themselves there or elsewhere.

Two important events intruded upon the campaign. President Lincoln's assassination, according to Drake, "opened the eyes of the nation to the dangers into which its big-souled magnanimity was about to plunge it." The new Chief Executive, Andrew Johnson, took a strongly vindictive stance in the wake of the tragedy, and Missouri Radicals expressed their hope that leadership more to their liking would be available at the national level. Sen. B. Gratz Brown wrote the President that "the loyal men of Missouri feel that today they have one at the head of this government who can sympathize in their struggles and privations and wants." This feeling would prove short-lived as Johnson became increasingly conservative in the months ahead.

The Ouster Ordinance was effected two weeks after Lincoln was murdered. Automatic suspension from office faced 842 officials across the state. Patronage, which had been Governor Fletcher's major problem since his induction, now mushroomed. Under the circumstances, he moved deliberately but not hastily, retaining in office those of undoubted loyalty, particularly if they had secured election the previous fall on the Radical ticket. Elsewhere he simply relied on recommendations from the local party committees.

In some instances incumbents refused to yield their offices readily. It became necessary for the Governor to call out the militia, which was, appropriately, a company of blacks, to oust recalcitrants in Lafayette County, a Conservative stronghold. Appeal to the local circuit judge brought no relief, as he had previously ascertained that Fletcher would have his way and, indeed, realized that his own job might be forfeit. In St. Louis County, one of the Governor's own new appointees, Circuit Judge James C. Moodey, upheld an appeal from the incumbent recorder of deeds on the ground that the Ouster Ordinance lacked legality because it was not part of the constitution. A German Radical active in the antiratification campaign, Moodey became the hero of the hour among his cohorts. But the Governor's choice as recorder took his case to the Missouri Supreme

Court, where the three recently installed Fletcher justices ruled in his favor.

Indeed, all of this controversy had been but a prelude to the struggle for control of the high court. A feeling had long pervaded the Radical camp that they had lost the judicial election of 1863 through the Provisional Government's manipulation of the balloting procedure. They also viewed the incumbent Conservative judges as potentially the greatest obstacle to the fulfillment of their program. Hence their desire for a change. The accomplishment of that task did not prove to be easy. The old court, with the help of Judge Moodey, sought to retain their authority and records in the face of demands for an orderly transfer from Fletcher's new justices. Once again the Governor found it necessary to summon the militia, who physically dragged the incumbent judges from the bench and seized the records from their protesting clerk. To ensure against further violence, troops guarded the courthouse while the new tribunal began deliberations. Each group held a public meeting to voice its sentiments and to denounce or sustain the Governor, but the Conservatives realized that theirs was a losing cause. Beginning with the September term, Fletcher's justices handed down a series of decisions upholding the Ouster Ordinance as an action of the duly elected representatives of the people.

By the time Missourians went to the polls in early June, Drake had secured the endorsement for his constitution—albeit not enthusiastic in some cases—of Missouri's two senators and all of her Radical congressmen. Still the balloting was extremely close, and for three weeks the fate of the new document hung in the balance as the returns trickled in. The Radicals were defeated in St. Louis by 5,926 votes, and then also saw much of southeastern Missouri turn against them under the combined influence of Germans and Conservatives. They had not expected to do well in the Missouri River counties along the central corridor, but with defeat staring them in the face, they began to raise the charges there of "pious perjury." This accusation involved the questionable taking of the oath by Conservatives who had decided to follow Edward Bates's advice. The Radicals contended that in the supposedly archconservative Kingdom of Callaway, many had not even bothered to take the oath before casting their ballots.

Returns from the northern and southwestern counties, where Radicalism enjoyed its greatest strength, showed sweeping victories for the constitution. Ultimately, however, its fate came to rest on the soldier vote, which was widely scattered and hence slow to arrive for tabulation. Since the early returns of the military canvass within the state indicated strong Radical majorities, the new constitution's opponents held a mass meeting at St. Louis and designated two of their number to go to Jefferson City and conduct their own canvass. The Radical *Missouri State Times* at the capital denounced this "smelling committee" and strongly backed Secretary of State Francis Rodman in his refusal to admit them to his office. Subsequently, the newspaper reported that there had been an attempt to bribe the Secretary and to break into his office. Since Rodman had safely deposited the returns in the state treasurer's vault, however, the intruders found nothing.

The official canvass finally occurred on the morning of July 1. Conducted by Rodman, Governor Fletcher, and State Auditor Alonzo Thompson, as required by law, it confirmed a bare majority of 1,862 in favor of the new constitution out of 85,478 ballots cast. It had been carried by the soldier vote, which gave it a margin of 2,827, while the civilian population was opposed by 965 votes. Drake and several friends had been anxiously waiting across the hall for several hours when Rodman emerged to announce the results. They broke into rousing cheers and hat waving as a party quickly got underway to celebrate the victory. Governor Fletcher promptly issued a proclamation putting the new organic law into effect as of July 4.

Promulgation did not mean the end of controversy, for, given the nature of the constitution's more proscriptive clauses and the closeness of the vote, both Conservatives and Radicals began to talk about a new convention or the consideration of amendments. Those in the government had no intention of seeing their newly won power diminished, however, and for the next five years they clung tenaciously to their spoils until a falling-out, reflecting somewhat the divisions of 1865, made possible the removal of the odious voting proscriptions and the return of the Democrats to power.

In the meantime, legal challenges quickly arose over the enforcement of the Iron-Clad Oath. Attorneys and the clergy in particular questioned the need for such a requirement in the practice of their professions. Under the new constitution, those required to take the oath had sixty days after Governor Fletcher's proclamation of ratification to do so. Early in August, leading members of the St. Louis bar announced that they considered the provision ex post facto in nature and that they would decline to abide by it. Someone sought the opinion of Atty. Gen. Robert F. Wingate, who ruled to the contrary. When the September 2 deadline passed with many non-Radical attorneys having failed to comply, enforcement varied, depending upon the court in which the lawyer practiced. In St. Louis, test cases before the various branches of the circuit court resulted in unfavorable decisions for those who balked at taking the oath, whereupon appeal was made to the Missouri Supreme Court. When that newly refurbished Radical body upheld the oath, one of the St. Louis attorneys, Alexander J. P. Garesche, filed a bill of exceptions to take his case to the United States Supreme Court. Most other St. Louis lawyers decided to comply in the meantime, however, to avoid the loss of their practice. Outstate enforcement varied, with some judges declaring the oath for lawyers unconstitutional and refusing to require it in their courts while others adhered rigidly to its proscription. The latter far outweighed the former, and one recalcitrant judge later was the target of impeachment proceedings in the legislature because of his attitude.

Missouri's clergy also searched their consciences in the matter and came up with a mixed response. The Reverend M. M. Modisett of Louisiana typified many when he wrote: "I confess that I am placed in a very unpleasant situation, not because of the fear of perjury or of doing violence to my feelings for any act of my life, by taking said oath, but on account of the seeming unreasonableness of the thing, and, as I now view it, as being an infringe [sic] of religious liberty, as well as a species of tyranny to which I dislike to submit." None of the alternatives of taking the oath, giving up preaching, nor going ahead and facing arrest if he failed to comply with the law had much appeal for him. No record exists of how he ultimately decided to "discharge my duty first to God & then to my country without doing violence to my feelings."

Many others concluded, however, that they could not in good conscience submit. The Most Reverend Peter R. Kenrick, Roman Catholic Archbishop of St. Louis, addressed a pastoral letter to his priests, which stated that he deplored the oath and expressed the hope that it would not be enforced among the clergy. He also urged his clerics to decline taking it if civil authority insisted on it. Those who suffered for their action were to seek his direct "counsel and assistance." Kenrick's Episcopal and Methodist counterparts, Bishops C. O. Hawks and Henry Kavanaugh, expressed similar feelings, although they left to each minister the right to decide his own duty in relation to his conscience.

The Baptists, not united by this kind of guidance, split over the issue. Their General Association met at Boonville in mid-August and adopted a lengthy address declaring the oath a violation of the federal constitution, an unjust attempt to punish ministers for crimes not committed, and a breach of their long-cherished principle of the separation of church and state. Most of the local associations followed suit at later gatherings. That October, however, the denomination's Radical ministers organized the Loyal Missouri Baptist Convention at Hannibal and endorsed the oath because it was a means of keeping wrangling out of the pulpit. This group continued an existence separate from the General Association for the next two years and apparently drew considerable support. It affiliated with the American Baptist Home Mission Society and undertook extensive work among the Negroes in St. Louis. When it reconciled its differences and returned to the regular Baptist fold after the test-oath controversy died down, it did so only on the agreement that there would be no racial discrimination in the new affiliation.

For those clergy who had hoped that their protests would encourage the Governor to disregard the test oath when they were concerned, Fletcher had a simple and disappointing retort. "Religious liberty is a political right," he asserted, "and when these outraged gentlemen go to the Supreme Court of the United States with their complaint, they will be told that there is not a sentence or a word in the Constitution of the United States which gives them the right to preach at all." This policy brought a protest from the Reverend Henry A. Nelson, a prominent Radical and minister of the First Presbyterian Church of St. Louis. Forwarding his letter to the Governor through Sen. B. Gratz Brown, Nelson reported that he had willingly taken the oath in connection with his service as curator of the state university. He questioned the state's right to exact it of him before he could preach, however, and urged that the legislature promptly submit an amendment to exempt the clergy. This action, he predicted, would win overwhelming approval by the voters. Brown endorsed the sentiments but hastened to reassure Fletcher that he had no desire to obstruct the constitution's operation in the meantime. Drake had also had qualms about this proviso at the time he accepted it from one of his outstate supporters in the convention, but he kept silent throughout the controversy.

A large group of ministers had not taken the oath by Saturday, September 2, the deadline for doing so. Many Missourians undoubtedly listened to "illegal" sermons the next day. Depending upon the zeal of local Radical officials, the offending clergyman might be hauled into court for arraignment. In these cases it became customary for the defendant to post bond and have his trial postponed until the spring term of court by circuit judges, who were content to let one of their colleagues hear the first case. How many ministers actually suffered for their convictions in this crisis is difficult to ascertain. The press frequently reported specific cases, and one leading Methodist pastor later declared that "hundreds of priests and preachers were indicted, arrested, and tried in civil courts for preaching the Gospel." Yet, one religious journal reported the following spring that as many as one thousand lawbreakers still preached throughout Missouri unhindered. It predicted the overthrow of the oath by the judicial process and urged those ministers who had been barred from their pulpits to stay in their parishes and attend to other pastoral duties. In an extensive study of the situation,[4] Professor

4. Thomas S. Barclay, "The Test Oath for Clergy in Missouri," *Missouri Historical Review*, 18 (April, 1924), 345–81.

Thomas S. Barclay found thirty-six specific indictments in approximately twenty-eight counties. The political sentiments of the area largely determined whether local clergy were intimidated into taking the oath to avoid facing adverse consequences if they refused. The situation affected ministers differently than it did lawyers, who had to deal with individual judges who could keep them out of court. No enforcement machinery existed to coerce the ministers if local officials declined or found it inexpedient to act.

It remained to an obscure young Roman Catholic parish priest to furnish the test case on which the fate of all of Missouri's recalcitrant clergy would be decided. Father John A. Cummings of Louisiana took the admonition of Archbishop Kenrick very much to heart. Although he had failed to take the oath, he preached as usual that Sunday morning, September 3. Indicted by a specially called grand jury, he appeared before Circuit Judge Thomas J. C. Fagg, a prominent Radical, the following Friday. Seemingly possessed of a martyr complex, Cummings refused to post bond and demanded an immediate trial. Judge Fagg reluctantly agreed, and, to the consternation of all those present, the young priest pleaded guilty. When asked if he wished to make a presentence statement, Cummings launched into "a religious stump speech," as one observer later characterized it. He implied that the Radicals possessed an anti-Catholic bias and compared his trial with that of Christ. Although he conceded that he was in violation of the constitution, he denied the state's right to interfere with his divine calling.

After further turmoil and the intervention of certain attorneys present, Judge Fagg allowed the priest to change his plea. But the following day when Cummings admitted preaching without taking the oath, Fagg found him guilty and fined him $500 as the law required. The priest refused to pay this penalty or to allow any of his friends to do so. Consequently, the judge had no choice but to remand him to the Pike County jail where he languished for a week with increasing aura of notoriety and martyrdom. With numerous offers of help pouring in and an expression of pleasure from Archbishop Kenrick at his young priest's behavior, Cummings quickly yielded to pressure from both Catholic and Protestant sources to allow his case to be made a test before the Missouri Supreme Court.

Meanwhile, with other arrests continuing, the Radicals launched an all-out campaign to gather declarations of loyalty by religious organizations through press and public meeting. The Loyal Missouri Baptist Convention was an example of this type of movement. The recently organized Missouri Congregational General Conference, made up principally of transplanted Northerners doing missionary work in the state, met at Hannibal and pledged its support for the principles of "true Unionism." Similar expressions came from the Northern Methodists meeting at Warrensburg and an interdenominational group called the Convention of Loyal Ministers, who gathered at Macon. All denounced those who balked at taking the oath and urged compliance with the law.

The Cummings case reached the state supreme court in late October. The priest's attorney argued that the Iron-Clad Oath represented both ex post facto legislation and a bill of attainder, both of which the federal constitution specifically prohibits. State's counsel denied each charge. The oath did not punish for past offenses but merely sought to regulate the practice of certain professions. Individuals were penalized, quite constitutionally, only if they failed to meet the particular qualification of loyalty. Nor could the oath be considered a bill of attainder, since it convicted no one of any crime and failed to require the forfeiture of any property. The Radical justices agreed and dismissed the deeper implications of the case by declaring, "It is not for the judiciary to inquire whether laws violate the general principles of liberty or natural justice, or whether they are wise and inexpedient or not."

Cummings's attorney immediately appealed to the United States Supreme Court, which heard the case in mid-March, 1866. Prominent national counsel had been obtained in the meantime with former Postmaster General Montgomery Blair heading Cummings's defense, assisted by David Dudley Field and Reverdy Johnson. All prominent Conservatives, they had been enlisted through Frank Blair, who was becoming a leader of the anti-Radical movement in Missouri. To counter this eminent trio, Governor Fletcher appointed George P. Strong, notable St. Louis attorney and convention delegate, and Sen. John B. Henderson to represent Missouri. Neither side presented any new arguments, but after hearing them, the justices took the matter under advisement.

An obviously closely divided court had not reached a decision on this and related cases by the time of its May adjournment. That summer, rumors flourished that the majority of judges favored Cummings but had held the case over until after the off-year elections. That contest resulted in a strong Radical victory in Missouri as elsewhere. In its wake, Governor Fletcher suggested to the legislature in his annual message that it consider submitting an amendment that would repeal the oath requirement for lawyers, teachers, and ministers. Admitting quite frankly that many members of these groups stood in open violation with little or no punishment, he warned: "The example offered by the disregard of unnecessary laws, especially by so intelligent and influential a class of citizens begets a general disposition to exercise individual discretion in obeying or enforcing laws—a disposition which leads to anarchy and impunity in crime."

Before any of the Governor's moderate supporters could effect such a plan, however, the Supreme Court resolved the issue. By a 5-to-4 decision on January 14, 1867, it announced that the test oath provisions as applied to professional groups constituted both a bill of attainder and ex post facto legislation. The majority contended that Father Cummings had thereby been barred from his ministry through legislative fiat rather than judicial proceeding and because of a supposed act that was not punishable at the time it might have been committed. All of this the minority denied in a vigorous dissent while upholding test oaths as occasionally necessary for the protection of the state.

Tied to the related case of ex parte *Garland*, which involved the constitutionality of an Iron-Clad Oath requirement for lawyers engaged in practice before the supreme court, this decision simultaneously resolved the problem of Missouri's attorneys who had been under the ban. These men were now fully welcome again before the various courts of the state. The pending cases on Missouri dockets that affected both ministers and lawyers were disposed of quickly and quietly. The state supreme court put its final seal of approval on the decision of its national counterpart in October, 1867, by reversing decisions on all test-oath cases that had reached it. Although the entire circumstance left some of the more ardent Radicals like Drake quite unhappy, the *Missouri Democrat* summed up the feelings of most: "The war is now over, and whether such restrictions were or were not legal and necessary during its continuance, the demand for them no longer exists, and the decision as confined to its legitimate scope and effect, will do but little practical harm."

The decision in *Cummings* v. *Missouri* did not affect one other case then pending before the Missouri Supreme Court involving Frank Blair and the Iron-Clad Oath, which dealt specifically with validity of the oath as a requirement for voting. Flank Blair, a leading Conservative politician, had issued a call for a mass convention of those who opposed the vindictive features of the new constitution and favored the magnanimous reconstruction program of President Johnson as it had emerged that summer. An avowed racist who scored heavily the Radicals' program of civil rights for Negroes and argued that this policy was the first step toward Negro suffrage, Blair toured central Missouri in early October to drum up support for the meeting to be held in St. Louis later that month. In gathering after gathering, Conservatives gave him a warm welcome and endorsed his sentiments for white supremacy and restoration of the *status quo.*

Nearly one thousand delegates, chosen by local assemblies, crowded into Verandah Hall on October 26 to begin a three-day session in which Blair, James S. Rollins, and other Conservative leaders harangued them with denunciations of Charles D. Drake, the Fletcher administration, and the new constitution. Out of this convention came the establishment of a Conservative party central committee, which was to lead the opposition in the 1866 elections. The delegates also sent a group to Washington to explain their stand to President Johnson and enlist his support.

After their return home, many of them called county meetings to endorse the sentiments expressed in Verandah Hall and begin the building of a grassroots organization for 1866. Blair continued speaking around the state at every opportunity. Then, at the November municipal election in St. Louis, he presented himself at the polls with his own oath, which simply declared his allegiance to state and nation. When the election judges rejected his ballot, he filed suit in circuit court asking $10,000 in damages from officials and contesting the legality of the Iron-Clad Oath. He could not take the oath, by his own account, because he had opposed the duly elected regime of Claiborne F. Jackson in 1861. Certainly none could doubt his staunch Union record during the war.

Still, Blair lost his case when it came to trial in circuit court in the late spring of 1866. With Drake serving as counsel for the election officials, the judges, in a split vote, affirmed the right of the state to require a stringent test for loyalty. The process of appealing to the Missouri Supreme Court consumed another year. Although many assumed it would find for Blair in the wake of the recent decision in *Cummings* v. *Missouri*, that tribunal unanimously declared that the state had the right to confer suffrage on whatever ground it deemed best. At the same time it also upheld the Iron-Clad Oath as a test for officeholding. Blair now appealed to the United States Supreme Court in the hope that the decision would be reversed before the 1868 elections.

This conflict came in the wake of the hard-fought 1866 contest. That encounter revealed the basic tactics by which the Radicals would seek to hang on to the power that was theirs. When the General Assembly convened in November, 1865, Drake personally appeared before the Radical caucus with a registry bill that he had prepared in line with the constitution. Inasmuch as his outstate supporters dominated that group he had little difficulty in having it adopted as a party measure. The beleaguered Conservative minority resisted, but in vain. By the terms of this act, each county would have a supervisor of registration appointed by the Governor to oversee the 1866 election. Subsequently, this official would be chosen by a popular vote. Under his general direction, "one competent and prudent person" of his own selection would handle the registration process in each district. This registration supervisor would have virtually limitless power to determine the validity of each test oath. While the right of appeal existed, the hearing board consisted of the supervisor and his assistants, which limited the possibility of successful challenge of their judgment. Indeed these boards could make whatever changes they felt necessary in the voting lists at the time of final review. Even before he signed the bill into law, Governor Fletcher was besieged with applicants for the supervisory posts. The Radical press had nothing but praise for this attempt to preserve the purity of the franchise.

The Conservative Unionists meanwhile pushed ahead with their party organization. They keenly felt the need for a new label to avoid the "Copperhead" stigma that had become attached to the name "Democrat." Combining a large number of prewar Whigs with those who had supported Thomas Hart Benton, they stressed their wartime fidelity to the Provisional Government and the Union cause. They picked up those of a pro-Southern bent who could somehow evade the registry officials, but they judiciously avoided seeking them out in any formal way. The Conservatives looked to President Johnson for leadership at the national level, especially after his veto of the Freedmen's Bureau bill in February, 1866. This action secured widespread endorsement from local Conservative meetings and created "Johnson Clubs" across the state. Making the most of this enthusiasm, the state central committee called a rally in St. Louis which attracted ten thousand.

The Radicals simultaneously denounced the President and read him out of the party. Many had been hoping through the winter that he would somehow be persuaded to yield to majority Republican opinion. At the same time they had attempted to make inroads into federal patronage positions still held by Conservatives who had been appointed by President Lincoln. Now with these hopes gone glimmering, the Radicals of Putnam County summed up the general feeling of their party: "Andrew Johnson, having abandoned the party which elected him, and the principles upon which he was elected, we unhesitatingly denounce him as a traitor, to said party, and to the great principles of our government."

With the registry act not yet in effect, the Conservatives scored well in municipal elections that spring and were encouraged about the campaign ahead. They fully realized that the new registration process would serve as the major block to their success. In seeking a way around it, they seized upon a provision which allowed those suspected of disloyalty to still be listed in the pollbooks and vote. Election officials simply took these ballots, marked them "rejected," and put them in a separate pile. Anticipating a decision on the test oath for the professions before fall that would be favorable to them, Conservatives hoped it might have repercussions on voting restrictions. In that case, if elections were contested higher authorities might accept the rejected ballots. So the word went out for every Conservative to attempt to register and vote, even if it meant the official rejection of his ballot.

That summer both sides attacked each other with vigorous rhetoric. Meetings frequently erupted in violence as one side or the other challenged its opponent's speakers. Nine men were killed at Madisonville in late July when the rival groups held meetings on the same Saturday and their partisans decided to turn the oral fights into the real thing. After a halt caused by a serious outbreak of cholera in St. Louis that August, both sides made a big final push to move the election campaign toward its November climax. Their leading orators crisscrossed the state, holding meeting after meeting. The Conservatives persuaded President Johnson to visit St. Louis in September on his "swing around the circle." And the Radicals brought in his bitter enemy, Congressman Benjamin F. Butler of Massachusetts, for a single appearance the following month. Both speakers gave memorable speeches as they lambasted the opposition without mercy.

An important part of Radical strategy was the cultivation of the veterans' vote. Their local leadership pushed the organization of soldiers' leagues and associations to ensure that this group, many of whom were Germans, would be loyal to the party. In St. Louis, in the call for an initial meeting, they warned: "The copperheads and rattlesnakes hidden under Union flowers . . . are endeavoring to swindle us out of our victories . . . and to destroy this Republic." For those inclined to follow their former hero, Frank Blair, the Radicals asserted that he had become a "false Moses" who had forgotten those who sacrificed so much, since he made common cause with the "Copperheads." Given the strong emotional appeals of their leaders, battle-hardened veterans could hardly resist casting their lot with "the party of freedom." Efforts of Blair and others to counter with their own rallies for the ex-soldiers' vote made little headway.

While political activity continued apace throughout the spring and summer of 1866, Missouri was confronted with renewed lawlessness similar in style, if not perhaps over-all intensity, to that which had plagued it during the war. Readjustment after such an upheaval is never easy. Many Missourians who had remained loyal might understandably resent the return of former neighbors who had served the Confederacy, especially if they had suffered from guerrilla depredations during the conflict. Indeed, notices were distributed from some communities that former rebels would not be welcome regardless of how penitent they might be. In Jackson County, highly partisan grand juries issued indictments against some of these men for wartime crimes after they had supposedly received pardons under President Johnson's amnesty terms.

Under these circumstances and given many of the routine economic difficulties of resuming normal pursuits, it is not surprising that many veterans took once again to the bush. Reports of robbery and occasional murder appeared in the newspapers. A group of armed men, possibly the James gang in its first major adventure, rode into Liberty on February 13, 1866, and held up the Clay County Savings Association. They escaped with $60,000 and killed a boy who ran into the street to give the alarm. The passengers of the Missouri River steamer *Ned Tracy* reported being stopped by bushwhackers at Waverly on March 30. Although no mention was made of robbery, the ruffians apparently shot up the boat in drunken boisterousness. These were only two isolated incidents among the many to be found in the public press. St. Louis suffered similarly, as the *Missouri Democrat* noted in November, 1865:

> Never in the memory of the most ancient citizen . . . has rascality stalked so boldly about our streets as at the present time. Houses are entered every night by burglars, and the inmates robbed, while a bolder class of rogues, who disdain the labor of climbing porches, picking locks, and experimenting with window fastenings, attack citizens on the public thoroughfares and cooly relieve them of their watches, jewelry and money. These operations are carried on by sun light and gas light.

By early February, 1866, Governor Fletcher felt compelled to ask Gen. John Pope, who commanded the Department of Missouri, for federal cavalry to assist certain sheriffs in executing writs against bushwhackers who threatened the peace. Pope declined, which forced the Governor to call out militia in some cases. Most of these men were Radicals, and their management of tense situations was far from evenhanded. In some places, voluntary groups of "regulators" began to appear, especially in the western counties. Such outfits as the Honest Men's League of Greene County usually acted first and talked later when trouble broke out.

With the situation out of control by late autumn, Conservative leaders went all the way to the White House to urge federal intervention. President Johnson replaced Pope with Gen. Winfield Scott Hancock, who persuaded Fletcher to reorganize the militia on a less partisan basis and promised that some federal troops would be available for support duty where needed. Eventually, three companies of Regulars performed spot patrols that fall.

Nor did the registration process go peacefully. Challenges were numerous on both sides, with Conservatives sometimes dredging up long-forgotten 1861 incidents to use against Radicals including Drake. Occasionally bushwhackers would invade registry offices, as much to create a nuisance as to actually prevent the supervisors from operating. More frequently, armed Radicals would offer their services to guard officials and thereby intimidate nervous Conservatives. Little uniformity existed in the proceedings. Zeal, courage, and the size of the safe Radical vote determined the extent to which registrars would exert a partisan conscientiousness in the different counties. Many a board of revision culled its lists judiciously before closing the books.

When the dust finally settled on November 6, it revealed a Radical victory of sweeping proportions. The party in power retained an overwhelming majority in both houses of the General Assembly—Senate: 28 to 8; House: 103 to 36. There would be many new faces, however, as a number of Radicals who had served in the previous legislature did not return, for reasons that are difficult to ascertain. The dominant party continued to be largely controlled by younger men with more than one-third of its legislative membership under age forty, while 40 per cent of its Conservative opposition exceeded age fifty. The number of lawyers increased markedly among the Radicals, to the extent that they constituted one-third of the new majority.

Since all state offices had been elected to a four-year term in 1864, there was only one contest at that level. Thomas A. Parker handily defeated his Conservative opponent for the newly created position of state superintendent of schools. In the congressional races the Radicals ousted Democrat John Hogan in St. Louis's First District and carried six of the eight remaining. Only in Third and Ninth districts did the Conservatives appear to have triumphed. Their victory there proved short-lived, however, as the Radicals revealed yet another tactic in their program to "purify" the ballot. The strongly Conservative pro-Southern Kingdom of Callaway had claimed 1,895 registered voters, yet the Radicals felt sure that there could be no more than a few hundred "loyal men" there. Hence, when Secretary of State Rodman canvassed the vote in January, 1867, he threw out all of Callaway's ballots, thereby turning an 1,122-vote majority for William F. Switzler, the Conservative congressional candidate, into an 178-vote deficit favoring his Radical opponent, incumbent George W. Anderson.

The Radical supervisor of registration in Callaway contended that he and his registrars had been openly intimidated throughout the county and consequently had left many names on the list that should have been stricken. Before forwarding it to Jefferson City, however, he had made such notations as "Enrolled disloyal," "Under Bond," or "In Rebel Armies" after various entries. The supervisor replied to a complaining Switzler that "the broth" stank of treason, and he felt compelled to send it to Jefferson City to be analyzed. There Rodman confirmed the suspicion. Switzler and the Conservatives protested the Secretary's arbitrary decision with considerable vehemence, citing the certification of county officers by the Governor after the same election. Making no headway at the state capital, they contested the results in Washington only to be turned aside after prolonged hearings. Meanwhile the General Assembly had also refused seats to both the senator and the representative chosen from Callaway. As a result, it was not represented in the legislature for the next two years.

In Lafayette County, the election was so close that the rival partisans came to blows over who would occupy the courthouse. There were also clashes between blacks and whites on the streets of Lexington as Conservative elements sought to take over the town by force. With turmoil prevailing in several other western counties in the wake of similar tight contests, Governor Fletcher found it necessary to call out the militia to restore order. In Lafayette they established the Radicals safely in power before withdrawing. Charges and countercharges followed, with a Conservative United States commissioner, who had recently been appointed by President Johnson, arraigning some of the Radical officials on a variety of counts only to have the Radical federal district judge dismiss the same.

A major beneficiary of the Radical triumph was Charles D. Drake, who had campaigned ardently throughout the state on behalf of the party's candidates. A colorful, albeit vindictive, speaker, Drake, in the process, had further cemented his hold on the outstate Radical partisans. Although desirous of defending "his constitution" and promoting the party's cause, Drake also had an ulterior motive. Sen. B. Gratz Brown had announced in late June that he would retire when his term expired that winter because of ill health. Should the Radicals triumph, as expected, Drake would be Brown's logical successor. No open mention was made of this possibility during the canvass, but the Radical press quickly put Drake forward for the Senate when the results were in.

Concerned by this action and by the increasingly vindictive tendencies of many Radicals, Brown decided to call a conference of party leaders in the wake of the election. In response to a letter from the "Acting Secretary of the Radical Union Executive Committee," twenty-nine men gathered at the Planters House in St. Louis on November 20. The group included Governor Fletcher, Drake, both United States senators, Missouri's incumbent and future Radical congressmen, several prominent state legislators, and the leading Radical editors. In all, it represented a substantial sampling of party leadership.

Brown quickly took charge of the meeting with the announcement that he wished to discuss party policy in anticipation of the forthcoming session of the legislature. He believed that the strong showing of the Radicals in the recent election put them in a good position to move toward reconciliation with their foes, thereby placing them on a sound footing for the indefinite future. For this purpose, he advocated "Universal Suffrage and Universal Amnesty," which would include extension of the franchise to both the Negroes and the pro-Southern element as well as the removal of the Iron-Clad Oath as a requirement for the practice of a profession. Brown caught Drake and the more ardent Radicals completely off guard with his proposals. Ten of them refused to stay, but Drake felt the necessity of remaining to protect his position. After a lengthy discussion, those at the meeting accepted Brown's proposals by a vote of 16 to 3 with journalist John F. Hume of St. Louis and Congressman Robert T. Van Horn of Kansas City joining Drake in the minority.

Drake wrote many years later that he "saw instantly that they meant an abandonment of all that the Radicals of the State had gained after an unequalled struggle, and a proffer of pusillanimous and unmasked surrender of the party, its principles, and its achievements to our adversaries." Although he favored a Negro suffrage amendment, which the General Assembly passed early in 1867, Drake opposed any relaxation of proscription of "rebels." When Brown's supporters prepared resolutions for the legislature, Drake strongly attacked them through two articles in Hume's *St. Louis Evening News.* In the session that followed, some opposition to Drake's Senate candidacy developed in the Radical caucus, but it proved insufficient to block his nomination or election. Only Governor Fletcher might have stopped Drake, but he realized that he did not have the strength to thwart the man who had become "Mr. Radical" in the eyes of the rank-and-file members of the party. Frank Blair put up token opposition for the Conservatives when the General Assembly finally voted. Drake had triumphed over all his enemies. He stood as the dominant figure in Missouri politics. His rise had been meteoric; his fall would be equally swift.

CHAPTER VI

MISSOURI'S BLACKS MAKE PROGRESS

The Twenty-fourth General Assembly, which sent Charles D. Drake to the United States Senate, instituted a program that Governor Fletcher and other Radical leaders had been advocating since the adoption of the new constitution, the granting of Negro suffrage. This issue had divided Radicals from the outset of their assumption of power. It had first been raised in a significant way for public debate by Sen. B. Gratz Brown in a letter to the *Missouri Democrat* on December 22, 1864. He urged that the state convention, which would convene soon, consider freedom and franchise as inseparable twins. In taking this position, he stirred up a hornet's nest, for only a small minority of white Missourians were prepared to give the black all of the rights of full citizenship. Many Radicals, quite cognizant of the importance of public opinion, held back for either political or personal reasons, although many of them were prepared to extend all other fundamental rights to the new freedmen.

When the convention met, Drake quickly proposed the following amendment to the emancipation ordinance:

> That no person can, on account of color, be disqualified as a witness, or be disabled to contract, or be prevented from acquiring, holding, or transmitting property; or be liable to any other punishment, for any offense, than that imposed on others for a like offense; or be restricted in the exercise of religious worship, or be hindered in receiving an education; or be subjected in law to any other restraints, or disqualifications, in regard to any personal rights, than such as are laid upon others under like circumstances.

When statements that were made concerning the matter during the debate indicated that this motion could not secure quick assent, the convention tabled it for later consideration and moved on to an issue on which there was near unanimity of opinion, the simple question of "freedom now."[1]

In pre-Civil War days, Missouri's free Negroes had the right to own property, including slaves, and to sue and be sued. They could testify in court against another of their own race but not against whites. Except for these rights, however, their actions were closely circumscribed either by law or custom. In particular, it had been declared unlawful, through an 1847 constitutional amendment, to teach any Negro to read and write. Contrary to Missouri's agreement with Congress at the time the area became a state, the General Assembly had begun to restrict the immigration of free Negroes into the state as early as 1825. Beginning in 1835, it required those in residence to have a license and provided apprenticeship for any free Negro less than twenty-one years old without one. As abolitionist controversy became heated in the 1850's, white Missourians came to fear the three thousand free blacks in their midst far out of proportion to their number within the total population. An 1857 measure forbade them to leave Missouri unless they were seamen, and only a pocket veto by Gov. Robert M. Stewart in 1859 saved them from being forced to choose between emigration or slavery.

For all their restraints and difficulties, a number of Missouri's free Negroes had prospered. Their success was particularly evident in the St. Louis area, where approximately two-thirds of them lived. There were approximately twenty Negro barbers in the city by 1860. Their "tonsorial parlors" must have had a large clientele because several of these establishments were valued at more than $20,000 in the census of that year. Other wealthy Negroes operated vegetable stands or meat markets, engaged in the cattle trade, or had river boat connections. Some had acquired an extensive amount of land from inheritance that could be traced to colonial times. Outside St. Louis, one of the most prominent free Negroes was Hiram Young of Independence, who acquired a fortune as a blacksmith and wagon manufacturer at that stopover for those going West. At the

1. Four votes were cast against the emancipation ordinance by William F. Switzler of Boone County, Thomas B. Harris of Callaway County, Samuel A. Gilbert of Platte County, and William A. Morton of Clay County.

other end of the social scale, most free Negroes were employed as domestics or laborers, particularly along the levee or on the many boats plying Missouri's rivers. In St. Louis, the Jesuits had provided a gallery chapel in one downtown church for a number of the wealthier Negroes who were strict adherents to the Roman Catholic faith. By far the greater number of free blacks belonged to the several Negro Methodist and Baptist churches in the city. One of these churches had a membership of more than a thousand, half of whom were free, by the time of the war. Its minister, the Reverend J. Richard Anderson, was one of the most prominent Negroes in the community. Although denied the right to participate in politics, St. Louis Negroes exercised a quiet influence, where they could, behind the scenes. They maintained ties with prominent white leaders, both political and religious, and took some credit, rightly or wrongly, for the increasing success of the local Republican party. One of them, in a highly interesting publication of 1858 concerning Negro society in St. Louis, predicted that when emancipation came, the community's free Negroes could be expected to be predominant among those seeking "an equal participation in the fruits of human progression and mutual development." This forecast was highly accurate.

On January 31, 1865, in the midst of debate over inclusion of his earlier proposals as a "Declaration of Rights" within the new constitution, Drake presented a petition from 94 "colored citizens of St. Louis" asking that the franchise be extended to them. A week earlier, there had been a similar plea from 600 soldiers of the Fifty-sixth Colored Infantry. Although Drake had no objection to Negro suffrage, he opposed its inclusion in the constitution at the time because of his fear that the provision would automatically bring about that document's defeat when submitted to popular referendum. During the debate at the convention, he maintained that franchise did not have to accompany freedom and pointed to women and foreigners as other examples of those free persons who could not vote. Drake stressed the need for education for Missouri's blacks as a prerequisite to this final achievement and expressed the hope that in time, existing prejudices might be overcome by the anticipated influx of immigrants from the free states. As it was, he had to repel numerous proposals for amendments that sought to eliminate or water down those rights for blacks that he had already proposed. In the end, he secured his "Declaration" with its original wording. It gave Missouri's blacks all civil rights except the vote and officeholding. During debate Drake had expressed his willingness to concede the latter to the blacks because he believed that no black could be elected to public office, but when his rural followers balked, he did not push the issue.

The bulk of those whites who favored enfranchisement of blacks were German Radicals and those who had ardently advocated emancipation before the war. Foremost among them was Governor Fletcher, who spoke out strongly in favor of equal rights on various occasions in the summer and fall of 1865. Another ardent enthusiast was State Rep. Enos Clarke of St. Louis, a young lawyer with strong abolitionist leanings who had emigrated from Ohio during the war and who championed the blacks' cause while he was in the legislature.

Both of these men worked closely with the leaders of the St. Louis black community. Early in October, this group called a mass meeting at one of their churches to launch the Missouri Equal Rights League. Speakers from both races proclaimed that the black could secure full equality before the law only through the possession of the franchise. The several hundred who were present adopted resolutions in support of this statement and appointed a seven-man executive committee of black ministers and businessmen to spearhead a statewide drive for support. In an eloquent appeal to the Missouri citizenry, they stated their case:

> Out of the fierce conflict which has just closed between an advanced civilization and a relic of barbarism, we at length have been released from chains, lashes, bloodhounds, and slave marts, and to us has a "freedom at large" been ordained. For this, in behalf of our long oppressed race, do we thank God and now ask that this liberty shall be secured and consecrated by those guarantees and privileges, which are enjoyed by every other American citizen, and which can only be found in the exercise of the right of suffrage.

The committee immediately started work. It invited John M. Langston, prominent black attorney from Oberlin, Ohio, to address a St. Louis rally in late November. Although the dollar admission price eliminated the attendance of many working-class blacks, the Ohioan spoke to an overflow audience. A popular spokesman for his race, Langston tempered his plea for Negro suffrage with a reminder to the blacks present that they must be prepared to assume the obligations of responsible citizenship. There followed a six-week tour, which took the black leader to Hannibal, Macon, Chillicothe, St. Joseph, into Kansas, and then back to Missouri for appearances at Kansas City and Sedalia. He climaxed this western swing with an evening speech in the Hall of Representatives at Jefferson City, which the reporter for the *Missouri Democrat* termed a simple but eloquent plea for the Negroes' cause. The members of the General Assembly attended en masse, and even the Conservatives "acknowledged frankly the fairness and justness of his argument." The Equal Rights League published this address in pamphlet form and sold copies for twenty-five cents each to help with the expenses of the campaign. The first anniversary of Missouri's Emancipation Ordinance occurred two days later, and the League enhanced the occasion with a long parade through the downtown streets of St. Louis. The enthusiasm was not dampened by the inclement weather as the various participating groups marched with festive banners and slogans to Washington Hall to witness one last appearance by Langston. Those who had invited the Ohioan to Missouri could be quite satisfied with the efforts of the past few weeks.

A petition campaign, which local committees had promoted simultaneously with the tour, yielded more than three thousand signatures of citizens asking that the General Assembly provide suitable schools for black children and eliminate the word *white* wherever it appeared in the new constitution. When the League's secretary, James Milton Turner, tried to inform the people of southeastern Missouri about his cause, however, he met with considerable hostility. In one home where he stayed, he was attacked by a mob and managed "to escape for his life at midnight, barefooted in the snow."

A fascinating individual, Turner rapidly emerged as the state's leading black Radical politician. Born a slave in St. Louis County around 1840, Turner later claimed that his father had been a nephew of the famous Nat and had come to Missouri after the unsuccessful rebellion in Virginia. The elder Turner learned the trade of a veterinarian and became well known in the area as "Black John, the Horse Doctor." Eventually he purchased his own freedom and that of his family. Young Jim first attended a "tallow candle school," which some Negroes had clandestinely established, until it was broken up by police. Later he spent three years in a class for Negro children maintained in open defiance of the law by Catholic nuns at the Old Cathedral. After working a few years, he saved enough money to secure additional education at Oberlin College.

Returning to Missouri shortly before the Civil War, Turner took employment with Madison Miller, a prominent St. Louis politician and railroad entrepreneur who, incidentally, was married to Tom Fletcher's sister. When Miller entered military service, Turner went with him as his body servant and saw action in the battles at Wilson's Creek and Shiloh. He received a hip wound in the engagement at Shiloh that caused him to limp for the remainder of his life. He returned to St. Louis, where he spent the rest of the war helping fugitive slaves escape into Illinois. Miller had been taken prisoner at Shiloh, and Turner unknowingly presumed him dead. He ingratiated himself with the Miller-Fletcher families, however, by transmitting a large sum of money back to Miller's wife. Undoubtedly these connections served him well in his postwar political career.

On March 7, 1866, Representative Clarke presented the Equal Rights League's petitions to the General Assembly and spoke for one and a half hours in support of their objectives. An accompanying memorial signed by 208 St. Louis blacks reminded the legislators that their race had proved "our undoubted loyalty" by furnishing 200,000 troops in the recent conflict. They also claimed the right to suffrage on the basis of the taxes they paid on approximately $2.5 million worth of real estate in Missouri "since taxation and representation are inseparable." The House remained unmoved, however, and the League's proposals died in the Committee on Constitutional Amendments.

Agitation continued sporadically throughout 1866. Then, soon after the Radical triumph in the fall elections, Senator Brown, who had raised the issue initially, brought it up again at the

Planters House conference. With his own election to the Senate assured, Drake backed the proposal, although he refused to link it to the rescinding of the test oath as Brown and other liberals wished. "If it is right to make the Negro a voter," Drake asserted, "let it be done because it is right, not as a swap with the rebels."

When the new General Assembly met, the Equal Rights League established a powerful lobby at the capital. It celebrated the second anniversary of the emancipation ordinance with another huge parade and rally in St. Louis, for which Governor Fletcher gave the principal address. The following month it brought in Frederick Douglass, the most distinguished black of his generation, for yet another St. Louis demonstration. A militant figure, Douglass did not mince words in calling for the black's full voice in government. A large audience made up of both races gave him an enthusiastic reception. Although far from united on how to handle the issue of Negro suffrage, the Radicals in the legislature finally hammered out an agreement in secret caucus. They turned aside the efforts of the liberals to eliminate the word *white* wherever found in the constitution or to tie the question of Negro enfranchisement to that of rebels. Rather, they agreed to submit, at the 1868 election, a narrowly worded amendment that provided for striking out all racial qualifications for voting. The minority Conservatives protested when the measure came to the floor of the House but to no avail, as the Radicals easily mustered the votes to push the bill through.

While Missouri's more articulate blacks struggled to secure their full civil rights, the vast majority concerned themselves with the all-important economic and social readjustments of day-to-day living in the aftermath of the war. Slavery died hard, especially in the rural areas of central and southern Missouri. Many blacks were uprooted from homes and the only kind of life they had known. They often served as readymade targets for marauding bushwhackers. Friendly whites sought to help with relocation, frequently outside the state; but such possibilities for a new start were limited by both cost and the ingrained prejudices of those among whom they would settle.

Although readjustment brought many problems to both races, Missouri progressed much more rapidly toward a lasting, harmonious solution than her Southern sisters. This difference may be explained in part by the relatively small proportion of blacks in her populace. According to the 1870 census, blacks constituted only 6.9 per cent of the state's population, so Missouri had the smallest number of blacks of the former slaveholding states, excluding Delaware. The Missouri Negro population had even decreased slightly; there were 3,572 free blacks and 114,931 slaves ten years earlier and 118,071 at the 1870 census. Many, of course, had emigrated during the last two years of the war. Of those who remained, the vast majority concentrated themselves in the counties along the state's two great rivers, while nearly one fourth settled in the St. Louis area because of its greater opportunities. In 1870, only twenty counties reported Negro populations in excess of 10 per cent; and only two of these had concentrations of greater than 20 per cent—Howard County in "Little Dixie" with 30 per cent and New Madrid County in the extreme southeastern corner with 22 per cent. Apparently, the state offered little attraction for Negro immigration as the census reported that 117,995 or better than 99 per cent of Missouri's blacks had been born within her borders.

Congress had created the Freedmen's Bureau in the winter of 1865 to assist both blacks and refugee whites in the problems of readjustment. Gen. John W. Sprague, a son-in-law of Benjamin F. Butler, served as its assistant commissioner for the Missouri–Arkansas District with headquarters at St. Louis. By early summer he had established posts at Cape Girardeau, Pilot Knob, Rolla, Cassville, and Springfield. Bureau records for July, 1865, indicated the distribution of about three thousand rations to needy freedmen. Thereafter, the reports showed a notable decrease in the number of blacks who required help each month. At the end of September, only 271 freedmen were still receiving direct aid from Bureau stations. Approximately fourteen hundred refugees remained on the rolls, but most of them were being sent back to their homes in Arkansas or were finding employment with farmers in southern Missouri.

Bureau agents performed many services for the freedmen. Their major concern was to supply enough clothing and rations to provide for those who were still destitute during the winter. They also helped arrange labor contracts for them with nearby farmers, and they assisted black couples in complying with the new Missouri law requiring them to be legally married if they had not had the benefit of a wedding ceremony while they were slaves. The agents made arrangements for Negro schools with instructors furnished by various benevolent associations. In Springfield, for instance, the Bureau sponsored Miss Emeline Howard and Miss Letitia Townsend, who had been sent by the Iowa Society of Friends and the Northwestern Freedmen's Aid Commission, respectively, to help with education for the blacks of that area. These two women enrolled approximately 150 pupils and climaxed their first year with ceremonies attended by Governor Fletcher and State Superintendent of Schools Parker. At Cape Girardeau, the Bureau's agent reported that about 80 had enrolled in a school taught by a black man, who toiled under very trying circumstances.

In late July, one of Sprague's assistants toured the St. Joseph and central Missouri areas. A large population of blacks and many pro-Southern whites lived in this region. With no permanent Bureau agent in the area, the blacks there had "been obliged to depend on themselves more fully" than in southern Missouri. The aide reported that there existed "abundant employment for all who can and are willing to work at remunerative prices." He found many blacks, however, who were "disinclined to labor except for a short time and then they remain idle until they have expended their earnings." Several schools had been started. Many black women with children, "some of them soldiers' families," would need help from the Bureau to get them through the winter. Most of the counties he visited had some program underway to assist needy freedmen, although they discouraged transients by restricting assistance to those known to have been resident for at least twelve months. The agent reported a general tendency for blacks to stay in the towns because "they are afraid to go into the country," but he added that "prominent citizens" believed "they will scatter through the county and support themselves" if some help could be given them that winter. All told, Sprague's aide thought "the prospects of the freedmen is good."

In spite of the work of the Bureau, much still needed to be done to implement the blacks' legal rights. Former Congressman

Sempronius H. Boyd wrote to Gen. Granville M. Dodge, the new departmental commander, from Springfield in June: "Hundreds of negroes from Arkansas have settled here and are industrious, well behaved and now constitute a large proportion of our laboring class and indeed is a great blessing to us. Yet I must say to you that they are cowered and frightened. They are persecuted & wronged, whipped and even killed and nothing done to prevent it or to hinder." Boyd cited the specific case: "One poor negro who was gathering a load of wood only half a mile from the court house was shot today by someone in soldiers clothes." A Negro church had been burned a few nights earlier and its members fired upon when they tried to put out the blaze. Black school children were stoned as they made their way to classes. Since the enlistments of the local garrison were about to expire, Boyd had a drastic solution—to send in black troops under competent officers. These troops would have a special interest in securing a respect for Negro rights. As the newly appointed judge of the Fourteenth Judicial Circuit, he promised to do all he could to secure justice for the new freedmen.

In central Missouri, a new Freedmen's Bureau agent, appointed in mid-October, reported some difficulty in helping his black charges redress their grievances against whites. Local law officials seemed hesitant "to open to them the doors of justice and law, and to render them the assistance necessary for their protection against oppression and wrongs." White employers, in some instances, had withheld wages they had agreed to pay black workers. In one particular case, the widow of a wealthy freedman had been driven from her home by a white neighbor after the death of her husband.

It is difficult to determine how many incidents such as these may have occurred. Relatively few were disclosed in the press, and the reports by Bureau agents tend to be far more positive than negative. Even Boyd admitted in his dispatch to General Dodge that the local troops had conducted themselves reasonably well. That commander was also receiving frequent complaints of harassment of whites by roaming bands of bushwhackers. He and Governor Fletcher continued a steady correspondence that spring and summer concerning coordinating the efforts of militia and Regulars to try to restore order, especially in a number of strife-torn areas of western Missouri.

By the winter of 1865–1866, many blacks began drifting back to the countryside. They returned because the economic opportunities in town proved insufficient. The unskilled especially had nowhere to turn except to that with which they were familiar. Many wandered back to the farms from which they had come, while others arranged labor contracts elsewhere. In many instances, especially when they lacked the benefit of advice from Bureau agents, they resumed work under conditions that left them hardly better off than they had been before the war. They were paid in monthly wages or by a share of the crop, and few of these laborers saved very much money, even when they had the opportunity to do so. As late as 1874, freedmen in some areas received wages lower than those paid hired slaves in the prewar era. The unskilled found themselves at the mercy of the white farmers who hired them. Reliable evidence exists to indicate that both parties frequently disregarded labor contracts. Arrangements in such circumstances became quite haphazard.

Some blacks did manage to save sufficient funds to purchase their own land, and most were as prosperous as anyone in their immediate environment could be. Others availed themselves of homesteads that Congress had offered without racial restrictions through an act of June 21, 1866, in Missouri and four other states. Gen. Oliver O. Howard, who headed the Freedmen's Bureau, reported that about four thousand black families had been able to take advantage of this opportunity in spite of the lack of teams and farming implements needed to start any large operation. By the early 1870's, the blacks in several counties had prospered sufficiently to hold their own agricultural fairs.

Those blacks who remained in town engaged in various trades or found opportunities for employment as servants. A survey of occupations of black parents with children in the St. Louis schools in the late 1860's showed a preponderance of laborers, laundresses, draymen, and boatmen. The 1870 census revealed that most of those outstate pursued similar endeavors. Few appeared to be very wealthy, although a substantial minority of them apparently owned homes valued from a few hundred up to two thousand dollars. Those who had prospered as free Negroes in St. Louis before the war with their barbering salons and other enterprises continued to do so. The National Freedmen's Savings and Trust Company opened a branch office in St. Louis on June 29, 1868. During its first eighteen months of operation, the association averaged a monthly gain in deposits of more than $1,400. By mid-1870, it had a total balance of more than $50,000. The cashier reported that the institution had "gradually ingratiated itself into the confidence of the people" and that it would soon move into a new banking room at "one of the best locations in the city." Although this bank catered exclusively to a black clientele, St. Louis's thirty-nine other banks also had a liberal share of Negro patronage.

The reorganization of the state militia during this period provided that all able-bodied blacks as well as whites could enroll. Each county had its own military organization. Separate companies of blacks were formed if there were enough recruits. They served quite readily and well when called upon, not without some grumbling in certain white quarters, especially in the postelection disturbances of the winter of 1866–1867.

Early in January, 1867, Radical Rep. Charles H. Branscomb, one of the leaders in the struggle for equal suffrage, received a letter from Isaac H. Sturgeon, president of the North Missouri Railroad. While commending him for his efforts on behalf of securing the franchise for blacks, Sturgeon called Branscomb's attention to the deplorable situation that plagued blacks in the use of public transportation in St. Louis. "As it is now," he declared, "the colored people have to stand on the platforms of the car in front of our street railroads or walk. I have seen neatly dressed colored females on cold days stand on the front platform with tender infants in their arms." Sturgeon urged that the state enact strong legislation to deny a charter to any company that failed to treat members of both races equally. Those who would "eject or attempt to enjoin a colored person from riding inside the cars" should be heavily penalized. In the meantime, he asserted, the mayor ought "to detail police along the lines where these roads run, to ride on the cars and see that the colored people were protected from injury or insult." Give the blacks protection, Sturgeon declared, "and if they deport themselves well as I am convinced they will, in six months the prejudice will wear away and there will be no further trouble."

Branscomb and others tried to push a comprehensive rights bill through the legislature that spring but failed because the majority of their colleagues did not want to endanger suffrage with side issues. Considerable agitation continued, however, for fairer treatment of blacks on public conveyances. The *Missouri Republican* suggested that St. Louis adopt the New Orleans plan, which provided that every fourth or fifth car be reserved for blacks. In these cars, they could enjoy the same privileges as whites had in the others. Early in June, the *Missouri Democrat* announced that an agreement had been reached to allow blacks to ride inside the streetcars. A day later it was discovered that there were two incidents in which blacks had been ejected, although in both cases a number of whites had come to their support. Matters finally came to a head the following month when Neptune and Caroline Williams filed suit against the Bellefontaine Railway in St. Louis circuit court. They sought an injunction against the line and $5,000 in damages on the grounds that one of its conductors had pushed Caroline, pregnant and with a baby in her arms, from a car when she tried to board it on July 21. The following May, the court agreed that public transportation companies could not discriminate and ordered them to allow blacks to ride inside their cars. The Williamses failed to secure damages, however, as the court allowed them only one cent for their inconvenience. From this time on there appears to have been little difficulty over this problem.

Apparently the ratification of the Fifteenth Amendment, guaranteeing Negro suffrage throughout the nation, had some favorable side effects. At least one black citizen of St. Louis wrote to Frederick Douglass's *New Era*, a leading weekly Negro paper: "The fifteenth amendment is working wonders. Streetcar conductors cannot tell whether you are black or white. I take a look in my glass sometimes to see if by some hocus pocus I have turned white, but it gives back the same old face, and tells me I am a citizen and not a chattel now. It used to be Old Pen, but now it is Mr. Pentalpha."

Accounts in newspapers indicate that most public meetings, particularly in outstate Missouri, had segregated audiences. Blacks generally sat on one side of the hall and whites on the other. Both races apparently accepted this practice as a matter of course. This type of seating arrangement had become the custom in many churches with mixed congregations before the Civil War. Although some all-Negro churches had existed in St. Louis and other large towns prior to 1861, most blacks in rural areas went to their master's church, if they attended at all. War and its aftermath brought increased separation by mutual consent. In the Negro churches there existed an opportunity for leadership training that was available in few other situations. Invariably, both before and after the war, it was the black ministers who took the first steps toward the education of their race.

In separating from their parent congregations, most black groups adopted either the Baptist or Methodist denominations from which they had come. An attempt in 1865 by the blacks of Columbia to raise subscriptions for an African Union Church that might be used by different congregations was unsuccessful, but within two years the Second Baptist Church and the St. Paul's African Methodist Episcopal Church had been started. In addition, local ministers had begun the First African Benevolent Society, an African Sunday School, and the Colored Temperance Society. The last named organized a Temperance Dinner for July 4, 1867, to raise funds for a Negro school. In nearby Mexico, where the blacks organized similar congregations, they at first alternated services in the Presbyterian Church on Sunday afternoons; then, in 1868, they received permission to use the courthouse. Two years later the Baptists purchased a one-room building, which had formerly been used as a sawmill, and continued to share with their Methodist brethren.

In addition to their churches and related organizations, blacks also established lodges and brotherhoods similar to those of whites. By August 1869, a sufficient number of chapters existed for the black Masons of northern Missouri to hold a conclave at Hannibal. One of the more interesting Negro groups to emerge in postwar Missouri was the International Order of Twelve of the Knights and Daughters of Tabor. Its founder, the Reverend Moses Dickson of St. Louis, had been active in the abolitionist movement before the war and had helped organize the Knights of Liberty, a secret Negro lodge designed "to carry to success the secret and great work of obtaining liberty for the bondsmen."

An active leader in the St. Louis black community, Dickson devised the idea of the Knights and Daughters of Tabor in 1868 to commemorate the memory of those who had served the prewar order. The organization had considerable appeal and grew rapidly in the 1870's.

A major concern for the black community was the matter of education. Since most of them had been barred from any kind of opportunity before the war and there was a high rate of illiteracy, their leaders early realized the importance of schools if any kind of economic, political, or social advance was to be achieved. Some clandestine educational activity had been carried on earlier in spite of an 1847 constitutional amendment forbidding the education of Missouri's Negroes. There is evidence that rural slaveowners did not hesitate to give their charges the rudiments of an education when they had compelling reasons for doing so and could accomplish it unobtrusively. Quaker schools with Negro enrollment had existed at Jefferson City and Glasgow in the 1840's, and Catholic nuns conducted classes for Negroes in St. Louis periodically, depending upon the stringency of law enforcement.

Apparently Hiram R. Revels, who later became the first black United States senator, started the earliest-known Negro-run school in St. Louis in 1856. Approximately 150 free Negro children paid a monthly tuition of one dollar. Although Revels operated his school for only a year, other subscription schools appeared in the next few years. Another such effort occurred in Hannibal when the Reverend Tom Henderson, a free Negro Methodist preacher, secured the Second Baptist Church, one of the few prewar Negro edifices, for classes. He also collected a monthly charge of one dollar. When war came, Henderson departed. Blanche K. Bruce resumed Henderson's work. He had been educated with his master's son while he was a slave. He later went to Oberlin College and then to Mississippi, whence the Radicals sent him to the Senate in 1875.

Revels returned during the war to reopen his subscription school. By the fall of 1863, three black women teachers had undertaken similar projects. The four had a combined enrollment of 187. Earlier that spring the American Missionary Association, a white philanthropic organization, had opened a school for blacks in the Missouri Hotel, only to have it burned three days later. At Benton Barracks, the Western Sanitary Commission had organized classes for black recruits that was quite successful. That winter Revels chaired a meeting of the interested citizenry of both races to discuss what could be done on a more systematic basis within the law's limitations. The group decided to establish a Negro board of education, which would take over the four subscription schools that existed at the time and add others that would not charge a fee, until such time as the General Assembly might change the law to permit the absorption of all such schools into the St. Louis system. In February, 1864, this group began operations with four hundred pupils registered in four schools located in rented accommodations that left much to be desired. A year later, enrollment had increased to six hundred, and eight teachers were employed. In addition, a high school for fifty or sixty "advanced scholars of the colored people" had been started in the basement of the Church of the Messiah. Supervised by two women from New England, it was sustained by contributions "from friends in Massachusetts."

From its outset, internal problems developed in the newly formed educational system. Hopes of hiring the teachers from the subscription schools broke down when the board discovered it could not pay them as much as they had been getting from the fees they charged. Some of these teachers had no difficulty keeping their private schools open, because many established black families had little desire to let their children mix with the poorer refugee element in the free schools. Some black Catholics continued to send their children to integrated parochial schools. Additional qualified black instructors for the new schools were hard to find, and for a time the American Missionary Association supplied and paid white teachers for the system. The Reverend George Caudee of the missionary organization agreed to serve as superintendent of the new arrangement temporarily, but he did not always see eye to eye with the black members of the board on curriculum and other problems. When it became evident that they preferred inadequately trained black teachers to qualified whites, he resigned. Thereafter he and the A.M.A. carried on independently. Faced with mounting difficulties, the board requested in February, 1865, that its official St. Louis counterpart at least provide them with financial support if indeed they could not take over the entire management of the Negro schools. The black leaders revealed that they had sustained the operation with gifts of $800 from the Western Sanitary Commission, $900 from two prominent whites, and $1,230.60 from the black community. The St. Louis board responded by granting the system $500, but it was too late to prevent the early closing of the Negro classes that spring.

Another school for black children was maintained by the Western Sanitary Commission as part of its Freedmen's Orphans' Home. This facility housed several hundred black youngsters during the first few years of its existence. The Commission sought to make it a temporary way station for the orphans and attempted to find more permanent situations for them by periodically announcing that "responsible persons, with good reference or recommendation, can obtain children from among the number to bring up, and have their service by assuming a proper obligation for care, support, clothing, tuition for three months each year, and moderate wages after they reach the age of fourteen years." When the Commission disbanded at the close of 1865, interested local citizens established a new organization to keep the home open. It still housed sixty children a year later; but by early 1869, the number of orphans there had dwindled to thirty-six, and it stood in dire financial straits. In their annual report of that year, the directors urged St. Louisans not to overlook these youngsters as they began to forget the conflict that had produced their plight. The plea proved successful, and the work continued.

While the General Assembly rescinded the old restrictions on education of Negroes in the spring of 1865, the action came too late to have much effect that school year. Although they urged speedy action by school trustees in rebuilding their systems with provisions for both races, the legislators made no monetary appropriations for the work. Instead, they decided to wait until the following session, when it would be easier to assess the total need. Consequently, most of the schools for blacks that were in operation that fall were maintained either by subscription or by white benevolent societies. Especially active among these societies was the American Missionary Association, which operated fourteen schools with eighteen teachers at various points throughout Missouri. The work of the Iowa branch of the Society of Friends at Springfield has already been mentioned. In addition, this group, cooperating with the Northwestern Freedmen's Aid Commission, conducted schools at Rolla, Warrensburg, St. Charles, St. Joseph, Weston, Sedalia, and Columbia. Many of these, as well as some subscription schools taught by black ministers, received additional subsidy from the Freedmen's Bureau. In St. Louis the Negro board of education struggled on for another year aided by the $500 subsidy from its white counterpart.

In his annual report to the General Assembly the following January, State Superintendent of Schools James H. Robinson remonstrated: "The education of the freedmen's child deserves the most liberal legislation." He thought it "astonishing to see such prosperous private schools, supported by the colored people, in many portions of our country" and warned, "Ere the State is ready to contribute the means to educate the colored man, many of them will be prepared to take places as teachers to assist in elevating the standard of his race."

The General Assembly responded with a series of comprehensive laws providing for the public education of the black. These measures would require each township or city board of education to establish and maintain one or more separate schools for black children within their respective jurisdictions where the number of such youngsters exceeded twenty. Each of these schools must be kept open for a winter term equivalent to that for white students, but if average attendance for any month should drop to less than twelve, the board could close the school for a period not to exceed six months. The school census must include the black children in the district, regardless of their number. Where there were fewer than twenty, their portion of subsequent tax money could be appropriated for their education as the board saw fit.

For all the elaborateness and seeming completeness of this legislation, public education for blacks ran afoul in many places because of apathy and evasion. With many citizens in conservative areas questioning the need for public schools at all, the plea for doing something for blacks fell on deaf ears. State Superintendent Thomas A. Parker pointed out in his annual report of 1867 the ease with which a hostile community or its officials might evade school laws, particularly since the legislators had not provided a penalty for noncompliance. Summarizing the progress of Negro education, Parker noted that fifty-six schools had been established in thirty counties. The majority of these institutions were privately run. Public schools for blacks existed only in the larger towns. Kansas City had set up the first in April, 1866, with J. Milton Turner as its teacher. That fall Turner transferred to Boonville to take charge of the Negro schools there. In St. Louis, the public education system absorbed those schools previously run by the Negro board of education. It opened three Negro schools in the fall of 1866 with an enrollment of 437. Of these, 45 students were over eighteen years of age—a common situation in the early black institutions. Two more schools for blacks were added the following year, while evening classes got underway to give working blacks an opportunity for special training in reading, spelling, penmanship, arithmetic, grammar, and geography. The 1867 report of the St. Louis board of education noted that "at the annual examination there were exhibited some fine specimens of penmanship; and several classes showed satisfactory proficiency in reading and spelling." The main difficulty was in securing the "degree of punctuality and regularity in attendance that is obtained in other schools." The board hoped to correct this problem, however, "as soon as these schools are established in localities more convenient to the population who patronizes them."

The establishment of public schools for Negroes in rural areas frequently was hindered by indifference, hostility, or lack of concentrated numbers of students. The report written by De-Kalb County's superintendent in 1867 was typical: "As there are but very few colored people in our county there is but little interest manifested in their behalf." In some instances, blacks found their efforts frustrated by malice of white opponents. This situation existed in January, 1867, when "some mischievous youths" burned their new school in Fulton. In this case, responsible elements rallied quickly to raise a subscription fund for its replacement. Amid the county reports of 1867, there were occasional hopeful signs. That of Daviess County in northwestern Missouri is especially noteworthy:

> There are but few colored people in this county and only one school organized, their number being insufficient to organize more than one school. There has been some interest taken in their welfare, and old prejudices are gradually wearing away. Their desire for and their efforts to obtain an education is truly commendable, and when their school is in operation they come from all parts of the county to attend and many of them have made considerable progress.

Two years later a Freedmen's Bureau agent reported that the number of Negro schools had doubled, and those of a public nature predominated. The 1870 census revealed that 9,080 Negro students attended classes "in churches and cabins with walls admirably adapted for ventilation and for admission of copious shower baths of rain." While these statistics showed a large increase over 1867, 55 counties with a total enumeration of 2,984 black children still had no Negro schools. With a potential of 42,000 black students for the entire state, the census indicated that about 21 per cent were receiving some kind of education. This proportion compared with 59 per cent of the eligible white children who were attending school.

The blacks of Missouri worked hard to promote their own progress. A typical example could be found in Columbia where the local board of education had opened a school for black children in the fall of 1866 under the direction of a black teacher, Charles E. Cummings. It met in rented quarters with an attendance of sixty-three the first year. Desirous of having their own building, the black community started to raise funds through a series of dinners, festivals, fairs, and picnics. The Freedmen's Bureau contributed $800. By the fall of 1869, a two-story frame structure named Cummings Academy, for the popular teacher, was ready for occupancy. Albert L. Aubin, the Freedmen's Bureau agent for Missouri, visited it in November and came away with high praise for both the facilities and the staff.

The Columbia effort was duplicated on numerous occasions across the state during this period. Frequent accounts of Negro fairs, picnics, and other fundraising activities appeared in the Radical press. One of the largest of these endeavors in the St. Louis area occurred during the summer of 1868, when the blacks of Kirkwood and Carondolet held a Freedmen's Fair of several days duration to underwrite the construction of schools and churches. Large crowds visited the booths and displays while enjoying entertainment provided by the Woodson family singers —the nine children of the Reverend E. S. Woodson, a former slave of Edward Bates, who had bought his freedom in 1848.

Unfortunately the blacks encountered continued resistance, as well as help, from the whites. The new school, which opened at Carondolet in the fall of 1869, burned a month later with a $10,000 loss. Scattered reports of other such incidents can be found in the state's newspapers and in Freedmen's Bureau reports. White teachers coming into communities to open Negro schools were sometimes subject to harassment. Many of them were women from outside the state—a preponderance were from New England. The tendency of conservative Missourians to question such female independence, especially in an endeavor already suspect, received further reinforcement when some of the teachers brought with them "Yankee missionary ideas" for remaking their new homes after a "progressive image." One such teacher at Linneus in northwestern Missouri resorted to an unsuccessful court action in an effort to redress her grievances against those who resented her teaching black children. Another, located at Roanoke in Howard County, wrote the Freedmen's Bureau of her increasing fears after some renegade whites had burned the Negro school in which she taught, together with a church and the farm buildings of the community's most prominent black leader.

In spite of the difficulties, however, progress continued to be made. In his annual report for 1869, Superintendent Parker, an ardent Radical, informed the General Assembly:

> The wise and liberal policy heretofore adopted has borne good fruit. Opposition to the education of the colored people is gradually disappearing. Their rapid improvement and good conduct help to disarm prejudice. The question of the capacity of the race is receiving a solution in these schools. . . . I have witnessed recitations in colored schools which were not inferior in enthusiasm, readiness

and grasp in thought to any I ever saw in a white school, considering the time the pupils had studied.

Under the prodding of Parker and his successors the legislators gradually closed existing loopholes in the laws concerning education for black children. The Twenty-fourth General Assembly in 1868 gave the state superintendent authority to assume school board powers in establishing and maintaining Negro schools where local groups had failed to act. Superintendent John Monteith, who served in the early 1870's, pursued this course rather vigorously and reported that he had started between fifty and sixty new schools in 1872. Two years later, he wrote: "I have levied taxes for negro schools in three instances. The medicine is good and effective, and I trust it will be administered in every similar case in the State until the colored people enjoy schools equally good in every way with the white schools." Perhaps the sharp decline in the amount of intervention during that period can be attributed to the passage of a law by which school officials found guilty of the persistent neglect of any duty could be fined $50 to $500.

The 1868 legislature also sought to eliminate another of the major obstacles in the path of Negro education—the sparsity of black population in some areas—by lowering the number of eligible students needed to begin a school to fifteen and by reducing the average attendance requirement from twelve to ten. The following year it allowed the establishment of a school by two or more districts together if their combined black population warranted it. Such consolidation became obligatory in 1874. Yet, for all of this, the scarcity of black students continued to cause difficulties. The 1871 reports from county superintendents revealed that thirty-nine counties lacked Negro schools because none of their districts had the required number of black children. The following year twenty-one superintendents called attention to this situation and its ensuing problems. The one in Clark County in northeastern Missouri advocated that black youngsters be admitted to white schools where there were too few of the children to establish separate schools. Apparently some districts did begin this practice where no objections were raised.

The question of training black teachers became a major problem almost from the outset of the program. Few whites cared to work with black children, and not many educated blacks were available to do so. Ten county superintendents, in their annual reports for 1873, mentioned difficulties in securing good instructors for their Negro schools. Prejudice existed on the part of both races against whites teaching black children. The self-righteous attitude of some of the early teachers from the benevolent societies was resented by blacks as well as whites. In the public schools white teachers did not always take the interest or have the patience that a black instructor might have in his pupils' training. The pay differential between white and Negro schools further complicated the matter. In 1873, average salaries ranged from $46.70 monthly for a male teacher in a Negro school to $82.72 in those for whites. By comparison, women teachers were victims of gross discrimination in both cases with a $40 monthly average in Negro schools and only $46.64 in white. The semi-annual report of the Freedmen's Bureau in July, 1869, further revealed that black teachers had been barred from attending local institutes and even the meeting of the state educational association because of their race.

In his annual report for 1869, Superintendent Parker disclosed:

> There is a school—Lincoln Institute—now in the fourth year of a successful operation, in Jefferson City, and possessing an endowment fund of $7,000, which, on a small scale and with limited means is doing good work in the right direction. It owns no building and is able to maintain but one teacher. . . . A valuable library of several hundred volumes has been obtained, and several good teachers have already been sent out.

Parker recommended that "this beginning, so auspiciously made, be encouraged by the State" with an annual appropriation of $5,000.

Lincoln Institute had indeed been doing good work under tremendous handicaps. As the Sixty-second Colored Infantry prepared to muster out at Fort McIntosh, Texas, in January, 1866, one of its white officers, Lt. Richard B. Foster, began discussing the matter of their further education with some of the other officers and men. Most of these men had been recruited in Missouri in 1863, and many of them had participated in the educational program conducted by the Western Sanitary Commission at Benton Barracks. They realized the importance of training for their race in the postwar world of freedom. From these conversations emerged a plan whereby the men of the regiment would pool their resources to start a school for freedmen in Missouri. Its purpose would be to "combine study with labor, so that the old habits of those who have neither capital to spend nor time to lose, may obtain an education." After Foster agreed to head the operation, a committee solicited the troops and raised $1,034.50 from the officers of the Sixty-second while the enlisted men gave $3,966.50. Another Missouri regiment at Fort McIntosh, the Sixty-fifth Colored Infantry, endorsed the program with gifts totalling $1,379.50. When one considers the small army pay of that day, particularly for black men in the ranks, this amount represented a considerable sacrifice on the part of these soldiers.

One of the many New Englanders who contributed so much to educational progress in Missouri in the postwar era, Richard B. Foster, was a native of New Hampshire who had graduated from Dartmouth College. He had taught in Illinois and Indiana before the war and then become involved with the abolitionist movement in Kansas. Volunteering for military duty in 1862, he had applied for a transfer to a Negro outfit when recruitment of black soldiers began. Now, with the support of his comrades, he returned to Missouri to begin his work for the education of their race. He quickly enlisted the support of James E. Yeatman, who had headed the Western Sanitary Commission, and a number of leading Radical politicians, including Governor Fletcher. After securing incorporation and establishing a board of trustees, they decided to locate the school at Jefferson City where land to be used as a farm could be acquired reasonably. Here the students might be profitably employed in line with the "study and labor" policy decided upon earlier. Foster then went East where he procured $2,000 from the Freedmen's Bureau for his enterprise. He found little additional interest, however, because "the ground [was] so entirely occupied by organized societies that I, an obscure individual, could not hope to make a successful appeal to the public."

After some difficulty in securing quarters, Foster began operations that fall in a dilapidated structure made available by the Jefferson City town council. Only two students appeared on opening day, but, as word of the school's existence spread, enrollment increased rapidly so that before the winter ended Foster had to hire two assistants. The following spring he reported to the Freedmen's Bureau that he had helped 235 different pupils while maintaining an average attendance of 70. With the help of several young blacks, including J. Milton Turner, Foster struggled through the next few years while using his political ties to agitate for some type of state support. The supporters of Lincoln Institute in the legislature annually sought to allocate to it 10 per cent of the income from the agricultural college land grants provided by the Federal Government. Justification for this financing rested on the supposed original purpose of the school's organizers to prepare the black for "study and labor." This proposal was never enacted, however, because the General Assembly could not agree on the distribution of any of the grants.[2]

In January, 1870, a number of leading blacks from all parts of the state gathered at Jefferson City for a convention to advocate legislative action for various concerns of their race. In addition to seeking some of the land grant funds for Lincoln, they endeavored to have the institute declared a state normal school. Declining to include Lincoln in the agricultural college bill that passed that session, the legislators, nevertheless, voted it a $5,000 annual subsidy providing its trustees would consent to convert the school into one designed for the training of black teachers. Its board would further have to certify that it held in trust for such a purpose buildings and grounds that were valued at not less than $15,000.

Under this impetus, Lincoln and its trustees forged ahead. The Radicals sponsored an exhibition by Foster's students in the Hall of Representatives on March 10, which raised more than $1,000 with $100 contributions from both the Governor and Lieutenant Governor. Within a year, sufficient funds had become available for Lincoln to erect its first building. Enrollment

2. For a complete discussion of the college land-grant problem, see pp. 183–85.

climbed steadily throughout the decade. Finally, in 1879 the state took over complete operation of the school.

Meanwhile, the General Assembly in 1875 had passed a bill allowing the St. Louis board of education to establish a Negro high school, which might include a normal department to help train black teachers. While the number of these institutions had been increasing outstate, the St. Louis system had yet to hire a black instructor. Not until the fall of 1877 did the recently formed Colored State Teachers Association manage to bring about the employment of the first blacks in the city's schools. Soon thereafter the instruction in Negro classrooms became largely a black endeavor.

By 1875, Missouri had a well-established Negro educational system with primary schools having been started in most areas. While it continued to be plagued with the problems already mentioned in the years that followed, it stood considerably in advance of those in the other former slaveholding states. No small part of this progress is due to the concern of Radical leadership in the postwar era and the cooperation these men promoted with a black community determined to advance its own best interests through the educational process.

Indeed, this combination had done much to foster the advancement of Missouri's blacks in every area of activity. Although they suffered a setback in the attempt to secure black suffrage at the 1868 election, the passage of the Fifteenth Amendment two years later brought fulfillment of a long-held dream for many leaders in both groups and found the blacks ready to participate fully in the political process.

CHAPTER VII

CULTURAL LIFE IN POSTWAR MISSOURI

The Radicals' efforts to promote Negro education in the postwar era represented only one part of their larger concern for a system of free public schools. Viewing their party as the protector of the Union and the champion of equal opportunity, the Radicals envisaged public education as the keystone for their program for a better Missouri. In January, 1867, the *Missouri Democrat* editorially advised former Confederates that their adoption of the Radical policies of "free labor, free schools, free speech, and the free ballot" could hasten the removal of all restrictions against them. The Radical press continually pointed out contrasts between those who stood in the vanguard of progress on this issue and those who would try to hold Missouri back. Conservatives, who already held reservations about the need for universal education, identified the public school movement with the Radical party and its "Yankee ideas" and, consequently, were not enthusiastic about the program.

The state convention of 1865 established the framework within which the new educational system emerged after the war. Considering "a general diffusion of knowledge and intelligence [as] being essential to the preservation of the rights and liberties of the people," it required the General Assembly to provide free public schools for all youngsters between the ages of five and twenty-one. That body could require sixteen months as minimum attendance by all eligible pupils at some time before they reached the age of eighteen. To coordinate Missouri's educational structure, the convention provided a state board of education made up of the secretary of state, the attorney general, and the state superintendent of schools. Most of the real authority rested with the state superintendent, who would be elected for a four-year term.

To undergird the new system, the constitution reestablished the Public School Fund, to be supplied by the usual sources.

The convention displayed progressive tendencies by requiring that the General Assembly in its disbursement "take into consideration the amount of any county or city funds appropriated for common schools purposes, and make such distribution as will equalize the amount appropriated for common schools throughout the State." The committee on education had originally recommended that the school monies be appropriated on the basis of the number of children enrolled in the public schools and the average time of their attendance, but this method proved to be too advanced. The convention struck this proposal without even subjecting it to a rollcall vote, retaining, in effect, apportionment according to the general enumeration of the school population. To be eligible for state aid, local districts were required to maintain free public schools for a minimum of three months each year. Should the regular Public School Fund be insufficient to provide for at least four months' schooling in each district, the General Assembly could raise the needed revenue through additional tax measures.

When the legislature convened that winter, the new state superintendent James H. Robinson reported:

> The condition of the common schools is difficult to describe. Many of the districts are unorganized. In these, two citizens are often unable to be found who can take the oath and thereby preserve their school organization. The towns and larger villages, for the most part, are enabled to continue the schools; but the country neighborhoods of many counties are wholly without them. The school houses are almost universally bad.

In St. Louis, the board of education established schools in rented facilities as quickly as they could be procured, but they still had to turn away two thousand white children for lack of accommodations. Superintendent of Schools Ira Divoll presented a blunt alternative in his 1865 report to the board: "The people must build school houses or prisons."

Using the guidelines provided by the new constitution, the General Assembly enacted a series of laws early in 1866 to establish a thorough and detailed public school system. The key man within the organization was the county superintendent of schools, whose functions were patterned after those of his counterpart at the state level. Unlike the county school commissioners of prewar days, who served as little more than transmitting clerks for the submission of annual reports, this new official had broad supervisory authority and was expected to provide real educational leadership at the local level. For this purpose, the law required him to "possess the qualifications of a competent teacher of public schools and be of good moral character." Among other duties, he must conduct two teacher institutes in his county each year and provide guidance in securing uniform textbooks. He also had to examine and certify all teachers. To qualify for a primary certificate, which remained valid for six months to a year, one was required to pass a periodic examination in spelling, reading in English, penmanship, arithmetic, English grammar, modern geography, and United States history. If a person planned to teach in a high school, he also had to be proficient in the higher mathematics and natural sciences. Certification for high school teachers was valid for two years. Unfortunately, in keeping with progressive ideas, the General Assembly made the office of county superintendent elective, so political considerations frequently took precedence over educational qualifications in selecting its occupant.

The same body of legislation established the most adequate, realistic basis for local tax support devised to that time. Local boards could tax their districts to cover the costs of building new schools without having to submit the levy to a popular vote. This policy greatly facilitated badly needed construction of schools, especially in areas where a dominant Conservative element might be recalcitrant. School taxes increased rapidly between 1865 and 1870 to accommodate the repair or rebuilding of many old structures and the erection of new ones. A later state superintendent, who began teaching during this time, recalled that "frame school houses sprang up like mushrooms in the night." State Superintendent Thomas A. Parker could boast in his 1868 annual report that 1,905 new buildings had been constructed over the previous year and the number of teachers had expanded by 838.

The typical country school erected in this period consisted of one room and usually measured approximately 24 by 36 feet. The side walls contained three or four windows protected by heavy shutters, with wainscoting from floor to sill and plaster above that. There was a high wooden ceiling under the shingle roof. A central flue was attached to the large box stove with drum, which heated the building. A "wall-to-wall" blackboard across the front of the room was behind the teacher's desk, which stood on a low platform. The pupils sat either on pine benches with backs or at patent desks, depending upon the local budget for such equipment. In some schools the entryway might have small separate rooms on either side used to store the students' wraps and lunches.

Where school boards could afford new furniture, blackboards, globes, or other instructional apparatus, they frequently secured them from James B. Merwin's Western Publishing and School Furnishing Company in St. Louis. Merwin established the popular *Journal of Education* in September, 1868, to disseminate progressive educational ideas to teachers and parents throughout the state. Much in demand as a lecturer at institutes and teachers' meetings, he often chose as his topic the need for modern equipment in the up-to-date schoolroom. "Our inventive genius, ingenuity, and skill," he boasted, "backed up by the laws of physiology, are constantly on the alert to devise new patterns, combining as far as possible, cheapness with comfort and durability." Another educator noted in mid-1869, however, that many pupils still attended schools that were "old dilapidated dry goods box structures" where they were "cramped by illy constructed seats, stifled by the foul, closely-confined air" or "else shivering for cold if enough of fresh be admitted to temporarily purify the fetid room."

Local school boards also held full powers to establish tax levies for the purpose of collecting general revenue to supplement state aid and keep the schools open for the minimum four-month period required. To maintain a longer school year, they had to secure approval at a general meeting of the eligible voters within their district. Once this acceptance had been given, that same group then had to provide the necessary supplemental revenues to finance this extension. The establishment of a high school required a similar procedure.

Most rural school districts followed the lines of the old congressional townships with subdistricts created where sufficient population warranted it. Incorporated towns or cities could maintain separate school districts with their own boards of education. These areas possessed virtually the same powers as their rural counterparts except that they had to secure voter approval for all new buildings and keep their schools open for at least thirty but not more than forty-five weeks each year.

All of these measures, reinforced by the vigorous leadership of State Superintendent Thomas A. Parker, stimulated the rapid development of the public school system throughout the state. A native of Indiana, Parker was only twenty-eight years old (two years younger than the statutory requirement) when Governor Fletcher appointed him to the post in late 1865. Little is known about his background, but he performed yeoman's work in directing the new school legislation through the General Assembly in the spring of 1866. That fall the Radicals elected him to a full four-year term. Thereafter he toured the state constantly, promoting progressive education.

Parker's annual report for 1870 revealed an increase in the number of public schools over the past three years from 4,840 to 7,547. The number of pupils enrolled had jumped from 169,270 in 1867 to 280,473 by 1870. Of course, laws do not automatically create a well-organized school system. Some counties and towns built excellent schools; others did practically nothing. Parker noted in this same report that he was concerned that taxes to underwrite the building boom were threatening to get out of hand. His office was being flooded with complaints, and he feared the way the taxpayers might react if school boards did not exercise more discretion. He questioned the wisdom of trying to "force any measure upon the people, however beneficial it might be," if its support would cause financial embarrassment.

The young superintendent's fears were partially realized in the mid-1870's, when conservative Democrats regained political power. With the nation in a state of economic depression, they were ready to oppose further expansion and high tax levies for "Yankee schools," which they believed had been imposed unfairly. In 1874 the General Assembly decentralized much of the Parker system, stripping the state and county superintendents of most of their powers and relegating them to paper-pushing functionaries. Local boards became virtually autonomous units with little or no direction from higher officials. The following year a new state constitution placed stringent restrictions on school financing at the local level in reaction to the excesses of the Radical era.

The better schools usually existed in areas where the partisans of public education placed heavy emphasis on the relationship between an enlightened citizenry and community prosperity. Such a situation existed in St. Joseph where the community began planning as early as 1864 for a vigorous campaign to improve public education once the war ended. It hired as superintendent Edward B. Neely, a native of Virginia and graduate of Washington College in Pennsylvania, who had been operating a private academy there since 1855. Neely served the St. Joseph schools for the next forty years. He brought in good teachers, advocated the construction of new buildings, and employed the latest educational techniques. Whereas St. Joseph had previously been "infested with private schools, by 1867 there was scarcely one in the city," since public education had, like the serpent of Aaron's miraculous rod, "swallowed up all the rest."

In Kansas City, a progressive town council initiated action by calling an open meeting of interested citizens early in 1867. "Well attested experience," it asserted, "has shown that a system of graded schools, supported by the community, and open to all children free of charge, is the most effective and enduring producer of security, peace, and prosperity in any community, and should have the hearty and united support of all good citizens." Finding enthusiastic backing, an energetic board of education began operation that fall of a uniform system of graded public schools, including a high school department with one teacher. Sixteen teachers conducted classes in rented quarters that had been hastily arranged and scantily furnished while the board pushed forward the construction of two new buildings and projected others. By 1870, the high school employed several teachers and was housed in a new building of its own, with provision for four full years of work.

St. Louis's public school system had enjoyed good leadership since 1838, when it began operations. It emerged from the Civil War in good condition, due largely to the efforts of Ira Divoll, who had become its superintendent in 1858. One of many New

Englanders who furnished strong educational leadership to the St. Louis community through these years, Divoll had overtaxed his energies during the war as he sought to keep a system of high quality operating on a shoestring budget while also planning for postwar expansion. When ill health forced him to take a leave of absence in the fall of 1867, the *Missouri Democrat* pridefully paid tribute: "Since the close of the war probably no other city in the Union has made such rapid progress in the cause of popular education as St. Louis." In only two years Divoll had opened twelve new schools, including three for blacks, and completed five new buildings. Approximately 250 teachers staffed the system's thirty-three schools, most of them having been trained at the St. Louis normal school, which was celebrating its tenth anniversary. Another postwar improvement, started by Divoll, was the public school library, which now had eleven thousand volumes and two thousand outside subscribers.

When Divoll retired the following spring, the superintendency passed to his youthful assistant, William Torrey Harris, who became one of the most forward-looking and respected educators of his day. A native of Connecticut and an alumnus of Yale, Harris had served a ten-year apprenticeship under Divoll. Building on the foundation laid by his predecessor, he made the St. Louis school system one of the most advanced in the country during the following decade. The new superintendent also exercised an influence throughout Missouri through his addresses at teachers' institutes and his articles in Merwin's *Journal of Education*. Harris held the Radical philosophy that the public school system was one of the agencies that would help break down class distinctions and prevent the growth of aristocracy. This viewpoint contrasted sharply with the attitude of many Conservatives who thought it desirable to produce an educated elite through private academies. Writing in the *Journal of Education* in September, 1869, Harris declared that the American educational system must be different than that of a nation whose society was stratified and asserted that it was the public schools that offered the best means for promoting social mobility through equality of opportunity.

Harris pushed the expansion of the high school, which had been established in 1853, as it became increasingly popular by

176

the late 1860's. Thirty-eight students graduated there in June, 1868, and over the next five years an average of 25 per cent of those who entered stayed to finish their work. He also persuaded the school board to acquire O'Fallon Polytechnic Institute from Washington University to serve as a center for practical education. About one hundred students enrolled in a variety of courses when it opened in the fall of 1868 under the new public sponsorship. Designed to supplement rather than supplant the basic educational program, it became a "real people's university," housing the public school library and the normal school in addition to its vocational classrooms. Harris also made rooms available to the Missouri Historical Society and other cultural groups, which he helped to organize in the community.

At the beginning of the educational process, Harris proposed the establishment of a public kindergarten to train small children in school skills before they started more formal classroom training. A German innovation to which many of St. Louis's immigrants had undoubtedly been exposed in their home country, there is some indication that the kindergarten may have existed in one or more of the private schools maintained by this group. Such an innovation took time for Harris to accomplish; three years elapsed between his initial suggestion and the opening of the first "public kindergarten" in the United States at Des Peres School in the fall of 1873. The Superintendent received help when Susan Elizabeth Blow, a member of a prominent St. Louis family who had studied the system in New York, volunteered her services providing the school board would make rooms available and give her a salaried assistant. Miss Blow had begun a private kindergarten in her home at Carondolet the previous spring and, for the most part, simply transferred it to new quarters. Aided by two unpaid apprentices in addition to the assistant, she enrolled sixty-eight pupils that first term. Within three years the program had proved so popular that the St. Louis schools operated thirty kindergartens throughout the city. Although private kindergartens became popular in other places, the public concept really did not develop extensively outside of St. Louis for another twenty years.

Another concern of Harris and other school leaders in towns with a large foreign-born population was the use of the public schools as a means of Americanizing immigrant children. Most important in this regard were the Germans. They constituted a large enough group that they could insist on the use of their own language, as well as English, in classroom instruction. With a German population of sixty thousand by the eve of the Civil War, the St. Louis Board of Education would have lost considerable support for the public schools had it not made concessions to this group in 1864. In the postwar era Harris justified the practice on the basis that the Germans paid their share of local taxes, but he increasingly steered instruction toward a more general use of English. Ordinarily not more than 20 per cent of classroom work was taught in the German language. In some rural areas where Germans made up the entire village population, however, less than an hour's instruction each day was devoted to English.

As Radical leaders and progressive educators sought to promote the various new educational concepts being developed in the postwar era, a major concern became that of sound teacher training. Too many Missouri teachers were "*keeping* school," according to an article in the *Journal of Education* for November, 1869. It took little preparation to "keep school," as the saying went, but skill and special training were needed to "teach school." "Let those be read out of the profession," urged the writer, "who have not prepared for the work and are not professional teachers."

To assist the average teacher, who barely met the meager standards for certification, in acquiring new educational ideas and techniques, Superintendent Parker pushed the concept of teachers' institutes. He pictured it for the legislators in glowing terms:

> The institute is a temporary training school for teachers. . . . It is the most effective means of vitalizing and popularizing the teachers' special work. At the session particular instruction is given in the various methods of teaching; of discipline; discussion of theories and their application; history of education, and such other subjects as tend to practical advancement; carefully excluding any mere displays in debate and harangues. The institute is a means of popular culture not only from the facts just stated, but also from the lectures which should be designed for that purpose.

The General Assembly, in its basic legislation of 1866, required the county superintendent to conduct an institute twice a year if he had enough teachers to make it worthwhile. Once established, attendance at this meeting became a routine expectation for each teacher in that county. By the close of 1867, Parker could report to the legislature that the program had been firmly established and well received. Approximately four thousand teachers had benefited from ninety institutes held throughout Missouri that year. Most lasted one week, although two or three days could suffice in areas where they were held more frequently. Most teachers welcomed these opportunities eagerly, and through resolutions of support, they endorsed them strongly. Local papers backed them with admonitions such as that in the *Sedalia Times.* "We would advise directors not to employ teachers who refuse to attend this Institute. No one can be fit to teach who is so lacking in the spirit of progress." The success at the county level encouraged Parker to establish a round of district institutes in the fall of 1867 as a means of promoting a broader sharing of ideas and providing more advanced instruction than the local meetings made possible.

All of this preparation merely served as a prelude to Parker's desire for a statewide system of normal schools to promote teacher education before certification. In the spring of 1866, he had reorganized the Missouri State Teacher's Association, which had been allowed to lapse during the war. The topics of teacher training and the dissemination of new ideas dominated the discussions at its annual meeting in late May. The delegates not only endorsed the institute program but they also appointed a special committee to petition the legislature for a normal school to serve needs of the rural areas. St. Louis had established such an institution within its public school system in 1857, but it primarily accommodated the local schools. That winter the General Assembly responded by appropriating funds for a normal department at the state university. It began operations the following fall with twenty-three students. Within two years its enrollment had grown to eighty-two, nearly double that of the rest of the university.

Not content with this accomplishment, Parker continued to work for a separate normal school system that would provide a teacher training institution in each congressional district. These schools would stand academically below the university, whose normal department could then offer more advanced instruction. Although the General Assembly was slow to act on the issue, several private normal schools came into being over the next few years in obvious anticipation that the state might eventually assume their control. The leaders of these institutions now joined Parker and other Missouri educators in pressing for legislative action, which ultimately came in March, 1870. The General Assembly divided the state into two normal districts (excluding St. Louis County) using the Missouri River as boundary. To establish and supervise schools in each area, it created a board of regents consisting of the state superintendent, the secretary of state, the attorney general, and two men from each district who would be appointed by the governor. According to the custom of that day, the board would "take bids" and locate the schools "in the counties offering the greatest inducements in buildings and lands."

The regents, meeting in December, 1870, originally selected Kirksville and Sedalia as the sites for Missouri's first two normal schools. Private institutions already in operation existed at both locations. The school at Kirksville had been started in 1867 by Joseph Baldwin, who had been connected with normal schools in Pennsylvania and Indiana. The one at Sedalia opened two years later under the guidance of George P. Beard, who had served as superintendent at Chillicothe and later taught in the St. Louis Normal School. Shortly thereafter the board changed complexion because of the election of new state officials elected the previous November and the resignation of Joseph Baldwin, who had been chosen to head the Kirksville operation (in reality the continuation of his private school on a public basis). Warrensburg and Johnson County had been challenging the Sedalia–Pettis County bid, but the matter had seemingly been settled by the old regents. Now, suddenly and without warning, the new board reversed its predecessor's decision and transferred the normal school for the southern district to Warrensburg. It also announced that Beard would head the new operation. Although Sedalians accused the board of foul play and political shenanigans, the decision stood; the Warrensburg Normal School began operations two weeks later. Its location at the far western edge of the state caused the citizens of southeastern Missouri to petition the legislature for a normal school in their area. The General Assembly agreed in March, 1873. Cape Girardeau outbid Ironton for the location of the new institution, which opened its doors in rented quarters that December.

In a measure of support for the new system, State Superintendent John Monteith recommended to county superintendents in 1872 that they certificate normal school graduates without examination. Six years later another state superintendent began issuing lifetime certificates to those who had completed the full normal school course of four years and temporary certificates to those who had attended two or three years. Yet the normal schools faced many of the same problems as the public school system as the reaction of the late 1870's set in. Although they weathered the storm, it was not always an easy task. Most importantly, however, they did fulfill quite well, in the years that followed, the purpose for which Parker and others had worked so hard to establish them.

The adjourned session of the Twenty-fifth General Assembly in 1870 not only marked the culmination of the struggle to establish a state normal school system, it also ended a five-year controversy over the future of the University of Missouri. The Columbia institution, while holding official state endorsement, had never received any revenues from the government.[1] It had suffered considerably during the war. By 1865, it was encumbered with a $20,000 debt, and its warrants were selling at a 40 per cent discount. To climax the distress, the president's home burned in November of that year with a complete loss and the destruction of many records.

The university's location proved a handicap in two regards. Columbia, located twenty-two miles from any railroad and twelve miles from the nearest river port, was isolated from major sources of transportation. Boone Countians proved that this drawback could be overcome by pushing to completion a spur line linking Columbia to the North Missouri Railroad at Centralia by the fall of 1867. The second problem and for the moment a more serious one, was political. Since Boone County was a stronghold of

1. See p. 82.

conservatism in the heart of "Little Dixie," many Radicals contended that it lacked the atmosphere essential to the education of the state's future leaders. They talked of reestablishing the university at Jefferson City, "where the State officers can at all times look after its interests," which meant political supervision of the faculty and curriculum. Although the 1865 constitution provided for the establishment of a state university with a science department, a normal school, and an agricultural college, the convention, by an overwhelming majority, rejected an attempt by the Boone County delegate to designate the Columbia institution as being it. A move in the legislature that same spring to give all university endowments and funds to an agricultural college, to be located elsewhere in the state with the help of federal land grants, failed by only the vote of the Speaker of the House.

The controversy continued over the next few years, while the university at Columbia struggled to maintain itself. In that time the school gained a number of important advocates including Governor Fletcher, who devoted several paragraphs of his 1867 annual message to its needs and stressed that it be made "worthy of our state and a source of usefulness and pride to our citizens." Most influential in aiding its cause, however, were James S. Rollins and Daniel Read. Rollins, though a Conservative, had served in Congress during the war and had acquired a record as a staunch Unionist. He had been instrumental in establishing the university, and Boone Countians sent him to the state legislature in 1866 to help advance their cause. He worked tirelessly to accomplish it over the next three years, bearing the brunt of the battle at Jefferson City. Because of his efforts, he is remembered as "the Father of the University of Missouri." Read became president of the institution in the winter of 1867. He was a respected educator who had lost a son to the Union cause in the fighting before Richmond, Virginia, and had come to Missouri from the University of Wisconsin at a critical time. He made a dramatic appearance before a joint session of the legislature early in 1867, emphasizing his loyalty to those principles for which his son had yielded his life and urging the revivification of the university to train the state's future leaders for useful service for those ideals. He presented a vigorous, straight-forward, and somewhat blunt appraisal of the institution's plight, especial-

ly as contrasted to more progressive states that had already acted
to set their universities on the "high road." Read's eloquence
converted many legislators who had been opposed, including
the sponsor of the 1865 resolution that would have stripped the
university of its endowments. Subsequently, the General Assembly appropriated $10,000 to rebuild the president's home and
repair other university buildings. Then, in unprecedented action, it set aside 1.75 per cent of the state's general revenues to be
used for the school's general operations.[2] That action tripled the
university's resources and made possible the establishment of the
normal department. It certainly indicated that the Columbia
institution had become, for all intents and purposes, "the state
university."

The only question that remained was where to locate the
agricultural college. To help underwrite this project, Congress
had allotted Missouri 330,000 acres of public land under the
Morrill Act of 1862. Designed to encourage the establishment of
state colleges for instruction in the agricultural and mechanical
arts, this measure provided each state that agreed to furnish such
training with 30,000 acres for each senator and representative
as of the 1860 apportionment. The state could choose tracts
within its boundaries of not less than 160 acres so long as public
lands remained available there. If a state no longer had sufficient
public domain, it could receive land scrip exchangeable for
tracts outside its boundaries for a limit of one million acres in
any one state. These lands could be held or sold by the state. If
it decided to sell, however, it was required to invest the monies
or land scrip it received in "safe stocks" yielding not less than
5 per cent.

Missouri's General Assembly had promptly accepted the Federal Government's benefice by joint resolution on March 17,
1863. Then the matter languished until March, 1866, when it
authorized the Governor to designate three agents to select lands
for this purpose. These men went to work promptly but found
that much of Missouri's better public land area had already been
taken by other states to the east, homestead claims, railroad land
grants, and other miscellaneous demands. Indeed, by June 30,

2. This money was to be paid only after 25 per cent of the state's general
revenues had been turned over to the Public School Fund.

1867, only 1,835,892 of Missouri's original 41,824,000 acres of public domain remained unclaimed. The state's agents consequently secured most of the agricultural college's land in the Ozark region near the southern border, where land values were relatively low. Although criticized by some for this action, these men did a good job, given the limited choice they had.

While the process of land selection progressed, so did the debate over where the college should be located. The 1865 constitution provided for the inclusion of an agricultural department within the state university, and the curators of the Columbia institution had promptly endorsed the idea of using the Morrill endowment to expand their school. Under the leadership of James S. Rollins and William F. Switzler, Boone Countians held a mass meeting in November, 1865, to pledge the necessary land for experimental farms and buildings. Switzler emphasized, through the editorial columns of his *Missouri Statesman* that, for the sake of efficiency and economy, all branches of higher learning in the state should be housed under one roof.

Others disagreed. Various communities countered the Boone County proposals with pledges of their own. Springfield, Jefferson City, and Kansas City particularly vied for the honor of having the agricultural college. Spearheading the opposition to the Columbia plan were the State Board of Agriculture and the State Horticultural Society, which served as the official voices of members of the agricultural community. Although dominated by Radicals who were naturally prejudiced against Boone County, both groups apparently feared that an agricultural college at Columbia would serve only as a minor appendage of the university with training in scientific agriculture held to a minimum. In other words, the university would get the Morrill endowment, which it badly needed, but the farmers of Missouri would receive little in return. Especially vocal in this regard were the Radicals with small farms in the Ozark area. They favored a policy of splitting the Morrill endowment among several small colleges conveniently located as service centers for various regions of the state. This policy, however, had the obvious disadvantage of slicing the melon too thin.

The Columbia proponents used the economy angle skillfully in honing their case. They secured an able ally in Norman J.

Colman, noted agricultural journalist, who was also active in Conservative politics and a member of the State Board of Agriculture. He and Rollins persuaded the state board to change its opinion in 1869. Gradually, Rollins adroitly picked up other important support, including editorial backing from the *Missouri Democrat* and several other Radical papers. Meanwhile, President Read worked closely with the state's educational leadership to create a progressive image for the university and secure broader support for its enlargement. After frustrating defeats in the 1868 and 1869 legislative sessions, the efforts of the Columbia group were finally successful in February, 1870, when the General Assembly voted to include the agricultural college at the university and give it three-fourths of the Morrill endowment. The remaining quarter of that largesse would go to support a separate school of mining and metallurgy in southeast Missouri. Rollins had agreed to this decision as a compromise with those from the mining areas who argued that technical schools should be located near the natural resources they would need. In the process he protected the university further by arranging that the new school would be a branch of the older institution and subject to the governance of its board of curators.

With Boone County promptly contributing its required $30,000 cash and 640 acres of land to support the agricultural college, that branch of the university opened its doors to students in the fall of 1870. The following year, the school of mining and metallurgy began operations at Rolla after a special committee of the university curators had taken bids from interested citizens at various locations. Both institutions were disappointments during their initial decade of existence. Although the university's curators appointed George C. Swallow, an energetic and dedicated geologist, to head the school of agriculture, it floundered for lack of money, as the curators had difficulty in disposing of the Morrill lands, and because of inadequate knowledge of how to effectively teach the necessary courses dealing with the technical aspects of farming. Swallow filled the curriculum with requirements in natural science and the liberal arts to such an extent that the State Board of Agriculture appointed a committee to investigate the lack of courses in technical agriculture. Its subsequent report only confirmed the fears of those who had distrusted the university situation from the beginning. Although no one disputed the need for a school of mines, given the importance of this industry to the state and the rapid advance in technology, it met many of the same problems as the agricultural college. Its leaders worked out a three-year degree in mining engineering but discovered few interested students. Consequently, they broadened the curriculum to include practical liberal arts and teacher preparation. They also established a preparatory school to make up for the lack of high schools in the area. All of these additions weakened the technical instruction. It was not until the 1880's that these problems were finally solved under new leadership. Then both schools slowly began the development that would make them leaders in their respective fields.

When viewed from the over-all perspective, Missouri made significant strides in the field of public education during the postwar years. For the most part, the Radicals at the 1865 constitutional convention and in the legislatures proved to be far-sighted. The wise leadership of such educators as Thomas A. Parker, Ira Divoll, William T. Harris, Joseph Baldwin, James D. Merwin, and Daniel Read helped enormously. Unfortunately, the return of the conservative Democrats to political power tended to put the rein to much that had been done. Although never strong enough to destroy the public school system, they frequently wielded enough influence to curtail support for it at both the local and state levels. Indifferent and careless administration of schools and school funds sometimes resulted. Those citizens seeking to boost public education often had to fight a rearguard action against destructive legislation at a time when they would rather have pushed for more progressive measures.

The Census of 1870 revealed that in addition to its public schools Missouri had thirty-seven private colleges and forty-five academies. The number of the academies had declined considerably over the preceding ten years, reflecting both the ravages of war and the trend toward public education. Still they represented the principal means of high school training outside St. Louis and a few of the larger towns. Generally, the private colleges operated academies in conjunction with them because of the paucity of public institutions from which to recruit and the need to maintain enough over-all enrollment to pay faculty salaries. The great majority were church related with enrollments largely drawn from their denominational constituencies or the surrounding area. They provided the traditional classical liberal arts curriculum, which nineteenth-century Americans considered essential to the pursuit of the various professions.

Most of these schools were struggling financially, however, with meager resources on which to draw. Many had received charters in the prewar era that exempted them from taxation because they were educational and charitable institutions. The new constitution stipulated that only government property and that used for public schools would receive such exemptions, which implied that charitable institutions and church property would be taxed. This was the interpretation of Charles D. Drake. It was accepted by the collector of the city of St. Louis, who imposed tax bills against the property of Washington University and the Home for the Friendless, both of whom had been granted tax exempt status under their charters. These institutions sought a court injunction. When the state supreme court upheld the assessment on the basis that a new governmental order had been established in postwar Missouri, they appealed to the United States Supreme Court. The financial repercussions severely threatened private education and charitable and religious institutions in the state. Consequently, they were relieved when the nation's Supreme Court reversed the Missouri decision on the grounds that the state had made the exemptions in contracts (charters) which could not be repealed unilaterally, whether by legislative enactment or a subsequent constitutional revision.

Washington University at St. Louis opened the state's first law school in 1867 and by the early 1870's had specialized programs for degrees in civil and mechanical engineering, chemistry, and mining and metallurgy. Missouri had six private medical colleges and three schools of theology, eight commercial schools, and three academies of art and music. Private day and boarding schools numbered 586, of which 62 were parochial and charity institutions. Missouri also maintained state schools for the deaf and dumb at Fulton and for the blind at St. Louis. In 1870, the institution at Fulton had an enrollment of nearly 100, while the one in St. Louis cared for 88 students. Both had been founded before the war, and Radical legislatures gave them generous appropriations. In addition St. Louis had a private school for the education of deaf children. From all sources, public and private, elementary and higher education received $4,340,805 in 1870. Of this, 75 per cent was obtained by taxation and from public school funds.

Most Missourians eagerly embraced the various cultural advantages that were available to them in the postwar era. The popularity of the teachers' institutes has already been noted. Many towns had established some type of subscription library by the early 1870's. That of California was typical with an initiation fee of two dollars and annual dues in the same amount. The county court made one of the vacant rooms in the courthouse available free of charge. Here a "lady librarian," hired for ten dollars a month during the winter, presided from three in the afternoon until ten at night. The collection consisted of books contributed by members and those "obtained by purchase as fast as funds allow." The library also made available all of the St. Louis daily newspapers and a number of journals, some of which had been donated. Missouri's two senators and the district's congressman had been made honorary members, in return for which they sent the library the *Congressional Globe* and other official publications. The reporter of one of the Jefferson City papers noted an obvious advantage offered by the library: "Here congregate the young men of town, who in former times were forced into billiard rooms because they had no other place to spend their time."

Another popular adjunct of public education that developed during this time was the lyceum circuit. A writer for the *Journal of Education* observed in December, 1868:

> So much is constantly done to cultivate the taste for sensuous displays, by the gorgeous spectacles which render our theaters perniciously attractive to the young, that we require a counteracting element that shall address itself, to the intellect with equal power of interest; and this we shall find in a course of lectures, given by

first class speakers, with the greatest possible variety of topic and style.

That winter the Public School Library Society of St. Louis was sponsoring its third annual course of lectures and had already engaged Josh Billings, the noted humorist; Paul Belloni Du-Chaillu, the African explorer; Henry Vincent, the English orator and political reformer; and the Reverend J. T. Hecker, the Roman Catholic writer and orator. Warrensburg, Sedalia, Kansas City, St. Joseph, Macon, Hannibal, and "several others of our growing young cities" had arranged for similar programs.

Although frowned upon by many clergy and others, such as the writer above, the theater and other popular entertainments attracted sizable audiences throughout the state. William F. West, Jr., in an extensive study of these diversions in rural Missouri during this period, counted 233 different troupes and individual artists traveling throughout the state at one time or another.[3] These groups included 16 companies performing legitimate theater—"popular comedies, farces, melodramas, and sentimental domestic dramas"—in more than thirty towns. They employed from 12 to 20 actors—who also maintained the costumes, changed the scenes, and performed other backstage duties —and traveled by wagon, stagecoach, steamboat, and rail. Not many towns had adequate stage facilities so that these hardy troupers frequently found themselves adjusting to a variety of makeshift conditions. St. Joseph had resident companies periodically in the late 1860's, which used an auditorium on the third floor of the Odd Fellows Hall that seated 500 to 600 on wooden benches. It also had two variety hall–saloons, which offered lighter entertainment with traveling artists on occasion. Amateur theatricals, both in English and German, were also popular there and in other towns. Of all the shows enjoyed by rural Missourians, none was more popular than the circuses that arrived each summer. Any number of them circulated through the state to enchant young and old alike.

3. William F. West, Jr., "The Legitimate Theatre in Rural Missouri from the Beginning of the Civil War through 1872," Ph.D. diss., University of Missouri, Columbia, 1964.

St. Louis, of course, had a variety of entertainments available on a regular basis because of its size and easy accessibility. Its five theaters grossed $272,462 in 1866, the Grand Opera House of Benedict DeBar leading the list. Although a Southern sympathizer, DeBar seems to have maintained a steady following throughout the war with his stock company, supplemented at times by visiting troupes and individual artists. His house featured primarily legitimate plays, while at George Deagle's Varieties Theater, musical comedy was introduced to St. Louis in 1867 with the performance of *The Black Crook*. Here those audiences who tired of Shakespeare and other more serious productions could find diversion in the loosely constructed plots that allowed the introduction of an endless variety of specialty numbers. By 1868, the Olympic Theater had taken the lead because of its inauguration of Saturday matinees, pantomime troupes, and a number of spectacular productions. In March of that year, it was offering a popular ballet while DeBar's featured an Offenbach opera. The Apollo presented dwarf actors—a departure from its usual German fare—and Wilson's Opera House provided its audiences with a burlesque of President Johnson's "Imp-each-ment" trial.

The Philharmonic Society continued its annual series of concerts, and other groups such as the Haydn Orchestra and the St. Louis Oratorio Society flourished briefly. In June, 1872, St. Louis played host to the eighteenth annual Saengerfest, a German-led festival of musical societies in the United States, which brought thousands of visitors to the city. A special hall with a seating capacity of fifteen thousand was built on Washington Avenue to accommodate the crowds for the various special events. These festivities got off to a good start with a long parade on the first day and speeches by Governor Brown and Senator Schurz. Businesses closed because a general holiday was proclaimed.

Banquets and balls at the Lindell or the Southern hotels—St. Louis's two leading hostelries—frequently entertained the members of the city's high society. These occasions were equally popular on a smaller scale among the ranks of the more common classes, as witness the various dances sponsored regularly by different labor and ethnic groups. Parades were a source of pleasure for everyone, and all kinds of organizations used them to add gaiety to the occasion when celebrating an anniversary or promoting a special project.

Sports enthusiasts, both participants and spectators, found plenty with which to amuse themselves. Cycling of both the three- and two-wheel variety became popular with both men and women. One newspaper reporter indicated his belief that the day was not far in the future when gentlemen of "moderate means and immoderate muscles" would use these machines for general transportation. The St. Louis Rink Association erected a building for ice skating, which could accommodate one thousand skaters and two thousand "watchers," in 1867. It was also used for a variety of other entertainments. The Laclede Association Track, among others, regularly held trotting and pacing races. In rural Missouri, any long and vacant strip of road might be the scene of an impromptu horse race on a Saturday or Sunday afternoon, and track competitions began to be advertised as a regular part of the attractions at many county fairs. For those who were thrilled by more elaborate spectacles, there was steamboat racing. The Missouri River's channel was not especially suited to this kind of competition, so one usually had to hie himself to the Mississippi to witness these extravaganzas. Such races could end in sudden death as an overly anxious captain "laid on the steam" to win the race. "With safety valve fastened down and furnace stuffed with pitch and tar, the order came for full speed ahead whether boilers burst or stayed intact." Explosions and other types of accidents became common occurrences under such circumstances and, occasionally, large numbers of people were killed. Although this sport had peaked in the 1850's, it reached an exciting climax in the famous 1870 race from New Orleans to St. Louis that the *Robert E. Lee* won by five and a half hours over the *Natchez*. Both boats were well-known favorites, so more than $1 million changed hands in this single contest—an indication of how popular gambling was in this era. It was a rare race of any kind in which wagers could not be found by those who wanted them.

The St. Louis Cock Pit on Chestnut Street still featured matches every evening in the late 1860's, but this sport was on the decline as its human counterpart became the local rage. Boxing was restricted by legislation in many of the Eastern states, so St. Louis became a principal center for what was then a rather grotesque sport. Bare knuckles were the order of the day. Following the rules of the London prize ring, boot spikes could be no longer than three-eighths of an inch and could not be used against a man when he was down. Aside from these mild restraints, they allowed nearly everything else, including all types of holds and techniques that are used in modern professional wrestling matches. Fighters thought nothing of using hot mustard on their knuckles or blowing a little red pepper into their opponent's eyes to add zest to the match.

Most fights took place in outdoor rings twenty-four feet square with a motley collection of enthusiasts urging on their favorite. Here, too, gambling was prevalent. The competions often served more as tests of endurance than the exhibitions of skill with which modern spectators are familiar. A round lasted until one fighter went down. At this time there was a thirty-second rest before the referee called "Time!" The two men were allowed eight seconds to toe the mark at center ring; if a fighter failed to do so, he lost the match. Since there was no limit on the number of rounds, these contests sometimes continued for hours. The local champion was a popular Irishman, Mike McCoole, who won his crown from Bill Davis in 1866 in a 34-round bout. Three years later the English champion Tom Allen arrived to challenge all comers. He and McCoole tangled on June 15, 1869, on one of the several Mississippi River islands used for this purpose. Allen had the upper hand until the local champion's supporters intervened with knives and pistols to force the referee to declare a foul in McCoole's favor. A rematch three years later went to Allen; but shortly after this fight, legislation was enacted to make boxing a felony in Missouri, because of public outrage at the sport's brutality and lack of organized control. The big money action now took place farther south while enthusiasts in the state had to be content with an occasional clandestine match between local amateurs.

Baseball emerged as America's "national pastime," during the decade after the Civil War, and Missourians were among those who enthusiastically received the new sport. The first known game in the state occurred at the St. Louis fairgrounds between the Cyclones and the Morning Stars on July 8, 1860. Baseball lapsed during the war, but shortly thereafter St. Louis had a traveling team known as the Empire Club. By the late 1860's several leagues had been formed, and town teams and college clubs were playing weekend games. Local newspapers gave an increasing amount of space to reports of contests in which scores as high as 47 to 42 and 56 to 29 were common. It was obviously a hitter's game. Supporters of the various nines followed their favorites to nearby towns to cheer them on to victory. One reporter noted that the "ladies kept up their courage during the trips with lively songs and winning smiles." Given the rough play, which marked baseball as well as other sports of this era, the girls no doubt needed plenty of spunk.

In a state still marked by considerable wilderness, hunting and fishing remained favorite pastimes. Rural Missourians loved to compete in shooting matches and would travel some distance to participate when one was announced for a given weekend. Prizes were sometimes cash but more frequently were turkeys or whisky. They also enjoyed making a contest out of almost any kind of community activity from barn raisings to corn huskings.

Fairs of all sorts became increasingly popular after having been curtailed during wartime. By 1870, about forty-four different counties and towns sponsored such events. Most of them occurred in late summer or early fall and provided an opportunity for both farmers and merchants to display their products. As already noted, trotting and racing frequently accompanied the proceedings. The St. Louis Agricultural and Mechanical Exposition, which had achieved considerable recognition before the war, resumed operations in 1866 and again proved highly successful. Within two years after it reopened, there were exhibits from all over the country. As many as ninety thousand visitors sometimes attended in a single day. By the mid-1870's it found an increasingly popular rival across the state in the Kansas City Industrial and Agricultural Exposition.

Missourians of the postwar decade were "joiners," attracted to a wide variety of organizations, old and new. The churches of the state were flourishing; the Census of 1870 revealed that number had more than doubled over the decade to stand at 3,229. They owned property valued at $9,709,358. The Methodists constituted the largest denomination, although divided into two major branches. Baptists and Presbyterians ranked next, and the Disciples of Christ, the Roman Catholics, and the Lutherans followed, in that order. Such interdenominational groups as the Missouri Sunday School Association also came into existence to promote the exchange of ideas and techniques, especially in the rural areas.

It was an era of protracted religious revivals that brought many adherents into the various denominational folds. The St. Louis Conference of the Methodist Episcopal Church, South, conducted one meeting at its campgrounds that lasted for over two weeks. A large tent, which stood at the center of the area, accommodated the preaching services. Smaller tents clustered around this, providing arrangements for the throngs of people who attended. Many enthusiasts came for only a few days and brought their own tents and cooking equipment. Approximately fifteen ministers led the meeting, which inspired more than one hundred professions of faith. The church's official historian, responding to the fervor of the occasion, reported: "The ministers seemed baptized with the spirit of the Master, and labored with unabated zeal for the conversion of sinners. Indeed, the whole Church seemed alive to her responsibilities and privileges, and on every side might be heard the voice of prayer and praise." Similar meetings on a smaller scale, but frequently for a more extended time, were a regular part of the life of nearly every Protestant church. Early in 1874 St. Louis had its first citywide interdenominational revival at which Parson Hammond was the featured speaker. In view of the dearth of adequate facilities to hold the crowds, the ministers apparently gave up their disdain of the theater long enough to hold the meetings at DeBar's Grand Opera House.

Fraternal organizations also enjoyed a considerable growth. Nearly every town with a population more than 600 persons had a lodge—in most cases either Masonic or Odd Fellow, sometimes both. The activity of most of these organizations had been drastically reduced during the war.[4] With the return of peace, their leadership took strong moves toward reconciliation and rehabilitation. The Missouri Grand Lodge, A.F. & A.M., gained

4. See p. 84.

steadily from a low of 175 lodges in 1865 (many of them inactive) and less than 10,000 members to 368 lodges and 18,443 members by October, 1870. In addition there had developed a Negro Masonic order in St. Louis before the war. It had spread to outstate Missouri in the postwar era, but no known statistics exist. The Missouri Grand Lodge, I.O.O.F., more than doubled its membership between the end of the war and 1870 as it grew from 4,052 members in 1866 to 8,897 by the end of the decade. Its women's auxilliary, the Rebekah Lodge, made its first appearance that same year. The Knights of Pythias also entered Missouri in 1870 and established chapters at St. Louis and Kansas City. A grand lodge was organized the following year.

Several organizations with exclusive membership based on national origins could also be found. The Irish in St. Louis had an active Fenian movement in the immediate postwar period and entertained James Stephens, the national commander, with a grand ball during his visit in October, 1866. Apparently some Fenian activity also existed in rural areas; reports are available of a meeting in Jefferson City that same year, at which Irish Republic bonds were sold at 6 per cent. The Germans had the Sons of Hermann, while Negroes enjoyed the Knights and Daughters of Tabor. B'nai B'rith lodges had made their appearance among the Jewish communities in St. Louis and Kansas City. Several other fraternal groups, unknown today, had flourishing memberships. In addition the Germans had their *Turnvereins*, originally physical culture clubs but more recently the center of family social activity. Both Kansas City and St. Louis had Y.M.C.A. and Y.W.C.A. groups.

The Grand Army of the Republic and other Union military associations were quite popular while the Radicals were in power only to go into eclipse with the return of the Democracy in the 1870's.[5] An even shorter-lived but important organization was the Missouri Southern Relief Association, established in the winter of 1866 to help "the suffering and indigent of the South." It sponsored a concert in St. Louis that April which was so "crushingly attended" that the affair had to be repeated. Various groups made donations, including the Colton Dental Association, which gave one day's receipts after advertising: "Let it be

5. See pp. 138, 237.

remembered that the teeth taken from the mouths in St. Louis today will furnish the means to place food in other mouths, to be eaten by other teeth, and also to clothe comfortably, worthy and needy women and children." In October the members of the woman's relief association held a great fair in St. Louis, which netted $130,000. As part of the proceedings they conducted a grand tournament in which the jousts of the chivalric days were reenacted. The "successful knight" received a prize and had the honor of choosing the queen of the ball that followed. This event, too, was so popular that the association held another a few weeks later. Similar affairs that took place elsewhere across the state, and by the end of the year nearly $150,000 had been collected and distributed. Having accomplished its purpose, the association dissolved soon afterwards.

There was a resurgence of organized union activity in the closing years of the war. Various professional groups also became established on a statewide basis. The Missouri State Teachers Association was reorganized during this period. Missouri's dentists formed a state association within a year of the war's end while medical doctors followed suit two years later with separate organizations of the state's allopaths and homeopaths. One of the most important of the professional groups, especially in helping to overcome the division within the state that was caused by the war, was the Editors' and Publishers' Association of Missouri, which was formed in 1867. It included both Radical and Conservative newspapermen in its membership and elected William F. Switzler, the highly respected editor of the Columbia *Missouri Statesman,* as its first president. It accomplished a number of benefits for the betterment of the press, including agreement for a set standard of printing rates to be used on a statewide basis. The annual gatherings came to be more social events than business meetings as the years went by. Following the 1869 convention in St. Louis, Switzler noted his agreement with a fellow editor, who had remarked: "Take it all in all, it was a big thing, a grand commingling of good drinkers, good thinkers, heavy feeders, a few blow hards, and a sprinkling of hard facts."

By 1870 Missouri had 279 newspapers with a circulation of 522,866. Of these publications 225 were weeklies, but 21 were dailies with 86,555 circulation. Led by the *Missouri Republican*

and the *Missouri Democrat* of St. Louis, whose very names be-
lied their political positions, the press, for all the congeniality of
its editors at annual meetings, was a highly partisan venture. In
the wake of the Radical split in the 1870 election, the *Democrat's*
owners had a disagreement over policy. Two of them, William
McKee and Daniel M. Houser, started the *Globe*. Early in 1875,
the latter bought out their original paper to give birth to the
St. Louis Globe-Democrat. At the other end of the state, Robert
T. Van Horn, prominent Radical civic leader and later a congressman, set the pace through Kansas City's *Western Journal of
Commerce*. With the resurgence of Democratic strength in that
area after the war, Conservatives organized the *Daily Kansas
City Times* in 1868 under the editorship of John Newman Ed-
wards, as rabid a Confederate partisan as ever lived. Also highly
influential within the constituency they served were the state's
two major German language papers: the *Westliche Post*, edited
by Emil Preetorius and Carl Schurz, which had a decided Republican bent; and Carl Daenzer's more conservative *Anzeiger des
Westens*, which usually followed the Democratic line. Joseph
Pulitzer, one of America's greatest journalists, received his start
as a cub reporter in 1868 at the *Post*.

Newspapers were the window to the outside world for most
of Missouri's citizens. There they found not only accounts of
political happenings with a heavy smattering of editorial opinion but also items concerning social gossip, advertisements of a
variety of services and goods, and stories of romance and nos-
talgia. The press promoted a multitude of good causes, both partisan and otherwise, and to peruse its pages gives one today an
interesting insight into the lives of those Missourians who walked
our streets a hundred years ago.

CHAPTER VIII

URBAN GROWTH AND ECONOMIC DEVELOPMENT

Missouri recovered from the devastation of the war in remarkable fashion in the late 1860's. From the outset of their campaign to secure political control of the state, the Radicals had combined the issues of emancipation and economic progress—free the slaves and Northern capital and population would flow into Missouri; maintain that deplorable institution, and progress would bypass the state, then economic stagnation and decay will result. Many a Radical was also an entrepreneur who saw unparalleled economic opportunity stretching before him. He also envisioned the votes of immigrants from the East as fuel for the Radical machine that would offset the old Southern conservative influence of prewar days.

Early in January, 1865, the editor of the St. Joseph *Morning Herald* exhorted:

> Missouri now lacks men. She has mines which await labor to develop. She has the finest agricultural breadth that the sun ever shone upon, only awaiting the ploughshare of the husbandman. . . . We want mechanics to improve our waterfalls. . . . A shrewd Yankee would compel every stream to strike a water wheel, and the hum of ten thousand spindles, and the merry shout of thousands of operatives would gladden, illumine, and make happy miles of the valley below. . . . Thus is Missouri's redemption to be made sure, and thus is she to be made the Empire State of the Mississippi Valley.

By late spring, as the war drew to its close, a flood of immigrants began to inundate the state. Land sales were booming in western Missouri where the Boonville public land office disposed of sixty-four thousand acres in the first six months of 1865, and a private agent at Independence reported $50,000 in sales during the first two weeks in July. The editor of the *Missouri Democrat* exulted: "If the rush of immigration to the State keeps on at the rate which is now witnessed for two or three seasons, the wild places of Missouri will soon blossom as the rose, and our population assume some fair proportion with the extent of our boundaries and agricultural resources."

This sudden influx of settlers did not occur accidentally. Responsible Missouri leaders and outsiders interested in the state's growth had been seriously planning for it since 1863. Large amounts of Missouri land, much of it good farming acreage, remained sparsely settled, especially in the western portion of the state. Men of both political parties realized early the desirability of attracting additional population to the state. It was estimated that Missouri's population had decreased by nearly one third because of the conditions during the war; many doubted that these people would return. Since the South was obviously losing, the state would have to depend on the East for capital and immigration. A westward movement was inevitable at war's end, and those who had a stake in Missouri's future prosperity determined to direct as many of these settlers to the state as possible.

Although Governor Gamble appointed an agent, whose expenses were underwritten by private businesses, to promote the state's interests in Europe during the closing years of the war, the legislature took no action at that time on his recommendation for a full-time immigration bureau. Meanwhile, private agencies of varying origins prepared and distributed promotional materials of different sorts listing Missouri's assets and urging would-be settlers to take advantage of them. One of the most efficient and effective promoters was George S. Harris, the land commissioner of the Hannibal and St. Joseph Railroad. Through newspapers, circulars, and traveling salesmen, he advertised the 500,000 acres available along his line as "one of the richest and healthiest agricultural and pastoral regions on this continent." Prospective buyers could have free transportation to search out potential homesites, an offer that many westward wanderers abused. Harris concentrated largely on immigrants from the East in his promotional campaigns, although he made some unsuccessful efforts to attract settlers from Canada. Two of his assistants worked as agents among the Welsh in 1864 and 1865 with some success, but Harris undertook no direct efforts on the European continent. He left that job to various emigration companies. By the end of the decade the railroad's land department, under Harris's efficient management, had disposed of more than 500,000 acres. Significantly, much of this land had been sold in relatively small tracts to actual settlers, and it has been estimated that the road directly or indirectly added approximately 100,000 people to Missouri's population.

A new legislature responded to Governor Fletcher's request for an official agency to promote the wonders of Missouri by creating the State Board of Immigration in February, 1865. The board was given an initial appropriation of $4,000 with authorization to seek additional funds from private businesses that might benefit from immigration. Soon after it was established, the organization sent agents to the Eastern states and to Europe to attract those who were interested in immigrating. It made a special effort to encourage German immigration by distributing promotional materials printed in that language. It also reached agreements with railroads and hotels to provide liberal discounts for those en route to Missouri locations. It further encouraged coordination within the state for local and private agencies engaged in the same type of work. As chairmen of the immigration board, Governor Fletcher took an active interest in its efforts and traveled extensively to promote the flow of settlers. He contacted numerous Eastern agencies, which channeled prospective immigrants to those areas with the most to offer. One such group was the Susquehanna Valley Emigrating Association of Oswego, New York, which boasted of southwestern Missouri: "The climate is the golden mean of the temperate zone. Its salubrity is proverbial. The elevation of the country above the ocean produces all the vitality of a more northern latitude, while none of the southern advantages are lost. Consumption and asthmatic complaints never originate here, and are often cured by the climate." With such a promising region luring him, who could resist the temptation to migrate?

In May, 1866, the commissioner of the General Land Office reported, in reply to a request from Congressman Henry T. Blow, that 247,249 acres of public land had passed into private hands in Missouri during the first four months of that year. Of this, 132,713 acres had been claimed under the Homestead Act, 25,238 acres bought for cash, 7,560 acres located with various kinds of warrants, and 81,738 acquired with scrip obtained through the land-grant college legislation. Blow, in forwarding this information to the *Missouri Democrat*, noted: "Nothing like the immense extent of these sales has occurred in any State in the Union excepting Minnesota, where something of the same spirit is manifested by the emigration." The statistics of the land office support his statement, and subsequent reports indicate that the trend continued until the end of the decade.

In his final message to the legislature in January, 1869, Governor Fletcher estimated that the population of Missouri had grown at least 50 per cent during the preceding four years, and he anticipated a bright future for the state. The official census shows Missouri's population in 1870 was 1,721,295—a gain of 539,283 or 45.6 per cent over 1860. When one considers the loss through wartime emigration, Fletcher was probably fairly accurate. St. Louis had an increase of 93.4 per cent from 1860 to 1870 and was the nation's fourth-largest city with and official count of 310,825 persons. Kansas City, with 32,254 inhabitants, ranked far behind in second place among Missouri's towns, followed by St. Joseph with 19,564 and Hannibal with 10,124.

Undoubtedly the St. Louis area retained many of the foreign immigrants who came to Missouri, because the 1870 census revealed that about half of the state's foreign-born population resided in St. Louis County. Missouri had witnessed a gain of 61,726 in this group during the decade, which marked a 38 per cent increase. A total of 222,267 persons of foreign birth lived in the state, more than half of whom were German. In St. Louis, during the closing years of the decade, the various national immigrant groups organized special societies to encourage their former countrymen to join them and to help them get settled once they arrived. One of those immigrants assisted by the *Deutsche-Gesselschaft* (German Emigration Society) was Joseph Pulitzer, who was given the post of warden of Arsenal (Quarantine) Island when he arrived in 1866 and then became secretary of this organization the following year.

Not all of the immigrants who came to St. Louis were as fortunate as young Pulitzer. Many of them crowded into the dingy tenement area north of Franklin Avenue. The men usually had no particular skill to offer, so they worked on one of the various construction projects around the city at an average daily wage of a dollar or even less. If they were lucky, their wives might find employment at equally low pay scales in one of the numerous factories that produced a variety of articles ranging from clothing to paper boxes.

St. Louis had all the problems of the rapidly growing city of this period. The coal smoke from the various industrial concerns combined with the brick and stone houses of its central district to give it "a somewhat Londonesque appearance." In the suburbs, on "the undulating lands west of Grand Avenue," there were pleasant homes as far as King's Highway and beyond. The only park in the entire city was Lafayette Park, on the near south side, until Henry Shaw donated part of his estate to create Tower Grove Park in 1867. Seven years later St. Louis purchased the 1,309 acres of Forest Park, which was then just beyond the city limits.

The city's leaders found themselves in a constant battle with the state legislature and the governor for greater control of their own affairs. Nearly every session of the General Assembly made some change in St. Louis's charter depending upon the political conditions of the moment. For instance, in 1866 the Radical legislators replaced the old unicameral common council with a bicameral board of aldermen and board of delegates elected from ten wards, in the hope of strengthening the party's control there. But that spring, because the test oath was not yet in effect, the Conservatives swept the city election, and the next session of the legislature promptly reversed the decision of its predecessor by reducing the council to a single body and gerrymandering a new twelve-ward setup in the Radicals' favor.

By longstanding arrangement, the governor appointed the St. Louis Police Board, which made the city's law enforcement agency completely independent of locally elected officials. Until 1867, the governor also assigned the posts of commissioners of the boards of health and water. After the cholera epidemic of 1866, the mayor was given the power to appoint these commissioners, but the legislators at Jefferson City consistently refused to yield their control over police affairs. As a result, the two authorities carried on a war of words—charges and counter-charges—concerning corruption and political meddling within the force. When the city council petitioned for an investigation in March, 1868, in the wake of the dismissal of several officers who were accused of collusion with gamblers, a joint committee of the legislature conducted hearings and then exonerated the police. This decision led, in turn, to an angry letter from Mayor James S. Thomas branding the legislators as being as corrupt as those whom they were investigating.

In an office of limited power, Mayor Thomas, an independent Radical elected in 1864 to fill a vacancy and then reelected in 1865 and 1867, was a dynamo of energy. He had planned to promote three main projects when he took office, and during his five-year tenure, he saw all of them on their way to completion. The first of these undertakings was the development of an adequate sewerage system. A haphazard arrangement had been allowed to develop during the rapid growth of St. Louis in the 1850's. Much of the city's sewage emptied directly into Mill Creek, an open stream. In summer it spread its obnoxious odors over the densely crowded population in an almost suffocating manner. As early as May, 1865, the mayor warned a moribund council of the need for precautions to repel a cholera epidemic such as was then raging in Europe. In addition to sewer improvement, he called for a general cleanup of the city's streets and alleys. This job had been neglected because of the inefficiency of the competitive bid arrangement by private companies and because of the general indifference of the citizenry in maintaining their own premises. The council finally ordered a crackdown in October, but cholera struck the following July with full force. The disease had probably been carried by an immigrant from New York, where it had hit some time before. Before the epidemic subsided two months later, more than 3,500 St. Louisans had died from its effects.

An alarmed Thomas urged the city council in early August to effect emergency measures to provide each district with a hospital and some type of volunteer committee to oversee its needs, but the aldermen balked for fear of panicking the people. As the epidemic spread, Thomas acted on his own to establish ward committees "to inquire into the condition of the infected neighborhoods, to use such remedies as necessity demands by supplying to the poor medical advice, having medicines made up for them, and using disinfectants." He provided for a morgue to care for the bodies of the poor and derelict prior to their transfer to Arsenal Island, and he could be observed constantly going about the city checking on drug stores, inspecting streets and alleys, and visiting cholera patients in the hospitals that he had helped set up. When the morgue burned and he had difficulty finding anyone to remove the bodies, the beleaguered mayor arranged to have prisoners from the city jail to do the job in remission of their fines and sentences. Thomas fell victim himself on the morning of August 19, "exhausted by the incessant work of the past four days during which he had only six hours of sleep." By then, however, his emergency program for the city's relief was operating smoothly. He and many other St. Louisans survived because of it.

Although cholera returned in 1867, its effects were much less severe because of the continued efforts of Mayor Thomas and his reorganized board of health to clean up the city. Aided by a general sewer tax, allowed under the 1867 charter, and bonds authorized by the legislature the following year, the city's sewerage system was gradually expanded to provide more adequate disposal for the densely crowded poorer sections, which had been particularly hard hit by the epidemic. Meanwhile, in late 1867, Thomas began the second of his projects, a new waterworks. This endeavor had also been inspired by the cholera epidemic and by frequent outbreaks of typhoid. Since the works built before the war had limited capacity, residents in the outlying areas of the city had to rely on wells for their water, many of which were contaminated.

The third item on Thomas's program got underway early in 1868 when the council passed legislation that provided for the condemning of sufficient land on which to build a wharf along the entire waterfront in the northern part of the city. The merchants and industries in the area, which represented an increasingly large and important segment of St. Louis business, had been forced heretofore to spend large sums for hauling merchandise and materials that were unloaded downtown. Nineteen blocks had been donated for the purpose by private owners, condemnation secured the rest, and an important business improvement went forward.

That same winter the mayor pushed through an ordinance which indirectly caused his political downfall. It provided for an investigation of the books of the various municipal departments, over which he had no appointive power and little real control. They disclosed "frauds positive and circumstantial" in the comptroller's office and resulted in the indictment of three current and former Radical officeholders. The Radicals purged the energetic and inquisitive mayor from their party, forcing him to run unsuccessfully for reelection in 1869 as the candidate of the Citizens' Reform League. In his valedictory address, Thomas urged a strengthening of the powers of the mayor. Two years later, his successor, Nathan Cole, helped push through a revision in the charter that not only expanded the mayor's control but also made important improvements in the fiscal operation of city government as well. This 1871 document remained the city's basic working agreement until St. Louis received a home rule charter five years later after the adoption of Missouri's new constitution in 1875.

If Jefferson City served as Missouri's political capital, St. Louis, standing at the confluence of the state's two great rivers, was certainly its economic focal point. The emblem of the steamboat dominated the city's great seal as a symbolic reminder of the river traffic that had long made it the dominant metropolis of the Mississippi Valley. But, by the 1860's, St. Louis was engaged in a bitter, continuing struggle for supremacy with its rapidly rising lakeside rival, Chicago. Chicago had tied its future to railroad extension during the previous decade, and this move had begun to pay off handsomely. While Missouri and St. Louis had not neglected this new means of transportation, the only railroad completed in the state prior to the Civil War was the Hannibal and St. Joseph, which proved detrimental to the interests of the river city. Although it received a $3 million loan from the state of Missouri, this road was built with mainly Eastern capital. Through its connections with the Burlington line, it provided a cutoff for Missouri River traffic across the northern part of the state and into Chicago. Residents and merchants of the upper Missouri Valley much preferred the certainty of rail traffic via Chicago to the frustrations and delays attendant upon the use of the river, which was plagued by frequent ice in winter and shallows at other times of the year. These same problems on the Mississippi caused many farmers along its upper reaches to ship their grain to New York via Chicago and the Great Lakes rather than by way of St. Louis and New Orleans, even though the river route allowed a savings of thirty cents per bushel of wheat.

Some dissatisfaction with the lake city did exist in that area, however, because of malpractices on the grain and livestock exchanges and the continuation of unduly high wartime railroad charges. St. Louis, determined to take advantage of the situation, opened its first grain elevator in the fall of 1865, and when this venture quickly proved its utility, plans for expansion promptly got underway. At the same time its commercial enterprises took steps to establish direct trade facilities with South America and Europe through New Orleans and to improve the Mississippi through the elimination of navigational hazards. Several conventions met at St. Louis during the late 1860's to work toward accomplishing this task. The need for federal aid quickly became evident, but progress toward attaining favorable congressional action moved slowly in this era of railroad expansion. While the representatives of the railroads grabbed the lion's share of land grants and subsidies, those interested in river improvement had to be content with the crumbs from the table. During the 1870's, there was some increase in appropriations as additional pressure built and the political complexion of Congress changed. An extensive program for bettering navigation on the Mississippi River from its source to its mouth was begun, but the work met numerous obstacles as the "Father of Waters" continued to defy control. Meanwhile, the railroads refused to cooperate in any way and drove resolutely toward an absolute mastery of the nation's transportation.

St. Louisans had also been agitating for some time to have their city declared a port of entry because the total duties paid on imported articles received there mounted rapidly after the war. Merchants and importers frequently encountered vexatious delays at New Orleans and New York, and the new status would greatly facilitate quick transit. To strengthen its case, the local Board of Trade made common cause with Chicago and Cincinnati. Their efforts were ultimately successful in late December,

1870; Congress passed the necessary legislation, although the new setup did not become fully operative until August, 1871.

Missouri had 810 miles of railroad track in operation by the eve of the Civil War. In addition to the Hannibal and St. Joseph, four other major lines and two minor ones had gotten underway before the financial difficulties of war caused construction to come to a grinding halt. None of the roads on which St. Louis pinned such high hopes had been completed even though the city and state governments had given generously of their resources, so they could begin operating. After ten years of building, with $2 million in initial state aid and an additional $1 million from the city and county of St. Louis, the Pacific Railroad, designed to link the state's two borders along the line of the Missouri River, extended only to Sedalia, 95 miles from its destination. The North Missouri Railroad, edging toward the Iowa border, had reached Macon early in 1859, where it provided a link with the Hannibal and St. Joseph. There construction halted until after the war. The St. Louis and Iron Mountain, stretching south from the metropolis into the mineral region, consisted of 86 miles of track to Pilot Knob, while the southwest branch of the Pacific, which was to extend from Pacific Junction on the main line of its parent through the Gasconade Valley to Springfield and beyond, had reached Rolla by the end of 1860. Efforts to persuade the Federal Government thereafter to extend it further on the ground of military necessity were unsuccessful.

All of these railroads had received subsidies of one kind or another, and by 1860, all had defaulted, except the Hannibal and St. Joseph. In most cases inexperienced and inefficient management caused high costs and resulted in poor construction and faulty equipment, which, in turn, increased the expenses of operation. All of the state's railroads suffered considerable damage as organized armies and guerrillas moved across Missouri between 1861 and 1864. It is difficult to ascertain the extent to which the Federal Government helped finance needed repairs during wartime, although it did undertake some.

Only the Pacific Railroad made any progress during that time. Seven additional miles of track from Sedalia to Dresden were laid in 1863 while the roadbed to Warrensburg was graded. Then it appealed once again to the General Assembly. In response, the state relinquished its first lien to the company in February, 1864, in the form of legislation enabling it to issue first mortgage bonds on the uncompleted portion of the road with the earnings of the entire route pledged to pay the principal and interest. When Sterling Price wreaked further havoc on the line during his raid that fall, the city of St. Louis came to the rescue with another $700,000 in bonds. It realized only too well the importance of this link to the western border as a competitor with the Hannibal and St. Joseph. At last, the final rail went down at two o'clock on the afternoon of September 20, 1865. The first passenger train left Kansas City the following morning at five and completed the run to St. Louis in exactly fourteen hours.

Meanwhile the North Missouri Railroad was stymied by its inability to dispose of a similar bond issue which the legislature had authorized at the same time it helped the Pacific. In agreeing to this arrangement, the General Assembly had stipulated that part of these monies be used for a branch line from Moberly to the western border, another move designed to curtail traffic over the Hannibal and St. Joseph. After numerous difficulties, a New York banking house representing European investors agreed to subscribe $6 million—the total amount allowable under state legislation. Construction resumed in July, 1866, and continued to advance at a steady pace, although the company again ran into problems with its bonds the following winter. After reorganization under a syndicate of St. Louis and Eastern capitalists headed by James B. Eads, the railroad made another appeal for relief to the General Assembly in January, 1868. This time the company sought release from the state's lien on the bonded indebtedness in return for a nominal cash payment. The directors of the railroad argued that such a program was necessary in order to have sufficient monies available to enable them to complete both the main line to the Iowa border and the branch to the west.

The General Assembly agreed to the request of the North Missouri's directors. In doing so, however, the legislature stipulated that the road must reach the Iowa border within nine months of the agreement and the western edge of Missouri within eighteen. It also required completion of a key bridge at St. Charles within three years of the date of the lien's release.

To assure their good faith, the directors would have to post bond with the state treasurer. Had the legislature declined the arrangement with the North Missouri, the government would have faced the unpleasant alternative of risking default by the company. As a result, the state would foreclose the road and then run it until a buyer could be found. Having already suffered through this process with several other lines, the legislators declined that route. But in settling for only $200,000 against a lien of more than $6 million with the balance passed on to Missouri's taxpayers for ultimate repayment, questions of probity naturally arise. This action was the first of a series of moves during the session that removed that state completely from the concerns of the railroad for a fraction of the various companies' debts.

John W. Million, who studied this general topic exhaustively,[1] indicated that the road did have sufficient earnings, for all its difficulties, to meet its interest to the state and other indebtedness in connection with its bonds. Whether the directors of the North Missouri employed the "boodle" (bribery) system at the legislature to secure their ends, as did the representatives of the Pacific Railroad, no proof exists. They did fulfill their commitments with regard to completion of the road. The main line reached Kirksville in mid-July and pushed on by late November to the Iowa border, where it linked with the St. Louis and Cedar Rapids Railroad. The following month the road's western spur met the Kansas City and Cameron Railroad just across the Missouri River from Kansas City. Meanwhile, work continued on the St. Charles bridge, which opened for traffic almost on schedule in May, 1871. In spite of the state's largesse, the North Missouri Railroad became insolvent that same year and was sold at auction to M. K. Jessup of New York. He, in turn, passed it on to the St. Louis, Kansas City, and Northern Railroad the following year. Ultimately, it became part of the Wabash system at the end of the decade.

The Pacific Railroad's failure to meet its debt payments also came before the General Assembly for resolution in the spring of 1868. The directors feared that the road would be foreclosed and sold to someone from outside the state, so they organized an

1. John W. Million, *State Aid to Railways in Missouri* (Chicago, 1896).

energetic lobby in the winter of 1868, whom they sent to Jefferson City with virtual carte blanche, to obtain release of the state's lien in their favor. The directors' minutes indicate that one member "expressed his disapprobation of the system of buying legislation & declared his unwillingness to adopt it But subsequently intimated that he might sanction an outlay of one hundred thousand dollars if it would secure what we desire." It took almost twice that amount to get the job done; but with "boodle" easing the consciences of key legislators, who would otherwise have proved reluctant, the General Assembly on March 31 released its lien to the road's directors on approximately $11 million in Pacific Railroad debts for a mere $5 million, payable in two installments within 180 days. This time the representatives from the railroad could not plead the necessity for the completion of the line, for it had been finished in 1865, although the directors pointed out that they would soon have to replace their entire track with standard gauge at considerable cost. The cost of this work was less than $400,000 and hardly justified the additional $6 million the legislators added to the taxpayers' burden.

In taking these actions, the General Assembly conveniently ignored, without any serious challenge, a provision of the 1865 constitution that forbade the legislature to release the state's lien on any road. Utterly dismayed by Missouri's reckless adventures with railroad financing in the 1850's and by its seeming inability to recover its investments at any time in the near future, a sizable majority of the members of the convention of 1865, in one of their more conservative moments, had moved to tighten the drawstrings on lending by state and local governments. The provision prohibited the use of Missouri's credit to assist "any person, association, or corporation"; nor could the state become a stockholder in any corporation or association except to secure payment for loans already extended. The constitution placed local governmental units under similar restrictions unless two-thirds of their voters gave approval. To provide for the orderly retirement of existing railroad debt, the convention had submitted a special ordinance requiring each road then under obligation to the state to establish a sinking fund with an independent fund commissioner in charge. Failure to meet this requirement could cause the railroad to be foreclosed and, subsequently, sold at public auction. The voters had approved this measure at the same time they ratified the constitution.

The four remaining railroads in which the state had invested were so hopelessly enmeshed in financial and other difficulties that the General Assembly, at its next session, had little choice but to pass legislation foreclosing Missouri's liens against the Southwest Pacific, the St. Louis and Iron Mountain, the Cairo and Fulton, and the Platte Country railroads. In doing so, the legislature authorized the Governor to appoint a board of three commissioners for each road to sell them at public auction. Should it be impossible to recover the full amount of the state's lien in this way, the commissioners could take title to the road for the state and then sell it privately, with the Governor's approval, under the best terms available. In each such case, the new owners must agree to a specific schedule for the completion of the line.

By the end of 1866, the commissioners had sold each of the four roads. The Southwest Pacific went for $1.3 million to John C. Frémont, who headed a syndicate of Eastern and Missouri capitalists of whom it was rumored that Governor Fletcher was one. The Governor had been actively advocating a change in management for this road for some time through speeches and letters in which he called it "the greatest enterprise of the age" because of its promise to ultimately furnish the desired rail link to California. Few were surprised to see his name among the incorporators for Frémont's parent company, the Atlantic and Pacific Railroad, when they were published in July, 1866. The same month Congress awarded the company 17 million acres in federal land grants, an action that touched off a flurry of speculative activity. Frémont and his associates entered into an agreement with the American Emigrant Aid and Homestead Company that September. The railroad would furnish half-fare transportation to the immigrants who wished to come to southwestern Missouri, and the homestead company would receive a 12 per cent commission on all of these sales. The new agents immediately began tapping the Scandanavian market with considerable success, but the railroad floundered in the face of mounting problems: strikes for higher wages, brittle English rails which "often broke while being put in place or with the passage of the first train," poor management generally. When the Frémont group defaulted on their first payment to the state in June, 1867, Governor Fletcher once again seized the road and turned it over temporarily to state management. In the whole process, twelve miles of new track had been added to the Southwest Pacific.

The people of southwest Missouri refused to be denied the transportation facilities that they needed. Speaking to a mass meeting at Springfield on July 17, Governor Fletcher called for another sale by the General Assembly under more liberal arrangements than those of the previous year. He predicted that the legislators would find no takers as long as they placed tight restrictions on the company's finances. When that body convened for its 1868 session, the speculators were lined up at the door seeking to share what promised to be a profitable pie. After considerable jockeying for position, the General Assembly agreed to dispose of the road and its assets in fee simple to a syndicate composed of various competing interests from St. Louis and the East that had shown a desire to take over the line. For services rendered in the process, Governor Fletcher and others received $3,000 in attorneys' fees.

Reconstituted as the South Pacific Railroad Company, the new group agreed to expend $500,000 within one year for the line's extension, with rails into Lebanon within two years and into Springfield within three and one-half. Target date for reaching the western border was June 10, 1872. To aid in financing this work, the legislature permitted the company to issue $7,250,000 in bonds and sell any of the lands already granted it. It could also extend the eastern end of its line from its present junction with the Pacific the remaining 37 miles into St. Louis, thereby relieving it of dependence upon that road. To assure compliance with all these provisions, the General Assembly required the South Pacific to post $1 million bond that could be forfeited. It also had to deposit with the state treasurer $1.5 million in either United States or Missouri bonds as a construction fund. These monies would be doled out in $100,000 blocks as needed, and $250,000 of the total would be retained for building beyond Springfield. Whatever the circumstances that surrounded this final disposition of the old Southwest Branch, work now moved rapidly forward. The line reached Springfield in May, 1870, and pushed on to the western border by the following October.

When the first train reached their city on May 1, the 5,555 citizens of Springfield held a giant celebration. They had worked hard over the past decade to secure this important link with the rest of the state. Time and time again their efforts had been thwarted. They believed their future prosperity depended on this connection, and in anticipation of the support the railroad would provide, the town and surrounding countryside had recovered remarkably from the devastations of war. Population had grown from 3,442 ten years earlier, and Greene County could now boast of ninety-six manufacturing establishments of some diversity and investment of nearly $245,000. The coming of the railroad would bring continued expansion. It particularly led to a tremendous boom in lead and zinc mining in the region just beyond Springfield, which benefited the whole area greatly. Meanwhile, the South Pacific pushed into Indian Territory after its purchase by the Atlantic and Pacific in October, 1870. The Atlantic and Pacific fell into receivership five years later, and in 1876, its Missouri trackage became a part of the St. Louis and San Francisco (Frisco) Railroad.

While the Southwest Pacific Railroad was going through its superficial boom under Frémont, Missouri's railroad commissioners disposed of two more lines to the same syndicate—the St. Louis and Iron Mountain and the Cairo and Fulton. That group bid low for the former and high for the latter and paid the state $900,000 for the package. The sale included the stipulation that the purchaser must extend the Iron Mountain line south from Pilot Knob, its current terminus, to link up with the Cairo and Fulton within three years and then complete it to a point opposite Columbus, Kentucky, on the Mississippi within five years. Although there were some protests that the board had received higher bids for the Iron Mountain, Governor Fletcher approved the sale on December 8, 1866.

Three days later the syndicate resold the roads for $1,275,000 to Thomas Allen of St. Louis, who had long been involved in Missouri railroad and banking circles. Charges of collusion had already been raised against the commissioners and the Governor for the initial sale; now they mushroomed. A legislative committee investigated not only Fletcher's connection here but also his involvement with the Southwest Pacific. While some wondered how the Governor could acquire a fortune of $100,000 and a house in his hometown of Hillsboro worth $40,000 on his $5,000 salary, the legislators found no concrete evidence of any wrongdoing. Nor has anything of this nature ever been proved against Fletcher.[2] While the legislature investigated, Atty. Gen. Robert F. Wingate acted by seeking an injunction against the sale. This action threatened to halt the construction that Allen had begun and was not received well by many of the people of southeastern Missiouri, who were as anxious to see the completion of "their" railroad as were their fellows in the southwest.

When the General Assembly reconvened the following January, 1868, Allen sought relief from the suit and confirmation of the title of his property. Suddenly, Governor Fletcher stepped in to muddy the water further by seizing the road, on the ground that the purchasers had defaulted on their agreement. After additional investigation, however, the General Assembly restored Allen's title on March 17, 1868, allowing him to consolidate the two roads and providing that the unpaid balance of $664,300 due the state be remitted to be applied to the completion of the road's construction. Following the pattern used for the Southwest Pacific, the state treasurer was to dole out this money at the rate of $15,000 for every mile of new track built. Allen had already made considerable progress beyond Pilot Knob and was proving himself one of the most able and efficient of Missouri's railroad entrepreneurs. By the middle of August, 1869, he had completed the St. Louis and Iron Mountain to Belmont, opposite Columbus, Kentucky, on the Mississippi. Three years later its tracks reached the Arkansas border, and by 1874, connections had been secured with Texas roads, which helped to bring much

2. Governor Fletcher filed $100,000 libel suits in St. Louis circuit court against the proprietors of the *Missouri Republican* and the *St. Louis Dispatch* in the spring of 1867. This action was taken because of their coverage of his handling of the disturbances in Lafayette County that winter (see p. 142) and his role in the St. Louis and Iron Mountain Railroad sale. Both suits were ultimately withdrawn.

of the trade of the southwest into St. Louis. The entire line passed into the control of the Missouri Pacific Railroad in 1881.

The remaining railroad in the quartette the state had acquired was the Missouri Valley, formerly the Platte Country. Designed to link Kansas City with St. Joseph and the Iowa border, many had considered this road essential to the initial program of bringing the trade of northwestern Missouri into St. Louis. This company had gone through a series of reorganizations involving entrepreneurs whose investments were mostly local and who also had railroad interests in northeastern Kansas. Now it too approached the 1868 legislature with alternative proposals: it would pay its indebtedness of $994,000, or it would complete its road. It could not do both. The General Assembly followed the established procedure and decided that it should be completed. To guarantee that the work would be finished, the legislature stipulated that the company pay into the state treasury $668,000 in equal amounts of Missouri and company bonds and $100,000 in stock certificates. The state would return $12,000 for every mile of completed track. When the line was finished to the Iowa border, the state would cancel the $100,000 of stock. The company barely met its deadline of December 1, 1869. In May, 1870, it consolidated with the St. Joseph and Council Bluffs Railroad to furnish a continuous trackage from Kansas City to a point opposite Omaha. Ultimately, the entire line was absorbed by the Chicago, Burlington and Quincy Railroad.

With all of the railroad activity occurring in the adjourned session of the Twenty-fourth General Assembly, there was an abundance of reports and charges concerning bribery and corruption at the capital during the final weeks. Considering the disposition of the Pacific Railroad's indebtedness, these accusations had obvious foundation. Although there is no direct evidence of the use of "boodle" in connection with the final arrangements with the other roads, it is logical to assume that the Pacific transaction set a pattern for the others that was followed to some extent. Just before adjournment, the legislators sought to put the rumors to rest by appointing a joint investigating committee to hold hearings on the matter. Obviously not anticipating really valuable results from these efforts, they instructed it to report back within twenty-four hours. One member of the group was Conservative Sen. John G. Woerner of St. Louis, whom the Pacific Railroad lobbyists listed as a valuable ally in their secret reports. After meeting through the afternoon and much of the evening of March 23, the committee, not too surprisingly, reassured their fellow legislators with the news that they had not obtained "one word of evidence" that any member of the General Assembly had "received or indicated a willingness to receive, directly or indirectly, a single dollar, or any valuable consideration as an inducement to support or oppose any railroad bill." Nor had any person "used or been authorized to use any money to secure the vote of any Senator or member of the House." As it turned out, most of those legislators on the Pacific Railroad's "good will" list did fail to benefit, for shortly thereafter some of the line's stockholders secured an injunction to thwart final payment of the promised "boodle." A shakeup of the railroad's management followed.

In the meantime, however, the 1868 legislature, having "exonerated" itself, passed into history. It had not only relinquished the claims Missouri had to her railroads, going back into the 1850's, but it also provided for their completion. The total railroad debt of the state stood at $31,735,840 in bonds and interest due on January 1, 1868. Only $6,131,496 was realized from the disposition of the various lines; $25,604,344 remained for Missouri's taxpayers to retire.[3] The roads that received such generous consideration from the General Assembly in 1868 had built only 914 miles of track, and very little had been constructed during the preceding two years. By the end of 1870, they had laid an additional 626 miles, and all of the lines had been finished to their original intended destinations. Missouri had secured 1,540 miles of railroad at a cost of $16,626 per mile.

John W. Million, in his thorough study of these intricate proceedings, concluded that the uncompleted roads could have been

3. Missouri's total state debt had been $36,094,908 in 1865. This figure included a war debt of $7,546,575. The Federal Government reimbursed $4,863,924.90 of the war debt in 1866 under wartime agreements concerning the expenses of the Missouri militia. By a variety of other means, including the sale of the railroads, Missouri had reduced its total indebtedness to $21,675,000 by January 1, 1869. This debt was not completely cleared until 1903.

finished without the legislature taking the action it did. This procedure, however, would probably have meant that Missouri itself would have had to undertake the work or wait until it could lure private capital at more favorable terms. Having gone through one series of foreclosures in which the state for a time actually ran two of the lines in question, most legislators had little desire to risk another such experience. For Missouri to have tried finishing the road itself would have added to the loss of bonds and interest even more costs at a time when its debt had already reached constitutional limits for such purposes. Finding new sources of private capital would take a great deal of time that could not be wasted, because the people were clamoring for completion of the roads, and the interest on the state's debt was mounting. The legislature acted in the most practical way it could to get the rail lines finished. Yet, it would seem that the railroad giveaway of 1868 could have been accomplished at a more beneficial price for the people of Missouri.

For all their involvement in stretching rails westward to reach all corners of the state and beyond, St. Louis businessmen also knew by war's end that they must bridge the Mississippi to tie Missouri more directly into the railroads on the eastern bank. Chicago, their great rival to the north, had been benefiting for a decade from the Rock Island Railroad's bridge at Davenport, Iowa, and would gain further when the Burlington completed its span over the Mississippi at Quincy, Illinois, in November, 1868. The St. Louis interests had to clear obstacles in Congress and both the Illinois and Missouri legislatures before surveys for a bridge there could finally be taken in March, 1867. Construction began that summer under the guidance of James B. Eads, the project's chief engineer. The same 1868 legislature that resolved the railroad burden agreed to allow the city of St. Louis to underwrite the bridge corporation's $5 million bond issue to raise the necessary capital if its voters approved, which they did. The work moved slowly with numerous engineering problems to be overcome and financial crises to be solved. The dogged persistence of Eads finally paid off when the bridge that bears his name was completed in the summer of 1874. St. Louisans celebrated the Fourth of July that year with its formal opening. A two-level structure, which could accommodate both rail and vehicular traffic, it was the first important bridge in the United States to use steel instead of wrought iron in truss construction.

The Eads Bridge, for all its magnificence, came too late for St. Louis to gain its trade position vis-à-vis Chicago. The United States Bureau of Statistics reported in 1878 that Chicago had received three and a half times as much grain as St. Louis, two and a half times as many cattle, four times as many hogs, five times as much butter, and six times as much lumber. Although St. Louis had become a major milling center, manufacturing six times as much flour as Chicago, the northern city still handled approximately 100,000 more barrels in shipment.

While still a long way from rivaling St. Louis, Kansas City was rising on the giant bend of the Missouri River at the other end of the state. It had grown rapidly during the 1850's because of its favorable position relative to trade and traffic into Kansas and the presence of forward-looking civic leaders. These men realized the importance of railroad connections for their town's future and set out early to surpass their up-river rivals—St. Joseph on the Missouri side and Atchison and Leavenworth in Kansas—and establish the crucial ties that would serve rail expansion to the west and southwest. As the Hannibal and St. Joseph reached completion in 1859, while the Pacific faltered in its westward drive, these men moved to connect Kansas City to the new line to the north. They negotiated a contract in 1860 with the Hannibal and St. Joseph whereby it would equip and operate trains between Cameron and Kansas City if a local group constructed the line. The town responded by voting $200,000 in bonds in exchange for stock in the proposed company. Across the river, Clay Countians followed suit with $150,000. Then came the war, and plans ground to a halt as guerrilla warfare wracked the area.

By war's end the Pacific was well on its way to completion with Kansas City as its western terminus. The town's business leaders, who remained remarkably intact as a group in spite of the turmoil of war, still viewed the connection to Cameron as important, however, especially since their rivals at Leavenworth had begun talking along similar lines. Led by Robert T. Van Horn, the editor of the *Western Journal of Commerce* and an increasingly important figure among the Radicals, they managed to interest James F. Joy, western agent for the Burlington

Railroad, in local real estate. His connections through that road with the Hannibal and St. Joseph ownership provided an important liaison at a critical moment. Like St. Louis, Kansas City needed a bridge to cross the Missouri River and make it possible for their proposed Cameron spur to come directly into the town. The Kansas Citians elected Van Horn, who had been serving in the state senate, to Congress in the fall of 1864 to obtain approval for the project. He worked closely with the Burlington lobby in Washington to push legislation authorizing the desired bridge and securing a land grant for the Missouri River, Fort Smith and Gulf Railroad, which he and his friends had recently chartered as a potential connection with the Southwest. After he had successfully completed these projects, the Kansas City entrepreneurs outmaneuvered their Leavenworth rivals. By 1867 construction of the Cameron spur had become largely a Burlington enterprise, which could tie that road into a southwestern link through Kansas City. As the "Hannibal bridge"—key to the whole scheme—slowly took shape, Kansas Citians eagerly looked forward to a bright future. Hopes became reality on July 3, 1869, as a gaily decorated train leading a two-mile procession made the first official trip over the newly opened span. More than four thousand trains crossed the bridge during the next eight months; the promotional efforts of Kansas City's business leaders had paid off handsomely.

The securing of good rail connections played a significant role in the initial development of Kansas City as a regional livestock center. Although some meatpacking had been done there before the war, few of these enterprises had survived the conflict. By war's end it appeared that St. Joseph would rapidly become prominent in this industry because of its existing rail tie to Chicago. It had become an important pork-processing center as early as the 1840's due to its key location on the trails leading west. High wartime prices in both the East and Colorado further stimulated both beef and pork production in the area. St. Joseph enjoyed an additional push in the spring of 1866 when angry Missouri farmers blocked the path of Texas cattle drovers, on their way to the Sedalia railhead on the Pacific, because of their fear that the longhorns carried Spanish fever, which could infect local cows. Most of the cattle were turned west into Kansas and

Missouri's major water and rail transportation systems in the
Reconstruction period.

headed toward St. Joseph from which they could transship into Chicago. Local entrepreneurs realized that this transfusion—25,000 head in 1866—could not be permanent unless they, too, bridged the Missouri and established rail connections to link with more convenient Kansas railheads that were beginning to develop. But the community spirit that stimulated the project in Kansas City was strangely lacking in St. Joseph, with the result that it did not secure its bridge until 1873. In the interim, Kansas City, with its connections to the Kansas Pacific Railroad edging westward across the prairie and its bridge giving it a tie to the Hannibal and St. Joseph on the north, had outdistanced its upriver rival.

One of the first major cattle buyers to realize Kansas City's value to the industry was Joseph G. McCoy, who was developing Abilene, Kansas, as a major railhead on the Kansas Pacific. When the Pacific Railroad refused to deal with him on shipping through to St. Louis, he turned to the Kansas City Cameron spur to carry his cattle into Chicago.[4] That foresighted entrepreneur, James F. Joy, joined forces with L. V. Morse, general superintendent of the Hannibal and St. Joseph, in 1870 to purchase a five-acre tract in Kansas City on which they constructed eleven cattle pens, fifteen unloading chutes, and a scale. These facilities quickly became inadequate as business boomed and as much as $3 million flowed annually into Kansas City banks from the livestock trade. By the spring of 1871 the forerunner of the Kansas City Union Stockyards had been organized. Its first year's receipts were 120,827 cattle (mostly Texas longhorns), 41,036 hogs, 4,527 sheep, and 809 horses and mules. The Chicago-based firm of Armour and Plankinton had opened Kansas City's first major meat packing house the year before and did such a good business that they were already expanding that summer with a new plant.

In addition to its fast-growing livestock-based industries, the

4. The Pacific and other railroads, in one of their more shortsighted moments, also refused to help St. Louis businessmen underwrite a union stockyards at this time, with the result that East St. Louis took the lead in establishing one in 1871. Only when it appeared that as a result much of the city's cattle market would be diverted across the river did those on the western bank of the river establish the St. Louis Union Stock Yards in 1874.

Kansas City area also had fourteen flour mills with a capital investment of $248,500, ready to begin processing the rolling wheat fields to the west. The decade ahead was to bring rapid expansion in both of these economic areas, as the saying made the rounds that Kansas City's prosperity rested on "bread and beef." The 1870 census also revealed a modest complex of metalware shops, brick plants, carriage shops, clothing factories, and other small industry to supplement the two major elements of the economy. The official population was 32,268—an eight-fold increase over ten years earlier—although A. Theodore Brown, who has written the most recent history of the city, claims this figure is too high and that 20,000 to 25,000 would be a more reasonable guess. Whatever the situation, Kansas City had begun the remarkable growth that was to make it the state's second metropolis.

Railroad development served as a key to the growth of St. Louis, Kansas City, St. Joseph, and Springfield. All four worked hard to secure their connections. Their efforts were emulated by scores of other communities and counties who believed that a tie to some rail line could mean prosperity or failure for their futures. Although the new constitution required a two-thirds vote before a locality could incur any bonded indebtedness against itself, this requisite was no obstacle in the postwar years. The "railroad mania" hit Missouri to such an extent that counties and cities subscribed $17,219,850 to in-state railways and another $1.1 million to lines outside the state between 1867 and 1872. The larger companies played off area against area in the race for subscriptions. But a great deal of the fever involved local schemes for feeder lines that would link a community to one or several of the already established main roads. The weekly newspapers contained numerous accounts of local railroad conventions designed to project this or that line through an immediate region, with bond issues, often in the hundreds of thousands of dollars, passing by overwhelming majorities. Nor is there any evidence of strong Conservative opposition, for in many of these elections the disfranchised, who frequently paid a large percentage of the taxes, were permitted to vote in an effort to promote county solidarity. A total of $3,080,000 was subscribed to railroads that, for a variety of reasons, were never built. Of this, the counties finally paid off $2,333,100. In the disillusioning 1870's, when hard times hit the country and the Granger movement spread over the Middle West, much defaulting occurred on these local railroad debts, and considerable litigation ensued. Most local governments eventually reached some kind of compromise with their bondholders, and a few continued to pay off their obligations well into the twentieth century.

Even though state and local governments in Missouri had paid a high price to secure an adequate rail network, the result had been a good one. Many towns and counties could attribute their growth and economic development directly to the coming of the railroad, as noted in the three outstate examples already given. The thirty-two counties most directly affected by railroad development in the 1860's accounted for 56 per cent of Missouri's total gain in population during the decade. Regionally, the Ozarks, which remained the last area to develop an extensive system of railroads, grew more slowly than the other sections of the state. Population density by 1870 is also revealing. The southern tier of counties had fewer than 5 persons per square mile, while the area between that region and the Missouri River contained an average of between 5 and 15. The rest of the state contained 15 to 40 inhabitants per square mile, and some counties along the Mississippi averaged as many as 40 to 75. In St. Louis County the density reached 125 persons.

By 1870, Missouri had 11,871 manufacturing establishments with a work force of 65,354. The figures indicate a threefold increase over ten years earlier. Capital investment had quadrupled to $80,257,244, with a total production of $206,213,429, a fivefold increase. As might be expected, approximately 75 per cent of this development centered in St. Louis County, where a wide variety of manufactories existed. That area's geographic position made it natural for an industrial complex to emerge there, and by 1870, the city of St. Louis stood third in the nation —led only by New York and Philadelphia—in the number and value of its manufacturing establishments.

Iron manufacturing had developed along both sides of the river before the war to an annual production exceeding $5 million. James B. Eads and others had taken advantage of this concentration to produce armored gunboats and other implements of combat. With the invention of the coking process and the discovery of bituminous coal in the region during the decade, there was an even heavier concentration of furnaces in southern St. Louis and adjacent Illinois to allow the industry to be near the source of supply. By 1870, total iron production in Missouri had attained a value of nearly $9 million on a capital investment of $6,130,000 with more than 2,300 workers employed, most of them around St. Louis. The county had 31 flour mills employing 684 hands and representing a capital investment of $3,850,-000. As it became known that wheat raised in certain Mississippi River counties possessed milling advantages over that grown farther east, St. Louis flour became increasingly popular throughout the nation. A large brewing industry developed in southern St. Louis, principally under the aegis of German capital. It absorbed the labor of 761 workers in approximately fifty establishments valued at $5 million. In 1873, the Anheuser Company was the first brewer to bottle beer for export on a large scale, and its business expanded accordingly. The manufacture of clothing occupied 3,900 workers in nearly 500 manufactories whose products were widely distributed throughout Missouri and the Mississippi Valley. A thriving furniture industry also developed a large rural market. At least nineteen industries in the St. Louis area claimed a capital investment in excess of $1 million each.

The county's industrial work force numbered 40,856 persons with an average annual wage of almost $600. Although unskilled labor was plentiful and worked cheaply, unions of the various craftsmen became quite active in the St. Louis area. The Workingmen's Union of Missouri, organized in 1864 to coordinate the efforts of the various craft unions, began publication of a weekly eight-page paper in the fall of 1866 to focus attention on the need for unity among laborers. It bore the name *Industrial Advocate* and proclaimed on its masthead: "Our aim is the Social Elevation and Mental Improvement of the Working Classes, by the Gradual Adoption of all Practical Measures of Labor Reform." The first issue carried meeting notices for the following: the Ship Carpenters and Calkers Protective Union, the Laborers and Helpers Protective and Benevolent Union, the St. Louis Stove and Hollow-Ware Moulders Union, Lodges No. 1 and

No. 4 of the Railroad Men's Protective Union, the Carpenters and Joiners Association, the Workingmen's Labor Union, the Journeymen Harness Makers Trade Society, the Journeymen Tobacconists Union, and the Eight Hour League. By the following week the list of notices had grown to twenty-six.

It is difficult to determine how many workers these associations reached or how effective they were on "bread and butter" issues over-all. An early editorial in the *Industrial Advocate* asserted: "It is the sheerest folly to suppose, for one moment, that the trades' unions of the present day are established as a means of conducting strikes, or that the more intelligent workmen favor the striking system, except as a means to be used, like war, only as a last resort, to effect objects that cannot be otherwise obtained." Apparently, the "last resort" frequently became necessary, however, for the columns of this paper contained news of numerous strikes by a variety of workers in St. Louis and outstate during the six and a half months for which copies are now available. Most were prompted by wage cuts or demands for higher pay by one group to keep it in line with another. The use of "scabs," including blacks, was not infrequent. The unions were seldom completely successful. Yet organizational activity continued with an abundance of meetings at some of which prominent national labor leaders appeared. Several local associations presented regular lectures covering a variety of topics on a weekly or biweekly basis for their members. They also sponsored such social activities as the Annual Workingmen's Ball and numerous picnics and other dances. To help their members cut food costs they organized the St. Louis Workingmen's Pioneer Cooperative Association in February, 1867. Established with an investment of $50,000 (2,000 shares at $25 each), it opened a grocery and provision store the following June, which proved an immediate success. Its books showed a net profit of $400 at the end of the first year's operation, which made possible a 7 per cent dividend to its 106 members.

Organized labor in Missouri, as elsewhere, attempted to use the political process to secure specific reforms of benefit to all workers. While it shunned creating a third party to accomplish this goal, it closely questioned various candidates, especially for

Congress and the legislature, as to their stands on matters that concerned it. As the 1866 elections approached, for instance, labor leaders from St. Louis took an active role in the Baltimore convention, which established the National Labor Union to serve as a forum for discussion of labor programs and means for the implementation of common goals. Four issues seemed paramount in the minds of Missouri's organized workers: public land for settlers only, the waste of the public domain by giveaways to railroads and other private interests, the unfair competition of convict labor, and the establishment of an eight-hour day for all working people.

The eight-hour day, particularly, became a burning issue. Agitation for a standard workday had gotten underway nationwide by the close of the war. Eight Hour Leagues sprang up in several industrial states. Their sponsors argued that such a program would eliminate competition between skilled and unskilled labor and at the same time increase productivity, raise wages, step up consumer demand, and create leisure for the workingman to enjoy a higher standard of living. Fifteen labor societies in St. Louis organized a local league in November, 1865, to push for action both in Congress and the General Assembly. They found a ready ally in Sen. B. Gratz Brown, who sought unsuccessfully to enact legislation limiting government workers to an eight-hour day. Late in March, 1866, they held a huge parade and rally to endorse Brown's proposal and promote the shorter working day for all laborers. "Eight hours for work, eight hours for rest, eight hours for recreation and mental improvement," proclaimed one banner. In an obvious appeal for press support, another urged: "We call on the press to advocate the system that will give us time to read their columns." A third warned aspiring politicians: "We will vote for no man who does not sustain the eight-hour law." Foreshadowing modern times was the argument that workers displaced by mechanization could find employment under a reduced-hour system.

The workingmen secured numerous endorsements in principle for their proposal by legislative candidates that fall. When the General Assembly passed an eight-hour law the following year, their hopes soared. They quickly discovered that it was a hollow

226

victory, however, because the new measure had so many loopholes that it was virtually unenforceable. Although it proclaimed
eight hours as the standard unit of a day's work, it permitted
longer hours if the arrangement were agreed upon by both management and labor. It further specifically exempted agricultural
workers and those employed by the month. When laborers of
St. Louis demonstrated for strict compliance with the law early
in May, 1867, they met with sharp rebuffs. Most manufacturers
were willing to go along if wages were cut accordingly. Since no
other nearby state had adopted such a law, their employers argued that it would work an unfair cost disadvantage. Appeals
to Mayor Thomas for an eight-hour day in city departments
brought the retort: "I require all persons under my control to
work as many hours as I do." A special committee reported that
fall to the National Labor Union concerning such legislation
passed by Missouri and five other states: "For all practical intents
and purposes they might as well have never been placed on the
statute books, and can only be described as frauds on the laboring
class." The union movement continued to struggle for recognition in Missouri as elsewhere but with little success.

   Although St. Louis was the industrial heart of Missouri, the
state's most important industry was mining, which, in its various
forms, could be found in every area. Wartime demands for lead
and iron had pushed production of those minerals to full capacity. Lead-mining operations centered in southeastern Missouri initially with limited expansion into the southwestern
corner of the state just before the Civil War. The ore was obtained from open cuts or shallow drafts. By means of the "dd
jigging" process, it was first crushed and then placed in a sieve
on the end of a long pole. This apparatus was balanced so that
several men could "jig" it up and down in water, the lead sinking
to the bottom and the residue remaining on top. The crude lead
was then smelted in reverberatory furnaces. Here six-man crews,
working in shifts, could usually process thirty-two pigs, each 72
pounds in weight, in 24 hours. An important advance came in
1869 with the introduction of a new diamond drill by the St.
Joseph Lead Company at its diggings at Bonne Terre. This instrument made it possible to go below the earth's surface and

work the deposits in a more sophisticated fashion and resulted in almost a sixfold increase in the company's production over the next five years.

The coming of the railroad in the 1870's brought boom times to an already expanding lead industry in southwestern Missouri. It also gave impetus to the exploitation of zinc, better known as "jack" or "blackjack" to the miners, who cursed it for the trouble it caused them in the extraction of lead. Its real value became recognized about 1870 just as large new quantities of both minerals were being discovered in the Joplin area. Speculators rushed to the region and overnight Joplin mushroomed from prairie grass to a tent city with all all its lusty rowdiness. By 1874, zinc production had reached 23,500 tons annually, with a value of more than $200,000. At the same time nearly 30,000 tons of lead were being extracted from Missouri soil.

Missouri was producing slightly more than 300,000 tons of iron ore a year by 1870. Forges and furnaces had early become established near the ore deposits in the Ozark hill region and greatly aided that region's economic development. These early enterprises were tightly run operations, much like plantations and the ironmaster, who owned the works, exerted a paternalistic sway over his employees and their families. Readily available timber on the nearby hills provided all the necessary materials for ironmaking, and narrow arable valleys close to the settlement furnished food for men and draft animals. By the early 1870's this paternalistic system began to break down under the impact of improved transportation and increased immigration, which provided a cheaper labor supply. Individual ownership yielded to corporate control, and company towns replaced the isolated plantation.

Gravel, sand, stone, and clay were abundant throughout Missouri. Yet, aside from the large-scale quarrying of limestone in St. Louis County, little mining in stone occurred prior to 1870. In St. Louis County, 433 men were engaged in 32 limestone quarries extracting $750,950 worth of the product annually. Their average annual wages of $675 were somewhat higher than that of $596 for the rest of the St. Louis area. Most of the stone they produced was used by the region's burgeoning construction industry. St. Louis County also had 85 brick yards to supply its building needs. Although they gave employment to 1,253 men, most of them, like their rural counterparts, were small, individually owned, hand-operated facilities. The Hydraulic Press Brick Company introduced the dry press process into the St. Louis area in the late 1860's and thereby gained a large proportion of the structural market.

Although Missouri had coal deposits underlying more than one-third of its area, commercial production did not get underway until the 1840's. It grew slowly during the prewar years, then mushroomed, through the discovery of new deposits, to exceed 1 million tons annually by the late 1860's. Until 1874, when Iowa passed it, Missouri was the leading coal producer among the trans-Mississippi states. Mining of bituminous coal centered primarily in two districts: the west central and the northeast. By the end of the Civil War the simpler methods of drifting and surface mining were replaced by slope and shaft methods where deposits were deep enough. Strip mining continued well into the twentieth century in many sections, however, especially where pockets of cannel coal were found. The face of Missouri is haunted by the familiar scars of these operations.

Mining operations were often precarious, working conditions dangerous, and the life of the miner exceedingly hard. It is not surprising that militant unionism first made its appearance among the coal miners at Gravois, several miles south of St. Louis, in the fall of 1863. A riotous strike over the hiring of nonunion labor ended in the temporary crushing of organizational efforts and the trial of the strike leaders. In Macon County, at the recently opened diggings near Bevier, approximately 250 miners of Welsh and English extraction, imported from Pennsylvania, struck because of a proposed wage cut and won because of the scarcity of labor. Once the war had ended, however, the owners moved quickly to squelch incipient unionism by calling in military forces, ostensibly to search for rebels. Bevier became a company town, and periodic attempts by the miners to improve their situation only met with stiff resistance backed by local police authority. One of those caught in this squeeze wrote the *Industrial Advocate* early in 1867: "Politicians may grow eloquent, armies may be raised to fight, and philanthropists may wail over 'the poor African,' but let me tell you, and through you the whole world, that never were the negroes in slavery, in so degraded and abject a condition as the miners here are, and for a long time have been."

Second to mining, milling dominated the outstate industry of Missouri. Twenty-two counties in 1870 reported a capital investment exceeding $50,000 each in this type of enterprise. Since the production of corn and wheat on Missouri's farms doubled during this period, both grist and flour mills sprang up in every area. But aside from the industrial operations and the mining interests previously mentioned, little industry existed elsewhere in the state except that which served the needs of an immediate vicinity.

Outstate Missouri remained predominantly rural. In analyzing the 1870 census, it becomes obvious that many of the new immigrants who were moving into the state after the war settled in the agricultural areas. The populations of thirty-six counties had increased more than 50 per cent over 1860. Another thirty-eight had experienced a growth rate of 25 to 50 per cent. By 1870 Missouri had a total farm acreage of 21,707,220, with 9,130,615 acres under cultivation. This area represented 148,328 farms averaging 146 acres, although the vast majority were still smaller than 100 acres. Implements and farm machinery had a value of $15,596,426—a marked improvement over the $9 million figure ten years earlier and an indication of the trend of agriculture toward mechanization to keep pace with the increasing need for food production in a nation with a growing urban population. In 1870, Missouri ranked seventh among the states in the value of its agricultural products with $103,035,759. More than four times as much corn was grown than the state's second most important crop, oats. The production of oats and wheat, however, had climbed noticeably, a response to demand and the availability of transportation. The farming of important prewar crops, tobacco and hemp, declined markedly in the 1860's with hemp disappearing altogether. The production of meat cattle doubled during the decade while that of hogs also rose significantly, another example of farming and processing facilities to satisfy a specifically developing need of the expanding population. Even though there was a trend toward mechanization in farming, the number of draft animals also increased as they were needed to accommodate agricultural growth generally. In the raising of mules, Missouri moved from seventh in 1860 to first in 1870. By the end of the century, the state would be the "mule capital of the world," and a writer for the *Kansas City Star* would suggest, tongue in cheek, that Missouri remove "the two uncouth and useless bears" from its great seal and replace them with "two mules rampant."

An active State Board of Agriculture, created by the Radicals in 1865, promoted the advantages of new techniques and machinery through its annual reports. But Missouri farmers benefited most particularly by the presence of Norman J. Colman. A truly remarkable and dedicated individual, he had arrived in the state in the mid-1850's to begin the development of experimental agriculture on a farm he purchased on Creve Coeur Lake in St. Louis County. Before long, he was publicizing the results in an agricultural paper, the *Valley Farmer*, later *Colman's Rural World*, and on the lecture platform. He promoted the growth of farmers' clubs, agricultural fairs, societies for specialized farming, and other means of bringing together in cooperative fashion those who tilled the soil. He served on the State Board of Agriculture for nearly fifty years and worked actively to see the agricultural college established at Columbia and then upgraded into a quality school. His decade of service in the General Assembly following the Civil War was also marked by a string of legislative proposals, not always successful, to benefit Missouri agriculture. A strong Conservative Democratic partisan, his party rewarded him with the lieutenant governorship in 1874. The following decade President Cleveland called him to Washington where his work as Commissioner of Agriculture led to the upgrading of the existing bureau into a separate executive department for which Colman, significantly enough, became the first secretary.

Those who farmed in postwar Missouri did not have an easy life, in spite of all the progress that was made. Like their counterparts everywhere, Missouri's farmers were caught in the vortex of industrialization and mechanization, which frequently confused them and by the 1870's left them swirling in a heavy sea of debt. They responded through the Grange and the People's party of 1874. Although there were scientific discoveries by Norman J. Colman and others, the Missouri farmer still had many natural problems to contend with, whether it be Texas cattle, which brought Spanish fever with them in the 1860's, or a plague of locusts, which decimated crops in 1875, or the ever-present cycle of drought followed by overabundant rain. Yet he, like most Missourians, at least until the Panic of 1873 struck in full force, seemed to have an unbounded optimism in his future and that of his state. This attitude was an important factor in the progress that Missouri enjoyed in all areas of the economy during the decade after the war.

CHAPTER IX

DIVISION WITHIN THE RADICAL RANKS

The Twenty-fourth General Assembly, which convened in January, 1867, quickly demonstrated its strong Radical bent. Although there was some disagreement within their ranks over the senatorial election of Charles D. Drake and the matter of amending the constitution to permit Negro suffrage, Radical leadership managed to patch up most differences behind the scenes and maintain a fairly united front. The Radical legislators refused to seat the newly elected representative and senator from Callaway County in support of the decision of the Secretary of State to discount the vote of the Ninth Congressional District. Three other Conservative house seats also went to Radical contestants. By special legislation the General Assembly abolished the county and probate courts of Adair County, whose debts had become unmanageable, and provided for a single judge to run its affairs. Governor Fletcher promptly appointed to the position D. S. Hooper, a strongly Radical partisan who had been lobbying for the measure. This arrangement continued until the General Assembly revoked it in 1870, while, in the interim, Hooper improved the county's finances through increased taxation. As noted elsewhere,[1] the Radicals also rewrote the St. Louis city charter to better enable their party to regain control of the local government there. Climaxing this exercise of power, they attacked several maverick members of the state's judiciary and ultimately convicted on impeachment charges Judge James C. Moodey of the St. Louis Circuit Court and Judge Walter King of the Fifth Judicial Circuit in northwest Missouri. Their enmity against both men went back to the 1865 controversies over the Ouster Ordinance and the test oath.

Since the Conservatives had been demoralized in many areas after their setback the previous fall and with the registry law of 1866 in full effect, the Radicals made significant gains in the

1. See p. 202.

municipal elections that spring. Although not totally enthusiastic about the reelection of Mayor James S. Thomas in St. Louis,
they united behind him to regain power on both the aldermanic
council and the board of education. They also triumphed at
Jefferson City, Sedalia, Boonville, Kansas City, Warrensburg,
and other outstate towns.

At the time of his departure for Washington to assume his
Senate seat, it appeared that Drake stood solidly entrenched in
power at home as "Mr. Radical" behind the facade of the test
oath and the registry law that he had created. His firm control
of the Radical caucus in the legislature had enabled him to sidetrack the efforts of the Planters House group, who had endorsed
B. Gratz Brown's proposals, to move the party along the path of
reconciliation. This success, coupled with the relative ease with
which he secured his election, strengthened his already existing
tendencies toward arrogance and inflexibility. Once at the nation's capital, Drake became embroiled in the quarrels between
the Radicals and the Johnson administration over the policy of
reconstruction. He neglected his political fences in Missouri and
failed to keep a fresh perspective of new issues that had begun
to attract some of his followers there. Other than his stand in
favor of Negro suffrage, which many Radicals found difficult
to accept, he seemingly remained intransigent to change. Since
Radicals and Conservatives outside the political sphere were
renewing associations, and Missourians were generally forgetting
old wartime animosities, Drake's insistence on standpattism behind "my constitution" simply became increasingly outdated.
Very slowly and imperceptibly his strength in outstate and, particularly parts of western Missouri, began to erode.

A strong anti-Drake minority had existed within the Radical
party since its inception. It centered around the more liberal
German element in St. Louis and eastern Missouri and looked
to Sen. B. Gratz Brown and Gov. Tom Fletcher for leadership.
Brown had never been extremely strong outside the St. Louis
area, and his ultraliberalism on "universal suffrage" for blacks,
women, and rebels, as well as on other issues, caused many hard-
core Radicals from rural areas to look at him askance. In announcing his decision to leave the Senate in June, 1866, Brown
had lashed out against the Drake constitution as too proscrip-

tive for the needs of a progressive Missouri. In a final act prior to his retirement, he had tried to persuade the party's leadership to pursue a more moderate course through the Planters House resolutions. The degree of support attained for these proposals at the meeting called by Brown should have been a warning to Drake that a considerable minority within the party favored change. Instead of altering his policies, however, he tried to defeat the challenge by directly attacking the Senator and others for trying to engineer what he called a "scheme of betrayal." Drake's success therein caused the liberal Brown to become politically inactive for two years, nursing ill health and a feeling of political frustration.

Governor Fletcher remains something of an enigma. A highly personable young executive at age forty and a popular speaker, he had proved himself a staunch friend of Missouri's blacks and counted many admirers and supporters among the liberal Germans. He had early and consistently advocated reconciliation. He seldom moved with the mainstream of his party, however, and many of the more ardent Radicals never forgave him for his opposition to the ratification of the constitution. The distribution of the spoils of office plagued Fletcher from the beginning of his administration as Radical partisans overran Jefferson City seeking public employment in the wake of victory and the enactment of the Ouster Ordinance. The Governor tended increasingly to leave patronage in the hands of his subordinates and department heads. Nepotism became a prominent feature in the statehouse, and rumors of corruption began to be circulated. Demands by Conservatives for investigations usually met with a whitewash by some Radical legislative committee or a complete refusal to even consider them. When he came under attack early in 1867 for his handling of the postelection outbreaks in Lafayette County and his questionable affiliation with the railroad, Fletcher retaliated with $100,000 libel suits against the *Missouri Republican* and the *St. Louis Dispatch*. Obviously feeling the pangs of harassment and frustration, he proclaimed to William M. Grosvenor, the editor of the *Missouri Democrat*, "I have sworn and never will recant that there is no office in the United States that I would accept under any circumstances. Never! Never! Once out of this I will be a Free Man and remain free." In answer to those who kept asking how he could live so well on his small gubernatorial salary, Fletcher informed Grosvenor that only considerable property holdings, against which he had to draw frequently, made it possible for him to bear the expenses connected with being Governor. Fletcher's refusal to challenge Drake in an active fight for Brown's Senate seat and his seeming desire to be done with political office made his "lame-duck" status during the last two years of his administration an increasing liability.

Sen. John B. Henderson, who might have filled the void left in the liberal leadership by Brown's retirement, pursued too independent a course in Washington to attract a large partisan following at home. An active Democrat in the prewar electoral battles, he had edged toward the Radical cause after his 1864 reelection only when it became politically expedient to do so. Although he gave nominal endorsement to the 1865 constitution, his outlook remained basically conservative. After the break between the Radicals and President Johnson, Henderson apparently continued to work independently with the White House in patronage arrangements. Nor did he seemingly participate in an overly active fashion in Radical party council in Missouri. In the spring of 1868 Senator Henderson was ousted from Radical party politics because of his convictions concerning the highly emotional issue of President Johnson's impeachment. Guided by a strong conscience, he joined the courageous phalanx of seven Republicans who voted against the President's conviction. This position made him anathema to Missouri's Radicals including the liberals. It ruined his chances for reelection, as the party cast around for someone to replace him in March, 1869.

As it turned out, that "someone" had arrived in St. Louis on April 16, 1867. Carl Schurz appeared at an opportune moment in the political life of Missouri's Radical party and rose rapidly during the next two years to provide the badly demoralized liberals with the kind of leader who could also communicate effectively with the dominant element within the party. Schurz was already a prominent figure on the national scene and within the councils of the larger Republican party when he moved to St. Louis to assume an editorial position with and part ownership of the *Westliche Post*, one of the largest German-language papers in the country. He had come to the United States fifteen years earlier as a German *émigré* in the wake of revolutions of 1848. Settling in Milwaukee, he assumed a prominent role among German Americans who were helping organize the fledgling Republican party. Equally adept at addressing audiences in English or German, he was a popular figure on the lecture circuit while he also produced a flow of editorials and letters. When war came, Schurz helped rally the Germans to the Union cause and then served briefly as President Lincoln's minister to Spain before returning to accept the brigadier generalcy of a troop of German volunteers. Thereafter he worked for the *Detroit Post* though continuing to lecture widely. It was while he was visiting Jefferson City and St. Louis on one such tour in March, 1867, that Emil Prectorius persuaded Schurz to join him at the *Westliche Post*.

With his background and national reputation, Schurz had little difficulty in gaining ready entry into Radical circles in Missouri. Preetorius introduced him into the German communities in and around St. Louis that summer. There he made a favorable impression both through personal contacts and public speaking. His editorial writing for the *Post* further enhanced this image. He assumed the post of district commander of the Missouri Department of the Grand Army of the Republic when it reorganized in late May. As such, in September he had the honor of welcoming to St. Louis Gen. Phil Sheridan, one of the "darlings" of Radicalism because of his stern military rule in Louisiana. The two men rode from the railroad station to the Southern Hotel amid a stirring torchlight procession of 4,200 veterans. A balcony appearance gave Schurz the opportunity to welcome the Radicals' hero with a stirring address praising his zealous course in Southern reconstruction, while the partisan throng below cheered lustily. The *Westliche Post* later printed the speech as a pamphlet, which was distributed widely. By the time Schurz went to Germany for a Christmas holiday with his family, he had strongly ingratiated himself with the German and other liberal elements among Missouri Radicals. It remained for him, upon his return, to move into a position where he could effectively challenge the more reactionary elements of the party on their home ground in the legislature. His prospects here were enhanced when the state's Radicals elected him in February, 1868, as a delegate-at-large to the Republican national convention that was to be held at Chicago in May. Out of deference to his national prestige, the other members of the delegation asked Schurz to serve as the group's chairman, which he readily agreed to do. Further recognition came his way when the Republican national committee designated him as the temporary chairman of the Chicago convention, which meant that he would deliver the keynote address. This honor did not go unnoticed in Missouri.

Since 1868 was a presidential election year, as well as the time for selection of a new set of state officers, the political fires had begun burning early in both parties' camps in Missouri. The Conservative Union party had virtually collapsed as an effective organization following its disastrous 1866 defeat. Its leaders scrambled after the federal patronage crumbs the Johnson administration had to offer, but increasingly they found their ambitions in this direction hampered by a Republican Senate in which Drake and Henderson could exercise senatorial privilege to block any nomination that displeased them. By February, 1867, a few leaders had begun to revitalize the slumbering Democratic party of Missouri. Frank Blair stood among them as he sought to consolidate a major position for himself within the developing Democratic circle. Blair excoriated his former ally James S. Rollins for deemphasizing partisanship in the General Assembly: "Instead of placating the damned Radicals, to get their support for your pet measures in the legislature, you should be giving them hell from every stump in the state. . . . You are wasting your ammunition on small game. Don't let your good nature or your interests in the Ag College, or any other University matter deter you from doing your plain duty at this time." Although many Conservatives of Whig origin, such as Rollins, showed little initial enthusiasm for coalescing the opposition, under a party label that had been a curse to them in prewar years, it became increasingly obvious that a rejuvenated Democracy offered the best hope for success against the triumphant Radicals.

In mid-March, the Missouri Supreme Court rejected Blair's challenge to the test oath for voting and also upheld that requirement for officeholding.[2] Blair immediately filed notice of appeal to the United States Supreme Court, which had recently handed down its decision in the Cummings case, hoping for a reversal before the 1868 election. If this could be secured, it would greatly enhance the anti-Radical chances in that contest.

As political activity among the opposition continued to build during the summer and fall of 1867, it found its manifestations increasingly within the circle of the Democratic party. The circulation of the *St. Louis Times*, a militant Democratic paper that had begun publication the previous year, increased considerably, indicating a resurgence of interest among the rank and file. By mid-October, the party had been reorganized under the banner of the State Democratic Association of Missouri with a call from a new executive committee to all "Democratic voters of Missouri" to organize at the grass roots in preparation for the 1868 campaign. In a special election the following month to fill a congressional vacancy caused by the unexpected death of Conservative Thomas E. Noell of the Third District, the Democrats sent Dr. James R. McCormick, a popular state senator from Arcadia, to Washington by a slim margin over his Radical opponent. The *Missouri Democrat* urged Secretary of State Rodman to check the returns for possible fraud, which could overturn the results. In view of the controversy over his handling of the last election, Rodman first sought an opinion from Attorney General Wingate concerning the constitutional powers of the secretary of state in such matters. Wingate advised him that he had no authority other than accepting and certifying the voting records presented to him by the county clerks, and Rodman therefore offered no challenge to McCormick's certification.

Democratic victories elsewhere in off-year elections that fall further encouraged the local Conservatives to take advantage of associating with the national party as the best hope for overthrowing Radical rule. In congratulating the New York Democracy for its recent triumph, the Missouri State Democratic Committee bewailed that their own organization had been "downtrodden and oppressed for a period of six years, hunted and hounded like wild beasts and [were] still bound to the iron

2. See p. 136.

hoofs of Radicalism by every species of test oaths and unconstitutional enactments that the brain of man could conceive and ultra Radical legislatures pass to deprive honest free-born men from the exercise of their rights." They were determined to overcome these adversities, however, and were encouraged by the success of their fellows elsewhere. By late February, 1868, Missouri Democrats had organized in nearly seventy counties, with Conservatives agreeing with one veteran leader that "names are nothing, principles are everything." This effort began to show results in the spring elections when the party was victorious in Kansas City, St. Joseph, Mexico, and other outstate towns and elected to office six of eleven aldermanic candidates, a street railway commissioner, and a majority of the school board in St. Louis.

In view of this Democratic resurgence, the Radical majority in the General Assembly moved to strengthen the registry law that spring. Effectively throttling all opposition from the hopelessly outnumbered Conservatives and Democrats, they pushed the new measure through select committees in both branches of the legislature to ensure for themselves a virtual stranglehold over the electoral process that fall. The purpose of the new act was to render ineffective a major loophole of the 1866 law: the popular election of county supervisors of registration. Fearful of what this stipulation might lead to in counties that supported the Conservative party under normal circumstances, the Radicals now provided a check through provision for thirty-four superintendents of registration—one for each senatorial district—appointed by the governor. These men would exercise general management over the registration process in the counties within their respective areas through the appointment of three-man registry boards to assist each local supervisor. These new bodies had the authority to appoint all election judges, a power hitherto reserved to the county courts. They also served, with the county supervisor, as a review panel to hear protests arising out of local registration. In this capacity, they possessed virtually unlimited powers in making up the final lists of voters. To prevent possible obstruction of these boards' activities through the normal channels of the circuit courts, the new law specifically forbade those judicial bodies to issue writs of mandamus or to compel the registrars in any other way to add or remove a name from their list of qualified voters.

The Missouri Radicals sought to capitalize on the impeachment of President Johnson that winter as an opportunity to stir up the masses while also gaining complete control of federal patronage in the state. The Grand Vice-Commander of the Grand Army of the Republic, John S. Cavender of Missouri, offered fifty thousand of the state's veterans "to carry out the action of Congress" against the President in the event it proved necessary. The editor of the *Missouri Republican* mocked this announcement but professed his dilemma as to whether the country should treat the whole affair as the ludicrous and absurd gesture of a few comic-opera generals or prepare for bloody revolution. The Missouri G.A.R., however, was deadly serious; a meeting of representatives from the various local posts unanimously adopted resolutions pledging their unconditional support to Congress should an open breach develop with the President. Congressman Joseph W. McClurg, who was already angling for the Radicals' gubernatorial nomination that summer, wrote a St. Louis party leader: "Your views as to the removal of officials in case impeachment succeeds (and it will) are correct, and I think every radical representative here will work, when proper time comes, to carry them out." But the Missouri Radicals had not counted on "betrayal" from one of their own. In spite of warnings of political retribution from his House counterparts, Senator Henderson voted his conscience when the crisis came in May. Because of his negative vote, the President escaped conviction and was able to complete his term.

In the wake of their harmonious national convention at Chicago, which had nominated Gen. Ulysses S. Grant for the Presidency, seven hundred of Missouri's Radicals gathered at Jefferson City in the sweltering heat of mid-July to nominate their state-wide candidates and draw up a platform. Would-be nominees had been maneuvering for the various spots on the ticket all winter in anticipation of another victorious sweep. Radical editors had met twice in St. Louis during May to better coordinate their propaganda efforts. According to the *Missouri Democrat*, they had a "full and frank" discussion on how best to sell the party's message to the electorate, and they came away determined to fight for their principles of "loyalty and progress." To help assure the veterans' vote and indirectly drum up enthusiasm for their own man, McClurg's managers organized a "soldiers' convention" for the day prior to the big event. It paid off nicely as Congressman McClurg responded to his party's call to head its ticket. The Radicals' choice for governor had seen service as a colonel of the militia during the war and had also been a member of the wartime state convention. Although trained in the law, he had spent most of his life at Linn Creek in southwestern Missouri as a merchant and trader. He had been elected to Congress in 1862 and had been a generally competent Radical legislator during the preceding six years. For lieutenant governor the Radicals selected Edwin O. Stanard, prominent St. Louis merchant who had liberal leanings. Virtually ignoring Governor Fletcher and his subordinates, the convention nominated only one incumbent, Secretary of State Francis Rodman. According to rumors "Count Rodman"—as some Democrats called him because of his adeptness at handling ballots—won support because of his threat to reveal the "real means" by which the constitution had been ratified. The others on the slate were chosen to assure even geographic distribution and secure the greatest possible party unity.

Although the convention's managers were primarily from the Drake wing of the party, they had done a good job behind the scenes to ensure harmony in both candidate selection and the adoption of the platform. The Radicals reaffirmed their endorsement of the Negro suffrage amendment, which their legislators had placed on the November ballot. This issue would be the most controversial of the campaign. They justified the continued disfranchisement of Southern sympathizers as the only means of protecting the "loyal" citizenry from abuse and depredation. This plank of the platform was worded, "We stand ready to restore every political privilege at the earliest moment consistent with state and national safety," thus consigning this issue to a vague future. Significantly, as the convention was about to adjourn, it called upon Carl Schurz to deliver the final address to send the hosts into battle.

The Democrats meanwhile had met in May at St. Louis to consolidate their organization and select delegates to their national convention at New York. There they worked hard to secure the presidential nomination for an eager Frank Blair, who had been making plans to seize the prize for over a year. The outspoken Missourian had to be content with second place on the national Democratic ticket that fall, however, as the party turned to former Gov. Horatio Seymour of New York for its standard bearer. Republican orators had little difficulty in painting Seymour in "Copperhead" hues because of his anticonscription activities during the war. As the party's vice-presidential nominee, Blair was equally controversial because of a preconvention letter in which he seemed to advocate usurpation of power by the President by calling upon the next Chief Executive to ignore the existing Radical legislation for the reconstruction of the South and unilaterally promote the restoration of Conservative rule there.

To offset the unfavorable image on which the Republicans had begun to capitalize, the Missouri Democracy sought to keep off their ticket anyone "who was not thoroughly identified with the Government during the rebellion." When they reconvened in August to nominate candidates for the statewide elections and to draft a platform, they chose John S. Phelps of Springfield as their gubernatorial nominee. A native of Connecticut, he had moved to southwestern Missouri as a young lawyer in the 1830's. The people there had sent him to Congress for nine straight terms beginning in 1845. He retired in 1863 to accept appointment from President Lincoln as Union military governor of Arkansas, where he performed well under trying circumstances. With a strong personal following in heavily Radical southwestern Missouri and an irreproachable Union record, Phelps seemed an ideal candidate. Second place on the ticket went to the popular agriculturalist Norman J. Colman, while the Democrats countered Rodman with another German, Mayor Bernard Poepping of Carondolet for secretary of state. In their subsequent district conventions seven of nine congressional candidates the Democrats nominated had active Union war records. They also carefully screened their nominees for the General Assembly in an earnest effort to avoid the "Copperhead" image at the local level. In their platform, they denounced Negro suffrage, called for the return of the ballot to all free whites, and scored the

Radicals for their arbitrary registration processes. The convention appointed a committee to devise some workable plan of opposition to the registry system.

In spite of their concern over the effects of the registry act or perhaps because of their fear that the franchise might be extended to blacks that fall, Democratic orators joined their Radical counterparts in crisscrossing the state to carry their message to the people. As rally followed rally it seemed that few Missourians had any interest in anything but politics. One prominent St. Louis businessman wrote a friend that there existed an "almost total stagnation in the movement of real estate, and general prostration in business," with little hope for improvement until after the election. He reported the canvass being waged "with unexampled spirit, almost to the neglect of general business." William B. Napton, former Missouri Supreme Court judge, noted in his diary that every night of the week there was a torchlight procession through the streets of St. Louis by one group or another. In amused fashion he commented:

> It would seem that men are after all but "children of a larger growth." Hundreds and thousands of dollars are expended on these fantastic shows—the members of each club being attired in some showy garb of bright colors, sparkling with tinsel, and looking for all the world like a parade on the stage in some spectacular play. Of course they have music and a crowd of urchins and loafers on all sides cheering them with their huzzas. It must be supposed by the knowing ones that these things make votes, or they would not go to such expense—and if they do, we see "with how much wisdom the world is governed."

Beyond the hoopla, Missourians concerned themselves with one central issue as speech followed speech and editorials piled up in the state's press. The Democrats attacked the Negro suffrage amendment, the heart of the Radicals campaign, with every racist argument at their command. They thundered that to give the black the vote was but the first step in a Radical program to promote complete equality of the races in social as well as political terms. The *Bethany Press* in northwestern Missouri put it bluntly: "Then it is with you, people of Missouri, whether you yet maintain your pride of race, or whether you will degrade yourself to the status of the negro, by voting for this infernal measure. Again we ask, will you do it? Let your voices be heard in thunder tones in opposition to this thrice damned proposition of your own degradation." *The Peoples' Tribune* at Jefferson City reminded its readers that Radicals had elected a black lieutenant governor in Louisiana and black legislators throughout the South with the strong implication that they had this move in mind for Missouri next. In their more rational moments, the Democratic press simply argued that it was too early to commit the ballot to a group that had been released from slavery less than four years earlier. As for the arguments that blacks paid taxes and had fought for the Union, Conservatives countered that women also fit the first category while foreigners and minors could be placed in the second, so why not lower the barriers to everyone. Of course, the amendment's opponents acquired a great deal of support when they reminded their adherents that large numbers of whites still remained outside the circle of political privilege because of Radical manipulations. Why should blacks have the rights that were denied to these citizens?

The Radicals countered with arguments in both a moral and a practical vein. Suffrage would complete the work that emancipation had begun in 1865 and assure the black those full rights of citizenship that were rightfully his because he was free. The editor of *The Missouri Weekly Patriot* in Springfield appealed to history with the information that free blacks had voted in every state of the Union at the time of the formation of the Constitution. Hence, adoption of the suffrage amendment was merely a return to the "principles of the revolutionary fathers." In yet another editorial, he dropped the pragmatic hint: "Let us then, while we can, do justice, and make Radicalism in Missouri so strong that it cannot be overthrown even by the enfranchisement of the rebels, which we know will be done whenever the Democratic party gets into power." The Radicals could not overlook the constitutional provision allowing the General Assembly, by absolute majority vote in each house, to drop the disqualifications for voters after January 1, 1871. If such a measure were passed, an estimated fifty-thousand ballots would be added to the strength of the Democrats. The Radicals had an obvious need for votes, black and white, to counteract such a potential avalanche. In typical demagogic fashion, Drake warned all who would listen: "This then is the one solitary and vivid issue: *Shall the people that saved the country rule it, or shall rebels and traitors?* ... Patriotism smothers Democracy, as Democracy smothers Patriotism. The question then is, whether we shall have patriotism without Democracy, or Democracy without patriotism?"

Throughout the campaign the Democrats expressed a genuine alarm over the highhanded system of registration that the Radicals sought to impose on the electorate. Their special committee on this problem urged every Democrat to try to qualify to vote in the hope that the United States Supreme Court might still rescue rejected voters through a favorable decision in the Blair case. Local watchdog committees should be established in every area to oversee the registration process. Whatever the strategy of their opponents, party members should avoid violence and comply with the law, even if this behavior caused all of them to be rejected. This admonition proved difficult for some in areas where rigid enforcement and seemingly underhanded tactics kept worthy Democrats off the registration books.

Although the Radicals tried to keep a firm hand on the registration process throughout the state, the strictness of enforcement varied from one area to another, depending upon circumstances and the depth of partisan feeling held by the local officials. The total number of registered voters in the state rose by approximately thirty thousand over 1866. This increase can probably be attributed to three factors: continued immigration from the Northern states; a large percentage of men reaching "maturity"; and, in many areas, a moderating atmosphere brought about by the passage of time. Whatever the case, the entire Radical ticket swept to victory that November by approximately twenty thousand votes, and the majority party retained nearly three times as many representatives in both houses of the General Assembly as the minority. Aside from bringing a few county governments into their camp, the Democrats registered their only gains in the congressional races, where they reelected McCormick in the Third District and picked up seats in the First, Sixth, and Ninth. The triumphs in the Sixth and Ninth districts were short-lived, however, as the Radicals' faithful "hatchetman," Secretary of State Rodman, refused to open and certify the votes of Monroe, Jackson, Platte, Dunklin, Wayne, Oregon, Shannon, and Ripley counties on the ground of illegal registration. Instead, he announced his intention of leaving the question of their inclusion to the General Assembly when it certified the total vote. That body simply accepted the results as they came from the Secretary and ordered new elections for local offices and the legislature in the counties in question. In the meantime, Rodman issued certificates of election on the basis of the remaining "official" vote to Robert T. Van Horn and David P. Dyer; the Radical candidates thus benefited in the Sixth and Ninth districts. Their Democratic opponents, James Shields and William F. Switzler, had to take their grievances to Congress—it was the second such trip for Switzler, and, after prolonged hearings, they came away emptyhanded.

The election of 1868 brought the Radicals to the zenith of their political power in Missouri. The amendment calling for Negro suffrage was strongly defeated, however, a failure that tempered the hopes of the party's leaders and sowed the seed for future dissension. Prejudice against the black among many rank-and-file members of the party had overcome all the moral and political arguments of the Radical leaders and resulted in the defection of a large number of them. This reaction, coupled with an almost solid opposition to the measure by Democrats, led to the rejection of the proposal by a count of 74,053 to 55,236. It carried in only 41 of Missouri's 114 counties, largely the Radical strongholds in the southwest and along the northern border. By contrast, McClurg outdistanced Phelps in 79 counties. The amendment took a particularly heavy blow in St. Louis County, which opposed it by nearly three to one while giving McClurg a 1,600-vote margin over his opponent. Missouri was not the only Northern state that opposed Negro suffrage. Connecticut, Wisconsin, Minnesota (twice), Kansas, Ohio, Michigan, Colorado and Nebraska territories, and the District of Columbia had preceded Missouri in rejecting similar constitutional referenda. Many Missourians undoubtedly feared being overwhelmed by black immigration, should their state prove more liberal than its Northern sisters.

It quickly became obvious that the Radicals could not agree on how to pursue the matter beyond this point. While the *Missouri*

Democrat proposed a compromise in which the Radicals yielded disfranchisement of whites in return for Democratic support of Negro suffrage, Drake, who had campaigned ardently for both the ticket and the amendment, insisted that Negro suffrage had to precede reenfranchisement. The editor of *The Missouri Weekly Patriot* proposed a third alternative—submitting an amendment giving the legislature sole authority to decide enfranchisement for Negroes, since it would have that power in the case of rebels after 1871.

A more immediate problem confronted the Radicals with the convening of the new Twenty-fifth General Assembly. With the defection of Senator Henderson on the impeachment issue just as his term was due to expire, the party's legislators had little desire to return him to Washington. For a while it appeared that his replacement would be Congressman Benjamin F. Loan of St. Joseph, a faithful party hack and the personal choice of Drake. Loan had been prominent in the militia during the war and had converted from Whiggery to intense Radicalism in the process. He had announced his candidacy early, but many of the more moderate party members had misgivings about sending a second partisan with Drake's convictions to the Senate.

Carl Schurz was working quietly behind the scenes to defeat Loan and secure his own candidacy. After an extensive canvass for the national ticket that summer, he had reserved the final six weeks of the campaign for a speaking tour of Missouri. While he talked about the justice of Negro suffrage, he also stressed the need for harmony in the building of a better Missouri. In the process, he made a sufficiently favorable impression that his name began to be mentioned as a senatorial possibility. While disclaiming personal ambition he assiduously promoted his own interests. He was concerned with more than his own advancement, however, as Schurz wrote his wife a short time later: "The battle in which I am engaged . . . involves the leadership of one or the other element, the narrowly despotic or the liberal people of Missouri." Shortly after the election he organized several of his liberal German and American friends into the Twentieth Century Club, a Saturday luncheon group that discussed politics and current events. From this group came the formal impetus for the Schurz candidacy. William M. Grosvenor, who had joined the editorial staff of the *Missouri Democrat* two years earlier, having left one of the New Haven papers, put out an initial feeler. The extent of the favorable response surprised even Schurz.

By the time the legislature convened in January, 1869, Grosvenor had stirred up sentiment to bandwagon proportions. Henderson renewed his hopes for reelection in the event of a Loan–Schurz deadlock, and Drake became sufficiently worried that he returned from Washington to personally lead the fight for Loan's election. This move stirred resentment in certain circles because it appeared that Drake intended to dictate the party's course. Those of his followers who had endorsed Schurz could not understand Drake's fear that this meant a repudiation of his leadership. Many of them looked on the German editor as one who could not only bridge the gulf within the party but also work to promote further immigration, railroad building, and other economic concerns. When the Schurz managers arranged a debate among Henderson, Loan, and their candidate on the eve of Governor-elect McClurg's inauguration at Jefferson City, Drake insisted on being included. Because of the festivities the next day, a large crowd packed the Hall of Representatives for the encounter. Drake became involved in such a long diatribe against his enemies within the party that it was necessary to carry the discussion over to the following evening. When his turn finally came, Schurz likened himself to "a young David, who, single-handed and without any weapon except his sling and a few pebbles in his pouch, had to meet in combat two heavily-armed Goliaths at once." As his listeners roared their approval, he dissected Drake with rapierlike efficiency, picturing him as a narrow, vindictive partisan who alienated the very people whose support he needed. He assured his audience that the day would come when Drake would stand "lonesome and forlorn, surrounded by an immensity of solitude, in desolate self-appreciation." After Henderson's anticlimactic closing remarks, the debate ended. Schurz was surrounded by enthusiastic well-wishers, and the other participants were largely ignored.

A deflated Drake caught the night train back to St. Louis, leaving the rest of Loan's supporters to fight what battle they could in the Radical caucus the next evening. All but one of the

115 Radicals from both houses were present at that meeting, and Schurz pushed through to a first-ballot victory by 59 to 40 with the remaining votes scattered among three other nominees. A survey of the balloting, as revealed later, showed that Schurz cut heavily into Loan's support in southwestern and west-central Missouri, while Loan held his own among the legislators of the northern tier of counties. The Loan men immediately closed ranks to make the nomination unanimous, and Schurz's election on January 19 over John S. Phelps, the Democratic candidate, became a mere formality. The victor appeared before a joint session the following day to accept his prize and pronounce his triumph as "evidence of the liberal and progressive spirit moving the people of Missouri." He reiterated his stand for Negro suffrage and offered reconciliation to the disfranchised whites if they would "come to us as men sincerely loyal to the new order of things." Although the vote in the Radical caucus could not be called a clear-cut assertion of leadership over all the party, Schurz's nomination did bring the liberal element to a position of strength and power it had not enjoyed before, while indicating that the tired old clichés would have to give way to the consideration of new issues.

In spite of this new direction, the Radicals showed little inclination to deal with the suffrage question at this session of the legislature. With the next election nearly two years away and an adjourned session intervening, they saw no need for haste in resolving the difficult problem that plagued them. Then, too, they hoped that two outside events that were taking shape in Washington might provide a solution that would eliminate the necessity of further action at Jefferson City. The first of these proposals involved the efforts of the Radicals in Congress to draft a constitutional amendment that would guarantee Negro suffrage nationwide. Such a move would help them avoid the "dangers" of unilateral action, which seemingly held back a number of Northern states, while assuring the Negro vote to support the Republican ticket in the 1870 election. On March 1, three days before the General Assembly's adjournment, word was received by telegraph that the measures were passed by both houses of Congress. Without waiting for official confirmation, the Radicals at Jefferson City rushed through resolutions of ratification, which Governor McClurg happily signed. They later discovered that in their haste they had omitted the second section of the amendment, and so had to repeat the entire process when they reconvened the following January.

In mid-March, 1869, the United States Supreme Court heard arguments in Frank Blair's appeal of the test oath for voting. The Democrats were confident of a favorable decision, which would, of course, resolve the issue of disfranchisement without the need for further legislative action. But as the Supreme Court prolonged its deliberation, their optimism faded. The Court finally announced that it would carry the case over to its October term. At that point it became doubtful that it would render a verdict before the reconvening of the legislature.

That body, meanwhile, had faced a challenge on the suffrage question from yet another direction. Early in February ten women alighted from the train at Jefferson City to apprise the legislators of the desire of their sex for the ballot. Their trip grew out of a movement that had begun two years earlier with the organization of the Women's Suffrage Association of Missouri. Leading the delegation were Mrs. John S. Phelps, wife of the recent Democratic gubernatorial nominee, and Miss Phoebe Couzins. Mrs. Phelps had long been active in promoting causes in her own right. During the recent conflict she had performed notable service in caring for the wounded after the battles of Wilson's Creek and Pea Ridge. At war's end she had established an orphanage at Springfield for the children of both Union and Confederate soldiers, and Congress appropriated $20,000 in appreciation of her many services to the war effort. Miss Couzins had worked with the Western Sanitary Commission in St. Louis during the conflict, where her experiences led her to the conclusion that women, if they possessed political power, could prevent war. She enrolled in the Washington University Law School that fall and received the bachelor of laws degree two years later, thereby becoming the first professional woman lawyer in the United States. Although one newspaper thereafter deridingly dubbed her "a female bachelor," she continued her course undaunted.

The women of Missouri, as well as of the rest of the nation, had become concerned with the possibility of exercising a larger and more direct political role as a result of the agitation over Negro suffrage at war's end. Many of their leaders, such as Phoebe Couzins, had worked with the Western Sanitary Commission and other wartime agencies, and they felt that their services warranted them some such consideration. When Sen. B. Gratz Brown announced that he favored a universal franchise regardless of "race, color, or sex" during debate over extending the suffrage in the District of Columbia in December, 1866, he struck a responsive chord at home. Mrs. Virginia Minor of St. Louis sent Brown a letter of commendation, which several others also signed. A petition from 355 women to the General Assembly later that winter brought no results in Jefferson City, but it did crystallize the movement into a formal organization in May, 1867, with Mrs. Minor as its president.

The association grew slowly, but its regular, biweekly meetings had a good attendance of both men and women. After fruitlessly sending another petition to the legislature in 1868, the women decided to have a delegation go personally to Jefferson City the following year. Their movement had been widely publicized in the St. Louis newspapers by this time, and some of the reports had been mildly favorable. Speaker John C. Orrick and Lt. Gov. Edwin O. Stanard met the delegation's train when it arrived at the capital and escorted them to a nearby hotel. The next morning they visited the governor's mansion where McClurg gave them a cordial welcome and signed one of their petitions. That afternoon the women met in informal session with legislators from both houses to present their case. The capital correspondent of the *Missouri Democrat* gave a favorable assessment of the meeting: "It is evident that the mission of the ladies has not been in vain. A serious attention was paid to all that was advanced, not as a matter of etiquette or show of gallantry to them alone, but as a matter of great moment and deep concern to the commonwealth." Others did not look so benignly upon the visit, however. One House member asserted disparagingly that the women had "unsexed themselves by coming here with their demands." Next morning the House tabled a resolution concerning equal suffrage by 64 to 50, on the ground that it was premature prior to the formal presentation of the women's petition. Subsequent efforts to revive the issue at this session were of little avail.

Undaunted, the suffragettes continued their agitation in St. Louis at the city hall but with as little success. The vociferousness of the group's leaders began to irritate some editors, and one complained: "Those who believe that the enfranchisement of women is desirable will wisely seek to convince the present voters of that position, by adopting a practical and sensible course. Unlimited orating to no practical purpose is not at all calculated to advance the object of the Association." The women had already moved out into a broader field, however, by holding periodic "working women's" meetings that spring. In July, they organized the Working Women's Protective Association for the purpose of promoting "the general welfare of each other, by lending our assistance in obtaining employment and ample remuneration therefor." That fall, the Missouri suffragettes played host in St. Louis to the movement's national convention, which adopted resolutions framed by Mrs. Minor asserting that the states by denying women the right to vote, had violated the letter and spirit of the Constitution.

While the women continued to agitate for equal rights, the Radical press kept up its debate over lifting the disqualifications against Southern sympathizers and enfranchising the blacks. Little had been resolved when the legislature reconvened in January, 1870. Governor McClurg, in his annual message, evinced some disposition to find middle ground by calling for a thorough airing of the question in the forthcoming electoral campaign and particularly emphasized the General Assembly's prerogative to restore political privileges by a simple majority vote after January 1, 1871. By this means, the Radicals could avoid the divisive question of Negro suffrage, inasmuch as the proposed Fifteenth Amendment had not yet been fully ratified.

The liberals, with strong editorial support from Grosvenor in the *Missouri Democrat*, showed little inclination for a compromise on this moderate position. Two Radical caucuses in January made no headway, although a good spirit generally prevailed among the participants. In the midst of this impasse, word came from Washington that the two outside events impinging on the

Missouri debate had reached a conclusion. In late January, the United States Supreme Court divided evenly, 4 to 4, in the Blair case thereby upholding the earlier decision of its Missouri counterpart through lack of a majority against it. Most of the Radicals believed the result justified their postwar course while the liberals now urged the more strongly that, although the test oath policy might have been necessary at one time, the moment had arrived for their party to end it in a gesture of magnanimity. When Secretary of State William H. Seward announced the final ratification of the Fifteenth Amendment a week later, many Radicals became more receptive to the liberal proposals. Even Drake, in response to an inquiry, agreed that the time had come to let the voters consider reenfranchising Southern whites now that Negro suffrage had been assured.

The Radical caucus had already decided by a vote of 51 to 22, with 26 members absent, to move ahead on the matter. The negative voices came largely from the border counties, where Radical extremism was still firmly entrenched. Undoubtedly many of the absentees were opposed and preferred not to lend any support to what one outstate paper called "the adroit expedients of the St. Louis schemers." Five days later the Democratic caucus endorsed the program unanimously, although some had earlier expressed the feeling that they should remain aloof from the whole proceeding. The proposal was approved in both houses by overwhelming margins; only a scattering of diehard Radicals, most of them from southwestern Missouri, voted against it. In its final form, the new program embraced three amendments: one would modify the constitutional provisions concerning the test oath for voting by eliminating the "ironclad" features and substituting a simple declaration of support for state and national constitutions; the second would rescind the test oath for jurors, a qualification that had seldom been required anyway; the third would repeal the test oath as a prerequisite to filing for political candidacy and for corporate or educational activity and would remove racial barriers to officeholding.

To help calm the misgivings of outstate Radicals during these proceedings, Grosvenor rationalized the effects of these amendments in the editorial pages of the *Missouri Democrat*. Following an already well established line, he pointed out that even if the amendments passed, the disfranchised could not exercise their new voting strength in state elections until 1872. By then, he contended, Radical voters would have been augmented by approximately sixty thousand through Negro suffrage and continued immigration, while the Democrats would be able to muster only about twenty thousand more if one did not count the disfranchised whom Grosvenor estimated at twenty-five thousand, undoubtedly a conservative figure. The editor argued that many of the disfranchised would not necessarily support the Democratic party. As old animosities died out, new issues would arise to divide the people; under such circumstances no one could predict how they would line up by 1872. Given the right strategy, the Radical party had just as good a chance of drawing their votes as did the Democrats.

Seeking to test the extent of the apparent Radical change of heart, the Democratic minority in the legislature began urging modification of the registry act in the direction of decentralized control. When their proposals came to the floor, they found the Radical majority not yet prepared to dismantle the elaborate machinery of control. Even such liberals as Grosvenor rejoiced when the General Assembly held firm because of their fear that it might open the floodgates too wide too soon. Given this failure, the minority had no hesitation in approving a course proposed by the state Democratic committee just before the legislature adjourned. This position was what became known as the "possum policy." Apparently the brainchild of William Hyde, editor of the *Missouri Republican*, it called for the Democrats to refrain from participation in statewide races—on the ground that a strict registry act made success there nearly impossible—and to concentrate instead on congressional and legislative campaigns. Some hope of making real gains in the legislature existed, should the amendments fail, the focus would really be brought to bear on that body which would then have the unilateral power of repeal. Although a few Democratic leaders questioned the possum policy, the others rather quickly persuaded them that it was valuable; late in July, the state committee made it the official stand of the party.

By that time, the Radical party had begun to come apart at

the seams over a variety of issues, looking to their state convention in August and the subsequent campaign. Although acknowledging the wisdom of submitting to a popular vote the amendments passed by the recent legislature, the regulars had no desire to endorse them. Given the divisiveness of the issue, they preferred simply to let each voter express his view without feeling party pressure. The liberals, on the other hand, led by Grosvenor through the editorial pages of the *Missouri Democrat*, argued that the party must commit itself to their passage in order to revoke a policy it had initiated. As the debate over this question became heated among the Radical press, Grosvenor and Schurz drew attention to another issue, free trade versus protection. Schurz had been fighting in the Senate to secure tariff reduction and hoped for support at home, but most party regulars favored continued protection in line with the general policies of the Grant administration. Regardless of the difference of opinion over the matter, most Missouri Radicals hoped to keep what they considered national issues out of state politics.

Far more critical, in the long run, to the future well-being of the Radical party was the question of leadership. With the gubernatorial term having been reduced to two years by the 1865 constitution, McClurg faced the prospect of a reelection battle in 1870. Grosvenor, at an early date, had considered the policies of the Governor and decided not to support him. In the eyes of the *Democrat*'s editor his renomination "would be absurd, because he is not competent to advocate the liberal policy, and could only make it ridiculous." The outstate liberal press took up the theme, which emphasized McClurg's seeming antipathy toward the amendments as a means of resolving the issue of reenfranchisement. A staunch prohibitionist, the Governor was suspected by the Germans because of his refusal to serve liquor at mansion receptions. They feared he might attempt to broaden this type of proscription throughout the entire state or at least seek to rigidly control the liquor traffic. Whatever his stand on other issues, McClurg earned Grosvenor's animosity because of his support of a high tariff. In short, the Governor was too much a regular, who had been allied to Drake from the outset of the struggle for power. As such, he showed too little inclination to move from the existing status quo. While the liberal press scored McClurg, the regular Radical papers came quickly to his defense, indicating their bitterness at what they considered Grosvenor's divisive tactics. During an informal gathering of Radical editors at the annual meeting of the Editors' and Publishers' Association, they deliberately ignored their colleague from the *Democrat*, and Grosvenor was infuriated.

By the time the Radicals gathered in convention at Jefferson City in late August, B. Gratz Brown had reemerged from retirement as the liberal contender for the governorship. The hostility between the two wings of the party had become so deep-seated that it was being widely predicted that should Brown not succeed in upsetting McClurg at the convention, he would lead an independent ticket. In light of this situation, the matter of selecting delegates had raised yet another divisive issue within the party. Following the usual procedure, the state committee had allotted each county one delegate for every 150 votes or fraction thereof that it had cast for Grant in 1868. Under the impetus of the Fifteenth Amendment and the prodding of J. Milton Turner, they also allocated additional delegates through a similar formula based on eligible black voters. The dispute came later over interpretation of "fraction thereof" and the separation of the two means of determining delegate slates. The liberals assumed that the term in question meant a minimum of 50 votes additional and that the number of black voters would be lumped together with the 1868 vote to make one determination on delegate strength. But the committee's secretary had interpreted "fraction" in a literal sense to mean one above 150. Ultimately, a compromise was reached in which the committee accepted the liberals' interpretation of the numbers while Turner prevailed on keeping the black delegate strength separate, so counties with less than 50 eligible black voters might still be represented by blacks at the convention.

The atmosphere was thus electrically tense as the nearly 800 delegates, including 180 blacks, gathered in the Hall of Representatives in the Capitol. After jockeying for position during two days of procedural decisions with neither side gaining a clear-cut advantage, it became obvious that the final showdown would be reached in the vote on the platform the third day. Behind-the-scenes efforts to work out a compromise came to naught as each side believed it had the strength to win for its plank on the amendments and its candidate for governor. Still, as chairman of the resolutions committee, Schurz managed to hammer out agreement on a vague platform down to the crucial issue of endorsing the amendments. He brought in a majority report favoring outright endorsement, while the minority of regulars on his committee, though supporting the issue of reenfranchisement in principle, wished to "recognize the right of any member of the party to vote his honest convictions." The liberals refused to accept this somewhat neutral ground; when the convention did, by a nearly 100-vote margin, 80 delegates from 35 counties bolted from the hall and moved to the Senate chamber to establish their own Liberal Republican organization.

While both groups adjourned for lunch, moderates sought to work out a compromise around the candidacy of Lieutenant Governor Stanard for the top of the ticket, but to no avail. That afternoon, many of them joined the liberal bolters and a number of bogus delegates, who had not participated in the regular proceedings, to launch the Liberal Republican party of Missouri. They nominated Brown for governor on a platform dictated by Grosvenor that contained every one of his cherished ideas: reenfranchisement, a revenue tariff, civil service reform, tax reduction, and opposition to the alienation of government land to private corporations. In climactic fashion, Brown appeared before the convention to accept their favor in a speech denouncing the regulars for their shortsighted obstinacy and condemning their methods for trying to secure Negro support. He closed with a strong positive statement of the Liberal position. The regulars meanwhile renominated McClurg and approved a platform whose plank on reenfranchisement repeated the vague statement of 1868. Ignoring the bolters, they promised to continue the programs that they claimed had brought Missouri unprecedented growth and prosperity during the past five years. They also included a complimentary endorsement of President Grant, whom the Liberals had chosen to ignore.

The various elements of the Radical Union party had come to a parting of the ways. From the very beginning, their coalition had been tenuous. They had bickered among themselves since the constitutional convention of 1865 about the dimensions of the new order they wished to impose upon Missouri. At first, unable to find a strong leader to cope with the magic of Charles D. Drake, the moderates had contented themselves with being a vocal minority within the party and had been able to secure a fair share of spoils because of their affinity with Governor Fletcher. With the coming of Carl Schurz, they had found a spokesman with broad appeal and political shrewdness. Drake's failure to modernize his image and his personal panic and ineptness before Schurz's challenge in 1869 had opened the door to the moderates' hopes for a more forward-looking party under their control. The breakdown of Drake's power, however, made both wings of the party increasingly adamant against compromise, fearing that any concession might result in a diminution of their own political influence. Many outstate regulars, in particular, regarded the liberal program of reenfranchisement as the beginning of the erosion of their power at the county level. In the refusal of the two wings to negotiate a settlement, they destroyed the Radical Union party of Missouri.

CHAPTER X

THE END OF AN ERA

With the election a scant two months away, the Liberals moved quickly to perfect an organization and launch their campaign. They issued a stirring manifesto on September 10 explaining the actions they had taken. They stressed the need for reenfranchisement now that the enmities of war had subsided, and they accused the members of the regular Radical party of being more concerned with spoils than with justice because of their refusal to endorse the amendments. They urged all men, regardless of party or color, to rally to their cause as a means of restoring full harmony among Missourians. While Grosvenor agreed to serve as state chairman of the new party, Schurz managed the campaign, somewhat to the disgust of Brown, who resented the heavyhanded direction of the fiery German. As the Liberal orators hit the campaign trail to carry their new message to the people, Grosvenor sought to inspire party workers with a real sense of urgency: "Republicans! . . . Waste no time in personal issues with the Proscriptives. Let them abuse you as much as they like. Present your principles to the people with the calmness, kindness and sure confidence of men who know that truth will conquer."

The Radicals reacted slowly. Although they still retained a generally strong organization, their leaders seemed hesitant to exert themselves. It took the arrival of Drake from Washington to stir them into action. Genuinely alarmed at what had happened and fully realizing the do-or-die nature of the struggle, he came prepared to pull out all the stops in his effort to rally the Radicals for the fray. He quickly began campaigning with his old vituperativeness, charging the bolting Liberals with having signed a covenant with the Democratic "rebels" whereby they would support each other in future elections, including the national one. He attacked the stand of Schurz and Grosvenor on free trade by accusing his fellow senator of being more concerned for the industries of his native Germany than those of the land where he now resided. With regard to the amendments, Drake, adopted the neutral position of his party by saying that every man must be free to vote his own conscience.

Drake did not hesitate to use the full power of the federal and state patronage to keep party workers in line. After he persuaded President Grant that the Missouri revolt marked the beginning of a general conspiracy within the party to defeat Grant in the 1872 election, Drake received virtual carte blanche to dismiss those Republicans who had indicated they supported Brown. Although for some reason he did not actively campaign, Governor McClurg followed Drake's lead by purging the dissidents among state employees. To prove one's loyalty, it became necessary for government workers to contribute 5 per cent of their annual salaries to the Radical campaign fund. Those employees who failed to respond were promptly dismissed from their jobs. As the campaign moved to a climax and the party's financial status appeared straitened, holders of federal offices also faced an assessment of 1 per cent on their gross receipts, from which they were usually paid on a commission basis. The notice requiring this donation concluded ominously: "The exigencies are great, and delay or neglect will rightly be construed into unfriendliness to the Administration."

As these matters came to their attention, the Liberal and Democratic press vigorously publicized them. They scored outside interference in Missouri affairs and the threat to everyone's right to a free vote. Certainly Schurz here found ample ground for continuing to support civil service reform that he had been advocating. McClurg further agitated the controversy by reorganizing the St. Louis Police Board midway through the campaign. He purged three Liberal members, on the grounds that secret reports indicated they had offered protection to certain gambling houses, but Grosvenor denounced this action as a political red herring and cited it as another link in the continuing chain of state interference with the city's affairs. It is certainly doubtful that all of this new proscription did the Radical cause much good.

Both groups meanwhile actively sought the support of Missouri's newly enfranchised blacks. The Fifteenth Amendment had been ratified that spring, just in time to allow the blacks the opportunity of voting in municipal elections. The jubilant blacks celebrated with parades and speeches in most of the larger towns. Approximately 20,000 turned out for a grand jubilee in St. Louis. Radical registrars promptly opened their books to the new voters, in spite of a scattering of Democratic protests. At St. Joseph two ancient blacks aged 100 and 101, "walked arm in arm . . . and asked to be permitted the exercise of the freeman's privilege before they died." The pro-Radical editor of the local *Herald* wrote movingly: "As the old men put their palsied hands to the pen that signed their names it seemed the consummation of a long-deferred justice—it was the breaking of the 'seal upon the tomb of hope,' and the glory of a perfect freedom issued out into the world." At Kansas City, the supervisor of registration had enrolled 228 blacks when the mayor and council enjoined him from further violating municipal law that made no provision for registering them. The Radical official ignored them, and there were no adverse effects. When election day came, the *Journal* there noted: "Our colored citizens are voting today, keeping the best of order themselves, provoking no disturbance, and encountering no opposition." Apparently the Democrats in that vicinity had decided to try wooing the black voter rather than obstructing him, for at this same time James D. Bowser of Kansas City wrote Frederick Douglass's *New Era*, a national Negro weekly, that he feared many blacks were supporting the Democrats because of the food and drink they had been distributing widely just before the election. He pleaded with the paper to work at informing his newly enfranchised brethren about the issues at stake.

That fall, Negro speakers crisscrossed the state with their white counterparts, holding rallies at which they urged full participation to secure the rights of citizenship. The Radicals proved far more successful in gaining black support than did their Liberal opponents. Their chief spokesman was J. Milton Turner, who had emerged during the past five years to a real position of respect and power in the black community because of his extensive tours on behalf of Lincoln Institute and the Equal Rights League. He had worked directly with the Radical State Committee to secure maximum black participation at the recent convention, and he now assured the regulars that he could deliver almost all the Negro vote into their camp. Not willing to yield this important segment of the electorate without a struggle, the Liberals enlisted Charles H. Tandy and George B. Wedley, two prominent St. Louis blacks, to counteract Turner's campaigning. They struck hard at Turner's opposition to reenfranchisement as a policy that encouraged needless antagonism between the races. In the midst of this debate, Bowser again wrote Frederick Douglass seeking advice on the best course for Missouri blacks to follow. The great national leader replied that they should vote for the amendments out of "genuine magnanimity" as well as "the dictate of sound political wisdom." At the same time he advised them to support the Radical ticket. "In that party the colored voter is a power," he reminded his readers. "There is no safety outside the ship."

For all their catering to the black voter, it was obvious to both sides that the Democrats held the balance of power in the forthcoming election. Their possum policy had paid off handsomely thus far. It left the feuding wings of the Radical party to fight among themselves; these circumstances had probably helped heighten the tensions prior to the Radical convention. Now the separate wings of the Republican party accused each other of making common cause with their "ancient enemy." Drake alleged a secret conspiracy between Liberals and Democrats going back to the preconvention period, while Grosvenor talked of a Radical sellout to the Democracy whereby McClurg would announce that he was in favor of the amendments in return for the Democrats' support. There was also considerable speculation about arrangements for splitting the legislative and congressional tickets yet to be nominated.

In reality, there is no evidence that the Democrats bargained with either of the rival groups until late in the campaign. But Democratic leaders, as well as the rank and file within the party, quickly saw that the Liberals' principles embraced much of what they had stood for over the past few years. Since the Liberals were an obvious minority within Republican ranks, they would need Democratic help to win the election. Consequently, Brown began receiving endorsements from prominent Democrats by late September. The Democratic press also aroused itself on his behalf. Many of these newspapers made it clear, however, that they were not abandoning their own party in so doing. Far from abdicating, they hoped, as William F. Switzler put it, to absorb the Liberals by 1872. Where possible, the new allies reached agreements with regard to congressional and county candidates. All such matters were handled at the local level, however, with no attempt to develop a statewide pattern. Wherever either party believed that it could elect its own men, especially in the legislative races, it did not hesitate to enter into competition against the other, as well as against the Radicals.

As they became increasingly aware of their danger, Governor McClurg and other Radical leaders sought to temper their positions that were abrasive to the Democrats. Most particularly they began to modify their stand on the amendments, indicating first their personal agreement with them and by campaign's end making an open endorsement. They also made efforts to encourage cooperative arrangements at the local level similar to those being consummated between Liberals and Democrats in the hope of salvaging McClurg's chances at the head of the ticket, but little came of this effort. Word went out from the Governor's office in late September that McClurg favored a liberal interpretation of the registry act by local officials, with challenges being made only where open and direct evidence of ineligibility existed. When the final registration figures were published, they indicated that the registrars had taken the Governor at his word. The number of those citizens eligible to participate in the electoral process jumped from 154,080 in 1868 to 199,297 by 1870. New black voters accounted for 18,000 to 20,000 of this increase. The continuing flow of immigrants also contributed. But a notable difference appeared in the figures for Democratic counties where the registrars had previously been unduly proscriptive. For instance, the three counties of Boone, Callaway, and Audrain in the heart of "Little Dixie" showed a striking gain of 4,000 registrants. On the western border the Democratic strongholds of Clay and Platte counties registered 1,100 and 1,700 more voters, respectively. Many Republican counties, on the other hand, revealed virtually the same registration as in 1868. Apparently, for all the excitement within the ranks of the Radical party, many eligible voters did not even bother to register, especially in St. Louis County. The *Missouri Democrat* complained continually during the closing weeks of the campaign about the lackadaisical attitude of the potential electorate. Final figures for St. Louis County showed 30,671 registered voters on the books, of whom 2,395 were black and 1,500 were new. This figure represented a decrease of some 1,300 registrants in comparison with 1868.

More than 160,000 voters went to the polls on election day as the Liberal ticket swept to a smashing victory. Brown swamped McClurg by 40,000 votes with a strong showing both in St. Louis and outstate. The Democrats, with considerable justification, contended that they had been largely responsible for his victory. Indeed, one county-by-county analysis indicates that they probably contributed about two-thirds of his vote total.[1] McClurg's strength came largely from the border areas, which remained true to the Radical cause to the bitter end. The *Missouri Weekly Patriot* of Springfield claimed that bad weather had held down the Radical vote in the southwest, but this made little real difference in the over-all figures.

The Democrats scored well in the congressional and legislative races. Four of their five nominees for congressional seats were elected—their sole loss being in southwestern Missouri. In the remaining 4 districts where they had no entries, the Radicals and the Liberals split evenly. The legislative races were most critical to the future of the Democratic party. Here they carried 77 of the 138 seats in the lower house while electing six senators to add to seven incumbents. Radical candidates won only 27 House seats with the Liberals picking up 21. In the remaining Senate races, six Liberals secured election. Three seats went to fusionists and two to Radicals. The Radical party had ten holdovers there. The Democrats thus held an absolute majority in the House and could control the Senate through coalition with the Liberals and the fusionists. The Democracy also fared well at the local level by winning nearly three-fourths of the various county races, which was a strong foundation for the structural rebuilding of the party.

The amendments passed by overwhelming majorities amid

1. Michael Burlingame, "Liberal Republicanism in Missouri, 1869–1872," seminar paper, Johns Hopkins University, May, 1966.

great rejoicing by the disfranchised. Many Conservative communities held parades and celebrations to herald the overthrow of the despised proscriptive measures. "The fetters which were forged in 1865 by the DRAKE Convention have fallen from the wrists of seventy-five thousand white men, and the ballot is free," exulted William F. Switzler. "Infamous registry laws, odious test oaths, and venal and villainous registry officers will be known to our State no more forever."

There was considerable speculation within Republican circles and among Carl Schurz's friends as to the future of Liberalism, since the leader of the rebellious wing of the Radical party was so prominent a party figure. Similar disruptions within the Radical camps in Tennessee and West Virginia the previous year had preceded the split in Missouri. Because President Grant strongly upheld the position of Charles D. Drake and the Missouri regulars, it became obvious that he feared general disruption in the party and had moved to quell it. Those who found the President less than satisfactory pondered all this activity as they looked to the elections of 1872. Some sought explanations from Schurz himself.

The Senator chose to make his explanation in Washington as he introduced a resolution calling for the removal of all national restrictions on "persons lately in rebellion." Explaining his pilgrimage from postwar proscriptionist to current antirestrictionist, Schurz declared: "It has always been my opinion that, although the new order of things had to be established under a pressure of force and restriction, other agencies than a continued protection by force and restriction—a system uncongenial to our principles of government—had to be relied upon for its development and perpetuation." As for the recent events in Missouri, Schurz pictured the battle there as a struggle of "inveterate prejudice and unscrupulous greed for office arrayed against fidelity to sacred pledges and sound statesmanship." With little need remaining for disfranchisement there, the more forward-looking Republicans had sounded the clarion call for the future. Did this mean that he and the others wished to make common cause with the Democrats or to start a new party? Denying the former, he asserted the need for the latter. He did not rule out the possibility, however, that this new party could be the Republican party if it would concern itself less with spoils and more with principles. Schurz pledged himself and his fellow Liberals to reforming the old organization.

The more practical of Schurz's allies in Missouri, however, realized that they represented a minority within Republicanism and that success in the election had been made possible only because of the coalition with the Democrats. Because there was little chance for remaking the Republican party on their terms or maintaining a successful independent existence as a third force, they did not hesitate to acknowledge the need for continued cooperation with the Democracy until the struggle for control was over and the positions of politicians and organizations on fundamental issues were clearer. Foremost among these practical leaders was Governor-elect Brown. When the Democrats of St. Louis congratulated him with a victory serenade at his home on the evening of November 14, Brown spoke quite candidly: "I can say to you, frankly, my fellow-citizens, that I am the last man in this nation to disregard the obligations under which I stand, and that in this election I recognize that my obligations are in the largest measure due to the Democratic party of the State of Missouri." The large partisan crowd, led by its state chairman, cheered heartily.

Brown's attitude dismayed Schurz in Washington. He wrote Grosvenor: "Here they quite generally put him down as having gone over to the Democrats—in consequence of his first serenade speech." Brown denied the charge. He was agreeable to trying to mollify "our Republican friends," if they would arrange a similar occasion. This opportunity was given to him on the evening of November 29. Although hampered by bad weather, a large group of Liberals appeared to receive the Governor-elect's praise for the singleness of their devotion to the principles that had triumphed in the recent election. A man of strong ambitions, already thinking of running for the Presidency two years hence, Brown would continue to walk a tightrope between the two groups responsible for his sitting in the governor's chair.

While the Liberals concerned themselves with principles and the Democrats enjoyed the prospect of a seemingly bright political future, many members of the discredited Radical party pressed the Grant administration for some kind of federal patronage job to ensure their security in the immediate future. The purge of federal officeholders continued after the election. Those in sympathy with the Liberal movement who had managed to survive the first onslaught now were required to surrender their offices to Radical stalwarts. Among those loyal party members rewarded for his services to the Radical cause was J. Milton Turner, who had kept his promise to deliver the black vote en masse in the recent election. President Grant appointed him Minister Resident and Consul General to Liberia, thereby making him the first black to enter the diplomatic corps.

Missouri's most prominent Radical also gave serious thought to his future and decided that it did not lie in his adopted state. On December 8, Grosvenor wrote disparagingly in the pages of the *Missouri Democrat:* "It is still reported that the President means to pension his faithful servant, Mr. Drake, by giving him a place for life as one of the Judges of the Court of Claims." The Missouri Senator had, in fact, been angling for the job of chief justice of that court since the announcement of the incumbent's resignation in early November. When Congress reconvened the following month, President Grant presented Drake's nomination to the Senate, which quickly confirmed it. Before leaving that body to move to the judicial bench, Drake took a final opportunity to deliver what might be termed his valedictory address as Missouri's "Mr. Radical." Defending the course of his party during its brief existence, he once again charged Schurz, who sat nearby trying to protest, and the Liberals with betrayal. Drake claimed that their actions had resulted in a Democratic triumph in Missouri and he recalled his father's words about those "who of old would rend the oak, but dreamed not of the rebound." He prophesied accurately that Liberalism, in the end, would prove a transitory phenomenon on the political scene. Having closed his political career, Drake departed amidst involuntary applause from the Senate floor and galleries for what had been one of his best performances.

Drake continued on the Court of Claims in Washington, far removed from the Missouri political scene, until his retirement in 1885. J. Milton Turner served with distinction in Liberia until 1878. After his return home, he engaged in a variety of business enterprises in St. Louis and Oklahoma including a successful attempt to see that the freedmen among the Cherokees, Choctaws, and Chickasaws received their just share of congressional allotments to Indian nations. After his defeat for reelection, Joseph W. McClurg retired to Linn Creek in Camden County, where he resumed his mercantile business. His predecessor in the governor's chair, Thomas C. Fletcher, pursued a successful legal practice in St. Louis and Washington. That Radical whom many Conservatives probably despised the most, "Count" Francis Rodman, left Missouri two years after his fall from power and spent the remainder of his life holding a variety of political appointments in Chicago. Most of the other men who had served Missouri under Radical rule slipped into political obscurity, although some occasionally enjoyed patronage positions in the national Republican administrations in the remaining years of the nineteenth century. In Missouri nothing remained of the brief political empire of the Radicals except control of a few courthouses in those areas where they had been able to consolidate their strength.

The Radical Union party of Missouri had ridden into power on the whirlwind of emotion generated by four long years of internecine strife. Led by men with many progressive ideas, it had set Missouri on the road to a postwar future brightened by prosperity and social advance. To help accomplish the better tomorrows, its leaders, especially Charles D. Drake, had thought it necessary to completely overhaul the state's basic constitutional framework. Yet, in carrying out their program, they went to vindictive extremes. Few Unionists would deny the necessity for some control over the remaining rebels and the disloyal who had remained at home to participate in guerrilla warfare. The example of Kentucky, where Conservatives entrenched themselves in power at the end of the war only to succumb to infiltration from ex-Confederates, contrasts markedly with Missouri. In Kentucky, economic and social stagnation characterized the five years after the conflict, and the state was long in recovering. Yet, the Radicals in Missouri had imposed such rigid restrictions on political freedoms that they needlessly antagonized many groups and individuals, as evidenced by the controversies that arose over the test oath required of lawyers and clergy. A group such as this party, which could secure a 40,000-vote mandate, hardly needed such ultraproscriptive measures to maintain itself in power. The illegal methods used by Secretary of State Rodman to secure elections where legal means had failed accomplished little of permanent value but aroused tremendous ill will as did the constant tampering with St. Louis's charter by the legislature.

More emphasis on the positive aspects of their program and less concern with extreme vindictiveness might have allowed the Radicals to build a strong progressive party of longstanding duration. As it was, they laid a good foundation for Missouri in the areas of education, Negro rights, and economic growth. If they had antagonized political opposition less, they could have accomplished much more. Even after their extreme measures of 1865 and 1866 the Radicals might still have salvaged the future of their party, had they been willing to move in the direction of the Planters House proposals of B. Gratz Brown when they were first suggested. The memory of war was still fresh, however, and partisans with newly won fruits of office feared lest these be lost. Succumbing to that fear proved their ultimate undoing and brought total eclipse except in a few scattered strongholds.

The announcement of Drake's resignation from the Senate intensified the excitement and speculation of the Democrats as they anticipated the convening of the new Twenty-sixth General Assembly. Their leaders and press had been working hard since the election to formulate a party program for the coming session, where they would be in control for the first time in ten years. Two issues dominated party thinking: a desire for a new constitutional convention to drastically revise the hated document of 1865 and a demand for major alteration if not the complete repeal of the equally despised registry system. The revived Democracy hoped that Brown and the Liberals would lend their support to both of these proposals.

The Democrats had little difficulty in organizing both houses of the legislature when that body convened in January, 1871. Although they had to share some offices with the Liberals and the fusionists in the Senate, the early rollcalls showed that many of the fusionists could be included permanently within their ranks. Of most immediate interest was the senatorial vacancy. Although various persons had been mentioned to succeed Drake, one quickly became the most prominent candidate, Frank Blair. From the earliest rumor that Drake might resign, Blair had began working assiduously behind the scenes to build up support for his candidacy. He claimed the right to the Democratic nomination on the grounds that he had played a major role in rebuilding the party in Missouri and that he would have been chosen senator in 1867, when he ran against Drake, except that disfranchisement made the Radical's election possible. The Democratic caucus was far from united behind the Blair candidacy, but he ultimately was victorious over three other opponents. He courted the added support of his cousin, the new governor, whom he suspected of having presidential ambitions if the new coalition of Liberals and Democrats could be made into a national movement by 1872.

The Liberals had been invited to participate in the Democratic caucus, but only four went. They later held their own meeting with an attendance of twenty-three present but could find no one willing to serve as their nominee. As a result many of them joined the Radical caucus when it met. Carl Schurz, suspecting that Brown would sell out to the Democrats, had been urging Grosvenor to work toward reconciliation of the two wings of the Republican party as the best hope of securing an acceptable moderate. The idea of Blair as a Senate colleague left him angry, for he realized the shallowness of the man's convictions in view of his overweening ambition for yet higher office. The demoralized Republicans also had difficulty finding a candidate. In the end, they turned to former Sen. John B. Henderson, whom they had driven out of the Senate two years earlier. Having already turned down the Liberals, he proved a reluctant nominee who made little effort on his own behalf. When the joint session met, Blair had no difficulty in securing election with 102 votes on the first ballot against 59 for Henderson. This total gave him 18 more than a majority and 12 more than the Democrats' total strength. Grosvenor tried to put the best face possible on a bad situation by writing Schurz: "He [Blair] went, I know, with an idea of cooperating as far as he possibly could with liberal Republicans like yourself; and I believe, if you encourage instead of fighting him you can do much to keep him straight or straighter." Blair did indeed desire to cooperate, but strictly to aid his own promotion in the presidential election of 1872.

Spurred on by Blair's easy victory, the Democrats sought to push forward the two main projects of their legislative program: the calling of a constitutional convention and the revamping of the registry law, both of which had secured the endorsement of Governor Brown in his inaugural address. After lengthy debate in the House, they pushed through a resolution providing for a May, 1871, referendum on the convention issue. But in the Senate, where the two wings of the Republican party had been drawing more closely together, a coalition of Liberals and Radicals turned it down; all Democratic efforts to enact the measure came to naught. The Republicans contended, with some insight, that such a vote now "would arouse all the slumbering passions of the past ten years" at a time when the recent adoption of the amendments made this agitation unnecessary. The Democrats were more successful with their second endeavor. Most of them had advocated outright repeal of the registry system during the campaign, but Governor Brown argued for the need to retain some type of simplified voter registration. After considerable consultation the majority party acquiesced, and a new law passed without much opposition. It provided for a registration process controlled by locally elected administrative and judicial officials. There would be no boards of review, nor could the secretary of state exercise any arbitrary functions. As if to augur well for their continued success, the Democrats swept the St. Louis municipal elections that spring while also carrying such outstate towns as Chillicothe, Clinton, Sedalia, Warrensburg, and the capital of the Radical southwest, Springfield.

The results of the legislative session left Liberals in a quandary as to the future of their movement. Many had become disillusioned with their independent status when they realized that the newly found strength of the Democracy put that group in the driver's seat. A prominent Liberal in southwestern Missouri, responding to Schurz's inquiry for an evaluation of the situation at home, wrote:

Our Liberal Republican members of the General Assembly threw away the opportunity to control this state, as you are aware. A portion went at once into the Democratic caucus and will remain with the Democratic Party, and the ballance [*sic*] with most humble deprecation and penitence went to the foot of the "Radical-Rad" class. The result was the election of Blair to the Senate and an exceeding great disgust among the better and purer men of both "wings" of our Party.

Schurz agreed with this sentiment and wrote his partner, Preetorius, at the *Westliche Post:* "The election of Blair has dealt the liberal cause a decided blow, from which it will not recover for a long time."

The Senator also heard grumblings from would-be officeholders and others that Governor Brown seemed to be favoring everyone but Liberals in his patronage appointments. This complaint undoubtedly stemmed from the Governor's strong feelings about upgrading the civil service "with a scrutiny as to the fitness of applicants, rather than to the political opinions they may have previously entertained." But to hopeful Liberals, who had joined the cause for personal gain as well as principle, it still left a bad taste. Almost universally Schurz's Missouri correspondents in the late spring of 1871 expressed concern over the supposed deal between Blair and Brown whereby the Governor quietly backed his cousin for senator in return for a chance at the Presidency the following year. When one Liberal queried the Governor about his ambitions for higher office, Brown replied with another question: "and why may not the campaign of 1870 in Missouri, be re-enacted in the Nation?" as he showed his listener a number of letters from other states offering support.

The beginnings of cooperation between the Liberals and the Radicals in the legislative session, especially in the Senate, seemed to some to hold out hope for a reunification of the Republican party. The *Missouri Democrat*, which had been such an ardent champion of the Liberal movement, now did a sudden about face. Early in 1871, its owners, William McKee and Daniel Houser, discharged their controversial editor, William M. Grosvenor, whose convictions were close to those of Schurz. Thereafter they hewed to the straight Republican party line with strong praise for President Grant and an appeal to Liberals to return to the regular fold. They sought to point out to the bolters that no one had profited by the revolt except the Democrats, who

273

now had a stranglehold on the state legislature and the St. Louis city government. Certainly none of them could be especially proud of having Blair in the Senate. The *Democrat* stated, "The question that every honest Liberal Republican MUST ask himself is: Haven't we done enough for liberalism just now, and isn't it time to do something for Republicanism?"

In reality, McKee and Houser had their own interests in mind. McKee had been unsuccessful initially in securing a patronage appointment from President Grant for his brother. Consequently, he and Houser had supported Grosvenor's move to the Liberals in the hope of playing a major role in the Brown administration. The new governor refused to deal with them, however, which forced them back into the regular fold. They now began to intrigue with John McDonald, Grant's appointee as supervisor of internal revenue, and others. These men were concerned for the future of the Republican party in Missouri as well as for their own economic well-being in a broader sense. Out of these discussions there emerged the infamous "Whiskey Ring," through which they defrauded the Federal Government of thousands of dollars of tax revenue over the next four years. With two anti-Grant men, Schurz and Blair, representing Missouri in the Senate, the ring also had a major say in federal patronage appointments for the state.

While the owners of the *Missouri Democrat* had ulterior motives in promoting the reunification of the Republican party, others had a more sincere interest in keeping the party as a really viable political option in the state. Foremost among them was John B. Henderson, who had reluctantly agreed to stand for the Senate against Blair. He joined Edwin O. Stanard and other leaders from both groups in sending out a call for an all-Republican gathering in mid-October at St. Louis to patch up party differences in anticipation of the 1872 campaign. The attempt was doomed before it started, however, as the Liberal Republican State Committee issued a statement in advance that it did not intend to sacrifice its independent existence. Although well attended, the mass meeting on October 18 made little headway because of the inability of the two contending elements of the party to agree on the support of Grant for a second term. Henderson finally secured a resolution that the two state committees act in harmony if possible. If this could not be done, the regular Republicans would move ahead on their own, joined by those rank-and-file Liberals who wished to return to their old loyalty.

Missouri's Liberal Republican leaders had been playing for time all summer. Their cause was receiving increased favorable sentiment throughout the country, and they had no intention of folding their tent for either the regular Republicans or the Democrats. Carl Schurz apparently continued to hope until late summer that the Liberals might somehow capture the Republican party at its 1872 convention thereby making Democratic support unnecessary. But by September 30, he was writing to Sen. Charles Sumner:

> Grant and his faction carry at present everything before them by *force majeure*. The organization of the Republican party is almost entirely in the hands of the office-holders and ruled by selfish interest.... But I shall not support him. Neither shall I support the Democrats. Far from it. But I think,—in fact I firmly believe,—in case of Grant's nomination we shall have a third movement on foot strong enough to beat both him and the Democrats. I have commenced already to organize it, and when the time comes, I think it will be ready for action.

More realistically, B. Gratz Brown anticipated that, if anything, the Missouri experience must be transferred to the national arena virtually intact, which meant they must choose a Liberal Republican ticket that would be acceptable to the Democrats. He had strong presidential ambitions and knew he needed their support to achieve these hopes. When interviewed by a New York reporter early in July about Liberal prospects, Governor Brown made a strong argument for the need of coalition with the Democrats to assure Grant's defeat. As for platform, he was willing to accept the so-called "New Departure" being put forward by a number of prominent Democrats. This program, adopted by many state Democratic conventions that year, called for acceptance of the postwar constitutional amendments as legitimate results of the conflict and then forgetting the animosities of the past to press on to the solution of the many problems of the present. Privately Brown wrote a Kentucky friend that he hoped the Democrats realized it would take more than

275

a platform to defeat Grant. The opposition must have a candidate who could embody that document in living form before the people. Meanwhile, the Governor pursued a broadly based patronage policy and cooperated with the Democratic leadership in the General Assembly. Having aided in the election of his cousin, Frank Blair, to the Senate by inaction if nothing else, he in turn looked to Frank to help him fulfill his presidential ambitions. Blair had designs of his own, but by late summer discovered that he had no hope of drumming up sufficient backing for another run at the Presidency. Hence, in August, he endorsed Brown and began to solicit support outside Missouri for his candidacy. Blair worked closely with James S. Rollins in the legislature to further the cause among Democrats there. He also joined the latter and Governor Brown on the platform when Cassius Clay of Kentucky spoke at the St. Louis Fair that October on the need for Democratic support of a Liberal Republican candidate to stop Grant. An ardent reformer, Clay had become disenchanted with the Administration when the President recalled him as minister to Russia.

That fall Blair traveled through the South on business for the Senate Committee on Outrages. He was well received everywhere and denounced Radical rule in that region and urged Southern Democrats to support the possum policy that had been used to such advantage in Missouri the previous year. Other Democratic leaders began to take up the cry. By mid-January, 1872, Blair was pushing it before the Missouri legislature. The local effort indeed was culminated that same month as Rollins secured its endorsement by the State Democratic Committee with an appeal to its counterparts in other states to go along. That group's letter indirectly praised Brown as it called for a Liberal Republican nominee whom the Democrats could support. A few days later the Liberal Republicans met in state convention at Jefferson City to chart their course. Amid ringing speeches from their leaders, they adopted a platform largely arranged by Schurz. It embraced the familiar planks on tariff and civil service reform, amnesty and suffrage for all, and a denunciation of big business and big government. Governor Brown gave the final address in which he excoriated President Grant for all the sins of his Administration. Most significantly, however,

Schurz persuaded the Liberal convention to issue a call to all Republicans who favored reform to gather at Cincinnati on May 1 to decide what course to follow in the national campaign.

Having satisfied their political appetites for the time being, the delegates and invited guests prepared to indulge their social tastes that evening at Governor Brown's open house in his new mansion on the bluff overlooking the Missouri River. Pressure for the building of a new home for Missouri's governors had been building for some time. The existing mansion had been built in the 1830's and had suffered from many years of wear and neglect. The legislature had appropriated $20,000 for a new home in 1861, but plans were cancelled because of the war. In their parting messages to the legislature, successive postwar governors had called attention to the need for somehow improving the accommodations of the executive. Governor McClurg had put it quite bluntly: "The present mansion is antiquated, dilapidated and uncomfortable; unsuited to the age and inadequate to the reasonable requirements of the public."

The Brown family spent much of their time at their St. Louis home in the weeks following his inaugural. By March, 1871, the legislature had approved a $50,000 appropriation. The General Assembly appointed the Governor, the State Treasurer, and the State Auditor to act as a commission to contract and superintend construction. After reviewing various plans submitted, they approved those of the St. Louis architectural firm of George Ingham Barnett and Alfred Piquenard. Gottlieb Martin of Jefferson City received the building contract for $56,500 and began work in early May on a site adjacent to the old mansion. That building was destroyed in late October while Mrs. Brown continued to spend most of her time in St. Louis. The handsome new structure taking shape attracted wide attention. One of its key features would be four pink granite columns for the portico, which Governor Brown had donated from his quarry in Iron County. Unfortunately, they were nine inches too short when they arrived for placing at the end of December, but a local newspaper reported that this "unlucky mistake ... will deter the work but little." In donating this gift, the Browns began a custom in which each succeeding first family has made some permanent contribution to the mansion as a remembrance of their occupancy. The total cost of the building when completed was $74,-960, which apparently included furnishings.

The Browns moved into their splendid new home on January 20, 1872. Three days later they held their first official reception in honor of the Grand Duke Alexis of Russia, who was touring the United States and had just completed a buffalo hunt in the West. He arrived in midmorning by special train to be met by state dignitaries and escorted to the mansion for a special luncheon. He departed after an open reception that afternoon at the Madison House across the street, while the Browns got ready for their big open house the following evening in conjunction with the Liberal Republican state convention. This occasion proved to be a magnificent beginning for a home that would continue to house Missouri's governors for the next hundred years. A few years later, one of the Jefferson City papers described the event thus:

> The ladies shone like a Louis XV salon, with high, light puffs of hair and nodding plumes, while the brass buttons and epaulettes of the State Guards outdid themselves and made their wearers look small in comparison. There passed through the parlors that night most of the notable men of the State . . . and others; yes, others, for the great house was packed from the front door to the roof.

As word of the actions of Missouri's Liberal Republicans spread throughout the country, a generally favorable reaction set in among reformist and anti-Grant groups. The Democrats began serious reconsideration of "playing possum." Unfortunately, the movement had begun to attract a variety of disparate elements, a situation that complicated the procedure of choosing platforms and candidates. Brown's name continued to be mentioned among those who might receive the presidential bid, but the increasing favorite by convention eve was Charles Francis Adams, scion of an old-line Massachusetts family and son and grandson of presidents. An ardent reformer, Adams had served with considerable distinction as American minister to Great Britain during the Civil War. Moving up on the outside was Horace Greeley, the erratic editor of the *New York Tribune* who hated Grant but also loved high tariffs. This stance on the tariff issue caused many Liberals of the Grosvenor-Schurz stamp to view him with alarm. It was most important that the Liberals nominate someone who would also have appeal to the Democrats, since by this time most of them realized that therein lay the key to success.

About seven thousand persons packed Exposition Hall in Cincinnati on May 1 as Grosvenor called the convention to order. Rumors had been circulating for some time that he and Schurz were trying to swing Missouri's delegation away from its loyalty to Brown and place it in the vanguard of the movement toward Adams. The correspondent of the *Missouri Democrat* promoted these stories for his own purposes. Soon actions began to confirm the rumors, and someone wired the Governor, who had remained at Jefferson City, that his presence was badly needed to stem the tide. Brown took the next train to Cincinnati, accompanied by his cousin Frank Blair, in an attempt to salvage his political fortunes. They arrived on the evening of May 2, shortly after the convention had evaded the tariff issue by making the platform statement that it really had to be decided within each congressional district, depending upon their industrial needs. Aside from this position, the national platform went right down the line with the principles of the Missouri Liberal Republicans.

Brown found the convention divided but rather quickly assessed his chances for the top nomination as dim, in view of his lack of support from Schurz and Grosvenor. He had long since come to resent these men, particularly Schurz, for virtually taking the 1870 campaign planning out of his hands and then working at cross purposes with him in his wooing of the Democrats. When Schurz, realizing the dangerous mood of the Governor, offered to compromise on an Adams-Brown ticket, Brown, acting apparently on Blair's advice, refused. Rather, he cast his lot with the other front-runner, Horace Greeley, knowing that the New York editor was anathema to the fiery German and his followers. After the first ballot the next morning and before the tallies were announced, Brown withdrew in favor of Greeley, who received the convention's nomination five ballots later. While the Governor did not carry all of the Missouri delegation with him, his announcement and subsequent efforts on Greeley's behalf were a turning point in the proceedings; Brown was rewarded with the vice-presidential nomination by Greeley's promoters. The stunned Schurz men stood almost speechless. After much soul searching during the next few weeks, they decided to accept the ticket and support it. The Democrats, meeting in July after the regular Republicans had renominated Grant, went along with the Liberals on both platform and candidates, although many did so reluctantly. Greeley had been one of the Democracy's strongest critics during the past twenty years, but party leaders realized that support for the Liberals represented their only hope of overthrowing Grant and the Republicans. If all went well, they might be able to dominate the coalition in the long run as their Missouri brethren were already doing.

Cooperation between Democrats and Liberal Republicans in Missouri was a foregone conclusion under the circumstances. By prearrangement the two groups held their state conventions simultaneously on August 21 in the separate legislative chambers of the State Capitol. Each kept informed of the other's proceedings by a conference committee; the two readily agreed to divide the slate of candidates they would put before the electorate that fall. Because of their numerical dominance, the Democrats were given the right to name the head of the ticket together with the state treasurer, the auditor, the attorney general, and the four judges of the state supreme court. Liberals received the positions of lieutenant governor, secretary of state, and register of lands. The two groups split the presidential electors fairly evenly. With several strong candidates in the running for the gubernatorial nomination, the Democrats finally compromised on Silas Woodson, who was chairing their convention. The new nominee could offer a strong background for the office he sought. He had served his native Kentucky in both a constitutional convention and the state legislature before migrating to St. Joseph in 1854 to establish a law practice in that growing community. There he had gained a good reputation as a trial lawyer, and as such became well known across the state. Woodson had made one unsuccessful try for the Missouri legislature in 1868. The circumstances were now much more favorable for his election to the governorship.

The regular Republicans supported Grant's renomination at their state convention and chose former Sen. John B. Henderson as their gubernatorial nominee. Although nationally their ticket swamped Greeley and Brown, locally the Republicans fared badly. Many of the original Liberal bolters apparently returned to the regular fold that fall,[2] but the number of reenfranchised Democrats more than made up the difference. About 110,000 more persons voted in Missouri than had done so two years earlier, and the Republican vote nearly doubled while the Democrat–Liberal ticket increased its total by 50 per cent over that which Brown had received in 1870. Continued immigration, as well as reenfranchisement, help to explain the difference, for new settlers continued to pour into Missouri throughout the 1870's. Woodson ran some 5,000 votes ahead of the Greeley–Brown ticket, grinding out a victory over Henderson by 156,777 to 121,889. The Republican gubernatorial nominee carried only 33 counties—the staunch bailiwicks along the Iowa border and those in the southwest. Missouri gained four seats in the House of Representatives after the 1870 census, and the Democrats captured 9 out of the 13 to which the state was now entitled. In the new Missouri House they would outnumber Republicans nearly 2½ to 1, while the State Senate would have 20 Democrats, 11 Republicans, and 2 Liberals. Missouri Democrats had returned to power in a decisive way. It would be thirty-five long, lean years before Republicans once again had a taste of it at the state level. Because of its debacle at the national level and its weak position within the local coalition, Liberal Republicanism folded its tent as an outright political organization, its members seeking shelter in whichever of the other parties suited them best. Probably the greater number remained within the Democratic column, both for spoils and out of principle, but an accurate estimate is almost impossible to make.

For all its outward prosperity and the reduction of wartime tensions in many quarters, Governor Woodson inherited a restive state from his predecessor in January, 1873. Lawlessness was on the increase, especially in western Missouri, as the depredations of the James boys and others continued apace. In the aftermath of war, many returning former Confederates had difficulty

2. Particularly noticeable in the gubernatorial returns was the swing back to the Republican ticket in those counties with large German populations. This trend was not as noticeable in the presidential returns because of the deep dislike of the Germans for both Grant and Greeley.

finding steady employment and had turned to armed robbery as a means of support. Still others had been "in the bush" too long and could not readjust to peacetime living. The general repressiveness of Radical rule during the postwar era in certain Conservative areas had fostered violence, frequently by partisans on both sides. Governor Brown had had to call out local militia in the Bootheel counties of Stoddard and Dunklin in October, 1871, to quell the activities of some Ku Klux Klan elements there, but aside from this incident he consistently refused to resort to the militia action his predecessors had used. He preferred to use local law enforcement agencies, and the records abound with reward notices he issued for a variety of fugitives.[3] As a result there was a marked increase in local vigilante groups to cope with the tide of lawlessness. Sometimes they worked closely with law enforcement agencies. Often they operated on their own with little concern for anything other than the protection of their own interests.

Violence also permeated political affairs. Many counties were becoming restive under their heavy railroad debts, especially where there had been default on construction. In the case of Cass County, a conspiracy developed between certain county officials and a railroad construction outfit involving $229,000 in county bonds. When the plot was uncovered, some of the guilty persons fled while others came under indictment. Those who were discovered boasted that they could never be convicted. In the face of a hastily formed vigilante committee, however, they decided to retire to Kansas City pending the opening of their trial. En route to safety on the evening of April 24, 1872, their train was stopped at Gunn City by an armed mob who took the three fugitives off and shot them. Although some attempt at an investigation was made, no one was ever brought to justice.

3. Governor Brown believed that the prison system was grievously outmoded as a means of reforming the criminal element. He favored some form of work programs for minor offenses. This type of system would reduce the number of incarcerated and supposedly make their rehabilitation easier. Brown repeatedly called upon the legislature, without success, to move in the direction of establishing reformatories "to rescue juvenile offenders from the vicious path that leads to the state prison." He also opposed capital punishment and stayed all executions during his term of office.

The railroads increasingly became a source of irritation among Missouri's rural population. As the construction mania died down in the early 1870's, many farmers and small-town businessmen began to feel the pinch of being served by noncompetitive lines. These railroads frequently discriminated against the small shipper on freight rates, gave shoddy service on shipments, and ignored or delayed dealing with claims on losses. Because of the high degree of competitiveness in certain areas, which lowered if it did not actually destroy profit margin there, the railroads sought to make up their losses or increase their profits at the expense of those who had no other recourse but to use their services. At the outset of his administration, Governor Brown had called for a "Board of Railway Commissioners" to offer some form of regulation over existing lines, but railroad lobbies proved too strong in the legislature for anything concrete to be accomplished. Brown did secure the establishment of a State Board of Equalization, however, to more equitably assess and collect taxes due from the railroads. Although railroad property was valued at $50 million in the state (approximately 10 per cent of Missouri's taxable wealth), the companies paid little or no taxes. With the great increase in the general tax burden as a result of the legislature's "giveaway" to the railroads in 1868, many resented what they considered basic inequities of a twofold nature: the benefits accruing to the lines in profits and the minimum return to the state in taxes. It was not until the Twenty-eighth General Assembly strengthened the Board of Equalization in 1873 by providing for enforced collection of taxes that Missouri began to realize its just share of railroad tax revenues. With this new legislation, the amount collected rose from $11,876.66 in 1873 to $306,656.03 in 1875.

Governor Woodson shared his predecessor's concerns with these and related problems. Tensions mounted increasingly during his first year in office, spurred in large measure by the financial panic that hit the country in mid-September, 1873. The following month representatives of all the various farm clubs and organizations around the state met in Jefferson City to air their grievances. These complaints included concern over discriminatory rail rates, high taxes, and dishonest public officials. They severely scored the retroactive pay raise which Congress had recently voted itself. To help offset the high rail charges, they called for congressional aid to improve navigation on the Mississippi River. Many of these groups were disparate in their outlook, however, because they represented a variety of local and special interests. Many realized the need for some unifying force of a more permanent type through which they might better exercise their influence.

Some believed they had already found such an organization in the Patrons of Husbandry, better known as the National Grange. It had begun in 1868 as a fraternal order for farmers through the efforts of Oliver H. Kelley, a former clerk in the federal Bureau of Agriculture. Two years later Kelley visited Missouri at the invitation of Norman J. Colman, who had done so much to promote agricultural interests through his weekly paper. With the full backing of Colman and his *Rural World*, Kelley spent two weeks in the St. Louis vicinity organizing two "subordinate granges" and a temporary State Grange. Thereafter growth was slow until November, 1872, when it became possible for Thomas R. Allen, who had been active in the Missouri movement from the beginning, to assume a full-time position as general deputy with responsibility for developing the organization throughout the state. Allen's appointment coincided with the mounting unrest previously mentioned. He had the full backing of *Colman's Rural World* and found that it frequently paved the way for him as he moved into a new area of the state. A meeting of some 300 farmers at Knobnoster in May, 1873, established a permanent State Grange in which 190 of the then existing 306 local groups were represented. Immediately thereafter Allen expanded his staff of deputies with phenomenal results. By February, 1874, Missouri had 1,732 subordinate granges; a year later, when the national movement stood at its peak, the state ranked first with 2,009. Within these local groups, and indeed throughout the entire structure, women had equal voting rights with men, making the Grange one of the first major organizations to grant this status. Membership was open to any boy at age sixteen or girl at age fourteen who made the pursuit of agriculture their principal concern.

The local granges improved the social and intellectual life of their communities by bringing people together for entertainment and discussion. The grange meetings helped break down the isolation of rural life. Songs, special music, book reviews, and debates and discussions on a wide variety of topics formed a part of most gatherings. The men might discuss such things as the best variety of seed to use or the most profitable breed of hog, while the women talked about the rearing of children, how to plan a convenient kitchen, or the care of poultry. The State Grange provided for each county lecturers whom it supplied with materials on matters of immediate concern. Most members subscribed to *Colman's Rural World*, which served as the official organ of the Missouri Grange until 1875 when the state executive committee established *Monthly Talk*, a paper devoted exclusively to the group's interests. Many of the newspapers reserved one or two columns weekly for Grange news.

The Granges took a great deal of interest in local schools and stressed the need for community concern and individual involvement in promoting improvements. They displayed a special interest in the agricultural college at the university with the complaint that it provided too much theoretical instruction and not enough practical training. After Allen visited the school in 1874 at the invitation of James S. Rollins, the state organization began urging its local councils to lobby with their legislators for increased funds to make possible a wider variety of programs. Although there is no indication that such efforts paid off in large sums, they did improve communication between the college and the agricultural community.

One of the Grangers' major concerns was the promotion of cooperative enterprises to enable the farmer to better utilize his economic power. In many areas they sponsored weekly stock sales at the county seats, in which farmers could display and buy or sell not only cattle but also any other item for which there might be a local market. Cooperative stores were established in a number of communities and some, such as that at Otterville in Cooper County, were highly successful. A few cooperative grain elevators and warehouses were also started, with mixed results. The major problems in these enterprises were finding enough good managers and securing sufficient support from area farmers to make them pay. The State Grange appointed a purchasing agent in 1874 to coordinate ordering and make arrangements with manufacturers and dealers on reductions for bulk orders. *Colman's Rural World* reported the following year that this officer had handled $500,000 worth of business at a savings of several thousand dollars to the Grangers throughout Missouri. That same year the organization opened a wholesale store in St. Louis for the benefit of local cooperatives and purchasing agents, which was doing an aggregate business of more than $1 million within two years. The rural press abounded with projections of other types of cooperative enterprises from banks to an implement factory to meat-processing plants. But there is no indication that any of these proposals got beyond the planning stage.

Although the National Grange's Declaration of Purposes, which the Missouri organization adopted in 1874, forbade political activity on the part of its member groups, it also stressed the importance of each member fulfilling his duty as a citizen by being active in politics. Hence, it is not too surprising that the Patrons of Husbandry began to play an increasingly larger political role in Missouri and elsewhere, especially with the worsening economic situation that followed in the wake of the Panic of 1873. Local units increasingly began passing resolutions on a variety of topics for the enlightenment of their legislators. These opinions embraced many of the concerns outlined earlier in this chapter. As they met with seemingly little response from either Democratic or Republican leaders in the legislature—albeit they received a sympathetic hearing from Governors Brown and Woodson—many farmers, including active Grangers, began to talk of organizing an independent third party. Colman and Allen worked actively to discourage such a move with the admonition that the Grangers could work more effectively as a "balance of power" between the two existing parties. But in view of Colman's active candidacy for the Democratic gubernatorial nomination, many felt that he was putting his own political interests ahead of theirs.

Sensing the urgency of the issue at the outset of an election year, Governor Woodson strongly proposed the establishment of a board of managers to regulate the railroads in the public interest. The railroad lobby defeated the measure, however, as the legislature went no further than requiring one road to accept the cars of its competitors at the same rate charged for its own. It was much more receptive to Woodson's recommendations for curbing lawlessness. This issue had taken a new turn on January 31 when a band of outlaws, presumably the James gang, robbed a train at Gads Hill in Wayne County—the first such occurrence in Missouri. As other incidents followed, the Governor sent a special message to the General Assembly deploring his lack of resources with which to combat the mounting crime wave that seemed to be threatening to overrun the state. Although the legislators refused to appropriate $25,000 for reactivation of the militia to deal with the problem, they did provide Woodson with $10,000 for a 25-agent secret police force. These detectives proved largely ineffective, however, as the James boys and others of their ilk seemed able to muster endless sympathy from large segments of former secessionists in spite of their depredations.

Some time in February, 1874, a gathering of farmers at Boonville, possibly meeting simultaneously with the annual State Grange convention there, appointed a six-man committee to determine if "the exigencies of the times and the desire of the people demanded the formation of an independent political organization which should be under the control of the people, and not partisan tricksters and wire pullers." Following the adjournment of another unproductive legislative session, the "Six Simpletons of Boonville," as the *St. Louis Globe* promptly dubbed them, decided that the time was indeed ripe for such a party. Consequently they issued a call to convention for the following September at Jefferson City. On the appointed day, 450 delegates, who had been chosen in local meetings across the state and including at least 100 Grangers, met to establish the People's party. They called, among other things, for the regulation of railroads and the improvement of water transportation, the reduction of taxes and tariffs with a strict economy in the administration of government. They opposed any further retraction of the currency and advocated the improvement of the public schools. Finally, they urged an end to the lawlessness that hindered Missouri's growth because of the bad image it gave the state. To represent them in the forthcoming election, the People's party nominated a slate headed by William Gentry, a prominent farm-

287

er from Pettis County who had been a prewar Whig and more recently a Conservative Democrat. In order to provide balance, they named as their candidate for lieutenant governor S. W. Headlee, "square Republican and not bigoted," who had served several terms in each of the houses of the legislature.

Now it was the Republicans' turn to "play possum." They had been thoroughly demoralized by their setbacks of the preceding three years and anticipated a third political group such as the People's party, so they had begun moving in this direction early in the year when their legislative caucus pledged to support "every movement which looks to the restoration of peace, prosperity, and good government for all." After the People's party convention, the Republican State Committee affirmed this position in August by calling a meeting of their own at which they ratified the idea of not having a statewide ticket that fall.

Freed of the necessity for coalition with the now defunct Liberals, the Democratic party ran a full slate of their own candidates for the first time in six years. They met at Jefferson City in late August and nominated Charles H. Hardin, prominent Mexico attorney and state senator, as their candidate for governor. With former Confederates now openly participating in party affairs, Hardin gained the nod over Francis M. Cockrell of Warrensburg, who had been a general in the Southern army. A veteran legislator, Hardin, too, had been a Whig before the war. He sat out the conflict on his Audrain County farm and was accused of sympathizing with the South, although he reportedly cast the only vote against secession at the rump legislative session at Neosho in October, 1861. After the conflict, he became active in the Conservative and the Democratic parties. He and Gentry then had similar political careers until they now confronted each other as rivals. The Democrats made a strong effort to hold the agrarian vote against the encroachments of "Farmer Gentry" and his followers by naming Colman as their candidate for lieutenant governor.

The campaign dealt largely with personalities as both sides uncovered some questionable dealings by the other's gubernatorial candidate. The People's party, taking up a longstanding Republican cry, tried to pin the blame for the state's widespread lawlessness on the Democrats, but with little success. Carl

Schurz, whose Senate term was due to expire that winter, saw the new organization as a reincarnation of the Liberal movement, "strong enough to carry to a successful end ... the task of completing the work of 1870." But other reformers, including Schurz's former lieutenant, Joseph Pulitzer, denounced the movement as a fraud and ended up in the Democratic camp. Since the Democrats derided their opponents as the tool of the discredited Republicans and Colman worked hard to hold the Granger vote, Hardin had little difficulty in defeating Gentry by 37,000 votes. Although Gentry bettered Henderson's percentages of two years earlier in 35 counties, indicating some Granger defections, he ran behind the 1872 Republican candidate in 53 others, which possibly meant that many of that party simply did not vote. The Democrats swept all 13 congressional districts and strongly dominated both houses of the new General Assembly. In one of its first acts, that body rejected Schurz's bid for reelection and replaced him with Cockrell, thereby pacifying the Confederate wing of the Democratic party.

The Grangers could be pleased with the election results in several regards. Although they had suffered some defections to the People's party, they had held their organization basically intact. They would peak in 1875 so far as political power was concerned, however, and thereafter other groups would become more prominent spokesmen for the farmers' discontents. The new legislature responded to the agrarian challenge, though, by establishing a board of commissioners to regulate railroad charges, both passenger and freight, and to exercise certain other supervisory functions with regard to the general conditions of the lines. A signal victory for the Grangers at the time, the new regulatory body soon proved itself more advisory than supervisory, to the disillusionment of those who had urged its establishment. While triple damages might be collected for rates that were in excess of those set by the commission, these reparations could be secured only by court action, which few farmers could afford.

As it turned out, the Grangers also had an opportunity to exercise a more permanent influence in the reshaping of Missouri's organic law as a result of this election, for among the other questions the voters had to decide was that of calling a new constitutional convention. After facing frustration on this issue in three successive legislative sessions, the Democrats had finally pushed it through in March, 1874; Governor Woodson, though not favoring a convention for economic reasons, agreed to go along. The question aroused little enthusiasm during the campaign, but the measure won approval by only 283 votes out of 261,670 cast—an indication that most Missourians had learned to live with the Drake Constitution, once its proscriptive portions had been removed.

Missourians again went to the polls on January 26, 1875, to elect two delegates from each of the state's 34 senatorial districts to revamp their constitution. The personnel who gathered in Jefferson City on May 5 to begin this task differed markedly from the last such body. Whereas it had been predominantly Republican, the new group contained only 8 of that party. Eighteen of the 68 delegates had seen service, either civil or military, with the Confederacy, while 15 had served in the Union Army. The group tended toward middle age. Most of them were men of substance with a naturally conservative bent. Two thirds were lawyers, and most had had some prior political experience at either the state or local level. Only 1 had sat in the 1865 convention, but 9 had served in the wartime one. Symbolically chairing the new group was former Sen. Waldo P. Johnson of Osceola, who had been expelled from the United States Senate in 1862 for desertion to the Confederacy. Thereafter he had served under Sterling Price as a lieutenant colonel before being chosen a senator from Missouri in the Confederate Congress.

Meeting for almost three months, the delegates produced a basically conservative document that reflected the changing mood of the times. It increased the power of the governor at the expense of the legislature. It extended the terms of many state offices and instituted the four-year term with no reelection for the governor, which helped provide greater stability. The governor received the power of item veto over appropriation bills, while the margin whereby the General Assembly could override any veto was increased from a simple to a two-thirds majority. Should it be necessary to call a special session, the executive would retain control over the subjects to be considered, as he had under the last organic document.

On the other hand, the legislature suffered sharp restrictions, an indication of discontent with what many considered the excesses of the past ten years. It was specifically forbidden to hold annual sessions—a practice that had developed by adjourning the regular session at the close of its business until the following winter. Severe curtailments were placed on the legislative proceedings and the powers of the General Assembly, including a list of thirty-two specific topics on which the legislators were forbidden to pass any local or special law. The convention was particularly sharp in its limitations on the exercise of fiscal power at both the state and local levels. Indeed the prohibitions on lending, debt, and taxation put the state in a literal straitjacket, which would hamper future growth while forcing the practice of false economy.

The Granger influence came in the article on corporations. Thirteen of its twenty-seven sections dealt with the railroads, which were declared public highways whose companies were common carriers. The legislature received full authority to set reasonable maximum rates and prevent various abuses of corporate power. The giving and receiving of free passes by any official was strictly forbidden. Further restrictions were also placed on the granting of special corporate charters.

Two important positive steps forward were the creation of a St. Louis Court of Appeals to help relieve the burden on the state supreme court and the granting of home rule through charter to St. Louis or any city with a population of more than 100,000. The home rule charter had emanated from the desire of many in St. Louis to separate the city from the county government and to lessen the interference in its affairs by the state legislature.[4]

The convention unanimously adopted the new constitution on August 2, 1875. It received voter approval on October 30 in an election that indicated general apathy over the question; only 105,000 even bothered to cast ballots. With its adoption, however, Missouri had come full cycle in fifteen years. During the next thirty years, conservative interests would be generally entrenched in state government through the unbreakable control of the Democratic party. Much of the leadership of that period

4. See p. 202.

had strong roots in prewar politics. While they could not undo completely the progress of the postwar era, they did slow it significantly. After a decade and a half of almost continuous turmoil, the basic conservatism of Missouri's people had reasserted itself.

ESSAY ON SOURCES

The purpose of this essay is twofold. First, it is designed to indicate the sources consulted in the preparation of this study, and second, it is offered as a guide for further reading. The list is necessarily selective, but an attempt has been made to include the most pertinent material dealing with Missouri's history from 1860 to 1875.

LIST OF ABBREVIATIONS USED

The Bulletin for *Bulletin of the Missouri Historical Society*
MHR for *Missouri Historical Review*

GENERAL HISTORIES AND REFERENCE WORKS

The most thorough account of the state's development is David D. March, *The History of Missouri*, 4 vols. (New York and West Palm Beach, 1967). It updates but does not supplant Floyd C. Shoemaker, *Missouri and Missourians: Land of Contrasts and People of Achievements*, 5 vols. (Chicago, 1943). Still helpful, especially for anecdotal material, is *Missouri: Mother of the West*, 5 vols. (Chicago and New York, 1930) by Walter Williams and Floyd C. Shoemaker. Also useful for details is *Encyclopedia of the History of Missouri*, 6 vols. (New York, 1901), edited by Howard L. Conard. The best one-volume work on the state's past is Duane Meyer, *The Heritage of Missouri: A History* (St. Louis, 1970). *Missouri: A Guide to the "Show Me" State*, rev. ed. (New York, 1954), compiled by workers of the Writers' Program of the Works Projects Administration in the State of Missouri, contains a good deal of Missouriana as well as general history. William F. Switzler, *Illustrated History of Missouri from 1541 to 1877* (St. Louis, 1879), is helpful because its writer participated in many of the events of the period under consideration here. Although no general study of Missouri during the Civil War exists, William E. Parrish, *Missouri Under Radical Rule, 1865–1870* (Columbia, Missouri, 1965) is a comprehensive treatment of the state during Reconstruction.

293

The best one-volume reference for the national scene during this period is James G. Randall and David Donald, *The Civil War and Reconstruction*, 2d ed. rev. (Lexington, Massachusetts, 1969). The most thorough, up-to-date treatment of the war years is Allan Nevins, *The War for the Union*, 4 vols. (New York, 1959–1971). To understand Missouri in relation to the other border states, one should consult Edward C. Smith, *The Borderland in the Civil War* (New York, 1927), and Richard O. Curry, ed., *Radicalism, Racism, and Party Realignment: The Border States During Reconstruction* (Baltimore and London, 1969). For a more complete understanding of wartime Kansas, with which Missouri engaged in so much fighting, one is referred to Albert Castel, *A Frontier State at War: Kansas, 1861–1865* (Ithaca, New York, 1958).

MANUSCRIPT COLLECTIONS

Both the Missouri Historical Society in St. Louis and the State Historical Society in Columbia have extensive manuscript collections, including good sets of miscellaneous Missouri Civil War papers, that are important to this period. In the Missouri Historical Society may be found the papers of Edward Bates, Henry T. Blow, James O. Broadhead, John F. Darby, James B. Eads, William G. Eliot, Hamilton R. Gamble, Charles Gibson, William B. Napton, William K. Patrick, Thomas C. Reynolds, George R. Smith, and George R. Taylor. The State Historical Society holds the manuscript autobiography of Charles D. Drake and the papers of James S. Rollins (currently closed to the public) and Robert T. Van Horn.

Key collections that include materials about Missouri at the Library of Congress are the papers of Presidents Abraham Lincoln and Andrew Johnson and those of the Blair family (the Francis P. Blair, Jr., and the Gist Blair papers), John M. Schofield, and Carl Schurz. In the National Archives may be found the personal papers of Attorney General Bates that were written during the war period, the records of the military Department of the Missouri and of the Missouri–Arkansas District of the Bureau of Refugees, Freedmen and Abandoned Lands. Additional archives collections that were valuable to the writing of this book were the Blair–Lee Papers at Princeton University, Princeton, New Jersey; the Grenville M. Dodge Papers at the Iowa State Department of History and Archives, Des Moines; and the papers of Henry D. Bacon and Samuel L. M. Barlow at the Huntington Library, San Marino, California.

PUBLISHED DOCUMENTS, PAPERS, AND CONTEMPORARY ACCOUNTS

The periodic census reports compiled by the United States Government are important to any understanding of Missouri and its people. These documents contain statistical breakdowns concerning all aspects of political, economic, and social life. In addition, the manuscripts of the censuses for all Missouri counties in both 1860 and 1870 are available at the State Historical Society in Columbia. Invaluable to a study of the war in Missouri is *War of the Rebellion: Official Records of the Union and Confederate Armies*, 4 series, 70 vols. (Washington, D.C., 1880–1902). Congressional debates and proceedings on issues concerning Missouri are found in *The Congressional Globe* for the 37th through 43rd Congresses (Washington, D.C., 1861–1875). The records for disputed congressional elections in postwar Missouri will be found in Chester H. Rowell, ed., *A Historical and Legal Digest of All the Contested Election Cases in the House of Representatives of the United States from the First to the Fifty-sixth Congress, 1789–1901* (Washington, D.C., 1901). A helpful report is Senate Document 412, 57th Congress, 1st session, *Missouri Troops in Service During the Civil War* (Washington, D.C., 1902). Yet another valuable federal collection is the *Reports of the Commissioner of the General Land Office to the Secretary of the Interior, 1865–1875* (Washington, D.C., 1865–1875).

Although they are not comparable to the record of debates that took place in Congress, the *Journal of the House of Representatives of the State of Missouri* and the *Journal of the Senate of the State of Missouri*, 21st through 27th General Assemblies (Jefferson City, 1861–1875) provide an official record for the state's legislative body. Its final acts were regularly published under the title, *Laws of the State of Missouri*. Those laws that were passed during this period are summarized in *The Revised Statutes of the State of Missouri*, 2 vols. (Jefferson City, 1879). The executive branch of state government provides a number of important collections. Official gubernatorial writings are found in *The Messages and Proclamations of the Governors of the State of Missouri* (Columbia, Missouri, 1922, 1924). Volume III, edited by Buel Leopard and Floyd C. Shoemaker, covers the Jackson and Gamble administrations. The writings of Governors Hall, Fletcher, and McClurg are found in Volume IV, edited by Grace G. Avery and Floyd C. Shoemaker. Volume V, with the same editors, deals with the Brown, Woodson, and Hardin administrations. Additional useful references are the *Annual Reports of the Adjutant-General of the*

State of Missouri, 1863–1874 (Jefferson City, 1864–1875), the *Reports of the Superintendent of Public Schools of the State of Missouri, 1865–1875* (Jefferson City, 1866–1876), and the *Annual Reports of the Missouri State Board of Agriculture, 1865–1875* (Jefferson City, 1866–1876). The work of the Missouri Supreme Court is covered in *Reports of Cases Argued and Determined in the Supreme Court of the State of Missouri*, Vols. 36–61 (St. Louis, 1866–1876).

The official records of Missouri's several conventions are in the *Journal of the Missouri State Convention Held at Jefferson City and St. Louis*, March, 1861–June, 1863 (St. Louis, 1861–1863); *Proceedings of the Missouri State Convention Held at Jefferson City and St. Louis*, March, 1861–June, 1863 (St. Louis, 1861–1863); *Journal of Missouri State Convention Held at St. Louis*, January 6–April 10, 1865 (St. Louis, 1865); *Journal of Missouri Constitutional Convention of 1875*, 2 vols. (Columbia, Missouri, 1921); Isidor Loeb and Floyd C. Shoemaker, eds., *Debates of the Missouri Constitutional Convention of 1875*, 12 vols. (Columbia, Missouri, 1944). The proceedings for the 1865 convention will be found in the *Missouri Democrat* and the *Missouri Republican* for that period both published in St. Louis.

In addition to federal and state documentary sources, useful material on wartime activities in Missouri may be found in Frank Moore, ed., *The Rebellion Record*, 12 vols. (New York, 1861–1868) and the *Final Report of the Western Sanitary Commission*, May 9, 1864–December 31, 1865 (St. Louis, 1866). References to the labor movement in Missouri during the 1860's are scattered through *A Documentary History of American Industrial Society*, 10 vols. (Cleveland, 1910), edited by John R. Commons and others. The rhetoric of the Radical movement in its early stages may be seen in Charles D. Drake, *Union and Anti-Slavery Speeches Delivered During the Rebellion* (Cincinnati, 1864). For an understanding of Conservative thought, one should consult *Speeches and Letters of James S. Rollins*, 7 vols. (St. Louis, 1876–1882), and *The Diary of Edward Bates, 1859–1866*, edited by Howard K. Beale, which is Volume IV of the Annual Report of the American Historical Association for the Year 1930 (Washington, D.C., 1933). *The Writings of Carl Schurz*, 6 vols. (New York, 1913), has been edited by Frederic Bancroft. Far more revealing of this key figure in the Liberal Republican movement are *The Intimate Letters of Carl Schurz, 1841–1869* (Madison, Wisconsin, 1928), edited by Joseph Schaefer. President Lincoln's heavy involvement with wartime Missouri is amply evidenced through the correspondence contained in John G. Nicolay and John Hay, eds., *The Complete Works* of *Abraham Lincoln*, 12 vols. (Cumberland Gap, Tennessee, 1894), and Roy P. Basler, ed., *The Collected Works of Abraham Lincoln*, 9 vols. (New Brunswick, New Jersey, 1953–1955).

There are numerous collections of selected letters that reveal the observations of various participants in the war in Missouri. Among the more interesting are C. B. Rollins, ed., "Letters of George Caleb Bingham to James S. Rollins," *MHR*, 33 (October, 1938), 45–78, (January, 1939), 203–29, (April, 1939), 349–84; Alexander Niven, ed., "The Private Papers of Dr. William M. McPheeters," *The Bulletin*, 19 (October, 1962), 51–56; Harvey L. Carter and Norma L. Peterson, eds., "William S. Stewart Letters, 1861–1862," *MHR*, 61 (January, 1967), 187–228, (April, 1967), 303–20, (July, 1967), 463–88; Albert N. Doerschuk, ed., "Extracts from War-time Letters, 1861–1864," *MHR*, 23 (October, 1928), 99–110; Nicholas P. Hardeman, ed., "Bushwhacker Activity on the Missouri Border. Letters to Dr. Glen O. Hardeman, 1862–1865," *MHR*, 58 (April, 1964), 265–77; Jared C. Lohdell, "The Civil War Journal and Letters of Colonel John VanDeusen DuBois—April 12, 1861 to October 16, 1862," *MHR*, 60 (July, 1966), 436–59, 61 (October, 1966), 22–50; Vivian K. McLarty, ed., "The Civil War Letters of Colonel Bazel F. Lazear," *MHR*, 44 (April, 1950), 254–73, (July, 1950), 387–401; William G. Bek, ed., "The Civil War Diary of John T. Buegel," *MHR*, 40 (April, 1946), 307–29, (July, 1946), 503–30; [Isaac Hockaday], "Letters from the Battle of Lexington," *MHR*, 56 (October, 1961), 53–58; Virginia Easley, ed., "Journal of the Civil War in Missouri: 1861, Henry Martyn Cheavens," *MHR*, 56 (October, 1961), 12–25; James E. Moss, ed., "Missouri Confederate in the Civil War: The Journal of Henry Martyn Cheavens, 1862–1863," *MHR*, 57 (October, 1962), 16–52; and Donald H. Welsh, ed., "A Union Band Director Views Camp Rolla, 1861," *MHR*, 55 (July, 1961), 307–43.

Many participants in Missouri's turbulent affairs of this period have written their reminiscences. The memoirs of three Eastern reporters who covered the war there in 1861 are Thomas W. Knox, *Camp-Fire and Cotton-Field: Southern Adventure in Time of War* (New York, 1865); Albert D. Richardson, *The Secret Service, the Field, the Dungeon, and the Escape* (Philadelphia, 1865); and two works by Franc B. Wilkie, *Walks About Chicago, 1871–1881, And Army and Miscellaneous Sketches* (Chicago, 1882), and *Pen and Powder* (Boston, 1888). Three of the Union's principal generals left their remembrances of the 1861 events in Missouri: Ulysses S. Grant, *Personal Memoirs*, 2 vols. (New York, 1885–1886); Philip H. Sheridan, *Per-*

sonal Memoirs, 2 vols. (New York, 1902); and William T. Sherman, *Memoirs*, 2 vols. (New York, 1875). The sole Missouri military commander to write a complete autobiography is John M. Schofield, *Forty-six Years in the Army* (New York, 1897). Two other Union generals who served in Missouri in 1861 published brief memoirs: Franz Sigel, "Military Operations in Missouri in the Summer and Autumn of 1861," *MHR*, 26 (July, 1932), 354–67, and James P. Jones, ed., "Campaigning in Missouri: Civil War Memoir of General Jefferson C. Davis," *MHR*, 54 (October, 1959), 39–45. Military memoirs by Confederate soldiers are those of Basil W. Duke, *Reminiscences* (New York, 1911), who helped organize the St. Louis Minute Men in 1861 and later became a general in the Southern armies, and Joseph A. Mudd, *With Porter in North Missouri* (Washington, D.C., 1909), who was one of the Confederacy's recruiters of 1862. Mudd also recorded his account, "What I Saw at Wilson's Creek," *MHR*, 7 (January, 1913), 89–105. Other narratives by participants in the various military engagements in Missouri may be found in Clarence C. Buel and Robert U. Johnson, eds., *Battles and Leaders of the Civil War*, 4 vols. (New York, 1887–1888).

The only one of Missouri's four wartime governors to leave a memoir is Thomas C. Reynolds, whose manuscript "General Sterling Price and the Confederacy" is available in his papers at the Missouri Historical Society. Another manuscript of considerable importance is "Autobiography" by Charles D. Drake in the State Historical Society. Unfortunately, it does not account for the time after his election to the United States Senate in 1867. The *Reminiscences of Carl Schurz*, 3 vols. (New York, 1908) are valuable for the later period of Radical politics that led to the Liberal-Republican split. Other political memoirs are those of a Radical congressman from northeastern Missouri, David P. Dyer, *Autobiography and Reminiscences* (St. Louis, 1922); a Conservative state supreme court judge who was ousted by the Radicals in 1865, William V. N. Bay, *Reminiscences of the Bench and Bar in Missouri* (St. Louis, 1878); a leading Conservative and prewar mayor, John F. Darby, *Personal Recollections and Many Prominent People Whom I Have Known, and of Events* (St. Louis, 1880); a wartime Radical mayor of St. Louis, Chauncey I. Filley, *Some Republican History of Missouri* (St. Louis, 1898); prominent postwar Radical editor in St. Louis, John F. Hume, *The Abolitionists* (New York, 1905); Democratic lieutenant governor under Silas Woodson, Charles P. Johnson, *Personal Recollections of Some of Missouri's Eminent Statesmen and Lawyers* (Columbia, Missouri,

1903); and the son of a prominent St. Louis Conservative during this period, Rolla Wells, *Episodes of My Life* (St. Louis, 1933). Also of interest from the political viewpoint is Cyrus Thompson, "Reminiscences of Official Life in Jefferson City, 1865-1875," *MHR*, 23 (July, 1929), 550-67. Thompson worked in the office of his brother Alonzo, who was state auditor during the Fletcher administration. Daniel M. Grissom, a prominent St. Louis businessman affiliated with the Pacific Railroad, has left several "Personal Recollections of Distinguished Missourians" for this period, including "Abiel Leonard," *MHR*, 18 (April, 1924), 400-403; "James S. Rollins," 18 (July, 1924), 546-52; "Sterling Price," *MHR*, 20 (October, 1925), 110-11; "Frank P. Blair," *MHR*, 20 (April, 1926), 397-98; and "Claiborne F. Jackson," *MHR*, 20 (July, 1926), 504-8.

A memoir with an excellent description of wartime St. Louis is Galusha Anderson, *A Border City During the Civil War* (Boston, 1908). Anderson was a Baptist minister and an active Unionist. Also valuable in this regard are the reminiscences of Hannah I. Stagg, "Local Incidents of the Civil War," *Missouri Historical Society Collections*, 4 (1912), 63-72. Although it is neither as complete nor perceptive, an interesting work about western Missouri is George Miller, *Missouri's Memorable Decade, 1860-1870: An Historical Sketch, Personal-Political-Religious* (Columbia, Missouri, 1898); the author was a Presbyterian minister in the Kansas City area. Another useful, brief memoir is William H. Wilson, "A Missouri Merchant Recalls the Civil War: Reminiscences of Thomas B. Bullene of Kansas City," *The Bulletin*, 18 (July, 1962), 305-9. For a postwar view of that growing metropolis, see Mary L. McCarty, "Recollections of Kansas City, 1866-1916," *MHR*, 45 (October, 1950), 35-46. A glimpse of Missouri journalism during this period is offered by William Hyde, "Newspapers and Newspaper People of Three Decades," *Missouri Historical Society Publications*, 1 (1896), 14-15.

NEWSPAPERS

The State Historical Society of Missouri in Columbia has the largest collection of state newspapers of any organization of its type in the United States, and most of the papers indicated here may be found there. A complete guide to all known Missouri newspapers located in both Missouri and out-of-state archives is William H. Taft, *Missouri Newspapers: When and Where, 1808-1963* (Columbia Missouri, 1964). The pace setters for the state press during this period were the

Missouri Republican and the *Missouri Democrat*, both published at St. Louis. Their very titles are fascinating because they belie their politics; the *Republican* had been a Whig journal in the prewar period and then became Conservative–Democratic, while the *Democrat*, beginning as a Democratic paper in the 1850's, turned Republican during the war years. The most important newspapers outstate were the Columbia *Missouri Statesman* with its strong Conservative bent and the pro-Radical Jefferson City *Missouri State Times*. Other strongly Conservative papers were the *Canton Press*, the *Carthage Weekly Banner*, the Richmond *North-West Conservator*, the *Sedalia Democrat*, the *Louisiana Journal*, the *Liberty Tribune*, the Fulton *Missouri Telegraph*, the Jefferson City *Peoples' Weekly Tribune*, and Lexington's *The Weekly Caucasian*. Important Radical journals were the *Kansas City Daily Journal of Commerce*, the *Gallatin North Missourian*, the St. Joseph *Morning Herald*, Springfield's *The Missouri Weekly Patriot*, the Oregon *Holt County Sentinel*, *The Chillicothe Spectator*, and *The Sedalia Times*. Even though the file of the St. Louis *Industrial Advocate* (August, 1866–February, 1867) in the State Historical Society covers a short period of time, it provides revealing insights into the Missouri labor movement, while the St. Louis *Journal of Education* does the same for the public school movement. The St. Louis *Christian Advocate*, a Methodist journal, is the only religious newspaper for this period in the Columbia archives.

BOOKS AND ARTICLES, DISSERTATIONS AND THESES

BIOGRAPHIES AND BIOGRAPHICAL STUDIES

There are only two full-scale biographies of the Missouri governors who are dealt with in this volume: Wilbert H. Rosin, "Hamilton Rowan Gamble, Missouri's Civil War Governor," Ph.D. diss., University of Missouri, Columbia, 1960; and Norma L. Peterson, *Freedom and Franchise: The Political Career of B. Gratz Brown* (Columbia, Missouri, 1965). All of the governors, however, described in brief sketches in *The Messages and Proclamations of the Governors of the State of Missouri*, previously cited; their wives and daughters are discussed most entertainingly by Jerena East Giffen, *First Ladies of Missouri: Their Homes and Their Families* (n.p., 1970). Biographical articles dealing with the careers of these governors include John F. Phillips, "Hamilton Rowan Gamble and the Provisional Government of Missouri," *MHR*, 5 (October, 1910), 1–14; Marguerite Potter,

"Hamilton R. Gamble, Missouri's War Governor," *MHR*, 35 (October, 1940), 25–71; John F. Phillips, "Governor Willard Preble Hall," *MHR*, 5 (January, 1911), 69–82 (Phillips was a practicing lawyer during this period who knew both Hall and Gamble well); Hugh P. Williamson, "Willard P. Hall, Lawyer, Lawmaker, Statesman," *Journal of the Missouri Bar*, 17 (April, 1961), 170–73; and J. S. Botsford, "Governor Joseph W. McClurg and His Administration," *MHR*, 6 (July, 1912), 182–91.

Complete biographies have been written about five of Missouri's United States senators who served in this period, all of them quite important for a variety of reasons. In addition to the Brown biography, there are the following studies: Arthur H. Mattingly, "Senator John Brooks Henderson, United States Senator from Missouri," Ph.D. diss., Kansas State University, Manhattan, 1971; Dorothy M. Merideth, "John Brooks Henderson as a Representative of Border-State Public Opinion," M.A. thesis, University of Missouri, Columbia, 1939; David D. March, "The Life and Times of Charles Daniel Drake," Ph.D. diss., University of Missouri, Columbia, 1949; Claude M. Fuess, *Carl Schurz: Reformer* (New York, 1932); and Leonard B. Wurthman, Jr., "Frank Blair of Missouri, Jacksonian Orator of the Civil War Era," Ph.D. diss., University of Missouri, Columbia, 1969. March and Wurthman have also presented their subjects in the form of condensed sketches: "Charles Daniel Drake of St. Louis," *The Bulletin*, 8 (April, 1953), 291–310; and "Frank Blair: Lincoln's Congressional Spokesman," *MHR*, 64 (April, 1970), 263–88. Blair is also thoroughly discussed in a family biography: William E. Smith, *The Francis Preston Blair Family in Politics*, 2 vols. (New York, 1933).

William E. Parrish, *David Rice Atchison of Missouri: Border Politician* (Columbia, Missouri, 1961) deals with a prominent prewar United States senator from Missouri who played a key role in gaining Confederate recognition for the Jackson regime. Marvin R. Cain, *Lincoln's Attorney-General: Edward Bates of Missouri* (Columbia, Missouri, 1965) details the career of an important figure on the Union side. A leading St. Louis Conservative is the subject of an article by an anonymous author, "James O. Broadhead: A Subject for Reappraisal," *The Bulletin*, 27 (January, 1971), 125–28. Missouri's artist–politician, George Caleb Bingham, has been the subject of several biographies. The best concerning his role as an artist is John F. McDermott, *George Caleb Bingham: River Portraitist* (Norman, Oklahoma, 1959), while his political career is thoroughly studied in Fern H. Rusk, *George Caleb Bingham* (Jefferson City, 1917). George F.

Lemmer, *Norman J. Colman and Colman's Rural World* (Columbia, Missouri, 1953), contains the story of Missouri's famous agriculturalist who also dabbled in Conservative politics. Leslie Anders, "His 'Radical Reverence' John H. Cox," *MHR*, 65 (January, 1971), 139–58, is an account of a Methodist minister turned Radical politician. Lewis O. Saum, "Donan and the *Caucasian*," *MHR*, 63 (July, 1969), 418–50, describes one of the most rabid of racist Conservative editors.

St. Louis's great engineer and bridge builder is studied in depth in Florence Dorsey, *Road to the Sea: The Story of James B. Eads and the Mississippi* (New York, 1947). Charlotte C. Eliot has told the story of her father *William Greenleaf Eliot: Minister, Educator, Philanthropist* (Boston, 1904). Kurt F. Leidecker, *Yankee Teacher: The Life of William Torrey Harris* (New York, 1946), covers both the career and the philosophy of St. Louis's noted educator. A prominent St. Louis physician, who served in both the wartime and the 1865 conventions and became a caustic critic of the Radical constitution, is described in William E. Parrish, "Moses Lewis Linton, 'Doctor of Epigrams,'" *MHR*, 59 (April, 1965), 293–301. A highly sympathetic contemporary treatment of a St. Louis Presbyterian minister who sought unsuccessfully to maintain a neutral wartime pulpit is John S. Grasty, *Memoir of Rev. Samuel B. McPheeters, D. D.* (St. Louis, 1871). Joseph Pulitzer, the Hungarian journalist who began his career as a Radical reporter–politician, has merited several biographical studies, of which the best is William A. Swanberg, *Pulitzer* (New York, 1967). Particularly interesting for the early period of his life is Thomas E. Eickhorst, "Representative and Reporter: Joseph Pulitzer as a Missouri State Representative," M.A. thesis, Lincoln University, Jefferson City, 1968.

The most thorough treatment of James S. Rollins, Conservative congressman and legislator who played such a large role in the development of the University of Missouri, is James M. Wood, Jr., "James Sidney Rollins of Missouri: A Political Biography," Ph.D. diss., Stanford University, Palo Alto, California, 1951. An earlier and highly sympathetic work is William B. Smith, *James Sidney Rollins: A Memoir* (New York, 1891). Also of interest is John V. Mering, "The Political Transition of James S. Rollins," *MHR*, 53 (April, 1959), 217–26. Rollins's fellow Columbian and political ally, who edited the *Missouri Statesman*, is ably presented in Elizabeth D. Hall, "William Franklin Switzler: Editor, Politician, and Humanitarian," M.A. thesis, University of Missouri, Columbia, 1951. Another politician, but of Radical convictions, is described in Samuel B. Harding,

The Life of George R. Smith, Founder of Sedalia, Missouri (Sedalia, 1904). The noted black Radical leader, James Milton Turner, has been the subject of two articles: Irving Dilliard, "James Milton Turner: A Little Known Benefactor of His People," *Journal of Negro History*, 19 (October, 1934), 372–411; and N. Webster Moore, "James Milton Turner, Diplomat, Educator, and Defender of Rights, 1840–1915," *The Bulletin*, 27 (April, 1971), 194–201. Another Radical congressman and a leader in the struggle to make Kansas City the dominant city of the western border is seen in J. M. Greenwood, "Col. Robert T. Van Horn," *MHR*, 4 (January, 1910), 92–105; (July, 1910), 167–81.

Full biographies have been written about all except one (Samuel R. Curtis) of Missouri's wartime military commanders: Logan U. Reavis, *The Life and Military Services of General William Selby Harney* (St. Louis, 1878); Ashbel Woodward, *Life of General Nathaniel Lyon* (Hartford, Connecticut, 1862); Allan Nevins, *Frémont, Pathmarker of the West* (New York, 1955); Stephen E. Ambrose, *Halleck, Lincoln's Chief of Staff* (Baton Rouge, Louisiana, 1962); James L. McDonough, *Schofield: Union General in the Civil War and Reconstruction* (Tallahassee, Florida, 1972); William M. Lamers, *The Edge of Glory: A Biography of General William S. Rosecrans, U.S.A.* (New York, 1961); and J. R. Perkins, *Trails, Rails and War: The Life of General G. M. Dodge* (Indianapolis, 1929). Also a useful resource for information about Lyon is William E. Parrish, "General Nathaniel Lyon: A Portrait," *MHR*, 49 (October, 1954), 1–18. Two important Union military men of lesser stature are dealt with in North Todd Gentry, "General Odon Guitar," *MHR*, 22 (July, 1928), 419–45, and James E. Kirby, Jr., "How to Become a Union General Without Military Experience," *MHR*, 66 (April, 1972), 360–76, which is the story of Clinton B. Fisk.

On the Confederate military side, Sterling Price has been the subject of two recent studies: Albert Castel, *General Sterling Price and the Civil War in the West* (Baton Rouge, 1968); and Robert E. Shalhope, *Sterling Price: Portrait of a Southerner* (Columbia, Missouri, 1971). Two of his subordinates are discussed in Daniel O'Flaherty, *General Jo Shelby: Undefeated Rebel* (Chapel Hill, North Carolina, 1954), and Jay Monaghan, *Swamp Fox of the Confederacy: The Life and Military Services of M. Jeff Thompson* (Tuscaloosa, Alabama, 1956). The guerrilla chieftain, William C. Quantrill, is portrayed in Albert Castel, *William Clarke Quantrill: His Life and Times* (New York, 1962). Still valuable is William E. Connelley, *Quantrill and the Border Wars* (Cedar Rapids, Iowa, 1910). The life and legend of one of Quantrill's raiders who went on to even greater fame after the Civil War is in William A. Settle, Jr., *Jesse James Was His Name* (Columbia, Missouri, 1966).

Sketches of all of Missouri's congressmen and senators may be found in *The Biographical Directory of the American Congress, 1774–1961* (Washington, D.C., 1962). Biographies of several postwar state officials and educators are provided in Paul O. Selby, *The Board of Regents of the Northeast Missouri State Teachers College* (Kirksville, Missouri, n.d.). Two other standard biographical reference works are *United States Biographical Directory and Portrait Gallery of Eminent and Self-Made Men*, Missouri volume (Kansas City, 1878), and Allen Johnson and Dumas Malone, eds., *The Dictionary of American Biography*, 20 vols. (New York, 1928–1936). County histories are excellent sources of biographical material for many local leaders. The State Historical Society has a thorough index to these biographies its reference room.

THE ONSET OF CIVIL WAR

The standard account of the election of 1860 in Missouri is Walter H. Ryle, *Missouri: Union or Secession* (Nashville, 1931). Also interesting is B. B. Lightfoot, "Nobody's Nominee: Sample Orr and the Election of 1860," *MHR*, 60 (January, 1966), 127–48. The aides of the major protagonists reveal their respective viewpoints of the events that followed in Thomas L. Snead, *The Fight for Missouri from the Election of Lincoln to the Death of Lyon* (New York, 1888), and James Peckham, *General Nathaniel Lyon and Missouri in 1861* (New York, 1866). The view of another participant may be found in Robert J. Rombauer, *The Union Cause in Saint Louis in 1861* (St. Louis, 1909). One of the Iowans who joined Lyon after the skirmish at Boonville tells their story in Eugene F. Ware, *The Lyon Campaign in Missouri: Being a History of the First Iowa Infantry* (Topeka, 1907).

Of the more recent accounts, the best from the vantage of state politics are those of Arthur R. Kirkpatrick: "Missouri on the Eve of the Civil War," *MHR*, 55 (January, 1961), 99–108; "Missouri in the Early Months of the Civil War," *MHR*, 55 (April, 1961), 235–66; and "Admission of Missouri into the Confederacy," *MHR*, 55 (July, 1961), 366–86. Taking a modified view of Jackson as being more pragmatic than Kirkpatrick paints him is William H. Lyon, "Claiborne Fox Jackson and the Secession Crisis in Missouri," *MHR*, 58 (July, 1964), 422–41. A strongly pro-Union view of the same events is Hans C.

Adamson, *Rebellion in Missouri: 1861: Nathaniel Lyon and His Army of the West* (Philadelphia, 1961). Yet another aspect of the Union effort may be seen in Virgil C. Blum, "The Political and Military Activities of the German Element in St. Louis, 1859–1861," *MHR*, 42 (January, 1948), 103–29. A most helpful study of the long-range issues behind the secession question itself is Douglas L. Craig, "An Examination of the Reasons for Missouri's Decision Not to Secede in 1860," M.A. thesis, University of Missouri, Kansas City, 1970.

WARTIME POLITICS

The story of Missouri in the Confederacy is thorougly detailed in Arthur R. Kirkpatrick, "Missouri, the Twelfth Confederate State," Ph.D. diss., University of Missouri, Columbia, 1954. A brief synopsis of this dissertation is Kirkpatrick, "Missouri's Secessionist Government, 1861–1865," *MHR*, 45 (January, 1951), 124–37. Missouri's wartime relationship to the Union and the political turmoil that tore the Unionist element apart after mid-1862 are discussed in William E. Parrish, *Turbulent Partnership: Missouri and the Union, 1861–1865* (Columbia, Missouri, 1963). Useful articles dealing with specific aspects of Union–state relationships are Marvin R. Cain, "Edward Bates and Hamilton R. Gamble," *MHR*, 56 (January, 1962), 146–55; and Bill R. Lee, "Missouri's Fight over Emancipation in 1863," *MHR*, 45 (April, 1951), 256–74. An older but still helpful study is Walter B. Stevens, "Lincoln and Missouri," *MHR*, 10 (January, 1916), 63–119. Also important to an understanding of the President's problems with Missouri is John G. Nicolay and John Hay, *Abraham Lincoln, A History*, 10 vols. (New York, 1890). For the over-all problems of Federal encroachment on states' rights in the North, see William B. Hesseltine, *Lincoln and the War Governors* (New York, 1955).

An important study of the emerging Radical party, which is especially valuable for its statistical analyses of the elections of the 1860's, is Ida M. Nowells, "A Study of the Radical Party Movement in Missouri, 1860–1870," M.A. thesis, University of Missouri, Columbia, 1939. The Radicals' involvement with Lincoln's reelection in 1864 has been examined in two articles: David D. March, "The Missouri Radicals and the Re-election of Lincoln," *Mid-America*, 24 (July, 1952), 172–87; and William F. Zornow, "The Missouri Radicals and the Election of 1864," *MHR*, 45 (July, 1951), 354–70. The Radicals' ties to the national Union League movement are depicted in Guy J. Gibson, "Lincoln's League: The Union League Movement During the Civil

War," Ph.D. diss., University of Illinois, Champaign, 1957. For information concerning the relationship of Missouri's Conservatives to the national movement, see Frank L. Klement, *The Copperheads in the Middle West* (Chicago, 1960) and "Midwestern Opposition to Lincoln's Emancipation Policy," *Journal of Negro History*, 49 (July, 1964), 169–83. Older political studies are Samuel B. Harding, "Missouri Party Struggles in the Civil War," in *The Annual Report of the American Historical Association for the Year 1900*, vol. 1 (Washington, D.C., 1901), 85–104; and Sceva B. Laughlin, "Missouri Politics During the Civil War," *MHR*, 23 (April, 1929), 400–426, (July, 1929), 583–618; 24 (October, 1929), 87–113, (January, 1930), 261–84.

THE MILITARY SCENE

The best survey of Missouri's military problems is Richard S. Brownlee, *Gray Ghosts of the Confederacy: Guerrilla Warfare in the West, 1861–1865* (Baton Rouge, 1958). Useful for studying the development of the wartime state militia is John G. Westover, "The Evolution of the Missouri Militia, 1804–1919," Ph.D. diss., University of Missouri, Columbia, 1948. Another book that is helpful on the militia situation is Parrish, *Turbulent Partnership*. A special problem within the militia is discussed in Howard V. Canan, "Missouri Paw Paw Militia of 1863–1864," *MHR*, 62 (July, 1968), 431–48. The enlistment of black soldiers in Missouri is dealt with in John W. Blassingame, "The Recruitment of Negro Troops in Missouri During the Civil War," *MHR*, 58 (April, 1964), 326–37. The career of one Missouri volunteer regiment, which served largely outside the boundaries of the state, is described in Leslie Anders, *The Eighteenth Missouri* (Indianapolis and New York, 1968).

Jay Monaghan, *Civil War on the Western Border, 1854–1865* (Boston, 1955), is a good overview of the Missouri–Kansas troubles. A contemporary account of those incidents, which is still useful, is Wiley Britton, *The Civil War on the Border, 1861–1862* (New York, 1890). Important supplements are Albert Castel, "Kansas Jawhawking Raids into Western Missouri in 1861," *MHR*, 54 (October, 1959), 1–11, and Hildegarde R. Herklotz, "Jayhawkers in Missouri, 1858–1863," *MHR*, 17 (July, 1923), 505–13, 18 (October, 1923), 64–101. The effect of the war on three western Missouri counties is well illustrated in Kathleen W. Miles, *Bitter Ground: The Civil War in Missouri's Golden Valley—Benton, Henry and St. Clair Counties* (Warsaw, Missouri, 1971). One of the most controversial events of the war on the western border is dealt with in three articles: Albert Castel, "Order No. 11 and the Civil War on the Border," *MHR*, 57 (July, 1963), 357–68; Charles R. Mink, "General Orders, No. 11: The Forced Evacuation of Civilians During the Civil War," *Military Affairs*, 34 (December, 1970), 132–36; and Ann D. Niepan, "General Order No. 11 and Border Warfare During the Civil War," *MHR*, 66 (January, 1972), 185–210.

The expulsion of the Confederates from southeastern Missouri is well handled in Jay C. Mullen, "Pope's New Madrid and Island Number 10 Campaigns," *MHR*, 59 (April, 1965), 324–43. Later Confederate cavalry forays into Missouri are discussed in Edwin C. Bearss, "Army of the Frontier's First Campaign: The Confederates Win at Newtonia," *MHR*, 60 (April, 1966), 283–319; Stephen B. Oates, "Marmaduke's First Missouri Raid," *The Bulletin*, 17 (January, 1961), 147–52, "Shelby's Great Raid, 1863," *The Bulletin*, 17 (July, 1961), 337–45, and "Marmaduke's Cape Girardeau Expedition, 1863," *MHR*, 57 (April, 1963), 237–47; and Paul M. Robinett, "Marmaduke's Expedition into Missouri: The Battles of Springfield and Hartville, January, 1863," *MHR*, 58 (January, 1964), 151–73. Stephen B. Oates discusses the larger context within which these raids were made in *Confederate Cavalry West of the River* (Austin, Texas, 1961).

Sterling Price's 1864 raid into Missouri is described in the two previously cited studies of his career. In addition, valuable insights may be gained from Howard N. Monnett, *Action Before Westport, 1864* (Kansas City, 1964), and Norman P. Morrow, "Price's Missouri Expedition, 1864," M.A. thesis, University of Texas, Austin, 1949. These works should be supplemented with the following: Paul B. Jenkins, *The Battle of Westport* (Kansas City, 1906); Cyrus A. Peterson and Joseph M. Hanson, *Pilot Knob: The Thermopylae of the West* (New York, 1914); Richard S. Brownlee, "The Battle of Pilot Knob, Iron County, Missouri, September 27, 1864," *State of Missouri Official Manual for the Years 1961–1962* (Jefferson City, 1962); Howard N. Monnett, "The Origin of the Confederate Invasion of Missouri, 1864," *The Bulletin*, 18 (October, 1961), 37–48, and "The Confederate Advance to Lexington, 1864," *The Bulletin*, 19 (April, 1963), 260–72; and Mark A. Plummer, "Missouri and Kansas and the Capture of General Marmaduke," *MHR*, 59 (October, 1964), 90–104. For an overview of the larger scene within which the raid took place, see Robert L. Kerby, *Kirby Smith's Confederacy: The Trans-Mississippi South, 1863–1865* (New York, 1972).

Beyond these major military occurrences, nearly every Missouri town and area was the scene of some type of fighting at one time or another during the war. Accounts of these raids, skirmishes, "battles" abound. A few are in scattered issues of the *MHR*, but the majority are recorded in county histories, local historical journals or bulletins, and newspapers. Good references for locating materials in the last two sources named are the two regular features in *MHR*: "Missouri History in Newspapers" and "Missouri Historical Data in Magazines."

BEHIND THE LINES

A major problem of the war in Missouri was that of dealing with a hostile civilian population. The best survey of the difficulties over constitutional rights from a national perspective is James G. Randall, *Constitutional Problems Under Lincoln* (New York, 1926). Brownlee, *Gray Ghosts of the Confederacy*, contains two excellent chapters on martial law and its enforcement in Missouri. A good study of one aspect of this problem is W. Wayne Smith, "An Experiment in Counterinsurgency: The Assessment of Confederate Sympathizers in Missouri," *Journal of Southern History*, 35 (August, 1969), 361–80. William B. Hesseltine, "Military Prisons of St. Louis," *MHR*, 23 (April, 1929), 380–99, handles that topic quite adequately. A highly emotional contemporary account of sufferings by pro-Southern sympathizers that uses a kind of case-study approach is William M. Leftwich, *Martyrdom in Missouri*, 2 vols. (St. Louis, 1870). For the treatment of the pro-Confederate press, one should read William F. Swindler, "The Southern Press in Missouri, 1861–1864," *MHR*, 35 (April, 1941), 394–400. The most ardent of pro-Union papers is dealt with in Lucy L. Tasher, "The *Missouri Democrat* and the Civil War," *MHR*, 31 (July, 1937), 402–19.

The work of the Western Sanitary Commission is outlined in W. R. Hodges, *The Western Sanitary Commission* (n.p., 1906), but a more modern assessment is badly needed. *The Western Sanitary Commission: A Sketch* (St. Louis, 1864) by J. G. Forman, one of its leaders, gives an official view of its activities. Also useful for brief biographies of some of its workers as well as a description of the general endeavors of the important auxiliaries is L. P. Brockett and Mary C. Vaughan, *Woman's Work in the Civil War: A Record of Heroism, Patriotism, and Patience* (Philadelphia, 1868). For the relationship of the Western Sanitary Commission to its national counterpart, see William Q. Maxwell, *Lincoln's Fifth Wheel: The Political History of the United States Sanitary Commission* (New York, 1956). An earlier account is J. S. Newberry, *The United States Sanitary Commission in the Valley of the Mississippi During the War of the Rebellion, 1861–1866* (Cleveland, 1871).

A very good contemporary view of wartime St. Louis is offered by Galusha Anderson, *A Border City During the Civil War* (Boston, 1908). For a more general survey, see Brenda E. Richard, "St. Louis During the Civil War," M.A. thesis, Washington University, St. Louis, 1934. These accounts should be supplemented by William G. B. Carson, " 'Secesh,' " *The Bulletin*, 23 (January, 1967), 119–45, for a pro-Southern picture. Additional articles of interest concerning other Missouri cities are Joe Klassen, "The Civil War in Kansas City," *The Bulletin*, 16 (January, 1960), 134–50, and Charles Radcliffe, "St. Joseph and the Civil War," *Museum Graphic*, 18 (Summer, 1966), 4–11.

POSTWAR POLITICAL DEVELOPMENTS

The standard treatment of the Radical party is William E. Parrish, *Missouri Under Radical Rule, 1865–1870* (Columbia, Missouri, 1965). Still valuable are Thomas S. Barclay, *The Liberal Republican Movement in Missouri, 1865–1871* (Columbia, Missouri, 1926), and Ida M. Nowells, "A Study of the Radical Party in Missouri, 1860–1870," M.A. thesis, University of Missouri, Columbia, 1939. A seminar paper delivered by Michael Burlingame, "Liberal Republicanism in Missouri, 1869–1872," at Johns Hopkins University in May, 1966, contains a good statistical analysis of the Missouri elections for the period covered. An important auxiliary of the Radical party is covered in James N. Primm, "The G.A.R. in Missouri, 1866–1870," *Journal of Southern History*, 20 (August, 1954), 356–75.

Several articles discuss the constitutional convention of 1865 and its resultant controversies: Frederick W. Lehmann, "Edward Bates and the Test Oath," *Missouri Historical Society Collections*, 4 (1923), 389–401; David D. March, "Charles D. Drake and the Constitutional Convention of 1865," *MHR*, 47 (January, 1953), 110–23, and "The Campaign for the Ratification of the Constitution of 1865," *MHR*, 47 (April, 1953), 323–32; and Thomas K. Skinker, "The Removal of the Judges of the Supreme Court of Missouri in 1865," *Missouri Historical Society Collections*, 4 (1914), 243–74. For a comparison of this convention and its constitution with that of 1875, see Isidor Loeb, "Constitutions and Constitutional Conventions in Missouri," *MHR*,

16 (January, 1922), 189–246, and William F. Switzler, "Constitutional Conventions of Missouri, 1865–1875," *MHR*, 1 (January, 1907), 109–20. The general effect of the test oath as it related to the ministerial profession may be found in Thomas S. Barclay, "The Test Oath for Clergy in Missouri," *MHR*, 18 (April, 1924), 345–81. Missouri's most famous court case that challenged the test oath is detailed in Harold C. Bradley, "In Defense of John Cummings," *MHR*, 42 (October, 1962), 1–15. For an assessment of the national framework of which Missouri's oath was but a part, see Harold Hyman, *The Era of the Oath: Northern Loyalty Tests During the Civil War and Reconstruction* (Philadelphia, 1954). The role of the United States Supreme Court in the controversy is discussed in Charles Warren, *The Supreme Court in United States History*, vol. 3 (Boston, 1922).

Monia C. Morris, "The History of Women's Suffrage in Missouri, 1867–1901," *MHR*, 25 (October, 1930), 67–82, gives the origins of that movement after the Civil War. The struggle of Missouri's agrarian element may be found in Alma B. Wilkinson, "The Granger Movement in Missouri," M.A. thesis, University of Missouri, Columbia, 1926. The climax of their crusade for political recognition is described in Walter B. Stevens, "The Political Turmoil of 1874 in Missouri," *MHR*, 31 (October, 1936), 3–9. A brief analysis by his secretary will be found in Frederick N. Judson, "The Administration of Governor B. Gratz Brown, 1871–1873," *Missouri Historical Society Collections*, 2 (April, 1903), 24–44. A major scandal is discussed in Lucius E. Guese, "St. Louis and the Great Whisky Ring," *MHR*, 36 (January, 1942), 160–83. Yet another aspect of the political scene receives attention in William F. Zornow, "The Missouri Germans and the One-Term Tradition," *The Bulletin*, 10 (October, 1953), 72–77. A brief recent résumé of the entire era is to be found in Fred DeArmond, "Reconstruction in Missouri," *MHR*, 61 (April, 1967), 364–77.

MISSOURI'S BLACKS

Although numerous studies have been written dealing with Missouri's blacks, most of them remain unpublished. Several of these works, both published and unpublished, are becoming out of date. The standard work on Missouri slavery remains Harrison A. Trexler, *Slavery in Missouri* (Baltimore, 1914). It may be supplemented with Emil Oberholzer, "The Legal Aspects of Slavery in Missouri," M.A. thesis, Columbia University, New York, 1949, and William W. Bogue, "Status of the Negro in Missouri as Determined by Law, 1719–

1875," M.A. thesis, Northeast Missouri State Teachers College, Kirksville, 1952. A few unpublished local studies exist: Laurence O. Christensen, "Black St. Louis: A Study in Race Relations, 1865–1916," Ph.D. diss., University of Missouri, Columbia, 1972; Esque Douglas, "The History of the Negro in Northeast Missouri," M.A. thesis, Lincoln University, Jefferson City, 1946; Daniel M. Hogan, "The Catholic Church and the Negroes of St. Louis," M.A. thesis, St. Louis University, St. Louis, 1955; and Jesse M. Small, "The Negro in New Madrid County," M.A. thesis, University of Missouri, Columbia, 1930. The only other one-county study, aside from county histories, is George R. Lee, "Slavery and Emancipation in Lewis County, Missouri," *MHR*, 65 (April, 1971), 294–317. A pioneer work is William W. Elwang, *The Negroes of Columbia, Missouri* (Columbia, Missouri, 1904).

The antislavery movement and Missouri's struggle over emancipation have been covered by a number of unpublished studies. The most recent, reflecting current historiographical trends, is Donnie D. Bellamy, "Slavery, Emancipation, and Racism in Missouri, 1850–1865," Ph.D. diss., University of Missouri, Columbia, 1970. Earlier works include Benjamin C. Merkel, "The Anti-Slavery Movement in Missouri, 1819–1865," Ph.D. diss., Washington University, St. Louis, 1939; Earl J. Nelson, "The Passing of Slavery in Missouri," M.A. thesis, University of Missouri, Columbia, 1932; and Hallie W. Smith, "The Anti-Slavery Crusade in Missouri, 1819–1865," M.A. thesis, Lincoln University, Jefferson City, 1958. Two of these authors have published summaries of their work: Benjamin C. Merkel, "Abolitionist Aspects of Missouri's Anti-Slavery Controversy, 1819–1865," *MHR*, 44 (April, 1950), 232–53, and Earl J. Nelson, "Missouri Slavery, 1861–1865," *MIIR*, 28 (July, 1934), 260–74. The end of slavery is dealt with in Bill R. Lee, "Missouri's Fight over Emancipation in 1863," *MHR*, 45 (April, 1951), 256–74. The adjustment of many Missouri blacks to military life is discussed in John W. Blassingame, "The Recruitment of Negro Troops in Missouri During the Civil War," *MHR*, 58 (April, 1964), 326–37.

A comprehensive treatment of the black in postwar Missouri will be found in Parrish, *Missouri Under Radical Rule, 1865–1870*. Henderson H. Donald, *The Negro Freedman: Life Conditions of the American Negro in the Early Years after Emancipation* (New York, 1952), contains some references to Missouri. V. Jacque Voegeli examines the problem of racism in the Middle West in *Free But Not Equal* (Chicago, 1967). The same subject on a national level is probed in

Forrest G. Wood, *Black Scare: The Racist Response to Emancipation and Reconstruction* (Berkeley, California, 1968). Both contain passing references to Missouri.

The work of the Freedmen's Bureau, including brief mention of its efforts in Missouri, is covered by George R. Bentley, *A History of the Freedmen's Bureau* (Philadelphia, 1955), and Paul S. Peirce, *The Freedmen's Bureau: A Chapter in the History of Reconstruction* (Iowa City, Iowa, 1904). Walter L. Fleming, *The Freedmen's Savings Bank* (Chapel Hill, North Carolina, 1927) is also helpful on a particular supplemental organization. Particularly useful concerning the later work of the Bureau in Missouri is W. A. Low, "The Freedmen's Bureau in the Border States," in Richard O. Curry, ed., *Radicalism, Racism, and Party Realignment: The Border States During Reconstruction* (Baltimore and London, 1969).

The efforts to promote Negro education in Missouri have received considerable attention, although again much of what has been written remains unpublished. Particular attention should be given to Robert I. Brigham, "The Education of the Negro in Missouri," Ph.D. diss., University of Missouri, Columbia, 1946; Pauline D. Knobbs, "The Development of the Separate System of Education in Missouri," Ph.D. diss., George Peabody Teachers College, Nashville, 1946; and George L. Mann, "The Development of Public Education for Negroes in Saint Louis, Missouri," Ed.D. diss., Indiana University, Bloomington, 1949. Additional brief published discussions may be found in John W. Evans, "A Brief Sketch of the Development of Negro Education in St. Louis, Missouri," *Journal of Negro Education*, 7 (1938), 548–52; W. Sherman Savage, "The Legal Provisions for Negro Schools in Missouri from 1865 to 1890," *Journal of Negro History*, 16 (July, 1931), 309–21; and Henry S. Williams, "The Development of the Negro Public School System in Missouri," *Journal of Negro History*, 5 (April, 1920), 137–65. A comparison of the institution in Missouri to that in other states may be found in "Legal Status of Colored Population in Respect to Schools and Education in the Different States," *American Journal of Education*, 19 (1870), 301–400. W. Sherman Savage, *The History of Lincoln University* (Jefferson City, 1939), tells the story of that institution adequately. Two other articles dealing with interesting aspects of Negro life in Missouri are Ralph Fletcher and Mildred Fletcher, "Some Data on Occupations Among Negroes in St. Louis from 1866 to 1897," *Journal of Negro History*, 20 (July, 1935), 338–41, and G. Hugh Wamble,

"Negroes and Misouri Protestant Churches Before and After the Civil War," *MHR*, 61 (April, 1967), 321-47.

EDUCATION

The only general study of education in Missouri is Claude A. Phillips, *A History of Education in Missouri* (Jefferson City, 1911), which is quite sketchy and now somewhat dated. A summary may be found in Phillips, "A Century of Education in Missouri," *MHR*, 15 (January, 1921), 298-314. The impact of new educational trends on postwar Missouri and the concerns of the Radicals for a progressive educational system are well covered in Maynard G. Redfield, "Some Social and Intellectual Influences in the Development of Public Education in Missouri, 1865 to 1900," Ph.D. diss., Washington University, St. Louis, 1956. The development of St. Louis public schools is treated in two articles by Dela Lange: "A Century of Achievement in the St. Louis Public High Schools, 1853-1953," *St. Louis Public School Journal*, 6 (February, 1953), 3-129, and "Information Concerning One Hundred Years of Progress in the St. Louis Public Schools," *Public School Messenger*, 35 (January 3, 1938), 3-86. For the origins of the kindergarten in St. Louis, see Selwyn K. Troen, "Operation Headstart: The Beginnings of the Public School Kindergarten Movement," *MHR*, 66 (January, 1972), 211-29. Teacher training, which also had its Missouri origins in St. Louis, is detailed in Monia C. Morris, "Teacher Training in Missouri Before 1871," *MHR*, 43 (October, 1948), 18-37. Missouri's first two teachers' colleges have their official histories: Eugene M. Violette, *History of the First District State Normal School* (Kirksville, Missouri, 1905), and Leslie Anders, *Education for Service: Centennial History of Central Missouri State College* (Warrensburg, Missouri, 1971). The former may be supplemented with Lucy Simmons and Paul O. Selby, "The Northeast Missouri State Teachers College and Its Founder, Joseph Baldwin," *MHR*, 22 (January, 1928), 157-70.

Most of Missouri's colleges have an official or unofficial history. Sketches of several nineteenth-century schools, including some no longer in existence, are included in Marshall S. Snow, ed., *Higher Education in Missouri* (Washington, D.C., 1901). The most recent history of the state university is Frank F. Stephens, *A History of the University of Missouri* (Columbia, Missouri, 1962). Still useful is Jonas Viles, *The University of Missouri, a Centennial History* (Columbia, Missouri, 1939). The story of the university's Rolla branch is told in Clarence N. Roberts, *History of the University of Missouri School of Mines and Metallurgy, 1871–1946* (Rolla, Missouri, 1946). This book should be supplemented with Harry J. Eisenman, "Origins of Engineering Education in Missouri," *MHR*, 63 (July, 1969), 451–60. The land-grant problems of the university are detailed in John J. Jones, "The Morrill Lands of the University of Missouri," *MHR*, 51 (January, 1957), 126–38. Other college histories include Frank C. Tucker, *Central Methodist College, One Hundred and Ten Years* (Nashville, 1967); Carl S. Meyer, *Log Cabin to Luther Tower: Concordia Seminary During One Hundred Twenty-Five Years* (St. Louis, 1965); George L. Peters, *Dreams Come True: A History of Culver-Stockton College* (Canton, Missouri, 1941); W. Sherman Savage, *The History of Lincoln University* (Jefferson City, 1939); Rita G. Adams and others, *St. Louis University: 150 Years* (St. Louis, n.d.); John C. Crighton, *Stephens: A Story of Educational Innovation* (Columbia, Missouri, 1970); William E. Parrish, *Westminster College: An Informal History, 1851–1969* (Fulton, Missouri, 1971); and Hubert I. Hester, *Jewell Is Her Name: A History of William Jewell College* (Liberty, Missouri, 1967).

RELIGION

Walter R. Houf, "The Protestant Church in the Rural Midwestern Community, 1820–1870," Ph.D. diss., University of Missouri, Columbia, 1967, gives a good overview of its topic with numerous examples from Missouri. State denominational histories include Robert S. Douglass, *History of Missouri Baptists* (Kansas City, 1934); George L. Peters, *The Disciples of Christ in Missouri* (n.p., 1937); and Frank C. Tucker, *The Methodist Church in Missouri, 1798–1939, A Brief History* (Nashville, 1966). Earlier works that are still useful are R. S. Duncan, *A History of the Baptists in Missouri* (St. Louis, 1882), and W. H. Lewis, *The History of Methodism in Missouri*, 3 vols. (Nashville, 1890). The impact on the Missouri synod of the wartime schism of Presbyterianism is discussed in Lewis G. Vander Velde, *The Presbyterian Churches and the Federal Union, 1861–1869* (Cambridge, Massachusetts, 1932). Information on the war's effect upon that denomination in St. Louis may be found in Milan J. Kedro, "The Civil War's Effect upon an Urban Church: The St. Louis Presbytery Under Martial Law," *The Bulletin*, 27 (April, 1971), 173–93. The story of blacks within the Protestant fold is presented

in G. Hugh Wamble, "Negroes and Missouri Protestant Churches
Before and After the Civil War," *MHR*, 61 (April, 1967), 321-47.

AMUSEMENTS AND SOCIAL ORGANIZATIONS

A general overview of the types of entertainment in Missouri in
the nineteenth century may be found in Lily Ann Dickey, "The
Pastimes of Missourians Before 1900," *MHR*, 37 (January, 1943),
134-49. Also helpful to the study of this subject is Mary Alicia Owen,
"Social Customs and Usages in Missouri During the Last Century,"
MHR, 15 (October, 1920), 176-90. The story of the theatre and re-
lated amusements in outstate Missouri is thoroughly discussed in
William F. West, Jr., "The Legitimate Theatre in Rural Missouri
from the Beginning of the Civil War through 1872," Ph.D. diss.,
University of Missouri, Columbia, 1964. Its urban counterpart is
Grant M. Herbstruth, "Benedict DeBar and the Grand Opera House
in St. Louis, Missouri, from 1855-1879," 2 vols., Ph.D. diss., Univer-
sity of Iowa, Iowa City, 1954. The latter should be supplemented with
John R. David, "The Genesis of the Variety Theatre: *The Black
Crook* Comes to St. Louis," *MHR*, 64 (January, 1970), 133-49, and
Alfred H. Nolle, *The German Drama on the St. Louis Stage* (Phila-
delphia, 1917). The theatre of Kansas City has been studied in Alice
J. Machey, "A History of the Coates Opera House, Kansas City, Missouri, 1870-1901," M.A. thesis, Central Missouri State College, War-
rensburg, 1964, and Phoebe Peck, "The Theatre in Kansas City,"
M.A. thesis, Kansas City University, Kansas City, 1940. A less genteel
form of amusement is detailed in Paul Magriel, "Missouri Prize-
Fighting in the 1860s," *The Bulletin*, 7 (October, 1951), 8-16. Surveys
of their respective topics are J .S. Ankeney, "A Century of Missouri
Art," *MHR*, 16 (July, 1922), 481-501, and Ernst C. Krohn, "A Century of Missouri Music," *MHR*, 17 (January, 1923), 130-58. Only the
Masons among Missouri's various fraternal organizations have recorded an official history: William F. Kuhn, *Centennial History of
the Grand Lodge, Free and Accepted Ancient Masons of Missouri,
1821-1921* (n.p., n.d.). It should be supplemented with Ray V. Dens-
low, *The Civil War and Masonry in Missouri* (n.p., 1930).

LITERATURE AND JOURNALISM

A valuable survey of this subject is provided by Elijah L. Jacobs
and Forrest E. Wolverton, *Missouri Writers: A Literary History of*

Missouri, 1780–1955 (St. Louis, 1955). Yet another shorter effort is Alexander N. DeMenil, "A Century of Missouri Literature," *MHR*, 15 (October, 1920), 74–125. A thorough topical reference dealing with literary production on Missouri is Joe W. Kraus, "Missouri in Fiction: A Review and a Bibliography," *MHR*, 42 (April, 1948), 209–25, (July, 1948), 310–24. A highly specialized subject is treated in John D. Lawson, "A Century of Missouri Legal Literature," *MHR*, 15 (July, 1921), 595–610.

William V. Byars, "A Century of Journalism in Missouri," *MHR*, 15 (October, 1920), 53–73, provides a brief introduction to that topic. A good survey of individual newspapers is contained in Minnie Organ, "History of the County Press of Missouri," *MHR*, 4 (July, 1910), 252–308. The effects of wartime conditions on the press are studied in William F. Swindler, "The Southern Press in Missouri, 1861–1864," *MHR*, 35 (April, 1941), 394–400, and Lucy L. Tasher, "The *Missouri Democrat* and the Civil War," *MHR*, 31 (July, 1937), 402–19. An interesting postwar newspaper is depicted in Lewis O. Saum, "Donan and the *Caucasian*," *MHR*, 63 (July, 1969), 418–50. The complete story of the *Missouri Democrat* is included in Jim A. Hart, *A History of the* St. Louis Globe-Democrat (Columbia, Missouri, 1961); while Harvey Saalberg, "The *Westliche Post* of St. Louis: A Daily Newspaper for German-Americans, 1857–1938," Ph. D. diss., University of Missouri, Columbia, 1967, details the history of Missouri's most influential German-language newspaper.

URBAN DEVELOPMENT

Missouri's two principal cities have been the subject of numerous studies. Two histories that provide especially good coverage of nineteenth-century St. Louis are William Hyde and Howard L. Conrad, eds., *Encyclopedia of the History of St. Louis*, 4 vols. (New York, 1899), and John T. Scharf, *History of St. Louis City and County from the Earliest Period to the Present Day*, 2 vols. (Philadelphia, 1883). Also useful is Walter B. Stevens, *St. Louis, The Fourth City, 1764–1909* (St. Louis, 1911). A survey written in sprightly style is provided in Ernest Kirschten, *Catfish and Crystal* (New York, 1960). Interesting as a contemporary propaganda piece is Logan U. Reavis, *St. Louis: The Future Great City* (St. Louis, 1875). Postwar developments are covered systematically in Catherine V. Soraghan, "The History of St. Louis, 1865–1876," M.A. thesis, Washington University, St. Louis, 1936.

More specialized topics regarding St. Louis have also received extensive treatment. An interesting analysis of St. Louis's principal ethnic group is to be found in Sister Audrey Olson, "The Nature of an Immigrant Community: St. Louis Germans, 1850–1920," *MHR*, 66 (April, 1972), 342–59. The growing competition that the city suffered from its rival Chicago is ably described in Wyatt W. Belcher, *The Economic Rivalry Between St. Louis and Chicago, 1850–1880* (New York, 1947). Daniel Gorjanc, "Cholera Epidemics in St. Louis, 1832–1873," M.A. thesis, Lincoln University, Jefferson City, 1965, details the effects of devastating disease and the resulting efforts at improved sanitation; the city's efforts at the regulation of prostitution in the 1870's is treated in John C. Burnham, "The Social Evil Ordinance—A Social Experiment in Nineteenth Century St. Louis," *The Bulletin*, 27 (April, 1971), 203–17. The successful struggle over separation of city and county governments, which was resolved in 1876, is described in Thomas S. Barclay, *The Movement for Municipal Home Rule in St. Louis* (Columbia, Missouri, 1943).

The best study of Kansas City for this period is A. Theodore Brown, *Frontier Community: Kansas City to 1870* (Columbia, Missouri, 1963). Older histories, which are still useful, are Darrell Garwood, *Crossroads of America: The Story of Kansas City* (New York, 1948), and Carrie W. Whitney, *Kansas City, Missouri: Its History and Its People*, 3 vols. (Chicago, 1908). Postwar economic development is well detailed in Charles N. Glaab, *Kansas City and the Railroads: Community Policy in the Growth of a Regional Metropolis* (Madison, Wisconsin, 1962). The industrial growth of the 1870's is told in Alice Lanterman, "The Development of Kansas City as a Grain and Milling Center," *MHR*, 42 (October, 1947), 20–33, and G. K. Renner, "Kansas City Meat Packing Industry Before 1900," *MHR*, 55 (October, 1960), 18–29. Howard F. Sachs, "Development of the Jewish Community of Kansas City, 1864–1908," *MHR*, 60 (April, 1966), 350–62, tells the story of that important group, while the start of the city's "beautification" process is described in William H. Wilson, "Beginning of the Park and Boulevard Movement in Frontier Kansas City, 1872–1882," *MHR*, 56 (April, 1962), 255–73. The development of home rule for the rising metropolis is discussed in Thomas S. Barclay, "The Kansas City Charter of 1875," *MHR*, 26 (October, 1931), 19–39.

Book-length treatment of outstate towns are Felix E. Snyder and Earl A. Collins, *Cape Girardeau: Biography of a City* (Cape Girardeau, Missouri, 1956); Dolph Shaner, *The Story of Joplin* (New York,

1948); and Larry W. Clark, "Moberly, Missouri: A Study of Promotion, 1866–1966," M.A. thesis, University of Missouri, Kansas City, 1966.

IMMIGRATION AND TRANSPORTATION

Norman L. Crockett, "A Study of Confusion: Missouri's Immigration Program, 1865–1916," *MHR*, 57 (April, 1963), 248–60, presents an accurate picture of efforts to attract immigrants to postwar Missouri. A more detailed account is Florence Kidd, "Efforts to Encourage Immigration to Missouri after the Civil War," M.A. thesis, University of Missouri, Columbia, 1933. The efforts of individual railroads in this regard are discussed in Howard F. Bennett, "The Hannibal and St. Joseph Railroad and the Development of Northern Missouri, 1847–1870: A Study of Land and Colonization Policies," Ph.D. diss., Harvard University, Cambridge, 1950, and H. Craig Miner, "John C. Frémont and the Southwest Pacific Railroad," *Kansas State Quarterly*, 2 (Summer, 1970), 40–45.

A résumé of the history of Missouri's railroad construction is provided in Margaret L. Fitzsimmons, "Railroad Development in Missouri," M.A. thesis, Washington University, St. Louis, 1931. A summary of the period is in Fitzsimmons, "Missouri Railroads During the Civil War and Reconstruction," *MHR*, 35 (January, 1941), 188–206. Another good survey is Paul W. Gates, "The Railroads of Missouri, 1850–1870," *MHR*, 26 (January, 1932), 126–41. Essential to the understanding of railroad promotion in the state are John W. Million, *State Aid to Railways in Missouri* (Chicago, 1896), and Edwin L. Lopata, *Local Aid to Railroads in Missouri* (New York, 1937). The efforts of one community to insure its future through railroad development are well painted in Charles N. Glaab, *Kansas City and the Railroads: Community Policy in the Growth of a Regional Metropolis* (Madison, Wisconsin, 1962). St. Louis's efforts to bridge the Mississippi are detailed in Calvin M. Woodward, *A History of the St. Louis Bridge* (St. Louis, 1881). The development of individual railroads is covered in H. Craig Miner, *The St. Louis–San Francisco Intercontinental Railroad: The Thirty-fifth Parallel Project, 1853–1890* (Lawrence, Kansas, 1972); Richard C. Overton, *Burlington West: A Colonization History of the Burlington Railroad* (Cambridge, Massachusetts, 1941); Robert E. Riegel, "The Missouri Pacific Railroad to 1879," *MHR*, 18 (October, 1923), 3–26; and L. L. Waters, *Steel Trails to Santa Fe* (Lawrence, Kansas, 1950). For the background of railroad building throughout the United States in this era, see George R. Taylor and Irene D. Neu, *The American Railroad Network, 1861–1890* (Cambridge, Massachusetts, 1956). The disillusionment of many Missouri communities in the 1870's after the railroad boom died down is well illustrated in Virginia R. Frazer, "Dallas County Railroad Bonds," *MHR*, 61 (July, 1967), 444–62, and H. Craig Miner, "Hopes and Fears: Ambivalence in the Anti-Railroad Movement at Springfield, Missouri, 1870–1880," *The Bulletin*, 27 (January, 1971), 129–46.

The place of railroad development within the entire system of transportation in Missouri is one of the subjects researched in "The Story of Transportation," a series of articles by Floyd C. Shoemaker in *Missouri Motor News* (1934–1935) and in Edward J. White, "A Century of Transportation in Missouri," *MHR*, 15 (October, 1920), 126–62. Studies on steamboat and road development center their attention on the prewar period primarily, but a good survey of the former will be found in Louis C. Hunter, *Steamboats on the Western Rivers* (Cambridge, Massachusetts, 1949).

BANKING, TAXATION, AND SOCIAL REFORM

Very little writing and research has been done on these topics and their effects on the postwar era. Timothy Hubbard and Lewis E. Davids, *Banking in Mid-America: A History of Missouri's Banks* (Washington, D.C., 1969), covers that topic adequately. An earlier brief summary is Breckinridge Jones, "One Hundred Years of Banking in Missouri," *MHR*, 15 (January, 1921), 345–92. Nineteenth-century tax policies are treated in Frederick N. Judson, *A Treatise Upon the Law and Practice of Taxation in Missouri* (Columbia, Missouri, 1900). George B. Mangold, "Social Reform in Missouri, 1820–1920," *MHR*, 15 (October, 1920), 191–213, provides a brief survey of various reform movements, while the role of state government is analyzed in Fern O. Boan, *A History of Poor Relief Legislation and Administration in Missouri* (Chicago, 1941).

MINING AND INDUSTRY

A good account of the wartime background and postwar economic expansion is provided in George W. Smith, "New England Business Interests in Missouri During the Civil War," *MHR*, 41 (October,

1946), 1–18. Various studies have been made of Missouri's mining enterprises. A good overview of lead mining and related activities will be found in Henry C. Thompson, *Our Lead Belt Heritage* (Flat River, Missouri, 1955). Developments farther west are covered in Arrell M. Gibson, "Lead Mining in Southwest Missouri to 1865," *MHR*, 53 (April, 1959), 197–205, and "Lead Mining in Southwest Missouri from 1865," *MHR*, 53 (July, 1959), 315–28. A long-time executive tells the story of one of the major mining companies in J. Wyman Jones, *A History of the St. Joseph Lead Company, 1864–1892* (New York, 1892). Isaac Lippincott, "Industrial Influence of Lead in Missouri," *Journal of Public Economy*, 20 (July, 1912), 695–715, shows the importance of the mineral, especially in the St. Louis area. A brief survey of Missouri's coal mining operations is found in Sam T. Bratton, "Coal in Missouri," *MHR*, 22 (January, 1928), 150–56. A regional study is Stephen E. Daniels, "Coal Mining in Northeast Missouri, 1850–1920," M.A. thesis, Northeast Missouri State College, Kirksville, 1968.

The production of iron is thoroughly covered by Arthur B. Cozzens, "The Iron Industry of Missouri," *MHR*, 35 (July, 1941), 509–38, and 36 (October, 1941), 48–60. An excellent view of one particular operation in outstate Missouri is furnished by James D. Norris, *Frontier Iron: The Maramec Iron Works, 1820–1876* (Madison, Wisconsin, 1964).

There are also good works concerning other industries in the state. Ronald J. Plavchan, "A History of Anheuser-Busch, 1852–1933," Ph.D. diss., St. Louis University, St. Louis, 1970, is a valuable study of the brewing industry. Clarence Roberts has provided two articles on closely related industries: "Developments in the Missouri Pottery Industry, 1800–1950," *MHR*, 58 (July, 1964), 464–73, and "History of the Structural Brick Industry in Missouri," *MHR*, 47 (July, 1953), 318–28.

Lee Meriwether, "A Century of Labor in Missouri," *MHR*, 15 (October, 1920), 163–75, provides a brief overview of that topic. A detailed account of this period is in Walter R. Houf, "Fifty Years of Missouri Labor, 1820–1870," M.A. thesis, University of Missouri, Columbia, 1958. Also useful is Russell M. Nolen, "The Labor Movement in St. Louis, 1860–1890," *MHR*, 34 (January, 1940), 157–81. Some references to postwar labor groups in Missouri will also be found in John R. Commons and others, *History of Labour in the United States*, 2 vols. (New York, 1918).

AGRICULTURE

A short survey of this topic is provided by F. B. Mumford, "A Century of Missouri Agriculture," *MHR*, 15 (July, 1921), 277-97. Also useful is George F. Lemmer, "Missouri Agriculture as Revealed in the Eastern Agricultural Press, 1823-1869," *MHR*, 42 (July, 1948), 325-42. John Ashton has contributed two studies on specialized areas of animal breeding: *A History of Hogs and Pork Production in Missouri*, Monthly Bulletin of the Missouri State Board of Agriculture, 20 (January, 1923), and *History of Jack Stock and Mules in Missouri*, Monthly Bulletin of the Missouri State Board of Agriculture, 22 (August, 1924). The cattle industry is well covered by Clifford Carpenter, "The Early Cattle Industry in Missouri," *MHR*, 47 (April, 1953), 201-15, and Virginia Sue Hutcheson, "Cattle Drives in Missouri," *MHR*, 37 (October, 1942), 286-96. Miles W. Eaton, "The Development and Later Decline of the Hemp Industry in Missouri," *MHR*, 43 (July, 1949), 344-59, deals with an important agricultural product of the prewar era, the importance of which declined rapidly after the war. It summarizes Eaton, "A History of the Hemp Industry in Missouri," M.A. thesis, University of Missouri, Columbia, 1938.

INDEX

election of 1870, 260–65; evaluation of, 269–70; efforts at reunification, 271–75; and election of 1872, 280–81. *See also* Republican party

Railroads: development of, 205, 207–23; efforts to regulate, 283, 286–87, 289, 291. *See also* individual lines

Read, Daniel, 182–83, 185, 186

Rebekah Lodge, 195

Refugees, 44, 68, 70–72, 101, 151

Registry system for voting, 122, 136–37, 140, 233–34, 240–41, 246, 255, 264–65, 272

Republican party, 2, 5–6, 89, 146, 288–89. *See also* Radical Union party

Revels, Hiram, 158, 159

Reynolds, Thomas C., 29, 33, 111; and secession crisis, 4–5, 17, 20–21; succeeds Jackson as governor, 49–51

Richardson, Albert D., 19, 23, 24, 88

Ripley County, Missouri, 247

River improvements, 206–7

Roanoke, Missouri, 164

Robinson, James H., 161, 171

Rodman, Francis, 128, 242, 243, 269; and manipulation of election returns, 141, 233, 239, 246–47, 270

Rolla, Missouri, 25, 29, 41, 45, 72, 79, 151, 161, 185

Rollins, James S., 79, 107, 112, 135, 238, 276, 285; and efforts to aid University of Missouri, 182, 184–85

Rosecrans, William S., 64, 78, 79, 84, 106, 110, 111, 113

Ross, John, 20

S

Saengerfest (St. Louis), 190

St. Charles, Missouri, 161, 208–9

St. Joseph, Missouri, 21, 25, 81, 85, 152, 161, 175, 189, 201, 215, 222, 262; effect of war on, 79; rivalry with Kansas City, 218–19, 221

St. Joseph and Council Bluffs Railroad, 215

St. Joseph Lead Company, 227

St. Louis, Missouri, 2, 3, 18, 22, 73, 111, 113, 117, 127, 129, 139, 194, 195, 237, 244, 253, 262, 265, 284, 286; and secession crisis, 5, 11–16; economic rivalry with Chicago, 8, 77–78, 205–6, 217–19, 221; as mili-

tary headquarters, 27–28, 39–40, 56, 65; application of martial law in, 44, 61–64, 68–70; refugee problem, 44, 68, 70–72, 89; military prisons at, 66–67; educational developments, 74, 81, 158–62, 169, 171, 175–78, 188; Mississippi Valley Sanitary Fair, 75–76; labor movement in, 78–79, 224–27; entertainment, 85–86, 189–93, 196; municipal elections, 94–95, 108, 135–36, 202, 234, 272; cholera epidemics, 138, 202–4; black community, 145–51, 154–62, 169; press, 196–97, 224–25; postwar growth, 201–5, 223–24; and home rule, 202, 205, 270, 291; and railroad developments, 207–8, 215, 217, 222

St. Louis and Cedar Rapids Railroad, 209

St. Louis and Iron Mountain Railroad, 17, 207, 211, 213–15

St. Louis and San Francisco Railroad, 213

St. Louis Board of Trade, 206

St. Louis County, Missouri, 64, 81, 180, 207, 223–24, 228–29, 231, 247, 265

St. Louis Dispatch, 214*n*, 235

St. Louis Evening News, 143

St. Louis Globe, 197, 287

St. Louis Globe-Democrat, 197

St. Louis, Kansas City and Northern Railroad, 209

St. Louis Philharmonic Society, 86, 190

St. Louis Police Board, 5, 12, 35, 64, 202, 261

St. Louis Times, 239

St. Louis Union, 107

St. Louis Union Stockyards, 221*n*

St. Louis University, 82

St. Louis Workingmen's Pioneer Cooperative Association, 225

St. Vincent's College, 83*n*

Schofield, John M., 44, 52–53, 55–58, 97–106

School for the Blind, 188

School of Mines and Metallurgy, 185–86

Schools. *See* Colleges and universities; Education

Schurz, Carl, 190, 197, 238, 242, 267, 271–74, 288–89; moves to Missouri,